CAMBRIDGE STUDIES IN
CHINESE HISTORY, LITERATURE AND INSTITUTIONS

General Editors
PATRICK HANAN & DENIS TWITCHETT

Region and Nation

Region and Nation

The Kwangsi Clique in Chinese Politics
1925-1937

by

DIANA LARY

Assistant Professor of History, York University, Ontario

CAMBRIDGE UNIVERSITY PRESS

Published by the Syndics of the Cambridge University Press
Bentley House, 200 Euston Road, London NW1 2DB
American Branch: 32 East 57th Street, New York, N.Y.10022

© Cambridge University Press 1974

Library of Congress Catalog Card Number: 73-793 12

ISBN: 0 521 20204 3

Printed in Great Britain
at the University Printing House, Cambridge
(Euan Phillips, University Printer)

For my parents, M. M. E. and E. A. Lainson,
with great love

Contents

Figures

Preface

Many people have helped me and encouraged me in the writing of this book, and in the research that preceded it. With a few people who have been most closely connected with my work have developed relationships of instruction and friendship whose value is difficult to express adequately. I hope that the following people will appreciate my special gratitude to them: my mentor, teacher and now colleague, Professor Jerome Ch'en, without whose generosity and erudite guidance this work would neither have been started nor completed; my father-in-law, Hal Lary, who gave invaluable textual criticism, and who tried to instil some understanding of economics into me; my long-time teacher, Professor D. C. Lau, who held before me a high example of rigorous scholarship; my supervisor, Professor Denis Twitchett, who guided me with humour and discipline through the obstacle course of thesis writing and book preparation; and my friend, Beryl Williams, who gave me critical advice and warm, constant encouragement. For the two people who have made my life a joy through the arduous task of writing, a special and different gratitude: Nikita and Tanya Lary.

I am indebted to Professor C. M. Wilbur, for his permission to quote from the 'Autobiography of Li Tsung-jen', part of the Oral History Project of Columbia University.

D. L.

March 1973

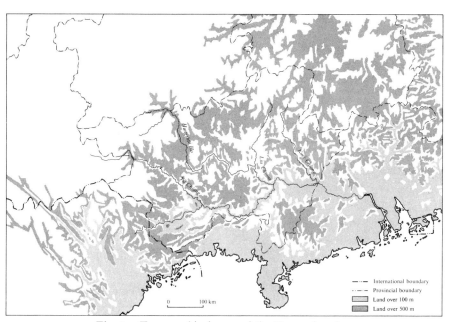

Fig. 1. Topographical map of the Kwangsi region

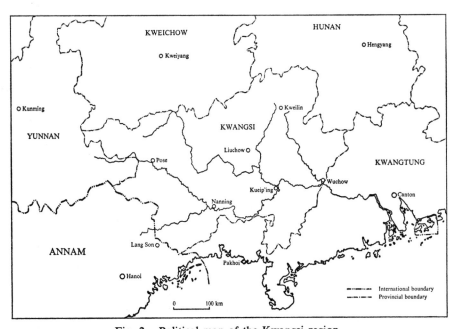

Fig. 2. Political map of the Kwangsi region

x

Introduction

'The stronger regionalism is, the weaker nationalism is. A man's feelings have limits, if he loves this he cannot love that. If we Chinese are extremely attached to our native regions, then we naturally have great difficulty in recognising the nation that stands above the region. We only know that we are from such and such a province, such and such a *hsien*, we give very little thought to the fact that we are Chinese [an identity], transcending the world of the province or *hsien*. In our work we are only concerned with advancing our region, and do not give thought to the interests of the nation. While the whole country is divided up along these provincial, *hsien* and *hsiang* lines [what hope is there] of easily producing a common national viewpoint? If we look at the government of China, we can understand the influence of regional colouring. Any Chihli Clique, Anhwei Clique, Fengtien Clique, even the proposals for federal autonomy, are all the natural manifestations of developed regionalism. When warlords and politicians see this kind of psychology, they have no qualms about using regionalism to pull together their strength. When ordinary people have drunk the poison of this kind of psychology, they also follow behind, and become their tools. Up to the Central Government, down to local government, virtually every *yamen* has become a *t'ung-hsiang hui-kuan* [regional association].'

Wang Tsao-shih's impassioned denunciation of regionalism skates around a crucial question in the understanding of the Chinese polity: is China a single entity, or is it both a collection of regions and a nation? Wang ignores the possibility that it could be the latter; he sees the nation and the region as antagonists, as mutually incompatible, the one good the other evil, negative regionalism working against positive nationalism. By ignoring the question, he is following an accepted pattern, Chinese and Western, traditional and modern, of regarding China as 'the whole China', of defining topics by discipline or by period, but regarding China

1

always as a homogeneous entity. The region is relegated to a lowly position, usually an irritant, sometimes a threat to the larger polity. The idea that China could be two things, both a high culture or nation and a collection of regions is unthinkable.

And yet in a polity as large as China, regional distinctions are enormous. The geographical and climatic diversity of China produces wide variations in food, dialect and social custom.[2] In a deeply-rooted society, where physical mobility is limited, attachment to a region and affection for it is natural. The region is a small cosy world within the larger world of China. Regionalism, as a strong sense of local identity and local integration, founded on common cultural ties, clearly exists, and provides local cohesion and a stability which can survive turbulence in the larger polity.

Why then is it seen as a threat? The answer lies in the function of regionalism. As a cultural manifestation alone, it is not a threat. Cultural regionalism, distinction of cuisine, of social customs, does not threaten the larger polity, as Chinese dialects do not threaten the written language. But when cultural regionalism slips over into political regionalism, when regional origins determine political behaviour, it can become a threat, of the kind that Wang rails against.

A high degree of political regionalism may threaten the cohesiveness of the nation, if it has reached a point where it amounts to local nationalism, to a desire to separate from the larger nation. Welsh nationalism, Basque nationalism, French-Canadian nationalism are expressions, in one region of a larger nation, of a sense of complete distinctiveness. They are also expressions of a separate historical identity, upon which they draw to justify their desire for separation. These nationalist regions have once been independent, they have been incorporated by force into the larger polity. Cultural distinctions are used to reinforce a sense of political separateness; the Welsh speak Welsh, wear leeks, hold eisteddfods to show how completely different from the English they are. The nationalism of the larger nation becomes the enemy, regionalism is nationalism-in-miniature.

All this is a long way from the Chinese experience of regionalism. Except in the Inner Asian frontier regions, the absence of major historical experiences of regional independence which preceded incorporation into the Chinese state has meant that regionalism as a desire for secession, for a return to a lost independence, has seldom been a problem, and that regionalism is not totally antagonistic to the state, since it does not threaten its fragmentation. But if this extreme version is absent, can regionalism, in either cultural or political manifestations, threaten the state in less drastic ways?

So powerful were the ties of cultural regionalism in traditional China that they could only be prevented from finding political expression within the organs of Central Government by artificial means. The development of 'regional nepotism' was aborted through rigorously observed laws of avoidance, through setting regional quotas for examination candidates, through distribution of Central funds by regional allotments.

These devices amounted to checking the political manifestations of cultural regionalism; they were not attempts to deal with fully fledged political regionalism. When that emerged, as it did periodically in Chinese history, it was a sign that the Central authority was waning, that a centrifugal process was under way, which the existing authority could not halt.

Did this latter kind of regionalism threaten the state in an absolute way? Wang assumes that it did. This study will try to show that it did not, that regionalism and nationalism were not necessarily antagonistic, that they could co-exist. We shall look at the political workings of regionalism in a period of extreme devolution of Central authority, the 1920s and 1930s, and in a province on the edge of China, Kwangsi. Kwangsi under the Kwangsi Clique represents regionalism in its most extreme form, both by period and place. There is a danger that Kwangsi regionalism is such an extreme phenomenon that it is atypical of other regions. There are very few studies of the regionalism of areas closer to the centre of China, which could confirm this danger; by default, we can only hope that it represents an extreme case of a common phenomenon.

We shall discuss the nature of regions, the constituency of regionalism, the cultural, political and economic workings of regionalism. We shall look at the relationship between region and nation, at the inter-action of the two elements within the Chinese polity. We shall examine the connection between regionalism and militarism, a crucial combination in Republican China. We shall use the term 'regionalism' fairly loosely, simply to mean a sense of regional identity. Regionalism in English translates a whole series of Chinese terms – *ti-fang kuan-nien, ti-yü kuan-nien, hsiao-ch'ün kuan-nien, chi-kuan kuan-nien, ti-fang chu-i, t'ung-hsiang kuan-nien* – which suggest subtle variations which cannot be translated into English, but which all imply attachment to a region and a sense of solidarity with natives of the same region. Our definition of regionalism will emerge from an attempt to define its various aspects, not in the form of a neat, dictionary-style definition.

WHAT IS A REGION?

Before we can discuss regionalism, we have to define the region, a task less simple than it seems at first sight. It is usually assumed that a region, in China, is a province; region and province are often used as synonyms. (Regionalism and provincialism are not, since provincialism, especially in English, carries strongly derogatory connotations. Provincialism is associated with benighted areas on the fringes of the civilised world, inhabited by provincial universities, provincial towns and provincial newspapers, all drab, parochial, gauche and second-rate. Regionalism is a neutral term.) Jean Chesneaux describes the Chinese provinces as distinct, natural regions, characterised by ' their geographical, political, sociological and economic cohesion '.[3] His description states in concrete form the common assumption that the provinces are the natural units of division within China, are natural regions.

This is not an unjustified assumption. The degree of geographical definition of provinces is high, especially in south China: most provincial boundaries fall on mountain ranges, on lakes or on rivers. The provinces are units of division for political and cultural loyalties which stress the region rather than the totality. Each province has its stereotype – the fiery Hunanese, the rats of Szechwan, the deceitful people of Hupei – all used of course by people of other provinces, but as a means of bolstering their own sense of provincial identity. ' Membership ' in a province is an honour, something acquired only by birth, and not even by one's own birth; several generations of residence are required before one can call oneself a provincial native. Cemented by such loyalties, the regionalism of the province is a potent phenomenon, whether as cultural regionalism or as political regionalism.

But there are other types of regionalism, which make an absolute identification of region with province impossible. These regions are not so conveniently defined as are provinces, their cohesive influence operates less consistently, but can still be very strong.

MULTI-PROVINCE REGIONS

These regions occur both naturally, as geographical phenomena, and artificially, as functions of administrative practice. The most important are both – natural regions, such as Kwangtung–Kwangsi, Hunan–Hupei, Szechwan–Yunnan–Kweichow – which were traditionally administered as joint entities, under a governor-general. The sense of regionalism generated in these regions was not overwhelming; it never precluded intra-regional hostility (nor did the regionalism of the province prevent hostility within the province). But in a specific context, of contact between the region and the larger world, it was an important force. Merchants, students and travellers from the region felt close ties to each other when they were outside the region. They frequently maintained joint *hui-kuan* (regional associations, *Landsmannschaften*); in a city where the activities of the natives of a single province were not important enough to justify an independent *hui-kuan*, there might be establishments of San-chiang (Kiangsu, Anhwei, Kiangsi, Chekiang), Liang-Kuang (Kwangtung and Kwangsi), Liang-Hu (Hunan and Hupei), etc.[4] These organisations operated as a focus of fellow-regional feeling, as a way of helping fellow-regionalists who might otherwise be isolated in the wide world.

In confrontations with the Central Government, the large region could exert a powerful integrative influence. Kwangsi and Kwangtung frequently fought each other, but they also stood side by side against the Centre. An external stimulus was needed to generate a feeling of regionalism, but the feeling was latent. Artificial large regionalism, the kind of conglomerations created by militarists in the twentieth century, could not generate such an identity. The ' Kwangsi Empire ' of 1928–9 was made up of a string of provinces from Kwangsi to Peking, but it was nothing more than that – a string of provinces held together only by the military might of the Kwangsi Clique, not by any natural ties, and it was easily snapped.

INTRA-PROVINCIAL REGIONS

However great the homogeneity of a province, it is no guarantee against the existence of distinctions within the province which amount to sub-regions. In Kwangsi, for example, there were ethnic distinctions, between tribal peoples and Han Chinese, between local natives and Hakka immigrants; there were distinctions of levels of cultural sophistication, as between residents of the provincial capital and backwoodsmen; there were geographical distinctions, between the plain of the southeast and the hills of the north and west; there were linguistic distinctions, as between the Mandarin speakers of the northeast and the Cantonese speakers of the south. All these distinctions could be submerged in a larger sense of provincial identity in a specific political or personal context: when the province saw itself in relation to other provinces, its natives felt a sense of provincial regionalism; when they were outside the province, they felt it too. But when the province was exclusively concerned with itself, the sub-regions became important; within the province a man was a Wuchow native or a Kweilin native.

Such loyalties had an important role to play in the formation of group-ings within provincial affairs.

BORDER-ZONE REGIONS

The areas where provinces meet often constitute distinct regions. Borders are seldom lines of absolute demarcation; the existence of a border does not preclude the existence of a commonality of social and political attitudes on both sides. Border zones tend to be isolated and poverty-stricken, their inhabitants are thrown together against the more prosperous inhabitants of the central areas of both provinces. Border zones were often less amenable to government control than inner-provincial areas; they were often the locus of rebellion, the haunt of rebels and bandits – a fact which the Communists used to their advan-tage when they set up their base areas in border zones during the late 1920s and early 1930s. Even where the border zones were not isolated, as with the Kwangtung–Kwangsi border, there were tight links across the border; the population on either side virtually ignored the border. Smuggling, of salt, opium, weapons, was a prime occupation for many border-zone residents; it demanded a secrecy and a mutual trust which created powerful links. In a specific context, such links could determine political behaviour. When, for example, two provinces were at war, the border regions would try to take themselves out of the hostilities.

Other types of region can be defined: dialect regions, agricultural regions, trade regions, economic regions. Economic regions are enor-mously important in so far as the organisation of Chinese trade and commerce is concerned; they frequently correspond to multi-province regions, centred around a major commercial city – the Canton region, which includes Kwangtung and Kwangsi, the Wuhan region, which includes Hunan and Hupei – but they can be smaller areas, the market-ing area surrounding a single *hsien*. As an abstraction, one may even define an ideal region, if one is a bold political scientist: ' As an objective entity and as a heuristic device for research, the ideal region will always be the composite region in which economic, political and cultural identity is evident.'[5]   But none of these regions has an independent political role to play, as do the regions we have defined above (though they may operate in supportive roles for political regionalism). Since we are concerned with the political workings of regionalism, we shall not discuss them in detail.

The definition of so many types of regionalism might suggest a hideous confusion of loyalties; in fact, none of the four main types we have defined is antagonistic; each comes into operation in a specific context, usually externally defined. They are part of a ladder of loyalties, starting with the family, and working up to the nation; any one can be called into play, as political regionalism, when a larger situation demands it; when the state is losing authority, large regionalism becomes important; when the state has collapsed, provincial regionalism is important; when two provinces are fighting, border zone regionalism emerges; when a province itself is disturbed, intra-provincial regionalism exerts itself. In all these extreme situations, existing loyalties are brought into play, for self-protection, as a retreat from confusion to the security of the known group. Regionalism responds to situations; the external situation decides which form is called for, not the regionalism itself. From a system of layered loyalties is selected the one which fits the situation best.

THE CONSTITUENCY OF REGIONALISM

We have talked as if the region, however defined, was a homogeneous entity, founded on a sense of common regional identity. But of course it was not; regionalism had its own form of class distinction. In traditional China, there were groups of people and institutions which transcended the region, whose identity was universal, unconscious of the region. The imperial administration was staffed by the Confucian elite, by men who lived away from their native places; of all bureaucratic regulations, the laws of avoidance were among the most strictly observed. The gentry, which administered the localities of China, shared the universalist identity of the scholar-bureaucrats, and knew their regions only to the extent that their administrative tasks demanded; they were in the regions, but not of them. Bureaucrats might call on regional ties in the choice of assistants and protégés, but they did this not because they felt themselves to be regionalists, but because they were more at ease with men from their native places.

For the mass of Chinese, however, the universal culture of Confucianism was a distant world. For them, the region – and even below that the locality, the *hsien* – was the major focus of identification. For the little people, the humble, the uneducated, the poor, the horizons of the region were the end of the real world. The culturalism of the elite was a dimly perceived, almost mystical vision. For them, travel beyond the region was seldom possible; if it was, the experience was unsettling and fearful. The twenty-five-year-old Li Tsung-jen was scared almost witless by a steam engine, when he emerged for the first time from the backwoods of Kwangsi into developed Kwangtung.[6] Even those who did travel outside their native regions found the outside world rather hostile, and stayed close together in *hui-kuan*; personal contacts were formed on the basis of common regional origin.[7] Only the members of the gilded elite felt really comfortable beyond the region – and they never saw the region.

Both in traditional and modern China, there are what amount to crude class lines in the development of regional identity. The mass does not think above the region, if it thinks that high; regionalism when used as a political tool of mass mobilisation tends to raise sights, not lower them – as the leaders of the Kwangsi Clique found in the 1930s when they used regionalism to unify the province. The constituency of regionalism is the mass, not the elite, who are drawn to the region only in times of Central (culturalist or nationalist) crisis.

REGIONALISM AS A POLITICAL FORCE

If regionalism was always present in traditional China, it was usually unimportant in political terms. It existed as a continuum, as a warm, comfortable identity, an underlying current to the universalist order, which it could not threaten because it did not impinge upon the functioning of the centralised political process. Regionalism was incoherent and ill formulated, incapable of competing with the self-confident, articulate universalism of the Confucian order. To the extent that it existed, it provided a potential retreat, a fall-back position. When the Centre could not hold, there was the region to resort to, a *faute de mieux*, but a real one nonetheless. When the Centre weakened, at the end of dynasties, the centrifugal forces created by Central weakness expressed themselves as regionalism, raised from incoherency to a political force, not fighting against the Centre, but providing a substitute for it.

Modern Chinese historians, both Communist and Kuomintang, have regarded regionalism as a negative, destructive force, as the creator of a weak and divided China. They have blamed it in part for China's sufferings at the hands of foreigners, and have seen it as an impediment to nationalism. In fact, it is not absurd to see its operation in almost a reverse light, to see regionalism as the sinews which held China together. If regionalism was the fall-back position, the response to Central weakness, it still allowed China to divide into pre-determined parts, without fragmenting arbitrarily. It did this because its proponents seldom saw it as more than a bridging phenomenon; they operated on the assumption that the Centre would reassert itself, and that regionalism as a political force would submit gracefully to the reborn Centre. It held the fort for the Centre, it provided a continuity between the order that had died and the new one which would emerge.

This was the tacit, unformulated definition of regionalism as a political force which the modern holders of regional power inherited. The case is deliberately over-stated. There are many regionalists in whom such ' regional altruism ' was manifestly lacking – crass, self-seeking warlords who considered neither the welfare of the region nor the nation. But in others, the sense of nation, and of region serving it, was strong enough to exercise a determinant influence on their actions.

THE REGIONALISTS

Who were the people who held political power as regionalists, specifically in the late Ch'ing and early Republic? They were seldom members of the elite, who might manipulate regional loyalties to serve the declining Centre, but who stopped short of setting themselves up as regional rulers, detached from the Centre. The regionalists were new men, soldiers who became increasingly powerful as the civil order declined; civilians lacked the desire or the ability to seize regional power. The late Ch'ing scholar-bureaucrats served only the universalist order; their successors, the intellectuals of the early Republic, inherited from them the assumption that political positions must be national in scale, self-conscious, coherent and assiduously cultivated. Regionalist attachments could never aspire to such heights; they and their proponents were unsophisticated, incoherent, unsystematic. They were not susceptible to organisation and refinement, their strength lay in their ability to bind without making demands for the adoption of specific political positions. When they were articulated, they ran the danger of becoming artificial and bogus, a form of play acting.[8] Expressions of regional ' racism ', like the following poem, are amusing rather than deeply moving; they suggest that though the authors may hope to make political capital for the region out of such declarations, they also have their tongues in their cheeks.

> ' The Kwangsi scenery is beautiful,
> Revolution is rooted there.
> First there was Shih Ta-k'ai,
> Then there was Li Hsiu-ch'eng.
> Talking of the heroes of today,
> We put forward first Li Tsung-jen.
> We throw the silken ball, waiting for
> a catcher, to the Kwangsi men.' [9]

The intellectuals and politicians of the early Republic recognised that regionalism could never be anything more than a stop-gap, that it existed below the level of philosophical discourse. They might use it as a temporary convenience – Sun Yat-sen played on fellow-Cantonese feeling to establish himself in Canton – but they despised it. So, too, in a quirkish way did the holders of regional power; they might use regionalism, but they could never take it as a supreme goal. Regional militarists sought national titles, they sought higher sanction for their regional independence. They fought wars to protect the constitution (*hu-fa*), to protect the country (*hu-kuo*). They spoke incessantly of national unity, they held reunification conferences, they struggled for Peking, the ' national ' capital. They applied to the incumbent ruler of Peking for approval of the titles they gave themselves. Lu Jung-t'ing, the first ruler of Kwangsi after the establishment of the Republic, assiduously requested Peking's confirmation of decisions which he in fact took quite independently. Absolute regional separatism was unknown, secession from China unthinkable. Lord Beresford might speak of the ' break-up of China ', the proponents of regionalism never. A well-informed foreign resident might imagine that ' logically, China must become a loose federation of autonomous regions ' [10] but this prescription went far beyond the ambitions of even the most extreme expression of regional devolution, the Federalist Movement of the early 1920s.

The sense of China as a single entity never lost its potency, even among the holders of regional power. Of the two dominant groups of political figures in the early Republic, the elitist intellectuals talked of the nation and fought vainly for it, while the regional militarists protected their regions, with the thought of the nation somewhere in the back of their minds.

REGIONALISM AND MILITARISM

If we say that the major proponents of regionalism as a political force were militarists, we must discuss the relationship between regionalism and militarism. The two phenomena depended on each other, and fed off each other. Military control was essential for regional independence, the region provided a locus for military independence. Once the civil order was gone, only military control was available to dominate a region and its income.

In its simplest lines, militarism means a dependence on military might for the maintenance of control; it means the subordination of civil organs to the military; it demands an economic organisation geared to military needs; it implies an authoritarian attitude towards the civilian population, and a deep suspicion of popular political organisation. It may serve a higher ideology – Fascism, *la gloire de la France* – but it may also act as a substitute for ideology; the military style may become an end in itself, as it did almost for the leaders of the Kwangsi Clique.

China has known two major forms of militarism: the centralised militarism of dynastic founders, where the dominant desire is to establish Central control through military means; and the regional militarism of periods such as the early Republic where regional militarism is a substitute for weak Central authority.

Centralised militarism was abortive unless its practitioners could make the transition from military to civilian rule. The old saw that China could be conquered by the sword but not ruled by it was generally true. Thus the Ming and Ch'ing founders established long-lasting dynasties, the Ch'in and Yüan disappeared quickly.

Regional militarism in the modern period is usually traced back to the local units which were raised to act against the Taipings in areas where Central authority no longer ran. The Hsiang and Huai Armies protected the regions *for* the Centre. But as Central authority failed to reassert itself, this form of regional militarism was transformed into a system which protected the regions *against* the Centre. Individual regions, under military control, detached themselves from the Centre, a process which reached its height during the Warlord Period (1916–28), when regional militarists protected their regions against all comers.

I shall not attempt here a specific discussion of militarism in the Warlord Period, of warlords and warlordism. Several important studies of the subject now exist – biographies of individual warlords, such as James Sheridan's study of Feng Yü-hsiang, Donald Gillin's of Yen Hsi-shan, Winston Hsieh's of Ch'en Chiung-ming, and theoretical discussions, such as Jerome Ch'en's work on warlord characteristics, and Andrew Nathan's on the nature of factions.[11] My main interest is to look at the relationship between regionalism and militarism; in the process it will be impossible to avoid glossing over many important subtleties and distinctions.

The term warlord is a problematic one, both in Chinese and in English, because it is explicitly derogatory. No militarist, regional or otherwise, ever called himself a warlord – that was what his enemies called him. To call a man a warlord suggests that his actions are dictated by self-interest, that he has no higher focus of loyalty.[12] The early Republic was clearly inhabited by many militarists of this nature – there were indeed very few who were not. There is no need to catalogue the vicious behaviour of some warlords – James Sheridan has already done an excellent job.[13] But if we use the term warlord to describe *all* the military figures of the Warlord Period, we run the risk of abusing more than we explain; since they have already had a full measure of abuse heaped on their heads, and are in any case no longer politically relevant, that is a waste of time. I shall therefore use here, for purposes of discussion, the neutral term militarist, suggesting neither praise nor blame. This does not prevent me from using the term ' warlord ' in the text, where it is appropriate and descriptive.

Regional militarism was a self-protective, conservative phenomenon. It protected the region by detaching it from the turbulent state. It protected not the inhabitants of the region but its military rulers. Regionalists might play on regional loyalties, might stress regional identity, but they subordinated the interests of the people of the region to their military ends. Regional power-holding meant not a cosy common cause, but a licence to the regional ruler to exploit its inhabitants.

Militarism, whether Central or regional, emerged in response to the disorder created by civil weakness, by the vacuum at the centre of the Chinese polity and in the regions; it quickly created new problems of its own. The economic consequences of militarism were devastating; the maintenance of large armies drained any economy. Militarism preyed on the population, making heavy demands for recruits, for lodging, for transportation. As a system, it tended to be unstable; there were recurrent problems with military control over the military. The absence of an overarching ideological commitment meant that militarists were hard put to retain the loyalty of their subordinates. Some militarists evolved complex clique structures to tie their subordinates to them,[14] but these were not fool-proof.

A militarist system demanded large armies to ensure its survival. The existence of large armies, under various independent commands, created a pressure for warfare, a pressure which manifested itself in a series of civil wars in early Republican China. No militarist could disband troops so long as his enemies kept their armies large. In any case, with China's agricultural crisis deepening, there was nowhere to send disbanded troops. There was no place for them in rural society; they could only become bandits, preying on the civilian population by turns with the militarists.

Where did the militarists come from, these people who had such devastating effects on modern China? In traditional China, the allocation of the soldier to the lowest rung of the social ladder kept him subservient to the civil elite; he was well aware that he was excluded from the higher culture. With the collapse of the traditional order, this sanction on the military disappeared.

The militarists of Republican China tended to come from lower social levels than the intellectual elite; they were commonly born in the less-developed areas of China, in the countryside rather than the town; very few of them were from scholar-bureaucrat families.[15] Many of them had some education; not a prestige, expensive education acquired at private universities and abroad, but military training in military schools, which were free. In the context of post-Imperial China, social disadvantages no longer made militarists feel so inadequate and inferior. They had the power to act, which their 'superiors', the politicians and intellectuals, did not. They were the 'class with guns' (*to-ch'iang chieh-chi*), against whom the 'gunless classes' (*wu-ch'iang chieh-chi*) were powerless.[16]

The worst burden of regional militarism on China was that it was self-perpetuating, that it induced stagnation, that it could not fill the ideological vacuum left by the collapse of the old order. Soldiers could not provide a stable and prosperous administration for China, but they could prevent anyone else from doing so. Militarism had the strength to crush the development of any new political force which might unite China and give its people a workable administration. China had to wait for some military force to unite it before militarism could be crushed; some form of centralised militarism was needed to dispose of regional militarism. This had to be a militarism committed to some higher ideological goal. Most existing militarists, committed to the *status quo*, would go to great lengths to prevent this from developing. In a negative sense, the regional militarists were united – against new political forces. Their immobility made it tempting for frustrated intellectuals to categorise China's civil wars as 'wars between the selfish militarists, by the selfish militarists, for the selfish militarists'.[17]

A CHRONOLOGY OF REGIONALISM

Up till now, we have spoken in fairly general terms, looking for general characteristics of regionalism and of the holders of regional power. We now move to the specific, and look at the growth of regionalism in late nineteenth- and early twentieth-century China.

The process we shall discuss was a more acute devolution of authority than any that had accompanied the fall of earlier dynasties, for it was part of the final collapse of the old order. In this particular process, regional power-holding was not tiding the Confucian order over a temporary weakness; it was filling a complete vacuum in the larger polity, bridging a gap which had no clear further side – there was no immediate substitute for the lost Confucian order.

The process of devolution of Central authority into regional hands started in the middle of the nineteenth century; the Centre was so weakened by the blows of the Taipings that it had to farm out its responsibilities to regional authorities. Regional armies were raised in

Hunan and in the Huai region. In theory, the Centre was granting short-term, returnable authority to various of its servants to save it from temporary weakness.[18] In practice, the Centre did not reassert its domination, and the authority was never returned. Instead, the process of devolution, accompanied by the growth of regional militarism, was accelerated.

During the Taiping Rebellion, it became common for provincial governors out of touch with the Centre to retain local tax income; after the end of the Rebellion, it proved very difficult for the Centre to regain control of some regional incomes.[19] Several regional officials, for example Li Hung-chang, built up formidable regional bases. This was not yet full-scale devolution. The men who held power in the regions still regarded themselves as servants of the throne, and they could still be removed from office by Imperial order – as Li was in 1895.[20] The process of devolution still had similarities to earlier periods of Central decline, when regional devolution, growing militarism and decay of the civil order were all functions of Central weakness.

But this time the process coincided with a massive assault on the Centre from outside; physically and psychologically, the Centre was losing its self-confidence. The question became not whether the Centre could reassert its authority, but whether it could survive at all. Distraught and battered, the Centre started to reform itself – having seen in the Boxer Movement the uselessness of blind reaction. The reforms which it thought would save it had the reverse effect – they contributed still further to the weakening of the Centre, and to the growth of regional autonomy. The provincial assemblies, set up by the Centre to placate the demands for popular representation in government and to bolster the support of the Centre in the provinces, worked instead as funnels for demands for autonomy. In 1911, it was they who issued declarations of independence from the Ch'ing, they who declared for the Republican Government.[21]

But the provincial assemblies, made up of civilians, were ephemera; they were swept away by the tide of militarism which was engulfing China. The military, led by Yüan Shih-k'ai's New Army, played an increasingly important role in Chinese affairs. The decline of the Confucian order meant also the decline of the civil order; the scholar-officials and the local gentry lost the high focus which had given them a ' natural right ' to rule. Their own loss of identity was paralleled by a growing lack of respect for them on the part of the new holders of power, the militarists. The Centre had gone, and so had the supra-regional class of scholar-bureaucrats.

The 1911 Revolution did not bring about an immediate devolution into regionalism. For a while, Yüan Shih-k'ai managed to preserve some semblance of centrality. His forces dominated enough of China to bring him within striking distance of being a Central militarist. But he was condemned to continue as a militarist; he could not transform his military control into civilian control, because there was no civil system to call up. Yüan gave way not to a resurgent civil order, but to regional militarism.

After Yüan's fall in 1916, the last vestiges of Central authority disappeared. China's intellectuals were frenziedly searching for a new political and ideological form which would restore China to itself, but there was little common cause on what it should be, and no means of imposing any civil order, in a situation where the military had the upper hand. The only major agreement of the searchers was that China's solution should be a national one, that its prime concern must be the re-establishment of unity; fragmentation, devolution of authority to the regions was regarded by all as the worst evil. A few radicals, disgusted by the failure of the May 4th Movement (1919) to consolidate its early success, toyed briefly with the idea of revival in a single province,[22] but they were exceptions, and their enthusiasm soon petered out.

The devotion of politicians and intellectuals to the nation flew in the face of the attitudes of the militarists, of the pre-Northern Expedition vintage at least. Many of them were unsophisticated men whose ambitions and concerns were short-term – and centred on the region that they controlled. In a situation of almost complete devolution, regionalism became almost an end in itself – though not quite, for the regionalists still sought higher sanctions, from the 'National' Government in Peking, and kept a desultory attachment to the vestiges of Confucianism.[23] The second generation of militarists, which began to reach positions of authority in the early 1920s, was rather different, in its political attitudes and identity, if not in its behaviour. It consisted of young men who had usually a modern military education, which differentiated them in two important ways from the militarists who emerged at the end of the Ch'ing, either in the New Army or in the provincial armies. In the first place, their military training allowed them to compete to advantage with the older generation – they were better soldiers. In the second, their education often exposed them to modern ideas; as regional power-holders they could not indulge in the unabashed regionalism of men like Lu Jung-t'ing, for whom the province was the beginning and end of the real world. They had a sense of higher identity, they wanted to cast their actions in a larger framework, one dignified by some ideological content. They were drawn to the world of national politics, in particular, in the mid-1920s, to the Kuomintang.

The distinction between the first generation and the second generation of militarists is a very loose one, looser than James Sheridan's distinction between 'warlords' and 'residual warlords'.[24] It is used to try to explain subtle distinctions which clearly existed, without forcing individuals into tighter categories, which may look neat, but are incapable of explaining the complexity of early Republican China. The worst abuses of warlordism disappeared with the 'reunification' of China under the Kuomintang, though regional militarism did not. The explanation for this must lie in a subtle but real distinction between the older and younger militarists.

Before the emergence of the Kuomintang as an organised political force, in the early 1920s, the relationship between militarists and politicians was one-sided; though both sides wanted to use the other, in practice only the militarists could do this. They could use politicians as their pawns, they themselves could not be used, as political leaders like Liang Ch'i-ch'ao and Sun Yat-sen found to their cost. After the advent of the Kuomintang to power, the situation changed. The Kuomintang itself became militarist, realising that in a situation where China was ruled by regional militarists, only Kuomintang establishment of a Central form of militarism would offer any hope of moving to a return to civil administration. The Kuomintang espoused the ideal of the Party Army, an army which served a political end. That the Party Army would soon degenerate into an army which dominated the Party was not apparent until well into the Northern Expedition, and by then the ideal had had a great impact beyond the Kuomintang, and had brought the Kuomintang many converts.

The younger regional militarists, men such as the leaders of the Kwangsi Clique, were affected by a desire for ideological attachment because they felt uncomfortable as regional militarists. They wanted to be part of a larger identity, which in 1926 seemed to be the Kuomintang.

The Northern Expedition (1926–8) technically reunified China, and brought the country under Centralised military rule. The reunification was illusory; it brought large numbers of regional militarists under the Kuomintang flag, but did not strip them of their regional independence. The Kuomintang, obsessed with its own internal wranglings and with a desire to move northwards as swiftly as possible, did not draw the teeth of the regional militarists; it transformed them not into members of a Party Army, but into 'Party warlords'.

Through much of the decade after the end of the Northern Expedition, regional militarism persisted. A rough diagram can be constructed of a series of concentric circles, with the hub in the Shanghai-Nanking region, each circle indicating a receding degree of Central control.

Chekiang, Kiangsu and Anhwei were firmly under Nanking control; Fukien, Kiangsi, Hunan, Hupei and Honan were closely linked to the capital at Nanking, but were kept loyal only through a judicious use of military control; Kwangtung, Kwangsi, Yunnan, Kweichow, Szechwan, Shensi, Shansi and Shantung were effectively independent for all or part of the decade, and sometimes actively hostile to Nanking. Further out, in Manchuria, North China and along the Inner-Asian frontier, the question was less one of regional independence of the Centre than of detachment through foreign invasion.[25]

The continuance of regional independence based on military control meant that the Kuomintang could not establish a unified civil administration for China. There was little sign after the Northern Expedition that its leadership even sought to do so. The Kuomintang had itself come under military domination – of its own generals. This was Party militarism, an elevated form of the beast, but one in which the military clearly dominated the civilian, and had little intention of allowing the situation to be reversed.

The 'reunification' of the nation did not blunt regionalism; in a perverse way it accentuated it, at least in some regions. Sun Yat-sen's ideal which called for 'the diminution of provincial authority, until in the end the province shall be little more than a postal link between the central government and the *hsien*'[26] was an ideal which implemented itself only on paper. The regional militarists under the Kuomintang flag had not surrendered their autonomy, the regions they controlled were as independent as ever. By contrast to the Warlord Period, they were now ranged against a real Centre; their regional power-holding became more self-conscious, found more concrete expression. If opposition to Nanking made them more regionalist, attachment to the Kuomintang made them more nationalist. In some cases the militarists were drawn, through their connection with the new orthodoxy of the Kuomintang, to pay more than lip-service to its ideals, notably to the ideal of nationalism and national rebirth. They set about reconstructing their regions, developing feelings of regional solidarity in the process. Many of the most serious attempts to modernise and reconstruct took place in the independent regions – in provinces such as Kwangtung, Shansi, Shantung and Kwangsi; in these places, regionalism was stressed, not as an end in itself, but as a stepping-stone on the way to nationalism.

REGIONALISM AND NATIONALISM

The idea that regionalism as a political force could persist under the aegis of the Kuomintang seems at first sight contradictory. The Kuomintang, the Nationalist Party, was *the* Party of nationalism, and regarded regionalism as the antithesis of nationalism. We shall try to show that though regionalism and nationalism were superficially contradictory, though the leaders of the Kuomintang always regarded them as such, it was in fact possible for them to complement each other. The contradiction can only be resolved by looking closely at the meaning of nationalism.

The Kuomintang established itself under the banner of nationalism. Nationalism, initially an urban, elitist phenomenon, grew in strength through the Republican period until it embraced every sector of Chinese society. Any belief so all-embracing had also to be imprecise, at least in its starting form. The early Kuomintang used the term nationalism in a very loose sense; it was a vague, sweeping ideological umbrella, useful for attracting support when feelings of nationalism were burgeoning, when the idea of the nation and its salvation was strongly present. But a loose definition became less useful once the Kuomintang had achieved power, and needed specific policies for action. To channel nationalism into practical action, the Kuomintang needed to define it specifically in terms of its economic, social and political policies. This the Kuomintang failed to do, after its reunification of China. Nationalism remained a loose conception, meaning many things to many people. The Kuomintang failed to make it its own, to seize its leadership. The leadership of nationalism was therefore up for grabs; every party and faction needed nationalism; whichever did most for the nation won it.

The Kuomintang, the political founder of nationalism, failed to demonstrate to the many varieties of nationalists that it alone possessed the capacity to lead the nation. It failed in the most crucial task of nationalism, that of defending the nation from external aggression. By failing to mobilise the nation against the invader, by failing to relate nationalism to specific programmes of internal rebirth, the Kuomintang forfeited the leadership of nationalism.

Eventually, the leadership of nationalism, now mass nationalism, passed to the Chinese Communist Party (CCP), in return for its organisation of the population of much of occupied China during the War of Resistance. But in the meantime, before the actual invasion from Japan, and before the emergence of the CCP as a significant political force, the Kuomintang's weakness as nationalists meant that other groups could lay claim to nationalism, even, ironically, the regional militarists, the perverters of national unity. Embarrassed by their crude regional power-holding, stirred by tenuous feelings of nationalism, some of the regionalists started to evolve a new definition of regionalism, that of regionalism at the service of the nation. Regionalism would serve the nation, by making its individual parts strong. Regionalism was immediate and practical, nationalism rarefied and distant. The regionalists would apply themselves practically, in the regions that they controlled, with the aim of serving the nation. Regionalism was thus elevated from a *faute-de-mieux* to a positive policy, justified by the high nationalist cause which it served. The idea of levels of loyalty was spelled out, in such a way that regionalism and nationalism could co-exist, as different, but inter-dependent levels in a pyramid of loyalties. The major proponent of this blend of regionalism and nationalism was the Kwangsi Clique, which linked its regionalism also to militarism, as the most efficient means of achieving regional reconstruction. By an extension of the process of justification, nationalism came not only to justify regionalism, but also militarism.

This vision of a nation whose members were both regionalists and nationalists, in a political as well as a cultural sense, is obviously an idealised abstraction. How much or how little it squared with the actual behaviour of the regionalists we shall see later on. The idea that there was no necessary contradiction between regionalism and nationalism was not, however, false – in its barest lines. But it overlooked the contradiction that when regionalism existed as an independent political force, backed up by military control, the regions could scarcely contribute to the rebirth of a united nation, since their existence prevented its emergence. It ensured that the ideology which would reunite the nation must come from outside the regionalist system, especially when the Centre itself showed signs of becoming a ' central region ', dominated by men of Chekiang and Kiangsu, working as much in the interests of their region as of the nation. (An examination of the biographies of Kuomintang leaders will show how many of those in authority at Nanking after the Northern Expedition came from these two provinces.) Regionalism had the capacity to work in many different ways on nationalism, as Joseph Levenson points out, of ' inhibiting nationalism, aborting it, indirectly abetting it, or submitting to its solvent influence '.[27] It could only work in the last two ways if the Centre was strong, if it offered a coherent ideological justification of nationalism. If the Centre was weak, if no other potential focus of nationalism existed, it was more likely to work in one of the first two ways.

The Kwangsi leaders might claim to serve nationalism by developing their own region, but they had little concept of who would lead this nationalism, except that it would not be Nanking. Their nationalism remained such a distant phenomenon that it existed almost on another planet. In practical terms, regionalism, instead of serving the nation, provoked inter-regional rivalry, and national weakness – in the face of external threats. So long as Kuomintang China was divided by regional militarism, so long as there was no real push to unity, nationalism, in any definition, remained in limbo, its creative potential stultified.

What changed this stalemate was the full-scale Japanese invasion after 1937. Nationalism was given a specific, external definition – it meant resistance to Japan. Regionalism was submerged in the national peril; some regions were occupied by Japanese troops; the rest became parts of Free China. Regionalism as a political force became massively irrelevant. The Kuomintang was given another stab at the leadership of nationalism; early in the War, with Chiang Kai-shek as the glorious leader of resistance, it seemed to have won it. But the War bogged down; there was little effort to mobilise nationalism, to push its penetration into the masses, stirred for the first time by the harshness of the invasion. The leadership of mass nationalism was lost by default – to the Communists, a far more potent threat than the divided regional militarists had been.[28]

After the War, the Communists maintained the momentum of the mass nationalism they had fostered, and defined it increasingly in terms of their own social and political aims. The Kuomintang, almost apathetic, fumbled along for another four years, until the Nationalists were driven from the mainland by the nationalist Communists.

Regionalism as a political force did not survive the War; the antagonists within the Kuomintang, whether of the Centre or the regions, were thrown unwillingly together in the struggle against the Communists who were not regionalists. Regionalism as a sense of cultural identity was not dead, and was even encouraged in Communist China. But there was now a clear stratification of loyalty and a functional division: regionalism was cultural, a tool of organisation, not an independent political force[29]; nationalism *was* a political force, channelled into the struggle for socialism. Regionalism could still emerge as a political force, as it did in the Cultural Revolution, when individual regions were taken out of the larger political realm, to protect themselves from upheaval, but it was only a stop-gap. Claims that 'independent kingdoms' had been set up much earlier, for example by Chiang Hua in Chekiang, sound suspiciously *ex post facto*, a means of attacking a man whose real fault was opposition to present policies in Peking.[30] Soon enough, the regions returned to the nation, the ultimate centrality of the state was not threatened. The ideological vacuum, which had given birth to regional independence, and which had been perpetuated by it, had been filled.

1

Descent into regionalism: Kwangsi province—the historical background

In 1903, a French officer visiting Kwangsi to attend the unveiling of a monument to a murdered missionary was appalled by the contrast between Kwangsi and the French colony of Tongking. He saw Kwangsi as 'a rugged, mountainous province, ruined by civil war, terrorised by piracy, impoverished by the exactions of mandarins, depopulated by poverty. . .'.[1] His observations touched on the two most distinctive features of Kwangsi: its extreme poverty and its persistent lawlessness.

To characterise a province under such broad headings, without a bow to historical specificity, may seem facile. Nevertheless, the area that is now Kwangsi has never known prosperity, except in a few areas of the province near the Kwangtung border. Nor have its people ever accepted authority easily.

Kwangsi's poverty and unrest stemmed in part from geographical factors, from the natural isolation and barrenness of the area. The province lies in the upper basin of the West River, whose tributaries rise beyond the borders of Kwangsi, and carve deep valleys as they flow east, segmenting the province. Until recently, the rivers were the only means of communication within the province; connections between individual segments were precarious. Progressive erosion, both natural and as a result of deforestation, has denuded much of the plateau region. In the limestone areas of the province, chiefly around Kweilin, this erosion has created the weird rock formations for which Kwangsi is famous.

'The very name of Kwangsi aroused in the minds of educated Chinese the idea of a place like no other, where the fairy landscapes – pine-clad mountains of fantastic shape rising abruptly from a lake-studded plain, and breaking through wreaths of mist to show glimpses of ravines and waterfalls – which for centuries haunted the imagination of poets and artists, really existed.'[2]

In the northwest, slash-and-burn techniques of agriculture have laid bare many hillsides; by the twentieth century, at least half of the original forest cover was gone.[3] The sub-tropical southern sections of the province are very fertile, but also disease ridden.

This rugged land is demarcated from its neighbouring provinces by a ring of mountain ranges, whose only natural break lies in the southeast, on the frontier with Kwangtung. Geographically and economically, Kwangsi is the hinterland of Kwangtung; the two provinces are isolated from the rest of China by the mountains and the sea, and share a strong regional integrity.[4] Traditionally, Kwangsi has had little connection with her other neighbours. The only major water-borne entry to the province is along the West River from Kwangtung; the difficulty of land communications between Kwangsi and Hunan, Kweichow, Yunnan and Indo-China has not encouraged other contacts. The province has remained on the periphery of China.

Like Kwangtung, the area that is now Kwangsi was brought late under permanent Han rule; it lies on the extreme southward edge of Han expansion. Ch'in troops advancing south through Hunan colonised the province for a time, but did not establish a lasting authority there. Not until the T'ang was Lingnan (Kwangtung and Kwangsi) brought firmly under Han rule, and settled with military farm colonies.[5] Kwangsi was constituted as a province during the Ming and only then did large-scale Han immigration into the province start.

Only the southern and eastern sections of the province were brought under regular bureaucratic administration. In the hilly northern and western sections of the province, local tribal chiefs were named administrators, with Han advisers. This system, known as *t'u-ssu chih-tu*, was a rationalisation of the fact that the tribal areas, like other border regions, were too disparate to allow easy Han rule. So long as the tribal people respected Han paramountcy, and so long as they did not cause trouble, they could be allowed a considerable degree of autonomy. Their relationship to the Centre was like that of foreign tribute states, with the exception that they had permanent Han advisers attached to them. The system was hereditary, and in many cases persisted well into the Ch'ing, though the scale on which it operated was reduced as individual areas became sinicised and were brought under regular administration.[6]

Han penetration into Kwangsi, as into other parts of south China, was not a process of vigorous conquest, but of slow absorption. The immigrants moved gradually up the river valleys, occupying land suitable for Chinese styles of agriculture, settling wherever the climate and the natural vegetation were not too inhospitable. Penetration of Kwangsi followed the opening up of the more fertile regions of Hunan and Kwangtung. In the southern and eastern parts of Kwangsi, the bulk of Han families trace their origins from Kwangtung, in the northern parts from Hunan. These separate routes of immigration have created sharp distinctions between the two regions of Kwangsi, both cultural and linguistic. Those whose ancestors came from Kwangtung still speak a dialect close to Cantonese, those whose ancestors came from Hunan speak a form of Mandarin.[7] Until the nineteenth century, Kwangsi's population remained very low [8]; then a period of population growth started, as surplus population from Kwangtung moved into the southern areas of the province. This surplus contained some of the displaced and discontented elements who helped to launch the Taiping Rebellion.[9]

Han immigration drove the indigenous inhabitants of the province, Chuang, Yao, Miao and other tribal people, up into the hills and into the northwestern sections of the province. Some of these people, especially the Chuang, were sinicised. Others resisted the Han occupation of their native lands; during the Ming there were 218 rebellions in Kwangsi, most of which must have been the rebellions of tribal people against the colonising Han.[10] But the process of occupation was not reversible, and except at the furthest limits of Han expansion, the tribal peoples were not able to withstand the encroachment. The dispossessed peoples lived in deep poverty, scratching a living in the infertile hill country.

The economic and social malaise of the tribal peoples was mirrored by the misery of other distinct groups in Kwangsi society – Hakka immigrants, boat people, miners, charcoal burners – all of whom played important roles in the early days of the Taiping Rebellion. Much of this misery found expression in hostility to and open rebellion against the local authorities, some of which came to be organised by the Taipings. Relations between recent Hakka immigrants and established Han immigrants (known as *pen-ti* or Punti) were very bad. Persistent feuding between the two groups led to the formation of many para-military groupings, which, on the Punti side had semi-official sanction, and were known as *t'uan-lien*. The provincial administration had become corrupt and inefficient; local officials, serving in what were regarded as some of the least desirable postings of the whole Imperial bureaucracy, tried to remain aloof from factional feuding, but almost always ended up siding with the local gentry, overwhelmingly Punti.[11] River pirates flocked into Kwangsi in the late 1840s, as a result of repression of piracy in Kwangtung, and exacerbated an already disturbed situation.[12]

This province, seething with rebellion, at the extreme limit of a weakening Central authority, was the birthplace of the Taiping Rebellion. We shall not discuss the Rebellion in detail here, since it is already well documented.[13] Its effect on Kwangsi was enormous, the scars it left were ineradicable; and yet after it gained strength and spread out from Kwangsi, the province became almost a backwater of the Rebellion, little affected by the social and political policies of the Taipings which aroused such excitement and fear further north. Until its suppression, when Kwangsi suffered hideously for having given it birth, it never dominated Kwangsi as completely as it did other areas. Even when the Rebellion was germinating, it was only one of many rebellious movements in Kwangsi, some loosely connected to the Taipings, many completely separate, some involving several counties, others only a few villages, some led by secret societies, some by bandits.[14] This activity continued after the Taipings had left for the north, though on a reduced scale, and flared up again when Shih Ta-k'ai returned to the province in 1858. The return of Taiping units to the province towards the end of the Rebellion, coupled with the conviction on the part of many Ch'ing generals that all Kwangsi men were Taipings, brought savage repression upon the province, plunging it into desolation and anarchy. The destruction of cities, the disruption of the economy, the slaughter of large numbers of the population, set the already poor backward province even further back.

But the spirit of rebellion was not crushed. The Kwangsi peasantry was driven again and again to rise in revolt, often blindly and fruitlessly.[15] The causes of the rebellions lay in the economic and administrative ills of the province. Recovery from the devastation of the aftermath of the Taiping Rebellion was hampered by crushing taxation and by bureaucratic corruption. Banditry was rampant, and unchecked; many of the regular troops were little better than bandits. The population was defenceless, its rebellions, unless organised by the still powerful secret societies, useless. The secret societies, mainly sects of the T'ien Ti Hui, formed the core of many risings, peasants, bandits and mutinous soldiers the following.[16] These risings tended to have greater staying power than those which were simply blind revolts.

Until 1904, all these risings were easily put down; but in that year the whole province rose in rebellion. Many of the local government troops mutinied and went over to the rebels. The rising was put down, but only after very large numbers of troops had been drafted in from other provinces.[17] The situation within the province had deteriorated to such a point that there was no longer any hope of raising local militia units or regular military units to help in the suppression of the rebels. The only course open to the Governor-general of Liang-Kuang, Ts'en Ch'un-hsüan,[18] was to co-operate with the less objectionable bandits to crush the rebels. He brought two bandit leaders, Lu Jung-t'ing and Lung Chi-kuang, and their men into his regular forces; both men soon became high officers. The distinction between bandits and regular soldiers was irrevocably blurred; many of Kwangsi's 13,000 old-style troops and

6,000–7,000 modern troops (in 1911) were closely associated with bandits, and behaved as bandits.[19]

Ts'en was not setting a precedent in using bandits as regular troops. His father, Ts'en Yü-ying, as Governor-general of Yunnan and Kweichow, had worked very closely with the leader of the Kwangsi Black Flags, Liu Yung-fu, during the Sino-French War of 1885.[20] Although Liu was operating in Tonking, having been driven out of his native province some time before by Ch'ing troops, he came to be regarded as a part of the Kwangsi military camp, and his role in the War was seen as a herioc act of *local* as well as national defence. Though China lost the War, Liu and the other Kwangsi men involved in the fighting were regarded as victorious heroes.

A much later Kwangsi account gives this somewhat biased version of the Sino-French War:

> In 1855, France was at war with China and had invaded Lungchow, Pinghsiang, etc. Those who fought the French invaders were Kwangsi men. Their Kwangsi commanders, such as Lin Yungtu, Su Yuanchung, Shun Yuying [*sic*] were intrepid and victorious generals. Though the Manchu court made the unbelievably ridiculous blunder of suing for peace after victory, the Kwangsi people had made their reputation as defenders of the nation.[21]

Liu joined a line of Kwangsi warriors, starting with the Taiping generals and endings with the leaders of the Kwangsi Clique in the 1920s and 1930s, who gave the province one of its principal claims to fame – as a breeder of outstanding soldiers, as a martial province.

It had little else to recommend it. Neither Chinese nor foreigners were interested in Kwangsi. Its poverty deterred foreign traders. The only foreign power with any concern for Kwangsi was France, acting in the interests of her colony in Tongking. The French pursued a vacillating policy towards Kwangsi; at times they seem to have hoped for some signficant contacts – they built a railway up to the Kwangsi border; at others they pursued short-term, opportunist policies – they sold weapons to the Kwangsi rebels in 1903 [22] – which could not improve relations with the provincial authorities. But the Chinese did not reciprocate by building a railway up to their side of the border, and although treaty ports were opened at Lungchow (1886), Nanning (1897) and Wuchow (1897), it was generally felt that there was little hope of developing trade.[23] ' Can the French find there [in Kwangsi] an outlet for their commerce? We do not hesitate to say: No! ' [24] One report claimed that the only trade which flourished between Tonking and Kwangsi was the trade in human beings. The ' cargoes ' were women and girls, kidnapped in Tongking (' chosen land for the supply of human flesh ') and smuggled across the Kwangsi border en route to Canton.[25]

French missionaries entered Kwangsi with higher hopes, but their optimism was not rewarded. In 1925 a veteran missionary reported that: ' In spite of fifty years of work, it [Kwangsi] is still far from having received even a veneer of Christian civilisation, few of its inhabitants having been attracted up to now by the beauty of the doctrine of our Lord and sovereign master.'[26] In the number of conversions to Catholicism, Kwangsi was one of the least rewarding of Chinese provinces; in 1921, it had only 5,000 converts, scarcely more than Tibet, at the bottom of the convert table.[27] Of 125 seminarians enrolled between 1893 and 1925, only 14 were ordained.[28] Converts often manifested dubious motives in attaching themselves to the church, understandable in a province beset by banditry and poverty. Catholic missionaries detected desire for the financial gain and physical security offered by foreign protection in many of their converts: ' Nothing is more common in Kwangsi than ingratitude . . . a cause of suffering for the missionary heart.'[29]

The Catholic missionaries did indeed suffer in Kwangsi; several were martyred, all lived in deep isolation, cut off from each other at their mission posts, and from their native land forever. But they committed themselves completely to ' ungrateful ' Kwangsi, and many acquired a profound understanding of the affairs of the province. Their records offer valuable information, far more than do the records of the Protestant missionaries who arrived in Kwangsi after the Catholics, and anguished the Catholics with their conversion techniques: ' The temporal advantages which the American sects offer their followers are a strong temptation for some of our new Christians.'[30]

The lack of success of foreign merchants and missionaries in Kwangsi confirmed the opinion of many Chinese that Kwangsi was a hopelessly backward and uncouth province, with nothing to recommend it beyond its extraordinary scenery, and its fame for bandits, rebels and fighting men. And yet this combination of poverty and rebelliousness, of which we spoke at the beginning of this chapter, had, by the end of the Ch'ing, created in Kwangsi a distinct regional character which was to shape the history of the province after 1911. As we have noted, there was already a strong identity between the army and banditry, a portent for the Warlord Period. This common identity appears to have developed rather earlier in Kwangsi than elsewhere, and may in part explain why the ravages of warlordism were so severe and so prolonged in Kwangsi. There was also a strong feeling of isolation. Though the province itself was deeply divided internally, by geographical and racial divisions, when looking outward Kwangsi felt itself to be (and was felt by other Chinese to be) only on the edge of the Chinese world. This was true not only geographically, but also in cultural terms; the people of Kwangsi were almost universally disparaged by men of other provinces – a province without even its own cuisine. This disparagement turned Kwangsi in on itself, created feelings of antipathy towards other provinces, and laid the foundations for strong feelings of provincial identity.

Kwangsi's poverty also worked in an obscure way towards cementing intra-provincial solidarity; it had the effect of levelling the population. In a province as poor as Kwangsi, it was difficult even for the landlord-gentry stratum of society to amass any significant wealth. Few figures are available for the late Ch'ing, but a survey in the early 1930s indicates that there was a very small distribution of income within the province. Only 6·6 per cent of the population were listed as rich peasants or land-lords; 21·3 per cent were listed as middle peasants, and 72·1 per cent as poor. Only 8·2 per cent of the population, including landlords, owned more than 20 *mou* of land. At the other end of the scale, the incidence of tenantry in Kwangsi was much lower than in more prosperous provinces, at 25·7 per cent of the population.[31] This levelling of the population produced in Kwangsi some community of interest across class lines; the naked distinctions between poverty and wealth found elsewhere were less apparent.

For all its poverty and isolation, Kwangsi was not cut off from larger political movements. Its tradition of rebellion against authority made it in the eyes of Sun Yat-sen and the T'ung Meng Hui a potential area of revolutionary activity. There was a T'ung Meng Hui organisation in Liuchow, where the 1904 Rebellion was centred. Several clandestine journals were circulated; a number of revolutionaries taught on the staffs of the new schools set up in Kwangsi towards the end of the Ch'ing. By 1910, 100 out of 500 military cadets in Kwangsi military schools were secret members of the Party.[32] Sun Yat-sen himself considered that with his guidance, the persistent outbreaks of anti-government activity in Kwangsi could be transformed from blind rebellion into constructive political acts.[33] But a T'ung Meng Hui attack into the province in 1907 from Tongking was easily repulsed by Lu Jung-t'ing. Contrary to Sun's hopes, the risings in Kwangsi were not susceptible to outside direction, nor could they become part of a larger movement. The level of political consciousness within the province was still very low.

After the 1911 Revolution, control of Kwangsi passed not to a revolutionary leader, but to one of the province's leading bandit-soldiers. Lu Jung-t'ing was provincial Commander-in-chief in the late summer of 1911. He was still not detached from his roots – he maintained contact with his former bandit friends – but he had a canny sense of the general direction of political movement within China. When, after the Wuch'ang Uprising, a group of revolutionaries (T'ung Meng Hui) and subordinate army officers prepared to declare their independence of the throne, Lu put himself briefly at the head of their movement, ensuring that when the formal declaration of the province's independence was made on 17 September 1911, he should emerge as its leader.[34] Within a few days of the declaration, he forced the departure of all Imperial office-holders within the province, and had himself declared Governor (tu-tu).[35]

There was no political conversion on Lu's part. There was no need for one; the revolutionary movement in Kwangsi was small and fragmented, centred among the intellectuals and students of the major cities, incapable of leading any sustained bid for local power. Lu's reading of the situation in 1911 told him that the Ch'ing dynasty was doomed and should be abandoned; there was no corollary to this that the revolutionary movement, which had contributed to the dynasty's downfall, was about to emerge as a major political force with which Lu should associate himself.[36]

Already as provincial Commander-in-chief, Lu had been playing a role which was unfamiliar, acting on a stage for which his bandit background gave him little training. Now with the collapse of the dynasty, he found himself in a completely unknown situation, where his only possible response was to escape from potential confusion by maximising the security of his own position. He did this by curtailing the activities of Kwangsi's revolutionaries, isolating and dismissing officers who showed signs of independent thinking, and by bringing more of his old bandit confrères into the regular army, ensuring loyalty through personal connections, building a warlord clique around his personal leadership.[37]

In the early years after the Revolution, Lu gave no signs of territorial ambition beyond Kwangsi. His rule, though rigid and antipathetic to political development, provided a degree of stability within the province, which seemed his only concern. But in 1915 and 1916, external events impinged themselves upon the province, and as a result, Lu found himself in control of Kwangtung and Kwangsi. The normal relationship between the two provinces was reversed; backward, poverty-stricken Kwangsi came to dominate its rich and advanced neighbour. Through the complexities of the Hu Kuo (Protect the Nation) Movement, which arose in response to Yüan Shih-k'ai's imperial adventure, Lu was drawn into inter-provincial political and military manoeuvring, an involvement which he did not welcome. Lu was linked to one of Yüan's principal supporters in the southwest, Lung Chi-kuang, by common background and by marriage – Lung's nephew was his son-in-law.[38] The civilian officials of Kwangsi were Yüan's appointees; Lu depended on Yüan for financial aid; his son was a hostage of Yüan's in Peking.[39]

These very powerful sanctions, coupled with Lu's disinclination to move beyond the relatively straightforward military domination of one province, should have been sufficient to keep him in at least a neutral position on the monarchical issue. But he came under increasingly strong pressure from the anti-Yüan movement in neighbouring Yunnan, where one of the leaders of the movement was his former chief, Ts'en Ch'un-hsüan, a long-time enemy of Yüan's.[40] Lu found the pressure difficult to resist. He petitioned Peking for sick leave, and asked for the return of his son to care for him. His son started south, but died in mysterious circumstances at Wuchang. It was generally believed that Yüan had had the boy murdered.[41]

In the southwest, the military situation was swinging against Yüan. By January 1916, Yunnan and Kweichow had declared their independence of Yüan, and bitter fighting was in progress in Szechwan. Lu wavered, then himself declared the independence of Kwangsi in March, and named himself Commander-in-chief of the Kwangsi-Kwangtung Hu Kuo Army.[42] With Lu's defection, the Hu Kuo Movement grew powerful enough to force the independence of all southern and southwestern provinces, and their long-term detachment from Peking. In Kwangtung, the position of the Commander-in-chief, Lu's old friend Lung Chi-kuang, became untenable; he was swept from power by Cantonese and Kwangsi forces. Lu Jung-t'ing became Military Governor (*tu-chün*), a *de facto* position of authority which was given *de jure* recognition by the new ' national ' government in Peking, headed by Li Yüan-hung.

The reactivation of the 1912 Constitution by Li's government nullified the pretext for the independence of the provinces which had supported the Hu Kuo movement, but though the open breach between north and south China was healed, individual provinces remained effectively independent. As a result of the Hu Kuo Movement, northern troops had been withdrawn from Szechwan and Hunan. T'ang Chi-yao, a Yunnanese, controlled Yunnan; Lu Jung-t'ing Kwangsi and Kwangtung. Other southern provinces were dominated by local men. The development of regional, militarist government was clearly perceptible. Lu quickly gave his administration of the two provinces an uncompromisingly military flavour by severing his connections with the politicians with whom he had been associated during the Hu Kuo Movement, and by establishing as his administrative organisation a military government.[43]

Until this stage, Lu had functioned as military ruler of his own region – Kwangsi province – and had ruled through an informally but tightly-linked group of subordinates, former bandits, relatives, connections by marriage and the like. His political pretensions were minimal; he was prepared to work within a framework established by Peking, one to which he gave something more than lip-service, though less than obedience. His behaviour was dictated by a pragmatic reading of the national and regional situation, not by any deeply-held beliefs; he responded to situations rather than creating them. He made little attempt to interfere with the civil administration of Kwangsi. High civilian posts, most without any authority attached to them, were held by Peking appointees. Local administration was in the hands of local magistrates and, in effect, of the local gentry. A sharp distinction emerged immediately after the 1911 Revolution in the pattern of appointment of local magistrates, as for instance in the case of Ch'aop'ing, an important *hsien* on the lower West River. All magistrates until 1911 were from outside Kwangsi, though most were from neighbouring provinces. Between 1912 and 1926, fifteen of the eighteen *hsien-chang* were Kwangsi natives, and seven were from Ch'aop'ing itself.[44]

Lu now had to respond to a new situation, one in which he had unexpectedly achieved independent control over two provinces. He made no substantive changes in the policies he had followed for the administration of one province; the only major difference was in the scope of his activities. He took little part himself in the administration of the provinces. He made his brother-in-law, T'an Hao-ming, *tu-chün* of Kwangsi, and Ch'en P'ing-kun *tu-chün* of Kwangtung; he himself became Commissioner of Liang-Kuang.[45] He gave no practical allegiance to Peking, though he still felt the need for official sanction; he went to the capital in March 1917, and obtained official confirmation of his appointments.[46]

This desire for recognition from the capital revealed the deep uncertainty of Lu's position. Though he was not prepared to renounce his independence in practice, he was not prepared to be blatant about its form. His conception of regional independence remained that of local authority conferred by a higher authority – that is, Peking. He felt uncomfortable operating outside a centralised framework, the framework within which he had operated as an officer of the Imperial armies. The capital had lost the power to control its provinces, but it had not lost a moral suasion, a capacity to confer legitimation, which worked strongly on men who lacked the intellectual self-confidence of revolutionaries, on men who had found no new focus of loyalty. Although Lu's actions helped to detach two provinces economically, militarily and administratively from the Centre, formal loyalty to the Centre was still important to him, as was formal Central sanction of his actions.

Lu's administration of the two provinces was authoritarian, unimaginative and static; its stability depended entirely on military domination. It was not, however, impervious to political influences, nor was it able to prevent the development of political movements. In the summer of 1917, Lu became involved in another large movement, the Hu Fa Movement (Movement to Protect the Constitution). Tuan Ch'i-jui's seizure of power in Peking after the abortive attempt to restore the Manchu Emperor sparked off waves of opposition, not least among important groups in Kwangtung, many of whom were followers of Sun Yat-sen. Bowing again to pressure, Lu welcomed Sun to Canton, and declared the independence of Kwangtung and Kwangsi, in protest against the dissolution of Parliament in Peking.[47]

Sun arrived in Canton in July, and began to prepare for the convention of an extraordinary Parliament in Canton, made up of members of the Peking Parliament who had come south after its dissolution. At the beginning of September, a few days after the first meeting of the extraordinary Parliament, Sun also established a military government in Canton. Sun's bravado in establishing ' national government ' organisations in an area where his practical authority was virtually non-existent, however great his prestige, stunned Lu initially. He did not oppose Sun, though he gave him no material backing.[48] But within a few months he demonstrated, by his attempts to reach a settlement with Peking, that he considered Sun's ' government ' of no consequence. In 1918, at Lu's instigation, the military government was transformed into a Directorate of Seven, two of whose directors, Sun Yat-sen and T'ang Shao-yi, left Canton, leaving it to be administered, as Lu's tool, by Ts'en Ch'un-hsüan.[49] Lu continued negotiations for a peace settlement with the north, though they never led to a settlement. They did, however, put an effective end to the Hu Fa Movement.[50]

Lu's encounter with Sun did not change his attitudes towards the administration of Kwangtung and Kwangsi; it certainly did not instil in him any interest in political or social innovation. He continued his *laissez-faire* policies towards local government, relying solely on his military strength to maintain his position. His forces, numbering between 50,000 and 70,000,[51] were commanded by untrained officers, most of whom had started their careers as bandits. The only exception was the Model Battalion (to be discussed below), commanded by a foreign-trained officer, Ma Hsiao-chün, and officered by young graduates of military schools. The bulk of the troops were ill-trained, and oblivious to modern military methods; they owed their domination of Kwangtung not to their own skills, but to the chronic disunity of Cantonese forces. But their alien presence constituted a unifying force for the disunited Kwangtung units; as the Kwangsi troops sated themselves on the riches of Kwangtung, impairing what fighting capacity they had, and arousing bitter popular resentment, their position started to slip.

By the summer of 1920, local nationalist desire to rid Kwangtung of its

' foreign ' oppressors had focused the loyalty of many of Kwangtung's own commanders. In Fukien, Ch'en Chiung-ming, then a supporter of Sun Yat-sen, was preparing an expedition into Kwangtung, and had gained the (temporary) support of T'ang Chi-yao of Yunnan. When Cantonese commanders rose in rebellion, and Ch'en launched his expedition, Kwangsi forces crumpled, and began to retreat into Kwangsi, their withdrawal hampered by the loot of four years' occupation which they carried with them.[52]

Sun Yat-sen returned to Canton, and set about reorganising his military government. It appeared at first that Kwangtung would be satisfied with the expulsion of Kwangsi troops. But now Lu could no longer accept his reduced status as ruler of one province. In 1921, he attempted a counter-attack into Kwangtung, which turned out to be a complete fiasco; his subordinates deserted him, his troops scattered; his province was laid open to Cantonese invasion. In the summer of 1921, Cantonese troops occupied all the major centres of Kwangsi, almost without resistance. Fleeing Kwangsi troops were subjected to aerial bombardment by Cantonese planes; since they had no bombs, the Cantonese satisfied themselves with dropping baulks of wood, which did little damage.[53] Lu fled from Kwangsi into his first period of exile, which was to last just over a year. The province, which his military rule had granted ten years of relative calm, was plunged into a prolonged period of anarchy which, in retrospect, made his rule seem actually benevolent, and which was only ended in 1925 when the leaders of the new Kwangsi Clique consolidated their hold over the province.

It is easy to see Lu Jung-t'ing as a venal, narrow-minded figure. This is unfair. Lu did not rise to power in Kwangsi through cunning manipulation, through deliberate suppression of the province to his will, but by default. He found himself, in 1911, filling a vacuum created by the collapse of Central authority; his skill at manoeuvring in a confused situation, coupled with his military strength, then took him gradually to the rule of two provinces. Lu was probably as much surprised by this process as was anyone else; his personal inactivity after the Kwangsi occupation of Kwangtung suggests that he was overwhelmed by the height to which he had risen. His rise was a function of the failure of any new political authority to emerge after 1911, rather than of his own conscious machinations.

Under Lu's rule, Kwangsi moved further and further away from Central control. The movement was less a self-conscious drive towards autonomy than a response to the weakening of the mechanisms of Central control. It was not a process which Lu and other Kwangsi natives welcomed whole-heartedly – as with Lu's continuing concern for

Central approval – but it led almost automatically to the creation of political regionalism, fortified by a specific regional identity. The elements of this identity were pride in military achievement, in stubborn resistance to imposed authority and in the 'virtue of poverty'. By an almost perverse logic, the outstanding characteristics of the province – militarism, lawlessness, poverty – underwent a transformation in which they become points of regional loyalty. The province was poor, unruly, but proud with it.

2

The country boys

Under Lu Jung-t'ing, Kwangsi remained on the periphery of China's political life. Though Lu himself ventured outside the province, and actually ruled Kwangtung for a while, not even the most strident local patriot would have claimed that Kwangsi exercised any crucial influence as a political force. But in the mid-1920s a group of young officers came to power in Kwangsi who came to be known as the Kwangsi Clique.* This group, with only one major change in its composition, held the province until 1949, and played a sporadic but important role in national politics. Its influence over the affairs of southwestern China was enormous, over the province of Kwangsi absolute. The Clique's determined and often belligerent refusal to accept higher authority, and its reliance on military strength to maintain its position make it a prime example of regional militarism.

From its emergence in 1925 to its retirement in 1949, when the mainland of China passed under Communist Government, the Clique showed one outstanding organisational feature: its internal cohesion. This cohesion contrasted with the shifting relationships which characterised much of warlord politics, especially in the years between 1916 and 1928, relationships which, as Jerome Ch'en has shown, were so unstable that only a blood tie provided a solid guarantee of permanence.[1]

The ties that bound the Kwangsi Clique were not familial ties, though family ties had some importance in the organisation of the lower echelons of the Clique.[2] Nor were they initially provincial ties. The Clique developed within the focus of one province, sharply divided itself into regions. It was not until the Clique became active in the national sphere

* We shall refer throughout to the Kwangsi Clique, the collective noun by which the leaders of Kwangsi after 1925 are usually known. It should be noted, however, that the Kwangsi leaders never called themselves by this name, which they regarded as highly pejorative, and never indeed thought of their group as a 'Clique'. The term was not used by anyone until 1927, and then chiefly as an insult. But it is a convenient and well-established way of referring to the group, and it would be pettifogging to avoid it.

that provincial origin became important; until that stage its unity existed in spite of *intra*-provincial regional distinctions, rather than because of a sense of provincial solidarity. Of the three early leaders, one, Huang Shao-hsiung, came from Jung hsien near the Kwangtung border, and was a Cantonese speaker. The other two, Pai Ch'ung-hsi and Li Tsung-jen, both came from the Kweilin region, but Pai was a member of a small but distinct community of Moslems. Finally, the Clique's early cohesion cannot be ascribed to a common political commitment. Though all three were later to be supporters of the ideology of Sun Yat-sen, this ideological interest only matured after the conquest of Kwangsi by the Clique. The formation of the Clique grew out of a series of fortuitous encounters of three young men who had much in common, but between whom there existed no links strong enough to encourage the formation of a Clique without this catalyst.

An examination of the early life of the three founders of the Clique, along with that of Huang Hsü-ch'u, who replaced Huang Shao-hsiung in 1930, shows a considerable degree of similarity in social and economic origins, and in educational background. This similarity may go some way to explaining the relationship of near equality which existed between the three; their equality of origin and education discouraged the domination of one of the three over the others. Their social and educational background was shared by the second echelon of the Clique, which gave additional stability and durability to the Clique (see Appendix I). The educational ties which bound the Clique together were formed in two military schools, the Kwangsi Military Elementary School (Kuang-hsi lu-chün hsiao-hsüeh) and the Paoting Military Academy. Kwangsi officers who were trained in Japan, or at the Whampoa Academy, had few links with the Clique.

Let us look now at the social and economic origins of the four leaders of the Clique. Considerably more information is available on Li Tsung-jen, Huang Shao-hsiung and Huang Hsü-ch'u than on Pai Ch'ung-hsi, and the greater space given to the first three reflects this imbalance rather than the relative importance of the four men.

LI TSUNG-JEN [3]

Li Tsung-jen was born in 1891, near Kweilin, into a family which had once been prosperous, but had been declining for some time, partly as a result of the aftermath of the Taiping Rebellion, in which Li's family home had been destroyed. Li's father was a failed scholar, a tutor and pen-pusher who left the running of the small family farm to his wife and her five sons. From the age of six, Li went to the village school, which was run by his father, spending half his time studying the classics with his father, and the other half working in the fields with his mother. His schooling was adjusted to the farming calendar; at harvest or planting time, he spent his whole day in the fields; at slack times, he went to school all day.

His experience of imperial repression, and his failure as an examination candidate, had made Li's father bitterly anti-Manchu; his awareness of China's humiliation before the foreign powers made him equally anti-foreign. At the same time he had a sense of the value of a modern education, in which Western subjects were included. When a modern elementary school was set up in Linkuei hsien, near Li's home, he sent his son to it. But Li did not respond well to the unhappy amalgam of partially understood 'new education' and incompletely reformed 'old education' that the school offered, and within a short time moved to another school, the provincial Cotton Weaving Institute in Kweilin. Li graduated from this school – to unemployment. The 'modern' school had trained its students for a type of work which did not exist. After a period of deep despondency, he decided to try for a third time to get a useful modern education, and in 1908 enrolled in the Kwangsi Military Elementary School. Li chose this school not because he or his father wanted him to become a soldier, a career that was still widely scorned, but because of all the modern schools in Kwangsi it was the best organised and offered the most certain prospects of employment.[4] It was also free, a decisive factor in the choice of education of a young man of impoverished family.

HUANG SHAO-HSIUNG [5]

Huang Shao-hsiung was born in 1896, in a village in Jung hsien, only a few miles from the Kwangsi-Kwangtung border. His father, like Li's, was a failed scholar. He earned his living as a school-teacher and as a practitioner of traditional medicine; he was also a small landlord. Like Li, Huang studied under his father, in the Huang clan school. His childhood was boisterous and unrestricted; he was a tough and daring boy. His father, again like Li's, had some knowledge of 'modern' ideas, and encouraged his son to question and even to attack the old society and its rulers. He had misgivings, however, when his headstrong child left for Kweilin in 1908 (at the age of about thirteen) to enrol in the Military Elementary School, determined to become a soldier.

HUANG HSÜ-CH'Ü [6]

Huang Hsü-ch'ü, like Huang Shao-hsiung, was a native of Jung hsien. His father was another failed scholar, a poor descendant of a once prosperous family. The family into which Huang was born in 1893 eked out a precarious existence while the mother ran the farm and the father tried repeatedly to pass the Imperial examinations. When he finally became a *hsiu-ts'ai* in 1900, his success turned sour; he could find no worthwhile position, and eventually enrolled with his son in the Wuchow Sericulture Institute. For Huang Hsü-ch'u it was an abortive experience, and served only to delay his entry into the Military Elementary School. When he arrived there in 1912, Huang Shao-hsiung, Pai Ch'ung-hsi and most of the students who subsequently became members of the second echelon of the Kwangsi Clique had already left.

PAI CH'UNG-HSI [7]

Pai Ch'ung-hsi was born in 1893, near Kweilin. His ancestors had migrated to Kwangsi from Nanking at the collapse of Taiping rule there. His family were members of the tiny Moslem community in Kwangsi, a religious attachment which gave Pai something of the air of an outsider, but was an important factor at various stages of his career. His father is described as a farmer, though he presumably also had some pretensions to education, since the family was literate. Little is known of Pai's childhood, beyond the fact that he studied in a primary school in Kweilin run by his relative Li Jen-jen, and that he entered the Military Elementary School at about the same time as Li Tsung-jen and Huang Shao-hsiung, that is, in 1908.

The most striking common feature in the early life of these four men is that three of them at least were sons of men who had failed under the old system, whose efforts to restore the lost prosperity of their families through success in the examination system had met defeat. In all three cases the mothers had borne the brunt of the support of the family while the fathers tried to establish themselves as scholar-bureaucrats. Only one father, Huang Hsü-ch'u's, actually managed to pass the first level of the examination system, but his achievement turned to ashes when this distinction became meaningless; the abolition of the examination system in 1904 negated his success. The failure of their fathers in literary careers must have exerted a strong influence on their sons, pushing them towards military school. In the decay of the old order, half-baked ' modern ' vocational schools, such as Li's weaving school, and Huang Hsü-ch'u's sericulture school, offered as little hope of a profitable career as did the moribund classical education system. Only an army career gave good and swift prospects for advancement. Modern military forces were being built up rapidly, staffed by the graduates of local military schools, and by those trained at Paoting or abroad. In Kwangsi, the main military school was the Kwangsi Military Elementary School.

THE KWANGSI MILITARY ELEMENTARY SCHOOL [8] (KUANG-HSI LU-CHÜN HSIAO-HSÜEH)

The Kwangsi Military Elementary School was set up in Kweilin in 1906, as part of a national programme to improve the calibre of the officers of the Chinese armies. The military elementary schools, set up in each province, were the lowest of three levels of officer training: at the next were four military middle schools, and at the top was the Paoting Military Academy.[9] All these military schools were financed by the Central Government; the prospect of a free education drew in many young men whose parents could not afford to educate them privately, either in China or abroad. They trained many of the major military figures of Republican China.

The purpose of the elementary schools was to give a foundation in modern military techniques and in ' modern ' subjects such as science, mathematics and foreign languages. They attracted as teachers men who had acquaintance with new ideas, which were frequently revolutionary. The first head of the Kwangsi school was Ts'ai O, later the leader of the 1916 anti-monarchist movement. Though the school was highly disciplined – spit-and-polish training and meticulous drilling were demanded – Ts'ai was tolerant of covert political activity – which meant at this stage only anti-Manchu activity. Many instructors had revolutionary leanings, revolutionary ideas were widely discussed. There were secret T'ung Meng Hui cells within the school, to one of which Li Tsung-jen belonged.[10]

The enthusiasm for revolutionary ideas within the school burst out into the open after the Wuch'ang Uprising (October 1911) and the declaration of Kwangsi's independence from Peking. The cadets welcomed the outbreak of revolution with wild enthusiasm and rushed to enrol in a small student group heading north with a force of the Kwangsi Army to participate in the fighting on the Yangtze.[11] Huang Shao-hsiung and Pai Ch'ung-hsi got into the group; Li Tsung-jen did not, and his exclusion meant that he missed the chance of further military training in central and north China which came to Huang and Pai. For though their military adventure came to little, some of the cadets who went north were able to enrol in military schools there, first at Wuch'ang, and then at Paoting. Huang and Pai graduated from Paoting in 1916, having received an inadequate and sketchy education – the academy was seriously affected by Yüan Shih-kai's distrust of its staff [12] – but with a handle to their name, as Paoting graduates, which was to increase their military standing enormously. They became part of one of the key old-boy networks of the military world of Republican China. While at Paoting they met many of the future generals of war-lord armies and of the Kuomintang armies, who were their fellow-cadets. The fellow-feeling of Paoting graduates was never as powerful as that of Whampoa graduates, but it was activated on occasion to cement nascent alliances; it was a bond which was useful if other circumstances favoured an alliance, but not one which of itself was strong enough to form them.[13]

After their graduation, Huang and Pai returned to Kwangsi to serve in the army of Lu Jung-t'ing. In doing so, they were following an expected pattern, that military school graduates serve in their native provinces; an identity of place of service with place of origin was almost standard now for military men. Some cadets from Kwangsi did not go back, however, but made their careers in other provinces, especially in Hunan. Amongst these were several men who were later closely associated with the Kwangsi Clique. Pai Ch'ung-hsi thought of going to Sinkiang, presumably so that he could work in a Moslem environment, but eventually decided to return to his native province.[14]

The failure of some of the Kwangsi Paoting graduates to go home was caused in part by uncertainty about their future careers under Lu Jung-t'ing. Many of Lu's senior officers, men of bandit origins, were hostile to young officers with modern military training, and saw them as a potential threat. Lu agreed, but was shrewd enough to see that they might represent an even greater threat if they were left unemployed within their native province. He hived them off into a new unit, the only unit with any claims to modern military organisation within Lu's army, the Kwangsi Model Battalion.

THE KWANGSI MODEL BATTALION[15]
(KUANG-HSI MO-FAN YING)

The Battalion was established in 1917, under the command of Ma Hsiao-chün, and officered by graduates of Paoting and of the Kwangsi Military Elementary School. Ma had been attached to Lu's forces for some time, but he was quite unlike the majority of Lu's officers. 'He stood out as the one red spot in a mass of green branches [that is, men of bandit origin].'[16] He was a *hsiu-ts'ai*, a graduate of a Japanese military academy, and a man with a revolutionary record. Into his unit were put all the best-trained young officers in Kwangsi, for whom there was no place in Lu's old-fashioned armies.

The Battalion formed in 1917 consisted of 30 young officers, all military school graduates, and about 500 soldier-cadets, many of whom had some previous education. Huang Shao-hsiung, Huang Hsü-ch'u, Pai Ch'ung-hsi and a number of other young officers who were later closely associated with the Kwangsi Clique served in the Battalion. (Huang Hsü-ch'u had recently graduated from the Peking Military College.) The Battalion was not conceived of as a fighting unit, but as a training unit, an *oubliette* for Kwangsi's potential dissidents. It saw no action until 1919, when it was sent to put down bandits in the west of the province.

A strong corporate identity existed within the Battalion, centred on personal loyalty to Ma. Ma's influence over his subordinates was very great. He commanded the kind of personal devotion from his young subordinates, which, if he had ever been able to establish a strong military and territorial base, might have helped him to a commanding role in the military politics of Kwangsi. Lu Jung-t'ing made sure that he never got the chance. The loyalty of his subordinates could express itself only in unswerving obedience to his instructions. When he surrendered to invading Cantonese forces in 1921, in order to keep the unit intact, his subordinates accepted his action, though it made them the following year the butt of attacks by the resurgent Kwangsi forces, now without any central organisation, and known as the Autonomous Army (Tzu-chih chün), a loose and feuding federation of Lu Jung-t'ing's former subordinates. Under attack, the Battalion fragmented, and individual units scattered. Huang Shao-hsiung and Pai Ch'ung-hsi led a small band into Kwangtung, Huang Hsü-ch'u left the Battalion altogether, and went home. When Pai went to Canton for medical treatment for a wound, Huang Shao-hsiung led his tattered remnants back into Kwangsi, and joined Li Tsung-jen, who now, as an independent military commander, controlled an area around Yülin hsien, near the Kwangtung border. The Model Battalion came to an inglorious end, unable to operate in what had become, after the defeat of Lu Jung-t'ing in 1921, a situation of great complexity, an almost copy-book example, within one province, of the worst abuses of warlordism. The young officers of the Model Battalion, whose association with it had kept them clear of warlord feuding, were unable to cope with the situation. Only one of the future leaders of the Kwangsi Clique, whose career after 1911 had been very different, could operate within this new framework – Li Tsung-jen.

LI TSUNG-JEN'S CAREER AFTER 1911 [17]

Li Tsung-jen failed to go north with his fellow-students in 1911, and had to be content with finishing his military training in Kwangsi. He graduated from the Military Elementary School in 1913, and found himself, after a short time, unemployed. There were apparently no openings for him in Lu Jung-t'ing's army. He was forced to become a physical-training instructor in a middle school. The job was well paid but it was not the career he had envisaged.[18] His pride took a severe battering; he appeared to have taken yet another blind alley. But if the Kwangsi Army would not employ him, others would. He managed to get taken on as a lieutenant in a Yunnanese unit, which was passing through Kwangsi en route for Kwangtung. He spent the years from 1916 to 1920 in Kwang-tung, serving in a variety of units, and rising to the rank of major. The regiment which he commanded as major was made up of Kwangsi natives, and when in 1920 Ch'en Chiung-ming drove Lu Jung-t'ing from Kwangtung, Li withdrew his unit into Kwangsi on his own initiative.

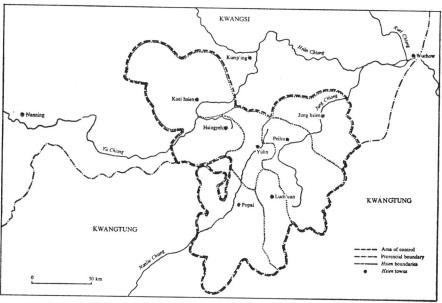

Fig. 3. Li Tsung-jen's area of control in south Kwangsi, 1922

The unemployed youth of 1913 now found himself in command of about 2,000 men, an autonomous, self-sufficient unit living off the land, and eventually, through accident and good management, controlling an area of seven *hsien* (see Fig. 3). The process by which Li acquired his force and his area of control is too complicated to describe in detail. It is enough to say that Li fought himself and schemed himself into this position by playing the warlord game: by allying himself for brief periods with whoever was temporarily on top; by exercising a strong personal control over his men; by exploiting the areas which he occupied;

by expanding his unit with disbanded men and deserters from other units; by taking advantage of confused conditions to extend his area of control.

If Li's career had ended at this stage, there would have been nothing to distinguish him from the very large number of petty warlords who beset Kwangsi at this stage. But Li was still very young – just on thirty – and he had had enough exposure to modern ideas to feel uncomfortable in his present role, though he had no intention of abandoning it until circumstances, or his own initiative, presented him with an alternative. The arrival of Huang Shao-hsiung in 1922 provided Li with the spur he needed to launch out on a different tack. Though he appears to have accepted Huang initially in the spirit of a petty warlord expanding his forces, and though three more years of essentially petty warlord activity elapsed before he and Huang gained control of all of Kwangsi in 1925, he was now working with an old school comrade whose horizons were much wider, whose military experience had been divorced from the kind of warlord manoeuvrings in which Li had been involved. The possibility of another course opened up, one which would eventually lead to a commitment beyond the simple aim of establishing and enlarging his own satrap. The two strands, of ' unreformed ' warlordism, and of politically-committed military control, continued to co-exist within Li, and within Huang, for most of their subsequent careers. The line between the two was fine, and, until 1925, the former appeared dominant.

3

Towards the revolution

Between 1921 and 1926, the province of Kwangsi passed through five years of chaos and isolation. A large number of petty warlords battled with each other, and sometimes with men from neighbouring provinces, for control of sections – frequently as small as one county – of the poverty-stricken province. In January 1923, for example, 17 separate major commands (with more than 1,000 troops) existed, totalling about 56,000 troops (see Appendix II).[1] This was not an exhaustive list, for it did not include smaller units. The number of troops in Kwangsi rose rapidly during the years of chaos; though exact figures are unobtainable, a figure of 118,000 for early 1925 seems plausible. This figure is far below that of 280,000 for Szechwan, or 220,000 for Kwangtung, but it was disproportionately high for a province as poor as Kwangsi.[2] Several of the units fighting in Kwangsi were not Kwangsi troops, but ' guest ' armies from neighbouring provinces, sometimes only in transit through Kwangsi, sometimes stranded in Kwangsi by vicissitudes within their own province, sometimes brought in by a Kwangsi commander to strengthen his own position. These ' guest ' armies were onerous for the local population; they had no local ties and they sequestered and plundered at will. Endemic warfare became a way of life, one which made the already crushing burdens of Kwangsi's peasantry even heavier. The instability of individual warlords added to the precariousness of the situation; at times, the division of local authority within the province shifted daily.

The nature of warfare was changing. Pitched battles were fought, often involving large numbers of casualties. The old style of warfare under which the two sides squared off, and the weaker side tactfully withdrew, disappeared with the demise of Lu Jung t'ing. The brutality of the Cantonese invasion in 1921 set the style for the next five years. Frequently, the battles between individual warlord armies revolved around struggle for control of sources of income, in particular of the opium traffic through Kwangsi. The economic life of the province was badly disrupted, first by warfare itself, and secondly by the effect that the warlords' constant demands for money had on the currency of the province; the only way, for example, that the Kweilin Chamber of Commerce could meet the demands of local warlords was to print its own money, unbacked by any significant metal reserves.[3] Individual warlords also printed their own notes to pay their troops. In September 1924, the *Yin-hang yüeh-k'an* estimated that the military in Kwangsi had issued $5,000,000,000 in virtually unbacked notes, the highest figure for any province (the next highest was Hupei, with $2,000,000,000).[4] Payment in these worthless notes turned transactions between soldiers and the civilian population into expropriation. Currency collapses also brought about large numbers of business failures, and sharply curtailed trade between Kwangsi and her neighbouring provinces. The expenditure on warfare devoured an enormous percentage of the official tax income of the province, not to speak of income raised by printing notes; figures for provincial income and expenditure for 1923, though only a limited guide to the actual financial situation, show that over 75 per cent of the province's expenditure went for military purposes.[5]

Regular taxation as a source of revenue gradually came to take second place to taxation on opium. Opium had been rigorously suppressed in Kwangsi during the late Ch'ing and the early years of the Republic; it was still not grown in significant quantities within the province, but opium in transit from Yunnan and Kweichow to Kwangtung was heavily taxed.[6] There were three main taxation points within Kwangsi, at Pose, near the Yunnan border, at Nanning, the provincial capital, and at Wuchow on the Kwangtung border; between Yunnan and Canton, the price of the opium was quadrupled by the taxation imposed on it.[7] These three cities were therefore frequently fought over. The controllers of the cities guaranteed the cargos of opium a safe conduct to the next taxation point, usually in the form of a military escort which supplemented the opium ships' own guards.

The traffic in opium (which will be discussed further below) was the one major form of commercial movement which continued. Other forms of water-borne trade were continually disrupted, since boats were commandeered to move troops. At times, the fragile communications of the province collapsed completely, encouraging still further the fragmentation of the province.

Other social evils flourished during this prolonged period of anarchy. Banditry became rampant. The interchange of men between bandit gangs and regular military units was frequent; expanding units sought new recruits from bandit gangs, the men of disbanded units returned to bandit careers.

The commanders of military units, whether former subordinates of Lu Jung-t'ing or not, were often illiterate former bandits. Of sixteen major commanders, only one or two had any modern training, one was a *hsiu-ts'ai*, and the others were all uneducated (see Appendix II). The various units were usually miserably armed and equipped; their weapons ranged from antique blunderbusses to more modern weapons acquired haphazardly, often from defeated forces, or in small consignments from Annam or Canton. Supplying these motley weapons with ammunition was an almost impossible task. This, plus the fact that commanders tended to value their better weapons more highly than their men, and therefore tried not to use them in critical situations where they might be damaged or lost, mitigated to some extent the blood-spilling of warlord engagements.

Some of the warlords probably had contact with secret societies – it would have been difficult for them to rise to positions of local importance without some connection with these organisations, which had exercised a powerful influence, though intermittent and localised, in Kwangsi politics. One can only sense the importance of these organisations at this stage, drawing from the knowledge of their importance at earlier periods, particularly before, during and after the Taiping Rebellion (see above, p. 24). They were now, as far as available source materials indicate, really secret, and those amongst the warlords who may have been associated with them kept their association quiet.

It was during this chaotic period that the nascent Kwangsi Clique established itself, and eventually won control over the whole province. It would be gratifying to think that the Clique's leaders were substantially different from the other warlords against whom they struggled for control of the province. But while they had within them potential for different patterns of development, as we have seen above, only an out-and-out apologist for the Clique could pretend that their behaviour during these five years differed materially from that of Kwangsi's other petty warlords. What ultimately differentiated them was their ability to co-operate with each other, their awareness of developments outside the province, and their leanings towards the forces of modernisation within China – in their case towards the Kuomintang in Canton. The alliance between Kwangtung and Kwangsi, signed by the Central Committee of the Kuomintang in March 1926, signalled the end both of the period of disunity within Kwangsi province, and of the careers of the leaders of the Kwangsi Clique as petty warlords. Before that their success was founded on their ability to play the warlord game better than their rival warlords.

Much of the detail of the rise to power of the Kwangsi Clique sounds petty and obscure. But it reveals the complexity of the situation, and suggests some of the modes by which power could be won – military skill, the formation of temporary but advantageous alliances, the reliance on personal connections – and some of the abilities which were required – tenacity, flexibility, a sense of timing. The Kwangsi leaders succeeded not by moving along a clearly-marked path, but by adapting to existing situations, by consolidating their own positions, and then darting out to take advantage of new opportunities. They had only one consistent goal: the domination of the province. Their modern military training gave them an edge over their rivals; it did not permit them to adopt a different mode of behaviour. They had to build themselves up, step by tortuous step, within the ill-defined but clearly understood war-lord mode of operation.

Kwangsi's descent into chaos began with the defeat of Lu Jung-t'ing in Kwangtung in 1920, and with the Cantonese invasion of the province the next year. By the end of 1921, Cantonese troops had occupied all the major centres in the province. Part of Kwangtung's intention in invading Kwangsi was to provide a starting-point for the northern expedition that Sun Yet-sen was planning; his idea was to attack north from the Kweilin region into Hunan, roughly along the route used by the Taipings.[8] Kwangtung was also pre-empting a threatened counter-attack by Lu Jung-t'ing, and avenging Kwangtung for its four years' occupation by Kwangsi troops. The campaign was brutal.

' The invaders pillaged everything in their route, abducting women and girls . . . there was a great fear almost everywhere; as soon as the Cantonese soldiers were seen arriving, the alarm was given, and a *sauve-qui-peut général* followed.' [9]

French missionaries in the province suddenly found themselves appreciated. Their compounds were crowded with refugees, and there were numerous conversions, ' non pas toutes déintéressés '.[10]

In many areas, no such protection was available. Between Nanning and Pose, a thousand hamlets were destroyed.[11] In the midst of the turmoil, Lu Jung-t'ing fled to Annam. His rule had given Kwangsi a decade of calm.

' There had been no serious natural disasters . . . nor had there been any currency collapse or advance collection of land taxes, nor any miscellaneous taxes to cause the people distress. The fact that the operations of the Kwangsi troops were all outside the province had brought about something difficult to achieve: no trouble from soldiers within the province. The only negative aspect was that the government had not been active in pursuing the welfare of the people, but because there was little of the oppression of bad government, the people could live their rough and simple lives without interference. . .'[12]

All that was now ended.

The Kwangsi Army disintegrated before the advancing Cantonese; its commanders either surrendered, fled the province, or took to the hills. Beyond the major centres and waterways of the province, many commanders were independent of any higher command. In these circumstances, the distinction between soldier and bandit was minimal. Kwangsi became ' an immense field of desolation '.[13] The economy broke down. The trade of the province for 1921 (according to Maritime Customs figures) was down by half over 1920, indicating that it must virtually have ceased with the Cantonese invasion in June.[14] The Kwangsi Bank collapsed, and its whole issue became worthless.

The Cantonese did not press their attack beyond the key regions of Kwangsi – the river valleys, the major cities, and the opium routes. There still remained many ' safe ' areas, where Kwangsi control continued, of which Li Tsung-jen's area near the Kwangtung border was one. Sun Yat-sen appointed as Governor of the province a close associate, Ma Chün-wu. Ma, a Kwangsi native, one of the few educated abroad (he was a doctor of Berlin University), was determined to bring good administration to his native province. But his good intentions could not extend the influence of his government beyond the walls of his *yamen* in Nanning. He was distrusted by the Cantonese as a Kwangsi man, and by the Kwangsi people as a Cantonese puppet.[15] He was the first of a series of weak or powerless Governors – there were six between 1921 and 1925 – whose claim to govern the province was never more than nominal. The fact, however, that the position continued to be occupied indicates that some sense of provincial unity survived, even at the periods of greatest disunity.

Ma did not last long. He was caught up in the growing hostility between Sun Yat-sen and Ch'en Chiung-ming over Sun's northern expedition, for which, at the end of 1921, Sun was preparing in Kweilin. Ch'en started to withdraw troops from Kwangsi, allowing control of Kwangsi to revert to local commanders, who moved into the areas vacated by Ch'en's troops. In the spring of 1922, Ma himself withdrew, taking with him the translations of European political thinkers on which he had worked during the long hours of inactivity entailed in administering an area he did not control.[16]

On the Cantonese withdrawal, Kwangsi was divided between an assortment of military units and bandit gangs. The economic burden of warlordism was terrible. Warlords financed their troops in part from tax revenue and note printing; but they also expected that their troops would loot and plunder, and 'live off the land' – that is, off the backs of the people. A semblance of unified authority remained, in that some of the military units were allied into a loose federation known as the Autonomous Army (Tzu-chih chün), which was set up in May 1922.[17] The authority of the commander, a former subordinate of Lu Jung-t'ing, Lin Chün-t'ing, was minimal; most of his 'subordinates' were genuinely autonomous, and ruled their own areas without reference to Lin. 'There were more battalion commanders than dogs, and the streets were full of commanders running around.'[18] Lin's only function was to negotiate lines of demarcation between the commanders of adjacent areas, though such matters were usually settled militarily.

Li Tsung-jen had a working agreement with the Autonomous Army, by which he maintained his local control over an area of seven *hsien* near the Kwangtung border (see Fig. 3).[19] When Huang Shao-hsiung joined him there in the summer of 1922, Huang established himself in the easternmost *hsien*, Jung hsien, his native place.

Huang's relationship with Li was not at first an easy one. Li had taken him in as a subordinate, not an ally; Li had 2,000 men and 1,000 rifles, to Huang's 1,000 men and 500 rifles.[20] Li had overhauled the civil and financial administration of the areas under his control, removing the traditional administrators – local gentry, tax farmers, etc. – from office, and substituting his own appointee, Huang Chung-yüeh, who was to serve with Li for the rest of his career. In this way he managed to raise the revenue of his area of control substantially.[21] His administrative reform was unusual; more typical warlord practice was to leave the old system of civil administration untouched, and simply to require local leaders to produce so and so much revenue. Li felt this was inefficient, and preferred to exercise direct control. His reforms were limited, dictated principally by a desire to increase revenue, not by a concern to institute social reform.

In this situation, Li clearly occupied a position of superiority to Huang. Li was slow and cautious, content to co-operate with the Autonomous Army, not concerned to expand his area of control. Huang was impetuous and eager for action. He did not want to break with Li, but neither did he want to be his subordinate for ever. In the event what the two men did was to officially sever their connection while maintaining covert links. Li remained an adjunct of the Autonomous Army, while Huang turned towards Kwangtung. For two years they took separate courses.

Early in 1923, Huang formed a superficially disadvantageous alliance with Shen Hung-ying, who controlled the port city of Wuchow on the

Kwangtung-Kwangsi border and the area adjacent to Huang's Jung hsien. Huang appeared to be subordinating himself to a notoriously untrustworthy ex-bandit, from whom he could expect no advancement. But Huang had relatives in Shen's entourage, and he knew that Shen was interested not in taking over more territory in Kwangsi (including Huang's), but in extending his power into Kwangtung by an attack on forces loyal to Sun Yat-sen.[22] Huang gambled on this enterprise failing, and on himself being able to seize Wuchow when it did, if he was first able to move troops there in the guise of allying with Shen. He was right. In April 1923, Shen attacked and was defeated by Cantonese troops. Acting in conjunction with Cantonese forces, Huang was able to take Wuchow in July.[23] He then officially 'surrendered' to the incoming Cantonese forces, thus allying himself for the first time with Kwangtung.[24]

This overt alliance was the culmination of a period of delicate negotiation between Huang and Canton, in which the go-between was Pai Ch'ung-hsi. Pai had been injured in 1922, when he and Huang were fleeing with the remnants of the Model Battalion. His injury, which left him with a permanent limp, was acquired not on the battlefield, but during a nocturnal inspection of his troops, to check that none of them were gambling in their bivouacs, a type of inspection which was characteristic of the disciplinarian Pai. His injury forced him to go to Canton for treatment. While there he became linked with the Kuomintang, and used this connection to act as liaison between Huang (and Li) and the Kuomintang.[25] Pai had arranged with Huang that he should now associate himself with the Kuomintang openly; he himself came to Wuchow with the Cantonese forces, bringing with him an instruction from Sun Yat-sen that Huang rename his forces the T'ao-tse chün (Anti-bandit Army).[26] Huang was to operate in Kwangsi, in close liaison with Cantonese troops of the First Division, under the command of Li Chi-shen, stationed between Wuchow and Canton. The new connection between Li Chi-shen and Huang was the start of a long association between Li and the future leaders of the Kwangsi Clique which eventually led to his complete identification with the Clique.*

Huang now controlled one of Kwangsi's key centres; his rear was secured by his *entente* with Canton, and the way was open to expand his control deeper into Kwangsi. He had risen in a brief period from a subordinate of Li Tsung-jen to a major figure in his own right. His

* Li Chi-shen was a native of Wuchow, who made his career in Kwangsi. His status in Kwangtung, however, was always that of an alien, and as the Kwangsi Clique became powerful, he naturally associated himself with it, to the point where he was considered the fourth member of its leadership. As ruler of Kwangtung from 1926 to 1929, his contribution to the Clique was considerable.

gamble had paid off. His impetuosity had not been, as it was later often to be, damped down by the caution of Li Tsung-jen.

Huang increased his forces after the capture of Wuchow by the standard procedure of amalgamating defeated troops. He also amalgamated another unit which had surrendered to Cantonese troops. To do this, he resorted to a stratagem which was more reminiscent of Chinese historical romances than of twentieth-century military technique. He invited the commander to a party held on board a 'flower-boat' in honour of a visiting Kuomintang dignitary, Teng Yen-ta, arrested him, threw him into the vault of the local bank and had him shot.[27] By these methods, Huang brought his troop strength up to three regiments (3,000 men).[28] Pai Ch'ung-hsi was his chief of staff, a critical appointment; Pai's ability as a tactician was considerable and undoubtedly had a great influence on Huang's subsequent military enterprises. Control of the opium trade passing through Wuchow gave Huang a substantial income. Huang had no intention of curtailing the trade; in fact he tightened up the operations of the Opium Suppression Board (the taxation agency) to make sure that no untaxed cargoes slipped through. The office was staffed day and night, and searchlights played on the river to prevent smuggling.[29]

Huang's reminiscences (Wu-shih hui-i) give the impression of a young man full of self-confidence and drive, of a man who had proved that he could outplay experienced warlords at their own game, and who intended from now on both to continue his warlord activities, and to develop in another direction – towards a closer alliance with the Kuomintang. In this he was disappointed. When he went to Canton early in 1924 to meet Sun Yat-sen, his expectations of a warm and grateful welcome were dashed. Though he made suitable declarations of revolutionary ardour, no additional recognition, and above all, no material aid was forthcoming. Sun made it clear to him that true revolutionaries must prove themselves by standing on their own feet – an indication that he felt that Huang had yet to display any genuine revolutionary commitment, and that he himself had no further purpose in mind for Huang.[30] Another year was to pass before Huang even joined the Kuomintang.

If Huang had established himself in a flamboyant way, Li Tsung-jen was still waiting cautiously in the wings. He was again allied with Lu Jung-t'ing, who had returned from exile at the end of 1922, and had re-established himself in the south and west of Kwangsi. Li did not believe that Lu would be strong enough to reassert control over the whole of Kwangsi – many of his subordinates were reluctant to accept his authority again – but he himself was not strong enough to oppose him.

For the moment, it suited Li and Huang to have a foot in both camps – one with Lu, the other with the Kuomintang. Their own private alliance must have been widely suspected, but in an atmosphere of constantly-shifting loyalties, it was quite possible to accept that the apparent split between them was a real one. It was in any case a very tenuous alliance; the two men did not meet, though they co-ordinated their strategy to some extent. Gradually they consolidated their areas of control in southern Kwangsi, by eliminating various petty warlords. Early in 1924, they linked their two domains together in a pincer action against the one remaining warlord. Their troops met at Fenghua on the West River, the place, formerly known as Chint'ien, from which the Taiping Rebellion had been launched.[31]

Though the meeting of the two armies was friendly, it was not an indication that a unified military grouping had been formed. Neither Li nor Huang were yet interested in full-scale co-operation. There was a degree of latent animosity between the two men, centring around Huang's virtual defiance of Li in expanding his own area of control; the two men were willing to co-exist with each other as long as mutual enemies still existed, but there was no guarantee that this co-existence would lead to closer co-operation.

The area the two men controlled was still small in absolute terms (15 *hsien*), but in strategic and economic terms it was very important. Li and Huang controlled the lower reaches of the West River within Kwangsi, and thus Kwangsi's connections with Kwangtung. With their rear protected by the entente with Kwangtung, and with a strong economic base within their region, they were in an excellent position to expand their control within Kwangsi. But before they embarked on any further schemes of expansion, the power balance within Kwangsi shifted rapidly.

Early in 1924, Lu Jung-t'ing had set out on a tour of inspection of his former subordinates. He took with him only a small force, his intention being to show the flag rather than to forcibly re-integrate units under his command. In the middle of April, however, he was unexpectedly besieged at Kweilin by his former subordinate Shen Hung-ying. The siege effectively neutralised the two strongest forces in Kwangsi – Lu's and Shen's – and it promised to be a long one. The topography of the Kweilin region made military operations difficult. The small plains, dominated by contorted hills which rose steeply from them, were easily defended. The besiegers were able to deflect the attacks of the reinforcements which Lu immediately summoned, and prevent them from relieving the city. The besieged on the other hand were safe behind the massive walls of the city; their chief enemy was hunger.

The siege started gaily, with a celebration in which the sound of fire-crackers competed with the sound of gunfire,[32] but as food supplies dwindled, it became unpleasant. Lu Jung-t'ing was impatient to be out, and had himself carried on to the walls, where 'rifle in hand, the old man . . . fired away at the foe'.[33] The foreign community was brought low by the death of the Reverend Cunningham, who was struck down by a stray bullet. His death occasioned the appearance of posters which proclaimed: ' Jesus God is not a strong spirit, that one of his missionaries has been killed.'[34] An attempt by a group of missionaries from Wuchow, led by the 'Cowboy Missionary', Rex Ray of Texas, to break through to the city to rescue missionaries caught in the siege ended in their capture by bandits, an incident whose settlement involved the execution of a large number of Chinese.[35]

The siege lasted three months. By the time it ended, Lu's authority within the province had been eroded, and it was time for Li Tsung-jen to break with him officially. He put his *de facto* autonomy on a formal basis by renaming his army the Ting-Kuei chün (Army to Settle Kwangsi), and with Huang Shao-hsiung launched a joint expedition against the provincial capital in June 1924.

Tactically, their task was easy: the bulk of Lu's forces was in the Kweilin region, attempting to extricate him from the city. But both men had apprehensions about attacking Lu. Attacking Lu promised them control of the provincial capital; in a province divided between several warlords, possession of the capital usually conferred upon the occupying warlord the symbol of legitimacy, plus the right to appoint civilian officials and to receive recognition from Peking. But it also involved them in an alliance with Shen Hung-ying, a man they regarded as of a much lower calibre than Lu. It went against the grain to attack Lu rather than Shen, and in particular to ally with Shen to do so – they had to protect their northern flank, which Shen dominated. But this was no time for moral scruples, and those that appear in the memoirs of the two men are probably *ex post facto*. At the time, they found it within themselves to overcome them.[36]

For their attack on Nanning Li and Huang marshalled about 8,000 troops.[37] Huang commandeered a large number of boats to transport his men up river; warlord armies did not concern themselves with sophisticated military organisation, certainly not with units such as transport corps; their transport was requisitioned from the local population. Additional financing was taken care of by a grant from Canton of $30,000.[38] Foreign sources believed that the attack was actually ordered by Sun Yat-sen.[39] It certainly had his support,[40] but it is unlikely that it was ordered from Canton. Li and Huang were still fighting under their own banners, and acting principally in their own interests.[41] Li had little idea of developments within the Kuomintang. When he joined the Kuomintang in October 1923, he was at first under the impression that he was re-registering in the T'ung Meng Hui, which he had joined in his youth.[42] That Canton was prepared to help the enterprise financially was merely an indication that it was also, coincidentally, in the interests of Canton.

In the event, the ' battle ' for Nanning proved to be a classic example of one form of ' silver-bullets ' warfare, though not of the kind which involved the attacking forces in large expenditures. To protect their city, which had frequently suffered, and was to suffer again, from the disastrous effects of warfare, the local Chamber of Commerce paid Lu Jung-t'ing's forces in the city $30,000 to evacuate the city peacefully.[43]

Li and Huang occupied Nanning, and then split their forces into two sections, one, under Pai Ch'ung-hsi attacking north towards Liuchow, a key city in central Kwangsi, the other pressing west towards Lungchow, Lu Jung-t'ing's old stronghold. Although resistance was expected in this region – the officers of the attacking army took their coffins with them – the defenders fled into Tongking, commandeering a fleet of taxis which had recently started operating between Lungchow and Langson (over the border). In the panic which preceded the arrival of the Li-Huang troops, the French consul at Lungchow enriched himself by extending consular territory to cover an area large enough to house such of the terrified local inhabitants as could pay his entry fees.[44]

THE FINAL CONSOLIDATION OF KWANGSI

The emergent Kwangsi Clique had succeeded, in their first major campaign, in occupying most of lower Kwangsi, and had scarcely extended their troops in the process. Part of the reason for their success lay in their tactical skill, in their ability to marshal their troops swiftly, and to press on rapidly from one success to another, without waiting, as many warlord armies did, to enjoy the fruits of success – that is, to loot and plunder the territory they occupied. This swiftness and manoeuvrability suggested a fairly high degree of discipline within their units. They had also proved themselves able manipulators in the making and breaking of alliances with other warlords – notably in their alliance with Shen Hung-ying – an indication that they possessed the fine sense of timing which was a prerequisite of success as a warlord. Their tactical and ' diplomatic ' ability gave them a high reputation as military men, and this reputation itself, which preceded them wherever they went, helped their enterprises, for it struck fear into their enemies.

The unity between Li, Huang and Pai gave them an advantage over other warlords; these three men were beginning to act as a team. Their unity was based, in practical terms, on the realisation that no one of them would ever come to anything without the other two, and that their forces were too small to allow them to operate individually. It was cemented by the ties of their similar backgrounds, and their school friendship. The three men's characters complemented each other: Huang supplied the dash and daring to keep them moving; Li's caution prevented Huang from over-reaching himself; while Pai's tactical abilities, which later gave him the nickname 'hsiao Chu-ko Liang', ensured their military successes.[45] (Pai had no independent command, and his position was for some time a step or two behind those of Li and Huang.)

As far as the emergence of the Clique was concerned, the summer of 1924 was a crucial period, for Li and Huang had to decide whether they wanted to transform what had been principally an alliance of convenience, in getting them both established, into a more permanent arrangement. They could no longer continue the haphazard and un-demanding co-operation which had worked while they were pursuing different, if parallel, aims. The size of their commands, both in terms of men and land, and their physical conjunction demanded that a formal structure be established, or that they split up – presumably to fight each other. The prospect of the second course was daunting. Both then commanded their own armies, and their own group of personally-loyal subordinates, but neither amounted to much without the other. A split now would cost them all they had won to date and would probably end with both being defeated – by Shen Hung-ying. A tighter unity, though still not a close one, served the interests of both men.

In July 1924, a joint headquarters was formed at Nanning, officially linking the two forces. Li became Commander-in-chief, Huang his deputy. Huang's subordination cost him hard; but he swallowed his pride, and in a typically dramatic gesture smashed his wine glass at the banquet to celebrate the establishment of the new headquarters, as a pledge of his loyalty to Li.[46]

Success brought no relaxation; threats were looming in several directions. There were many petty warlords to be mopped up; Shen Hung-ying was a dubious ally; and an attack from Yunnan threatened. The first threat to be encountered, however, was not a military one; it concerned the nature of their relationship to Canton.

Sun Yat-sen was desperately trying to curtail the power of the Yun-nanese and Kwangsi troops who had returned him to Canton in 1923, and who had now taken over control of Canton and its rich revenues. A plausible solution appeared to be to send Liu Chen-huan, the Kwangsi Commander in Canton, back to Kwangsi, and make him Governor. (As was frequently the case with Sun's actions, the question as to whether it lay within his jurisdiction or power to do such a thing does not seem to have concerned him.) Sun ordered Liu's appointment to this post shortly before he left for Peking, in November 1924.[47] Li and Huang were indignant at Sun's solution of his problem; they had believed that their efforts to reunify Kwangsi would lead to closer co-operation with Canton, not to a rebuff. Rather than accept Liu as Governor, they named themselves Rehabilitation Commissioner and Deputy Commissioner (*Shan-hou tu-pan*, *hui-pan*) of Kwangsi.[48] Huang then went to Canton for consultations with Hu Han-min, in charge at Canton in Sun's absence. On Huang's insistence, the Kuomintang leadership accepted the principle that he and Li Tsung-jen, of all Kwangsi generals within and without the province, would have sole right to Kuomintang recognition and co-operation. Their new appointments were confirmed, and their armies renamed the First and Second Kwangsi Armies. The new relationship between Li, Huang and the Kuomintang was symbolised by Huang's admittance into the Kuomintang at a special ceremony while he was in Canton.[49]

At the beginning of 1925, Kwangsi entered into its fifth consecutive year of civil war. The province was over-burdened with troops, the trade of the province was still badly disrupted, and the currency was hopelessly unstable. Bandits were active in many of the rural areas, while the cities were periodically looted by warlord armies; the military techniques of siege warfare and of arson bore directly on the urban population.[50] These sufferings did not concern Kwangsi's warlords; there was no sign that they would decrease. The year 1925 started with Li and Huang fighting on two fronts, against Shen Hung-ying and against T'ang Chi-yao of Yunnan.

Shen, now in control of Kweilin and Liuchow, attacked in February. T'ang Chi-yao entered Kwangsi in January, en route for Kwangtung, where, he claimed, he intended to take up the post of Deputy Grand Marshal of the Kuomintang, which Sun Yat-sen had unwisely conferred upon him the autumn before. (T'ang, one of the major warlords in southwest China, was *not* a devoted follower of Sun's; his interest was in expanding his own area of control, in increasing the influence of the Federalist Movement, with which he was so closely associated,[51] and in gaining control of the opium traffic through Kwangsi.) Fortunately for Li and Huang, T'ang was delayed at Pose while he tried to dispose of the large stock of opium with which he proposed to finance his expedition.[52]

Shen attacked in strength between Wuchow and Nanning, planning to divide the forces of Li and Huang. His attack was driven back, and forces under Pai Ch'ung-hsi occupied first Liuchow and then Kweilin, bringing northwest Kwangsi into the Li-Huang sphere of control. But the campaign against Shen had dangerously depleted forces at Nanning, which fell to the advancing troops of T'ang Chi-yao in mid-February. Li and Huang called up reinforcements from Kwangtung (actually Yunnanese trops under Fan Shih-sheng interested in returning to Yun- nan), making a combincd force of 20,000 men, supplied in part from Kwangtung, which laid siege to Nanning in early March.[53] Nanning now found itself besieged by its recent occupiers. Under siege, it became a 'city of mourning'.[54] It was not the only city suffering at this time. Counter-attacks by Shen Hung-ying in north and central Kwangsi led to the looting of Kweilin and Liuchow.[55] The people of the cities of Kwangsi were undergoing greater hardship than at any time since the Cantonese invasion in 1921.

But the end of civil war within Kwangsi was near. Shen Hung-ying's counter-attacks failed; T'ang's allies in Canton, Yang Hsi-min and Liu Chen-huan, were driven from the city in June; his own force at Nan- ning was worn down by hunger and disease. In July, the Yunnanese broke out of the siege, and fled back to Yunnan, pursued by Fan Shih- sheng, off to try to reconquer his native province.[56]

The province of Kwangsi, exhausted after five years of continuous civil war, was now unified under what came to be known as the new Kwangsi Clique (to distinguish it from Lu Jung-t'ing's group) – led by Li Tsung-jen, Huang Shao-hsiung and Pai Ch'ung-hsi.

THE ALLIANCE WITH KWANGTUNG

These three men had completed the first – and at that time probably the only – stage of their grand design. They had become rulers of their native province, and had raised their status from that of petty warlords to that of provincial warlords. Their power and their authority depended entirely on the armies they commanded. No civilian authority was func- tioning within the province, except the Maritime Customs, run by foreign nationals. Their achievement differed little from that of other men who had fought their way to control of their native province, except in the time that it had taken. The situation in Kwangsi had been so confused for so long, there were so many petty warlords, that their struggle for power had been protracted.

But, as we have noted above, these three men possessed within them- selves the potential to develop further. There was no indication that the conquest of Kwangsi would be the culmination of their careers. They were still young; none of them was much over thirty. Their military education had made them aware of the need to train troops properly, and they devoted considerable attention to this. Their armies were pruned of dead wood after their conquest. Of the twelve senior commanders of Li Tsung-jen's First Army at the time of reunification, only six continued their careers in the Kwangsi Armies; of the eighteen in Huang Shao-hsiung's Second Army only eight continued.[57] Those whose careers continued were almost all graduates of military schools; most of those who were phased out were not, but were men of less desirable origins who had become attached to Li or Huang during their period of growth. Whether this process extended to other ranks as well as officers is impossible to tell. The Kwangsi leaders were well aware, however, that good officers could not command bad soldiers, and were insistent on proper training and discipline in the ranks; their success in instilling such virtues had helped them appreciably against their warlord enemies. It is unlikely that they would have ignored other ranks in culling their forces.

The most notable distinction between Li, Huang and Pai and more typical provincial warlords was that they were interested in the modern ideas and ' isms ' which were circulating in China. Their horizons extended beyond the boundaries of Kwangsi. Their birth, into educated if declining families, gave them some pretensions to higher values, originally to the universalist values of Confucianism, now to the concept of the nation; their education had introduced them to a new concept of the role of the soldier; and their experience outside the province had attracted them to the revolutionary ideas of the Kuomintang. They lacked the unconscious provincialism of men such as Lu Jung-t'ing, for whom Kwangsi was a world on its own. But their identification with their province was still far stronger than was that of most educated Kwangsi natives, men such as Ts'en Ch'un-hsüan and Ma Chün-wu, whose roots were not provincial, but were set in the broader world of Chinese culturalism. Li, Huang and Pai were, in 1925, amalgams of provincial warlords and young men with immature but strong interests in modern, nationalist ideas. They felt themselves to be quite distinct from the crude, illiterate middle-aged Kwangsi warlords they had just defeated; they were young and educated. They found this amalgam uncomfortable. The only way out of this discomfiture, the only way of making the two strands compatible, was to cover the position they had won for themselves with more seemly clothing, to associate their warlord dominions with a modern, nationalist force outside the province, that is, with the Kuomintang. They would do this without compromising their local power. They would offer their military strength to an alliance, in return for the granting of respectability as associates of a nationalist enterprise.

It appeared, in the summer of 1925, that such an alliance was about to be formed. They were still not exclusively committed to such a course of action, as their sending of representatives to Tuan Ch'i-jui's Shan-hou hui-i (Rehabilitation Conference) in Peking in early 1925 indicated,[58] but Kwangtung and the Kuomintang was clearly the main focus of their interest. The Kuomintang now seemed prepared to enter into a formal alliance, to supersede the various types of informal recognition it had granted Li and Huang in the past. In his speech to the Military Committee of the newly-formed National Government in July 1925. Chiang Kai-shek outlined plans for the complete unification of the two provinces. He saw Kwangsi as the first stepping-stone of a future northern expedition (as Sun Yat-sen had done in 1921), and proposed the establishment of military schools, arsenals and even an aeroplane factory in Kwangsi. Strategic roads linking the two provinces would be built. Chiang referred to the geographic importance of Kwangsi for Kwangtung, and to its 'very close connection with revolutionary history', which he coupled with the loyalty of the present Kwangsi leaders to Canton. He made it clear that any alliance would involve the incorporation of the Kwangsi Armies into the Kuomintang Armies on an absolute basis. His tone was severe; he was not contemplating an alliance of equals, but the submission of one to the other.[59] (It is worth noting that Chiang's proposals for the incorporation of potential allies in 1925, with their emphasis on submission and transfer of military control, were terms which he did not, or could not, apply to warlord armies during the course of the northern expedition. The indiscriminate incorporation then of units which remained effectively autonomous created huge problems for the Kuomintang, which will be discussed below.)

Though Chiang's proposals cannot have embodied the kind of alliance that the Kwangsi leaders would have proposed themselves, or which they would respect in practice as well as in theory, they accepted them for the moment.[60] On 6 August the Kuomintang Government ordered Li and Huang to prepare for the reorganisation of the province's government.[61] Li Chi-shen and Wang Ching-wei visited Kwangsi separately to discuss full-scale unification of the two provinces, and Kwangsi participation in a future northern expedition.[62]

The negotiations did not immediately bear fruit. Many Kuomintang leaders were wary of an alliance with the new Kwangsi leaders, whose revolutionary commitment they regarded with scepticism. The assassination of Liao Chung-k'ai at the end of August, and the start of the second expedition against Ch'en Chiung-ming diverted Kuomintang attention, and for a while there was no progress towards unification. The question was shelved.

Nevertheless, in some ways Kwangsi was rapidly drawing closer to Canton. Kwangsi supported the Hong Kong-Canton Strike, and encouraged the anti-foreign and anti-imperialist movements within Kwangsi. In Wuchow, on the Kwangtung border, the anti-foreign boycott was rigid. The Labour Federation, organised there in December 1924, was strong enough to demand compulsory membership. It was also strong enough to force the local military authorities to arrest vessels suspected of breaking the boycott.[63] British residents withdrew from Wuchow in July, on the advice of their consul; shortly afterwards the consulate was wrecked during an anti-imperialist demonstration.[64] Even in Nanning, further removed from Cantonese influence, a workers' syndicate was formed in the summer of 1925.[65]

How much this activity arose spontaneously in response to activity in Kwangtung, how much it reflected the re-opening of good communications with Kwangtung, or how much it developed as a result of a conscious policy on the part of the Kwangsi leaders, is difficult to gauge. Certainly all three factors were important. The demonstrations and boycotts were tolerated and frequently encouraged by the Kwangsi leaders. Foreigners believed that they had become ' bolsheviks '.[66] In February 1925, Huang Shao-hsiung personally led a demonstration against the Catholic mission in Nanning.[67] Whatever resident foreigners felt about the arrival of the ' red peril ' in the province, Kuomintang officials were less sanguine about mass activity there. The manifesto of the Second Kuomintang Congress, held in January 1925, reported that the mass movements in Kwangsi were poorly developed, and that no proper revolutionary basis had yet been established.[68] The Kwangsi leaders were not interested in social or economic reform, and had no intention of allowing the mass movements to develop an independent base. Their espousal of modern ideas meant the espousal of nationalist ideals for the re-establishment of national unity, and for the expunging of China's humiliation at the hands of the Powers. There was no commitment to social or economic change, and in the absence of strong popular opinion, no felt need to respond to pressure. The Kwangsi leaders in fact succeeded in deflecting the development of such pressure, by encouraging mass movements, but at the same time channelling their activities into anti-foreign agitation, which represented no threat to the existing social and economic order.

Kwangsi was also moving closer to Canton on the military front, and sent troops to participate in two campaigns, one in the North River valley, one in the southwest Kwangtung, which helped in the final re-unification of Kwangtung province. Having built up large forces to fight their internal enemies, the Kwangsi leaders now had surplus military capacity which they could deploy to help their neighbour. From these two campaigns they were able to expand their own forces further, and to increase their armaments through captured weapons. Kwangsi was still dependent on external supplies of armaments; the Kwangsi arsenal at Kweip'ing only produced bullets.[69]

By the beginning of 1926 Kuomintang power had been extended over the whole of Kwangtung; the time had come for the Kuomintang to expand still further, and to start on the implementation of its grand design to reunify the whole of China. As a first stage, negotiations began again to bring Kwangsi into full alliance with Kwangtung.[70]

In his article, 'Military Separatism and the Process of Reunification under the Nationalist Regime, 1922–1937', Professor C. Martin Wilbur has described the background to this process of expansion from the Kuomintang side.[71] Let us see what the alliance meant to the new Kwangsi leaders.

At the end of January 1925, Wang Ching-wei (Chairman of the Canton Government) and T'an Yen-k'ai paid a visit to Wuchow, as a prelude to official negotiations. The two men made a round of speeches and visits, and were enthusiastically received by the people of Wuchow. Informal discussions were held with the Kwangsi leaders, who again signified their willingness for an alliance, and their desire to participate in a northern expedition. It remained only to draw up a detailed agreement. Pai Ch'ung-hsi, the Kwangsi leader who knew the Canton political world best, went down to Canton to negotiate individual points, and to act as chief Kwangsi delegate on the Kwangtung-Kwangsi Unification Committee which was established in Canton.[72]

If Pai had expected a quick settlement, he was disappointed; the negotiations did not go smoothly. The Kuomintang negotiators were tough, demanding from the Kwangsi leaders concessions which would ensure their subjugation to the Kuomintang. There were three main points of dissension: the number of armies Kwangsi would contribute to the National Army; the granting of financial aid to Kwangsi by Kwangtung; and the amount Kwangsi should pay its soldiers. Kwangsi wanted to contribute two armies to the National Revolutionary Army, the Seventh and Eighth; the Kuomintang wanted only one. (At this stage, the National Revolutionary Army consisted of six armies – army corps, of which only two, the First and the Fourth, were unquestionably loyal to the Kuomintang; the other four were made up of former warlord troops stationed in Kwangtung, some of them poorly converted.[73])

Kwangsi wanted financial aid from Kwangtung, which the Kuomintang was unable and unwilling to offer. The Kuomintang advocated a payment of ten *yüan* per month to common soldiers, which Kwangsi could not afford to pay without financial assistance.[74] Deadlock was reached, and Pai returned to Kwangsi at the end of February. The suspicion in certain circles in Canton that Kwangsi only wanted financial aid from Kwangtung was strengthened. In other circles, it must be said, the standing of the Kwangsi leaders, particularly of Pai Ch'ung-hsi, who was best known in Canton, was high. Michael Borodin apparently had a higher respect for him than for many local figures.[75]

The Kwangsi leaders were determined to continue negotiations, and they were also prepared to compromise. They drew up a new set of preconditions, whereby they undertook to finance themselves independently, provided that they were allowed to establish two armies. In March, Huang Shao-hsiung went down to Canton, and an agreement was finally reached, though not even on the revised Kwangsi terms. Only one army was established, the Seventh. In return for this concession, Canton gave vague promises about financial help, though it is doubtful that much was ever given. Half of Kwangsi's troops were reorganised as the Seventh Army, commanded by Li Tsung-jen; the rest remained under the Kwangsi Military Bureau, and were later reorganised as the Fifteenth Army. No specific provisions were made, however, for the submission of the Seventh to the National Army headquarters in Canton. This was an important omission, and one which the tone of negotiations had not foreshadowed; it was the first of many bows by the Kuomintang to what were seen to be the realities of the military situation – that where the imposition of authority would be difficult, an acceptance of an imperfect alliance was to be preferred to no alliance.

On 15 March, an official act of unification was passed by the Central Political Committee of the Kuomintang.[76] Huang Shao-hsiung returned to Kwangsi with a crowd of young political workers and a Russian adviser, a former steel-worker, Mamaev, who turned out to be incompetent both as a military and as a political adviser.

The unification was achieved. If it caused any excitement in Canton, it was overshadowed almost immediately by the SS *Chung-Shan* Incident, where crucial questions of revolutionary direction were involved, questions which scarcely figured in the Kwangtung-Kwangsi alliance.[77] The final form of the alliance suggested that it was a marriage of convenience, and a quiet one at that. By linking Kwangsi to the ideology of the Kuomintang, by enrolling their armies into the Kuomintang *en masse*, as the leap in Kwangsi Party enrolment between 1925 and 1926 suggests that they did,[78] the Kwangsi leaders increased their already commanding position within their province, putting themselves at the head of the nascent revolutionary movement. As far as a closer political integration with the Kuomintang outside Kwangsi was concerned, the Kwangsi leaders held back. Canton was already seething with factionalism and intrigue. Li, Huang and Pai looked quizzically at the factions and cliques of Canton, and responded to what they saw by tightening their own unity, moving towards the foundation of their own separate military clique within the Kuomintang.

Three months after the signing of the act of unification, Kwangsi forces were already in action on the Northern Expedition. Over the next three years, Li Tsung-jen and Pai Ch'ung-hsi established themselves as national figures. But they kept their base inviolate, under the control of Huang Shao-hsiung. They were able to retire there when they were defeated on the national scene in 1929, and to revert to the role they had shunned in 1926 – that of provincial warlords. They had cause to be grateful that the unification of 1926 had been so superficial, and that the Kuomintang had not enforced its hegemony over the province.

The alliance with Kwangsi was the first which the Kuomintang Government made with another province. For a variety of reasons – lack of time, lack of funds, lack of personnel, distaste for forcible incorporation of Kwangsi, the relative unimportance of Kwangsi – the Kuomintang failed to establish any significant control over its first convert. The alliance departed from the principles for alliance laid down by Chiang Kai-shek in 1925 (see p. 58), and from the spirit of the final negotiations, a departure which apparently went unnoticed at the time. It set a pattern for the treatment of provinces incorporated under the Kuomintang banner as the Northern Expedition proceeded. In almost every case, government of the province was entrusted to existing provincial power-holders. This pattern was less true of provinces seized by military action, but it was true almost without exception of the provinces which submitted voluntarily. It was a tacit recognition of the Kuomintang's inability to impose any other settlement in the first instance; it was also a contribution of the gravest importance to the failure of the Kuomintang to establish a genuine hold over the areas it came to control in name.

With Kwangsi, the Kuomintang ignored in practice the question of unity. It would have been difficult to do anything else. Canton could send in young activists to encourage political work, but it could not force the submission of pro-Kuomintang but still independent military commanders, without crushing them militarily; and the Kuomintang was not strong enough to fight potential allies, however qualified their loyalty. It did not pursue actively the one policy which might have undermined the independent stance of the Kwangsi militarists from within – the policy of attaching forceful political commissars to the newly-allied forces. A political commissar was attached to the Seventh, but more as a window-dressing than as an intention of politicising the army; he was given no authority. His anomalous position may have been a reflection of the unwillingness of the Kwangsi leaders to see their men become politically aware, and therefore less tractable. It may also have been an indication of the suspicion of Chiang Kai-shek, now firmly in control of the National Revolutionary Army, of the work of political advisers, whom he regarded as trouble-makers, men whose function was to curb the absolute authority of the officer over the soldier.[79] Far from being politicised, Kwangsi troops continued to fight under the personal banners of their commanders.[80] The failure either to exert effective authority over the Seventh Army, or to detach its men from their personal allegiances to their commanders, was a dangerous precedent.

4

Soldiers of the revolution

The Northern Expedition, the principal military aim of the Kuomintang for many years, finally got under way in the early summer of 1926. Sun Yat-sen's picaresque attempts to launch it earlier had been defeated by ' betrayal ' in the rear – more accurately by the refusal of loosely-allied militarists to risk their forces on Sun's impractical and grandiose schemes. But in 1926, the Kuomintang had achieved a position in which a northern expedition seemed to have an outside chance of success; it had its own army, the Party apparatus had been reorganised along Leninist lines, it controlled a strong base in Kwangtung, and it was beginning to collect allies.[1] There was general enthusiasm within the Kuomintang for an expedition; the only serious question at issue was its timing. In the event, the Northern Expedition started almost accidentally.

The account of the Expedition which follows has unavoidably to cover familiar ground.[2] But it discusses the expedition not in terms of the Kuomintang or the CCP, not in terms of mass movements and revolutionary upheaval, but through the eyes of one of the many warlord converts who came to make up the bulk of the ' revolutionary ' forces, and who at the end of the Expedition still controlled most of China. It focuses on the experience of the nascent Kwangsi Clique and its Seventh Army, and shows how it reacted to the tortuous events of 1926 and 1927. Though the detail of the story is almost unbearably complicated, the main line is clear: that the Kuomintang drew huge numbers of converts under its banner, but failed to remould them. For the Kwangsi Clique, the Expedition was a strangely circular process; the Clique started on the Expedition apparently anxious to become part of a national movement, to escape from its regionalist identity, and ended up more regionalist than ever, and in control of a much larger region.

The Kwangsi warlords were the first warlords not based in Kwangtung to ally with the Kuomintang; T'ang Sheng-chih of Hunan was the second. His independent activities in Hunan during the first four months of 1926, which started as an attempt to seize control of Hunan, and ended with his seeking emergency aid from his southern neighbours, played a key role in starting the Northern Expedition.

T'ang in early 1926 was *Shan-hou tu-pan* (Rehabilitation Commissioner) of south Hunan, one of the four division commanders of the Hunan Army. He was an uneasy blend of the traditional and the modern, a devout Buddhist, whose actions were often dictated by the advice of his personal priest,[3] but also a graduate of the Paoting Military Academy, who used the old school network to keep up connections with fellow-graduates serving elsewhere. T'ang's ambitions to conquer Hunan had led him to seek a defensive alliance with the Kwangsi leaders (two of whom were Paoting graduates) in order to secure his rear before he attacked north. His first overtures were made in the winter of 1925.[4] In January 1926 a man already linked to the Kwangsi leaders, Yeh Ch'i, appeared in Wuchow. Yeh was a Kwangsi native who had made his career in the Hunan Army; he was a *t'ung-hsiang* (fellow-native) of Huang Shao-hsiung, and a Paoting classmate of Huang and Pai Ch'ung-hsi.[5] Yeh was not in fact acting for T'ang, but for the Hunan Governor, Chao Heng-t'i. He had come to Kwangsi to try to persuade the Kwangsi leaders, still not officially allied with the Kuomintang, to support Chao's Federalist cause.[6] What changed the nature of Yeh's visit, and changed his principal from Chao to T'ang, was that it coincided fortuitously with the visit of Wang Ching-wei. Yeh was impressed with the pro-Kuomintang demonstrations in Wuchow, and with the new-found revolutionary enthusiasm of the Kwangsi leaders. He wavered in his support for Federalism. The Kwangsi leaders then spread rumours that he had come to negotiate T'ang's alliance with the Kuomintang.[7] Yeh accepted this new role, without apparently consulting T'ang. He was taken down to Canton and given an official reception at the Whampoa Academy.[8]

This kind of bizarre manipulation was quite in character with the negotiations between warlords; go-betweens such as Yeh were constantly on the move between warlord headquarters; it was usual for a man contemplating any major move to have discussions with several potential allies at the same time. The Kuomintang had no scruples about indulging in such activities itself. Its emissaries were in contact with a wide range of potential converts or allies, selected not on the ground of revolutionary potential, but for possible strategic value. Negotiations (which subsequently broke down) were in progress early in 1926 with Sun Ch'uan-fang, overlord of the five southeastern provinces of Kiangsu, Chekiang, Anhwei, Fukien and Kiangsi, to see whether at the least a pact of non-aggression could be reached between the two parties.[9]

The Kuomintang even used the converts it got through such devices to bring in other converts. A Kwangsi Clique subordinate, Chang Jen-min, was sent to Szechwan to try to secure defections of warlords there whom he knew personally.[10] Yeh's elaborate reception in Canton therefore surprised no one. T'ang Sheng-chih, who found himself allied to the Kuomintang without ever having planned such a development, saw no harm in it. Strategically, it protected his rear, and was therefore convenient. In March, he drove north and took Ch'angsha.

His association with the Kuomintang did not change the character of his enterprise – to establish himself as provincial warlord of Hunan. He adopted the slogan of the provincial warlord, *pao-ching an-min*,[11] proclaimed himself Governor of Hunan, paid lip-service to the Federalist Hunan constitution, denied his connection with the Kuomintang, and started negotiations with Wu P'ei-fu to have Wu confirm his status.[12] But Wu would not play; he put his support behind Chao Heng-t'i, and prepared to attack T'ang. T'ang abruptly changed tactics, and reasserted his devotion to the Kuomintang cause, hoping for aid against the attack from the north which he knew he would not be able to withstand.[13]

The counter-attack started in April, and by early May T'ang had been driven back to Hengyang, where he dug himself in on the edge of the hills. He called desperately for help from the Kuomintang, and, since T'ang's almost certain defeat would leave the Kuomintang facing Wu P'ei-fu, Kuomintang military leaders decided, on 24 April, to send troops to his aid.[14] Kwangsi troops had been massed on the Hunan-Kwangsi border since T'ang first started north, and heavy recruiting was going on in north Kwangsi.[15] Kwangsi would be seriously affected by a defeat for T'ang; there were exiled Kwangsi troops in Hunan, who would threaten Kwangsi if Wu did move south.

It was thus in the immediate interests of both the Kuomintang and of the Kwangsi leaders that Kwangsi forces should go to the aid of T'ang. The Kwangsi leaders lobbied strenuously for an immediate start.[16] In the first week of May, the Kuomintang Military Committee ordered the Seventh Army into Hunan, the first troop deployment of the Northern Expedition.[17]

There was dissension within the Kuomintang about the timing of the Northern Expedition. On the one hand, there was the feeling that an expedition should only be launched when the Kuomintang had consolidated its hold over Kwangtung, and had established a firm political base for its future rule; this feeling was strongest among the Left-wing of the Kuomintang, and among the Soviet advisers.[18] On the other hand was the desire to start it immediately, to extend the Kuomintang's geographical control as quickly as possible, and to worry about political stabilisation afterwards; this was the view of the Military Committee, dominated by Chiang Kai-shek. The Hunan operation strengthened

Chiang's already commanding hand, for by extending the Kuomintang's operations into Hunan, the Expedition had in effect been started. The question now was to get it started officially. On 21 May, the Second Plenum of the Kuomintang Central Executive Committee declared its intention of embarking on an immediate expedition.[19]

By mid-May, Kwangsi troops were in action in Hunan, and at the beginning of June they were joined by units of the Fourth Army. T'ang Sheng-chih's army was renamed the Eighth Army, and he himself became Field Commander of the Kuomintang forces (Ch'ien-ti ts'ung-chih-hui). By mid-June, there were 50,000 troops in Hunan under the Kuomintang flag.[20] The Kuomintang found itself in the anomalous position of having its great revolutionary enterprise led, at the front, by a man who only a few weeks before had been an undistinguished warlord, and staffed in the main by troops of other recently-converted warlord troops – of Kwangsi.

At the beginning of July, Kuomintang forces in Hunan attacked north, meeting little resistance. The summer floods in Hunan were so severe that the enemy had not expected a Kuomintang attack, and was caught off balance.[21] Kuomintang forces took the Hunan provincial capital on 10 July, two days before the Northern Expedition was officially launched in Canton.

The political activists who moved north with the armies from Kwang-tung started work immediately, organising mass movements, and bringing together existing revolutionary organisations within the province. This work was in the hands of the lower echelons of the Kuomintang and CCP cadres, and was immediately successful.[22] At the top of the political scale, revolutionary enthusiasm was less apparent. T'ang Sheng-chih was made chairman of the Hunan Provincial Committee of the Kuomintang, but his political commitment was non-existent. He allowed no effective political work within his army, appointing as political commissar one of his own subordinates, Liu Wen-tao; his troops were encouraged to worship Buddha, not the Three Principles of the People.[23]

After the fall of Ch'angsha, there was a hiatus while the next moves for the Northern Expedition were planned. Operations continued to mop up all of Hunan south of the Tungt'ing Lake, but there was no serious fighting. There were however further conversions. Other Hunanese units declared for the Kuomintang, as did the armies of neighbouring Kweichow.

Chiang Kai-shek, Commander-in-chief of the Expedition, left for Ch'angsha at the end of July. A top-level military meeting was held there on 13 August, at which it was decided to attack Wuhan immediately, taking advantage of Wu P'ei-fu's preoccupation with Feng Yü-hsiang.[24] Chiang moved to impose his authority over T'ang Sheng-chih and Li Tsung-jen, who had acted independently on the campaign to date. Their plan for the continuation of the Expedition was rejected, and their subordination to General Headquarters, and to Chiang Kai-shek, spelled out.[25] They agreed, somewhat resentfully, to accept Chiang's supremacy.[26]

The Fourth, Seventh and Eighth Armies were to bear the brunt of the fighting for the attack on Wuhan, while the Ninth and Tenth Armies were to make a flanking attack from Kweichow. With the exception of the Fourth Army (with only half its troops in Hunan), these armies were all recent converts, and the Kuomintang cannot have had any confidence in their revolutionary character. In speeches delivered to the Seventh and Eighth Armies in Ch'angsha, Chiang Kai-shek attempted to instil some revolutionary spirit into the men, by praising their courage and their achievements in conquering Hunan; he even held them up as examples for the whole National Revolutionary Army.[27] Whether his speeches had an effect on the men is dubious; they left T'ang Sheng-chih, whose chief concern now was that the rich plum of Wuhan should fall into his hands, unmoved.

The attack on Wuhan saw the first heavy fighting of the Expedition. The Fourth Army, fighting up the railway line, met heavy resistance. But the Seventh Army, advancing through wooded, sparsely-populated country, led by local guides, was able to break through behind Yochow, forcing the surrender of the city to the advancing Kuomintang armies. In the last week of August, the Fourth Army was involved in heavy fighting for a series of strategic railway bridges, the last defensive positions before Wuch'ang. Wu P'ei-fu was so determined to hold them that he came to the front himself, and ordered that any men who broke ranks should be beheaded on the spot.[28] But his threats could not prevent his forces from being driven back; the gates of Wuch'ang were closed for a siege on 1 September.

The investment of Wuch'ang struck terror into the hearts of the Kuomintang's enemies, who had never considered it a serious threat. ' The southerners whose preparation for the attack on Yochow was regarded with a smile of indifference a week ago are now hammering on the gates of Wuchang. . .'[29] The siege held; though the Fourth and Seventh Armies launched a series of attacks on the city, they were unable to break in. But T'ang Sheng-chih's Eighth Army crossed the Yangtse up-river without opposition, and on 6 September occupied the unwalled cities of Hankow and Hanyang, across the river from Wuch'ang. The local commander, Liu Tso-lung, defected to the Kuomintang, and was made commander of the Fifteenth Army.[30] This appointment aroused the fury of the Soviet adviser Teruni, who believed that Liu could easily have been defeated, and that bringing a ' scoundrel ' like Liu into the ranks of the Kuomintang was laying up future trouble.[31] Liu showed no signs of imminent political conversion; shortly after his appointment, he forced the local Political Department to release one of his supporters, a local ' kung-tse ' (scab) who had been arrested by Hankow workers.[32]

THE PROBLEM OF CONVERTED WARLORDS

A contradictory situation was developing in the rapidly-expanding Kuomintang Armies, a situation which for the time being was masked by the excitement of the Kuomintang's advance, by the growth of the mass movements, and by political struggles within the Kuomintang. At the beginning of September 1926, the Kuomintang found itself with fifteen armies under its flag, only six of which had any long-standing connection with the Kuomintang. The other nine were converts:

' there had been very few engagements during the original northward drive ... in which the National Army had not been assisted in or presented with victory by the treachery of troops either in the actual fighting army of the enemy or in the rear '.[33]

Many defections were brought about on Kuomintang initiative; no one who offered to defect was spurned. The speed of the expansion of the Kuomintang Armies made it impossible to bring these converted armies under Party control without temporarily halting the northern expedition. The leaders of the Kuomintang realised this, but tacitly decided against a pause for consolidation. The impetus of success drove them on; the warlord converts were left to their own devices.

There was at least a formal acceptance of the ideal of revolution on the part of the converts. Many of them believed that it was the force of ideological commitment which had enabled the ill-equipped, outnumbered Kuomintang forces to defeat Wu P'ei-fu. They were also aware of the impact of the Kuomintang's ideology beyond its own armies.

' Mercenary armies were no longer always reliable. Soldiers, recruited from the pauperised masses, were liable to be infected by the spirit of revolt spreading through the peasant masses. Minor militarists tried to exploit that psychological atmosphere for promoting their own ambition. They declared their adhesion to the Kuomintang and the anti-imperialist movement, in order to retain the loyalty of their soldiers. . .'[34]

Few were as blatant in their contempt for the mass movements as was Liu Tso-lung. They wanted political instructors attached to their armies, for they had grasped the connection between political training and military efficiency.[35] As an anti-Kuomintang commentator in the *North China Herald* put it: 'It is felt that the Southerners in some degree are fighting for an ideal, which however erroneous, gives them an enthusiasm entirely lacking among the Northerners.'[36]

The desire to instil a modicum of political enthusiasm into their troops did not mean that the converted warlords intended to remould themselves. Their primary concern remained the retention of regional control. Their regions had been affected to a greater or lesser extent by the waves of revolutionary excitement sweeping China; to maintain their position, they had to compromise, at least temporarily, with this phenomenon. Most of the warlords who were transformed into generals of the National Revolutionary Army were neither revolutionary nor nationalist. Their local functions and their political attitudes changed little in their transformation. But they gained respectability within the new political situation in China, a respectability which was bought very cheaply. They could no longer be called 'warlords', a category now reserved for military figures who were opposed to the Kuomintang. They found their new titles comfortable; old-style warlordism was increasingly unfashionable in a country stirred by nationalism. As Lu Jung-t'ing had sought official sanction from the government in Peking for his independent position in Kwangsi (see p. 28), so the new converts sought an alliance with what promised to be the new orthodoxy in China. The fact that they could acquire these alliances without surrendering local control made them doubly attractive.

The retention of local control aggravated an already serious problem for the Kuomintang Armies: the problem of finance and supply. Kuomintang finances, inadequate before the Expedition began, were not improved by the fall of Hunan, for the provincial treasury was empty.[37] The considerable revenues of Wuhan (which fell off as production declined in response to the organisation and strikes of Wuhan's workers, and as the foreign powers imposed a blockade on Wuhan's trade) had to supply the Hunan and Hupei troops; Kwangtung's surplus revenues were earmarked for the forthcoming campaigns into Kiangsi and Fukien.[38] There was no spare money to support troops without local bases. To maintain his own troops, therefore, the converted warlord had to keep his original sources of income, and thus could not afford to surrender local control. A vicious circle was created, which made the establishment of a centralised financial system impossible.

The Seventh Army, operating away from its base, found itself in constant supply difficulties. Though the Seventh had been promised financial aid from Kwangtung, this did not materialise; Kwangsi had to bear a major part of the cost of the upkeep of the Seventh on the Expedition, a task made difficult both by the poverty of the province, and by the increasingly large distances separating the troops from Kwangsi.[39] The Seventh was chronically short of weapons, ammunition and clothing; the troops, who had started out from Kwangsi in summer uniforms, suffered badly from the cold as the autumn wore on. Requisitioning from the local population was forbidden by the Kuomintang, so the Kwangsi troops resorted to the traditional warlord practice of forcing unbacked paper currency on the people.[40]

At this stage, the problem of the effect that this sort of behaviour would have on the image of the Kuomintang, the problem in fact of the continuance of warlord practices in a revolutionary army, was veiled. But as the area controlled by the Kuomintang increased, and as more warlords converted, it became more open, though it still attracted far less attention than the internal problems of the Kuomintang.

THE KIANGSI CAMPAIGN

Early in September, the menacing activities of Sun Ch'uan-fang in Kiangsi and on the Yangtse made it clear that the Kuomintang would have to attack into Kiangsi or be attacked itself. The siege of Wuch'ang showed signs of being a long one, since the Kuomintang lacked wall-piercing artillery; it was continued, but with a reduced force. The campaign into Kiangsi started in the first week of September with the bulk of the attacking force moving in from Hunan; the Seventh Army moved east from Hupei along the Yangtse, while further units attacked north from Kwangtung up the Kan Valley. The campaign, which started off on a note of wild enthusiasm, quickly got bogged down. Nanch'ang, the Kiangsi provincial capital, was taken, but not held; the attackers were thrown back in confusion. On the Yangtse the Seventh found itself cut off by enemy troops landed in its rear, and out of contact with headquarters.

With the Kuomintang forces in disarray, the situation was suddenly turned in its favour by threatened defections in Sun Ch'uan-fang's ranks. Sun pulled back into Chekiang and Kiangsu, and Nanch'ang and Kiukiang fell into Kuomintang hands. The fighting, though brief, had been severe. The Kiangsi Campaign lacked the easy successes and low casualties of the Hunan Campaign. The Sixth Army took fifty per cent casualties in its first, abortive attack on Nanch'ang.[41] The Kuomintang troops were demoralised by such casualties, by continuing supply difficulties, and by the onset of winter. For the time being, the impetus of advance slowed down; the only fighting was now in Fukien, where Ho Ying-ch'in was advancing with part of the First Army.

The end of the Kiangsi Campaign might have been a good time to increase political work in the recently-converted armies, to restore the morale of troops facing a hard winter in alien surroundings, and to turn the men and their commanders into genuine revolutionaries. But this kind of work would require a temporary freezing of the size of the Kuomintang Armies, and a massive expenditure of time and energy. Again the Kuomintang chose not to delay overall growth, but to continue to expand. The Kuomintang continued to welcome all defectors, and its emissaries continued to pay secret visits to susceptible enemy generals to arrange their future defection. In October and November, a number of warlords from Fukien, Kiangsi and Chekiang joined the Kuomintang Armies. These men included stereotypes of the venal warlord – men such as Yang Sen of Szechwan and Fan Shih-sheng of Yunnan. In the short run, it was easier for the Kuomintang to welcome them than to fight them. How must it cost the Kuomintang in concessions, or in terms of cash is difficult to assess. Some of them undoubtedly converted as a result of ' silver bullets '; others converted because they feared extinction by the Kuomintang Armies; others joined what they thought was the future – they put themselves in tune with the general trend of events within China. The Kuomintang made massive concessions on the degree of local control which converted warlords would retain. By allowing them to retain virtually independent control, it left itself with no future avenues of development within their areas. The warlords had been converted, but not transformed. They were in reality undefeated. To gain control of their areas, the Kuomintang would still have to defeat them at a later date; its apparent conquest was only a postponement of real conquest.

The majority of the Kuomintang leaders seemed unconcerned about this situation, and uninterested in incorporating the converted warlords into the activities of the Party and army leadership. There was no attempt to use the converts to bolster individual factions within the Kuomintang, now developing very strongly. All factions seemed to be agreed on two things: first, that the question of the converted warlords was a rather unimportant one, lying in the sphere of vulgar military problems, not in the elevated sphere of political controversy; and second that the converts were not to be involved in the Kuomintang's internal problems. This disdain and neglect played into the hands of the converts; while they were treated as outsiders, they could continue to pursue their well-established practices, attached to the Kuomintang, but not of it. The whole question of their incorporation was left unresolved.

More conversions were scheduled; for its attack towards the lower Yangtse cities, the Kuomintang depended upon the pre-arranged defections of Chou Feng-ch'i of Chekiang, and Ch'en T'iao-yuan of Anhwei. By the end of 1926, the Kuomintang had 260,000 troops under its banners (see Appendix III).[42] These troops were chiefly in converted warlord armies. There was no gain for the radical elements of the Kuomintang and CCP in this enormous growth. Only one regiment in this whole complex, that of Yeh T'ing, was Communist dominated.[43]

Much later, at the end of its rule in Wuhan (July 1927) the Left-Kuomintang issued a pronouncement on the dangers of residual warlordism, of ' party' warlordism; it attacked unconverted warlords who pursued their aims under the guise of the new orthodoxy of the Kuomintang, while in fact acting against the true interests of the Party.[44] But by then the damage was done.

' A pitfall in the path of the Nationalist Government is the old-fashioned but seemingly converted warlord... The encirclement of the Nationalist Government by a band of friendly *tuchuns* is as much a menace to civilian government as a direct attack by enemy *tuchuns*... The observer [George Sokolsky] wonders whether the Kuomintang will have enough time to whip these acquired armies into shape, or will find itself in the maelstrom of *tuchun* politics.' [45]

Even at the end of 1926, the process had gone so far that the answer to this prophetic question was debatable.

THE SPLIT IN THE KUOMINTANG

At the end of 1926, the divisions within the Kuomintang – the tension between the Communists and some elements of the Kuomintang, the rivalries between individual leaders, the divergence of opinions over future military and political developments – which had been fomenting since the death of Sun Yat-sen, came out into the open, and the superficially-cohesive Kuomintang political and military structure was fragmented.

The first major issue over which they surfaced was the question of moving the capital – whether the Kuomintang Government should move from Canton to Wuhan or, until Nanking was captured, to Nanch'ang. Chiang Kai-shek was opposed to a move to Wuhan, to an area controlled politically by Communists and Left-wing members of the Kuomintang, and militarily by the opportunistic T'ang Sheng-chih. He kept his headquarters at Nanch'ang, and gathered around him a group of Central

Executive Committee members unwilling to go to Wuhan, while a majority of the Central Executive Committee established itself in Wuhan. Relations between Wuhan and Nanch'ang deteriorated during the early months of 1927; in April, when Chiang turned on the Communists, and set up his own government at Nanking, the split became absolute. These developments took place against a background of success for the Kuomintang; the victories of its armies, the social revolution, and the forceful diplomacy of the Wuhan Government established the ascendancy of the Kuomintang throughout south China.

At the end of January, the advance into Chekiang got under way. (Pai Ch'ung-hsi, who until now had been acting chief-of-staff to Chiang Kai-shek, was given command of the campaign.) There was considerable fighting for the province. In one important battle, Pai's surname played an important part. His personal standard, the character 'Pai', was flying in the Kuomintang ranks. One of the enemy commanders was Pai Pao-shan, with an almost identical standard. When enemy troops saw the Pai standard flying on the opposing side, they jumped to the understandable conclusion that Pai Pao-sun had defected, and fled.[46] An interesting aspect of this incident is that, unless a deliberate trick was intended, Pai's Kuomintang troops were still fighting under the personal standards of their commanders, essentially a warlord practice (see above, p. 52).

After the fall of Hangchow, the Chekiang provincial capital, in February, only the Shanghai-Nanking area remained outside Kuomintang control south of the Yangtse. A multi-pronged attack on the area, aided by the defection of Ch'en T'iao-yüan in March (arranged in advance, allegedly at the cost of 600,000 *yüan*) [47] culminated in the fall of first Shanghai and then Nanking at the end of March.[48] The Nanking Incident, which occurred as Nanking was occupied, was successfully but dubiously blamed on Communists in the occupying Sixth Army, and gave Chiang Kai-shek a pretext for the purge of the Communists three weeks later.

THE PURGE

With the fall of Nanking and Shanghai, the split between Wuhan and Chiang was intensified. Chiang now controlled Chekiang, Kiangsu, Anhwei, Fukien, and most of Kiangsi; Wuhan controlled Hunan and Hupei; Li Chi-shen dominated Kwangtung; other provinces were still under their original overlords.

The newly-converted warlords within the two major blocs threw in their hands with the bloc controllers. Li Tsung-jen, whose troops were in Anhwei, naturally turned to Chiang. Politically the Kwangsi leaders were in favour of Chiang's rightward moves, and they gave Chiang their support during the Purge of the Communists. This was the first occasion on which the Kwangsi leaders worked together as a clique on the national scene, and the term ' Kuei Hsi ' (Kwangsi Clique) dates from this period. Up to this point on the northern expedition, each Kwangsi general had performed a specific and separate task, under the auspices of the General Headquarters; but now Li Tsung-jen, Pai Ch'ung-hsi, Li Chi-shen and Huang Shao-hsiung acted in unison against the Communists.

The first to take an openly hostile stance to the Communists was Pai Ch'ung-hsi, who became garrison commander of Shanghai immediately after its fall; he went out of his way to reassure the foreign community, in a state of hysteria after the Nanking Incident, that he would protect their lives and their property, and would rigorously suppress all ' unorthodox activities in the city ' – a clear reference to Communist and labour union activity.[49]

Pai shared with the other Kwangsi leaders a strident antipathy to Communism whose origins are obscure. Communist activity did not threaten their personal positions; there had been very little either in Kwangsi or in the Seventh Army. Li Tsung-jen had kept a strict hand on the political department of the army, and had not permitted its original political commissar, the Communist Huang Jih-k'uei, to march north with the Seventh; he had taken with him instead a much less radical figure, Mai Huan-chang.[50] A Russian adviser had been attached to the Seventh in December 1926, but there is no indication that he exercised any influence within the army.[51] Li and Huang Shao-hsiung had earlier taken strong exception to what they regarded as the patronising attitude of the chief Soviet adviser, Michael Borodin, towards them, but personal animosity alone would not explain their bitterness towards the Communists.[52] Perhaps Li had been alarmed by incidents in Anhwei in March, when clashes between Kuomintang and Communist elements resulted in the sacking of the Anhwei Kuomintang and Union Headquarters.[53] He must certainly have been concerned with the decline in discipline within his own army, a result of the privations the men had suffered through continuing supply difficulties, and have feared that this might make the men more open to Communist influence. (In January, men of the Seventh had looted at Kiukiang, and had gained the reputation of being ' a particularly lawless lot.' [54])

Most probably, the anti-Communism of the Kwangsi leaders stemmed from a deep uneasiness at the manifestations of social unrest that the mass movements engendered, and from a fear that increased mass organisation, led by the Communist Party, would seriously compromise their own positions. In operating within the Kuomintang framework and, in particular, in operating close to Chiang Kai-shek, they were playing a game whose rules they knew; the Communists were an unknown quantity. They suspected that if the Communists were ever in a position to deal with them, they would not accept the kind of superficial compromises that the Kuomintang had.

Whatever pushed the Kwangsi leaders towards extreme anti-Communism, the fact of its existence was a crucial asset to Chiang Kai-shek in his attacks on the Communists. All four Kwangsi leaders (Li Tsung-jen, Pai Ch'ung-hsi, Huang Shao-hsiung and Li Chi-shen) attended the preparatory meetings for the Purge (*Ch'ing-tang*) held in Shanghai at the beginning of April, and gave their full support to the measures which Chiang proposed.[55] Without their support, it would have been virtually impossible for Chiang to carry out the Purge. Pai Ch'ung-hsi was garrison commander of Shanghai, Li Chi-shen controlled Kwangtung and Li Tsung-jen commanded a large body of troops in the Nanking region, who were little affected by Communist influence. These were the three centres chosen for the start of the Purge.

In Shanghai, the Purge started on 15 April. Pai Ch'ung-hsi maintained his official adherence to the Kuomintang policy of co-operation with the Communists (*jung-kung*) until shortly before that day, but his actual position was so well known that reports of an interview in which he spoke of ' *jung-kung* ' were footnoted to say that there must have been a mistake in reporting, since Pai was a known anti-Communist.[56] As the Purge drew near, Pai dropped his pretences: ' the approach of zero-hour could almost be plotted graphically in the half-page advertisements run daily in the Chinese press by the political department of Pai Ch'ung-hsi's headquarters '.[57] On the day itself, Pai's troops disarmed labour union pickets and workers in the city, but left much of the butchery to the sinister and obscurely-directed Shanghai gangsters. Pai, who seems to have regretted the scale of the slaughter, later adopted the predictable and debased excuse that he was ' only obeying orders '.[58] He apparently performed one charitable act, in releasing the arrested Chou En-lai, whom he had known in Canton.[59]

Li Tsung-jen's contribution to the Purge was to move troops from Anhwei to Nanking, and to eradicate Communist elements from the First Army stationed there. There was also a slight purge in the Seventh Army, and at Wuhu.[60] In Kwangsi, the Purge was less brutal, and was confined to the cities along the West River; it did not touch the Communist-dominated area in the northwest of the province.[61]

In Kwangtung, Li Chi-shen's well-laid plans were put into operation two days after the Shanghai Purge started. Li himself was still in Shanghai, but had prepared a ' Doomsday Book ' of those he wanted eradicated before he left Canton.[62] The Canton Purge was the culmination of Li's anti-Communist activities, which had started as soon as the Kuomintang Government departed for Wuhan in December 1926. In the same month he had issued ordinances forbidding the Canton workers to make arrests, to demonstrate carrying weapons, or to seize or boycott factories and shops.[63] This had been followed by a series of repressive measures against the labour unions. Li's early moves against the Communists probably had a strong influence in shaping the anti-Communist attitudes of the other Kwangsi leaders. His relationship to them at this stage was critical. The identification between Li and the other three had become much stronger since their official association with the Kuomintang. It was a paternalistic relationship, for although Li was only a little older than they, he was much more experienced, politically and militarily; as a fellow-provincial, the Kwangsi leaders turned to him naturally for advice and guidance.[64]

In Nanking, in Canton and in Kwangsi, the Purge followed very swiftly upon the heels of the Shanghai Purge. Other areas followed suit more slowly, the first being Shansi, in mid-May. The fact that the Kwangsi Clique were emboldened to take such an open political stance suggests that they were beginning to acquire a degree of political self-confidence which was to lead them very shortly to another daring ploy – that of forcing Chiang Kai-shek's resignation. In an environment of great confusion, there was nothing to prevent them from taking the initiative; they need no longer simply respond to situations, but could create them themselves.

CHIANG KAI-SHEK'S RESIGNATION AND THE WUHAN-NANKING RAPPROCHEMENT

The government established by Chiang Kai-shek at Nanking on 18 April depended for its political support on the Right-wing of the Kuomintang, for its military support on the First Army, the Seventh Army and a group of recent warlord converts from Chekiang and Anhwei, and for its economic support on the wealth of Shanghai.

Nanking was faced immediately with two serious military threats: from Northern troops across the Yangtse, and from Wuhan troops up-river. The second threat was less pressing, for though the split between Wuhan and Nanking was now absolute, in the wake of Nanking's actions against the Communists, there was still a tacit understanding that the continuation of the Northern Expedition should take precedence over internecine fighting, though it could not now be a joint expedition.[65] To counter the first threat, Nanking troops crossed the Yangtse at the beginning of May, while Wuhan troops pushed north through Hupei. At the same time, Feng Yü-hsiang, the most powerful pro-Kuomintang militarist in north China (he had declared for the Kuomintang in September 1926) moved into Honan from the west. It was clear that his support for either Nanking or Wuhan would tip the balance for the survival of either one. After negotiations with both sides, he threw in his lot with Nanking, a terrible blow for Wuhan, but from Feng's point of view, the most practical course.[66] Feng's alliance with Nanking, and that of Yen Hsi-shan which soon followed, were the first that the Kuomintang formed with large warlord groupings. As in the case of smaller warlords, neither Feng nor Yen was required to make anything more than nominal concessions to the ideology of the Kuomintang. It was accepted that these alliances were based primarily on military considerations, and that they were not political conversions to a revolutionary ideology.

Wuhan was now in a desperate position; many of its commanders were openly disloyal, and were primarily interested in their own territorial gains; economically, Wuhan was almost at a standstill, with its trade curtailed by the hostility of the Powers, and by Nanking interdiction of river traffic; politically, an open breach between the Communists and the Left-Kuomintang was in the air.

Nanking's ascendancy over Wuhan created by its alliance with Feng Yü-hsiang proved only temporary; the situation was reversed in July when Northern forces counter-attacked and easily pushed Nanking forces back to the Yangtse. This was the first serious military set-back that Kuomintang forces had suffered during the entire Northern Expedition, and though the blame for it was put on Wang T'ien-p'ei, a converted warlord from Kweichow (Wang was executed), it was clear that a large part of the blame lay with the inept strategy of the Commander-in-chief, Chiang Kai-shek, who had allowed his unreliable converted warlord troops to become strung out along the Tientsin-P'uk'ou Railway with little protection on their flanks.[67]

The futility of the defeat had the effect of slackening the war threat on the Yangtse. Both in Wuhan and in Nanking, the leaders were losing the support of their subordinates. In Wuhan, Wang Ching-wei's purge of the Communists in July had not halted the downhill slide in his position; his move had not brought him increased support from the local military, led by T'ang Sheng-chih. All it had done was destroy the main point at issue between Wuhan and Nanking. In Nanking, Chiang Kaishek also found his military support dwindling; the defeat in the north, and the heavy casualties which accompanied it, had discredited him as a general. Feng Yü-hsiang was again taking a more independent stance, pressuring both sides to reach a settlement.

Above all, the strategic deployments of both sides had placed facing each other on the Yangtse front two armies which were deeply opposed to fighting each other. On the Wuhan side was Chang Fa-k'uei, with the Fourth, Eleventh and Twentieth Armies, all formerly parts of the Fourth Army; on the Nanking side Li Tsung-jen with the Seventh. Though the two armies were a long way apart politically – Chang's army was in part pro-Communist, and had been deeply disturbed by the Wuhan purge of the Communists, while Li's was apolitical, and followed the anti-Communist position of its commander – there was a great fellow-feeling between the two armies. The Fourth had originally been commanded by Li Chi-shen, its men were raised from West Kwangtung, near the Kwangsi border, and it had helped the Kwangsi generals during the consolidation of their province. (Provincial ties were not always strictly related to provincial boundaries; there were frequently strong ties between people from either side of a provincial border.) Both armies were exhausted, and had recently taken heavy casualties, the Fourth in the attack north from Wuhan in May, when it won the name of the Iron Army,[68] and the Seventh in the retreat from the north. The Seventh was bitter about the retreat; there was a feeling that all that the Seventh had gained from a year's fighting was 'the name of the Steel Army and 20,000 casualties'.[69] When Chiang Kai-shek ordered the Steel Army to attack the Iron Army, when Kwangsi troops were being asked to attack Kwangtung troops 'to satisfy the Napoleonic ambitions of a Ningpo man', Li Tsung-jen refused.[70]

Li's refusal to fight was the culmination of increasing disharmony between the Kwangsi generals and Chiang Kai-shek, centring chiefly on the deteriorating relations between Pai Ch'ung-hsi and Chiang Kai-shek. The two men were probably too close in character ever to co-operate easily. Pai, like Chiang, was outwardly self-confident to the point of arrogance. He was fully aware of his worth as a professional soldier, and was aloofly contemptuous of those he considered his inferiors as tacticians and strategists; he was an astringent, distant character, not given to flattery and political manoeuvre. Working under a man who shared many of these characteristics, Chiang Kai-shek, inevitably gave rise to friction. Li Tsung-jen was more conciliatory; though his auto-biography suggests that there was a powerful personal animosity between himself and Chiang even at this stage, this is probably a reflection of later hostility. There is no contemporary evidence to suggest that he was personally hostile to Chiang. But he felt no involvement in the enmity between Nanking and Wuhan, certainly not after the purge of the Communists at Wuhan, and he was not prepared to see his army, his only capital, destroyed in factional fighting. At the beginning of August, he emerged as a leading figure in moves to secure a rapprochement between Wuhan and Nanking.[71]

His refusal to fight Chang Fa-k'uei was, in the event, unnecessary, for on 1 August, the Nanch'ang Uprising occurred, and split Chang's forces. This development acted as a spur to negotiations between Wuhan and Nanking, especially since it was not immediately clear whether all Chang's forces would join the Communists, or whether they would move south or north. The fear of a Communist attack on the Yangtse galvanised both sides into action. Telegrams flew back and forth between Wuhan and Nanking. For a while it seemed that Wang Ching-wei would be able to maintain his position as leader of the Wuhan side. Chiang Kai-shek however was clearly on the way out. From the end of July, articles questioning his continuance in office had been appearing in the Chinese press, and posters attacking him were on display in Nanking itself.[72] The Kwangsi generals no longer acknowledged his authority, and though he bitterly opposed their negotiations with Wuhan, he could do nothing to stop them.[73] Finally, his most trusted subordinate, Ho Ying-ch'in, also abandoned him, leaving him without any loyal troops in the Nanking-Shanghai region, a Commander-in-chief without commanders.[74]

With a Northern counter-attack mounting across the Yangtse, a stormy meeting of the Military Committee took place at Nanking on 13 August. Chiang was openly defied, resigned on the spot and left for Shanghai. The Military Committee assumed all political and military authority at Nanking; Li, Pai and Ho were in control.[75]

The new leaders at Nanking moved swiftly to secure a formal rapprochement with Wuhan, concentrating their efforts on the more moderate leaders there, T'an Yen-k'ai and Sun Fo.[76] On 22 August Li Tsung-jen met these two men and Wang Ching-wei at Kiukiang. Wang, believing that he would now become the overall leader of the Kuomintang, agreed to transfer the Wuhan Government and the Central Executive Committee to Nanking, on the understanding that the existing regime at Nanking would be wound up. At the end of the meeting T'an and Sun left for Nanking with Li, ostensibly to prepare for Wang's arrival. But Wang's only authority was political; he was talking basically in political terms, of a re-establishment of governmental and political orthodoxy, of a return to Party rule. (One of his major demands was that the Fourth Plenum of the Central Executive Committee should meet immediately, to clarify the Kuomintang's situation, and assert his leadership.) Political authority, however, was now subordinate to military authority; Wang had discovered this at Wuhan, and now found it again at Nanking with an added twist: whereas the military leaders at Wuhan had tolerated his presence, the new Nanking leaders would not.

He was to be excluded from any office. He made his way disconsolately to Shanghai.

Most of Chiang's political supporters left Nanking with him.[77] It was a wise time to leave; the city was being shelled by Northern forces, and seemed about to fall to them.

THE SPECIAL COMMITTEE

When they took over control at Nanking, neither the Kwangsi leaders nor anyone else imagined that their authority would last, that it would be anything more than a stop-gap. They commanded no support in either of the main factions of the Kuomintang. These two factions, led by Chiang Kai-shek and Wang Ching-wei, soon drew closer together, in a joint effort to oust the Kwangsi leaders. In spite of the bitter divisions between them, the two sides still felt an even stronger antipathy to outsiders such as the Kwangsi Clique.

But, in the short run, the Kwangsi leaders had an urgent task to perform, to defend Nanking against invasion. A major counter-attack was repulsed, but not without heavy casualties. The Kuomintang found many of its recently-converted troops changing sides again, so precarious had its position become.[78]

Once the immediate military crisis was past, the political and governmental situation had to be sorted out. The only faction of the Kuomintang on which the Kwangsi Clique could rely was the Right-wing Western Hills group, a group which had detached itself from the mainstream of the Kuomintang in November 1925. This group had been disappointed in Chiang Kai-shek's failure to reopen relations with them after his own attack on the Communists in April 1927, and was now willing to ally with anyone who would give its members a taste of political authority, provided only that that ally was staunchly anti-Communist.[79] The Kwangsi Clique gave them a chance for a reappearance on the national scene.

The Kwangsi Clique hoped at first that a broader spectrum of the Kuomintang could be induced to come to Nanking, and at the beginning of September launched joint negotiations with all three factions in Shanghai. It was decided, as a result of the negotiations, temporarily to suspend the Central Executive and Supervisory Committees, to reorganise the Military Committee, and to set up a Special Committee to take over the functions of the Executive and Supervisory Committees until the Third Congress could be called – within three months.[80] This Special Committe was set up at Nanking on 15 September. Its inaugural proclamation blamed all the recent troubles within the Kuomintang on the Communists, and vowed to continue the Northern Expedition and to purge the communists.[81]

The impression that the Special Committee had been set up as a result of a tripartite agreement was an illusion. No major supporters of either Chiang Kai-shek or Wang Ching-wei attended the joint meeting of the Central Executive and Supervisory Committees which actually set up the Special Committee – indeed only thirteen of the thirty-four eligible participants were there.[82] The Special Committee was attacked from its inception as illegal; technically only a Plenum of the Central Executive Committee was empowered to make such sweeping changes in Party and governmental structure, and no such Plenum had been called, for the very good reason that it would not have sanctioned the Special Committee. It had at best a quasi-legal status in terms of the Kuomintang statutes. But by this stage of 1927, these statutes had been so much abused, both in the letter and in spirit, that the only ' legal ' solutions were those which a substantial body of Kuomintang leaders would accept. The Western Hills group was quite sanguine about this state of affairs, and stated explicitly that ' legality ' had become meaningless, and that the only possible solution to the present confusion was a pragmatic one, a reasoned response to objective circumstances.[83] The only drawback to their ' pragmatic ' solution was that very few other Kuomintang leaders accepted it, and it therefore lacked even the new version of ' legality '. The establishment of the Special Committee satisfied only those who supported it; it had no authority for those who considered it illegal. Its fiat only ran in the areas directly controlled by the troops commanded by the Kwangsi generals and Ho Ying-ch'in – about 200,000 men in the Nanking region.[84] Various other military commanders in the lower Yangtse Valley threw in their lot with Nanking, but these were all recently-converted warlords, who were presumably only forming yet another temporary alliance. Even the members of the Kwangsi Clique not in the Nanking region – Li Chi-shen and Huang Shao-hsiung – appear to have been dubious about its establishment.

On paper, the Special Committee had thirty-two members, and from these, again on paper, a new Executive Committee and a new Military Committee were named. But many of the ' members ' were not in Nanking; Chiang Kai-shek was in Japan, Wang Ching-wei back in Wuhan and Hu Han-min in Shanghai. The only well-known political figures in Nanking were T'an Yen-k'ai, Sun Fo and the members of the Western Hills group (Chang Chi, Tsou Lu, Lin Sen, Hsü Ch'ung-chih). Only two of the five members of the new Executive Committee were there, T'an Yen-k'ai and Li Lieh-chün.[85]

The inability of the Special Committee to gain any support from the two major factions of the Kuomintang doomed it to impermanence. The only field in which the Committee could operate effectively was the military. On the diplomatic front, none of the Powers was prepared to deal with an administration that they regarded as temporary.[86] Economically, the Special Committee was very weak: the contributions from Shanghai which had bolstered Chiang Kai-shek's position at Nanking had been secured on the basis of Chiang's personal relationships with members of the Shanghai financial world. While Chiang raised $40,000,000 in Shanghai between May and July 1927, Pai Ch'ung-hsi could only persuade the Shanghai Chamber of Commerce to donate $300,000 towards the establishment of the Special Committee.[87]

However, in September and October military problems were still uppermost, and they did something to disguise the other weaknesses of the Special Committee's position. The Northern Expedition got under way again, and was pushed into northern Kiangsu. Some of the most blatantly unreformed warlords in the Nanking forces were arrested, and their units disbanded.[88] (Such men could not be simply dismissed, since their forces were personally loyal to them, and they were able to resist commands to resign. However, once they had been arrested and removed from their troops, the leaderless troops were disbanded without great difficulty.)

The major military action of the Special Committee was against T'ang Sheng-chih in Wuhan. T'ang had extended his authority eastwards from Wuhan to include Anhwei, and had set up a Branch Political Council at Wuhan, in accordance with an earlier decision of the now defunct Wuhan Government.[89] T'ang was defeated by Nanking troops without great difficulty, at the beginning of November, the defection of many of his units having been secured in advance, in traditional style. Wuhan passed under the control of the Kwangsi Clique, through Hu Tsung-to, a leading second-level member of the Clique who was coincidentally a Hupei native, one of the few non-Kwangsi men ever associated with the Clique.[90]

Nanking was on the point of negotiating a settlement with T'ang's subordinates in Hunan, which would have brought Hunan as well as Hupei under Nanking control (and therefore under the sway of the Kwangsi Clique) when the whole position of the Clique was suddenly threatened by developments in Kwangtung. Li Chi-shen's authority there had already been badly undermined by the return to the province in the late summer of Communist troops, and, more importantly, of Chang Fa-k'uei. For while Li had little difficulty in crushing the Communist troops, it was quite impossible for him to do anything but welcome Chang Fa-k'uei, one of Kwangtung's favourite sons, who had powerful military friends in the Kwangtung armies. He was also Li's former subordinate, but the distance between the two men was now very great, with Chang a close supporter of Wang Ching-wei, and Li associated with the Kwangsi Clique.

When Chang arrived in Canton, to a triumphal welcome, Li's position became very precarious. He could not prevent the establishment in Canton of a Branch Political Council, set up under the same regulations as the one in Wuhan, which, from the end of October, was dominated by Chang's chief, Wang Ching-wei. Even the conservative merchant class of Kwangtung, formerly Li's staunchest ally, especially in his attacks on the Communists, was now abandoning him, alienated by his oppressive taxation.[91]

The Canton Branch Political Council launched a barrage of attacks on the Special Committee, denouncing its illegality and demanding the immediate convention of the Fourth Plenum. Li was forced to echo their demands, even though it meant attacking his colleagues in Nanking. The call for the convention of the Fourth Plenum was taken up in Shanghai, where Chiang Kai-shek was living after his return from Japan. Wang Ching-wei left for Shanghai in mid-November, to discuss the Plenum with Chiang, their recent hostility brushed under the carpet. He took Li Chi-shen with him, and before he left he secretly laid plans with Chang Fa-k'uei to destroy the basis of Kwangsi power in Kwangtung.

In 16 November, the day after Wang's departure, Chang launched a *coup* in Canton. Huang Shao-hsiung, deputising for Li while he was away, was attacked in his home, but managed to escape, disguised as a peasant.[92] The Whampoa Academy, the Shih-ching Arsenal, the Humen Forts and other key installations were taken over by Chang's troops. A military campaign was launched against Kwangsi itself.[93]

Chang's *coup* delighted many Cantonese, who were disgruntled with alien rule. For the Kwangsi Clique it had very serious implications. The *coup* undermined the whole position of the Clique, for its base, Kwangsi province, was threatened by Cantonese occupation. The province was the cornerstone of the Clique's structure of power. Ultimately, the Clique depended for its survival, not on its acquisitions outside the province, but on its base. So long as the Clique held it, it had a firm foundation from which to launch its wider activities and a haven for temporary retirement. If the Clique lost Kwangsi, it would become rootless, its troops wandering ' guest ' armies, vulnerable and unwelcome everywhere. (Some of the vicissitudes of Feng Yü-hsiang's career can be seen in this light, as a warlord with a very large personal following, but no permanent territorial base.[94]) Indeed, even as the Clique lost power in the south, its position at Nanking was slipping.

Chiang Kai-shek, back in Shanghai, was actively working for the downfall of the Special Committee, as were the majority of Kuomintang politicians. Alongside the calls for the convention of the Fourth Plenum, there was a movement to reinstate Chiang.

The Kwangsi Clique was sanguine about the chances of survival of the Special Committee, and did not oppose the calling of the Fourth Plenum. Now that Kwangsi was threatened, Li and Pai were much more concerned with saving the province than with saving the Special Committee. They laid plans for an expedition south from Wuhan to Kwangsi, to aid Huang Shao-hsiung. On 19 November, only two days after the *coup* in Canton, Pai handed over his command of the Shanghai garrison and started to transfer his troops to Wuhan.[95] All the Clique's pretensions to a national role melted away when their home base was threatened. This concern with their base betrayed the extent to which the Kwangsi leaders were still thinking in purely military, regionalist terms, and underlined the shallowness of their involvement in Kuomintang politics.

For the Western Hills group, however, the collapse of the Special Committee could not be viewed so lightly. Its members agitated vigorously for its continuation, but their attempts to persuade the Kwangsi Clique to continue to support it were brushed aside.[96]

The pressure to dissolve the Special Committee was irresistible. Early in December, preparatory meetings for the Fourth Plenum were held in Shanghai, and it was decided to wind up the Special Committee at the end of December. This decision represented a consensus of both major factions of the Kuomintang, in spite of the fact that it was becoming apparent that Chiang Kai-shek, not Wang Ching-wei, would emerge as the Kuomintang's new leader. His unpopularity of the summer was forgotten and his prestige as a national leader was reborn. In a speech of statesmanlike solemnity on 10 December, Chiang threatened the development of a new warlordism unless the Party's authority was reasserted over its armies. (That this authority had never been exerted over the bulk of Kuomintang forces he conveniently ignored.) He bitterly denounced the Kwangsi generals for their failure to obey Party orders, and for their disregard of the welfare of their troops and of the population as a whole.[97]

Another crisis in Kwangtung interrupted the progress towards the re-establishment of Chiang's authority at Nanking, and finished Wang Ching-wei's hopes of a new start to his career. A Communist rising in Canton led to the establishment of the Canton Commune. The situation

of the Kwangsi Clique in the south was radically changed again. Chang
Fa-k'uei's troops put down the Commune, but were then themselves
driven from the province by reorganised troops of Li Chi-shen. The
threat to the southern dominions of the Kwangsi Clique was removed.[98]
The incredibly rapid change of events in Kwangtung gives an indication
of the complexity of this period, and of the impossibility of forecasting
from one week to the next who would be in power in what area.
Alliances shifted constantly, the relationship between Party factions
and military units was highly unstable. The last four months of 1927
look in fact like one of the worst four months of the whole Warlord
Period. There was only one retreat from this chaotic situation – the re-
assertion of some kind of Central authority.

This was provided in some measure by Chiang Kai-shek's return to
Nanking on 5 January, 1928, ' in martial splendour, in a special train
escorted by three armoured trains '.[99] The Special Committee was dis-
solved. The members of the Western Hills group went abroad, while the
Kwangsi leaders established themselves at Wuhan. ' The rowdy Kwangsi
generals went behind the scenes, and only faint whispers of their off-
stage operations reached Nanking.' [100]

The Kwangsi Clique was not dejected by the loss of Nanking. If the
past few months had proved anything, it was that the Clique did not
constitute a faction strong enough to run a national government. The
Kwangsi leaders were able generals, and they were later to prove effective administrators of a single province, but they were lost in the tangled
fabric of national political life. They had no solid backing within the
Kuomintang. Their alliance with the Western Hills group was only a
temporary one, based on a fleeting chance that the political prestige of
the one could be reinforced by the military strength of the other. The
only common ideological commitments were negative: antipathy towards Chiang Kai-shek and vehement anti-Communism. (Li Tsung-
jen's anti-Communism reached new heights during the period. The
North China Herald stated approvingly (and improbably), that ' nothing
that has appeared in these columns as to the menace of Soviet influence
in China has been couched in stronger terms than those used by General
Li in his excoriation of the Soviet regime in China '.[101]) The members of
the Western Hills group at least had respectably-long records within the
Kuomintang, which the Kwangsi Clique, with the exception of Li Chi-
shen, did not. In 1927, Pai Ch'ung-hsi still had no position within the
Kuomintang hierarchy, while Li Tsung-jen and Huang Shao-hsiung were
only alternate members of the Supervisory Committee, elected at the
Second Party Congress in 1926.[102] They were justifiably regarded by
many Kuomintang men as upstarts.

This long account of the career of the Kwangsi Clique in 1926 and 1927, and of its relationship to the Kuomintang, seems excessively complex and confusing. It is in fact only an outline of the actual picture. The hideous confusion of 1927 almost defies untangling. Only one thing can be said with any degree of certainty – that the Kuomintang which emerged from this terrible year had largely failed in the aims of unification which it had set itself at the beginning of the Northern Expedition. It had not imposed any degree of centralised control upon the areas brought under its banner during the course of the expedition, it had failed to amalgamate and transform the converted warlord armies, it had not checked existing regional power-holding, it had not established the ascendancy of the Party over the military. Political training of troops had been virtually abandoned. Generals mouthed the credo of the Three Peoples' Principles, but the common soldier was still an illiterate peasant, steeped in tradition and superstition, not political ideology. While the ideology of the Kuomintang remained ill-defined and rarefied, another ' ideology ' was reasserting itself, an ideology-of-default, that of regionalism.

It is difficult to imagine that the Kwangsi Clique started on the Northern Expedition with the idea of establishing a regionalist base in central China, linked to the home base in Kwangsi. Nevertheless, this is what the Clique was doing at the beginning of 1928. Its leaders still paid lip-service to the Kuomintang, but without any feeling of immediacy. Their adherence to the Kuomintang was not expressed in any form of subordination to the Party or its government, but only through the colours of the flag.

5

Revolutionary regionalism: Kwangsi, 1926-1929

In the previous chapter we discussed the role of a militarist clique in the Kuomintang's drive to reunify China. We saw how the failure of the Kuomintang to exert pressure for transformation on its converted warlord allies allowed and indeed obliged the Kwangsi Clique to operate essentially in its own interests. Let us now look at the situation in Kwangsi during the period between the departure of part of its forces on the Northern Expedition, and their return in flight early in 1929, to see how a province nominally under Kuomintang rule was administered, and how much its new allegiance affected its development.

When the Seventh Army left Kwangsi in the late spring of 1926, two of the three Kwangsi leaders, Li Tsung-jen and Pai Ch'ung-hsi, left too, Li to command the Seventh, and Pai to act as Chief-of-staff to Chiang Kai-shek. The third leader, Huang Shao-hsiung, stayed behind to administer Kwangsi. Huang was bitterly disappointed that he was not to leave his remote corner of China, and go forth to make his name on the national scene. But neither he nor the other two leaders were prepared to see control of the province which they had fought for for five years pass to an outsider (presumably a Kuomintang appointee). If one of them were to stay behind, it was logical that it should be Huang, for he already held the position of head of the Office of Civil Government. Huang's natural resilience asserted itself, as it had done before on the occasions when his career took an unwelcome turn. He set himself to develop Kwangsi, and to form close links with Kwangtung.[1] His positive attitude to his disappointment is an indication of the strength of the co-operation between the three men. There was an understanding that responsibility should be shared, and that at times one would have to take a less attractive role for the sake of the other two.

For the next three years, Huang ruled Kwangsi independently of his two colleagues, and strove to imprint his energetic and expansive character on the province. His activities were set within the framework of Kuomintang policies, but since he neither asked for nor was given

88

direction from the Central Kuomintang authorities, his rule took on an individualist aspect. It was authoritarian, militarist, and politically Right-wing, but it was not static, as a combination of these three characteristics might lead one to expect. Huang's ambition was to drag Kwangsi out of its abysmal backwardness, and set it on the road towards modernisation.

Until 1926, the Kwangsi leaders' conduct of civil government had been haphazard. Before the unification of the province, Li and Huang had left the administration of their areas of control to existing local authorities, appointing new county heads where necessary from the local gentry, a system, which Huang observed, was 'genuine local self-government'.[2] In 1925, when they took Nanning, the provincial capital, and had to set up some form of provincial government, they simply appointed the head of the Kwangsi Provincial Assembly, Chang Yi-ch'i, as Governor.[3] (The occupier of the provincial capital in a much-divided province such as Kwangsi assumed responsibility for the administration of the province, whether or not he controlled the whole province; he was expected to make appointments to senior civil posts within the province, whether these appointments carried any authority or not. The ability to make such appointments enhanced the prestige of a warlord, and was one reason – though material considerations were usually much more important – why intra-provincial warlord struggles often centred around struggle for control of the provincial capital.)

However, Chang fled when Yunnanese troops took the city early in 1925, and when in the summer of the same year the Kwangsi leaders finally consolidated their hold over the province, they were again faced with the problem of installing some form of provincial government. They recognised neither the Peking Government nor the Kuomintang Government in Canton, and could not ask either for a nominee. Nor did they want another Governor from among the tradition-bound elders of the Provincial Assembly. They therefore established an Office of Civil Government (Min-cheng kung-shu), of which Huang Shao-hsiung became the first head in September 1925. This was, as Huang noted with disarming honesty, equivalent to 'setting oneself up as king' (*tzu li wei wang*).[4]

Initially, the new administration made little impact. Much of the province was still disturbed, and local government remained in the hands of existing local leaders. Some headway was made in the unification of tax collection, but the administration continued to depend for the bulk of its income on the tax on opium in transit through the province. Huang's chief concern in late 1925 and early 1926 lay in mopping up remaining areas of resistance within the province, in improving the standard of Kwangsi's troops, and in forming closer ties with Kwangtung and the Kuomintang. His primary preoccupation was with military matters; civil administration was a secondary matter. Not until after a new provincial government was set up in June 1926, in accordance with the Act of Union between Kwangtung and Kwangsi, did Huang pay more attention to non-military affairs.

PACIFICATION

As far as disorder within the province was concerned, Kwangsi faced three separate threats: the first was from the huge number of bandits who infested the province; the second was from dissident troops; the third was from Yunnan. To cope with these threats, Huang had at his disposal about half of the troops originally under his and Li Tsung-jen's command. Two of Huang Shao-hsiung's subordinates, Hsia Wei and Yü Tso-po, went north with Li Tsung-jen, their units incorporated into the Seventh Army. Li left behind in Kwangsi his own immediate subordinate, Huang Hsü-ch'u. Of the four brigades left behind in Kwangsi, two were commanded by Huang's own men (Wu T'ing-yang and Lü Huan-yen), one had formerly been attached to Li (Huang Hsü-ch'u's), and one was commanded by a defeated warlord, Liu Jih-fu.[5]

This complicated rearrangement of fighting forces – detaching units from their original commanders and transferring them to another – indicates the kind of canny manipulation which was necessary to keep relations between the Kwangsi leaders sweet. For though we have stressed the mutual understanding between them, and their willingness to co-operate rather than fight each other, goodwill alone was not enough to carry them through times when difficult decisions had to be made. Each man had his own troops (though not Pai Ch'ung-hsi at this stage), each man had what amounted to an informal sub-clique attached directly to himself. The distinctions in strength were fine, but nevertheless real – Li Tsung-jen had a slight edge over Huang Shao-hsiung which allowed him to come out with what was usually a slightly superior position. The overall strength of the Kwangsi Clique lay in its members' ability to live with these subtle distinctions, to put the common interest over the individual. Some safeguards were still needed, and the rearrangement of troops in 1926 represents one. By leaving some of his personally loyal troops behind, Li could make sure that Huang did not take Kwangsi entirely to himself; by sending some of his men with Li, Huang could be guaranteed at least a second-hand participation in the Northern Expedition.

Huang was reasonably successful in coping with unorganised bandits –

that is, with small bandit bands, not linked to larger military forces. Some were hunted down and exterminated by regular soldiers; some were incorporated into the regular forces; others were mopped up by militia units organised by local leaders, whose chances of crushing banditry had been increased by the new stability of the province.[6] The main lines of communication were cleared, and larger rural centres protected from bandit attacks (bandits had never bothered the major cities), though sporadic bandit attacks continued for many years.[7] Dissident soldiers, chiefly former subordinates of Lu Jung-t'ing, had in most cases already been brought under the nominal control of Li and Huang. The problem now was to draw their teeth and ensure their docility, if not their loyalty. Huang achieved this by sending large numbers of his own troops into the western areas of the province, where Lu's troops had surrendered, robbing them of the chance to establish strongholds from which they could launch divisive movements.

The threat from Yunnan was settled more easily; a faint-hearted Yunnanese attack in the late summer of 1926, timed to coincide with Wu P'ei-fu's final defence of the Wuhan region, was repulsed.[8] The Yunnan warlord T'ang Chi-yao was overthrown the following year by internal enemies, and Yunnan allied itself with the Kuomintang. Kwangsi's recurring problems with Yunnan were settled, as were her relations with her other three neighbours, Kweichow, Hunan and Kwangtung, all of which were connected with the Kuomintang. But the settlement was only temporary; there were reservoirs of bad feeling between Kwangsi and her neighbours, which later re-appeared, and contributed to inter-provincial warfare.

THE PROBLEM OF FINANCE

Huang faced formidable problems in the re-ordering of Kwangsi's finances. His commitments were enormous; he had to maintain a force of between 15,000 and 20,000 men within the province, and to contribute to the upkeep of the Seventh Army fighting outside the province.[9] He also had to stabilise the currency, to restore trade and commerce, and to start on the reconstruction of the ravaged province.

The amount of money that Kwangsi contributed to the Seventh Army is uncertain, and must have decreased as the Seventh moved further north and acquired its own garrison areas with their own sources of income. But until it reached the Yangtse, it was dependent on remittances from Kwangsi, which probably totalled 20–30 per cent of the provincial revenue.[10] Military expenditure was a crippling burden for Kwangsi, as for China as a whole; even in 1928, when the province was completely stabilised, and was presumably remitting very little to the Seventh, it accounted for 60 per cent of provincial income – a conservative estimate.[11]

Huang depended on two sources of revenue to raise the money he needed to fulfil all his obligations: regular taxation (principally the land tax) and the tax on opium. Given the progressive image he was trying to project, he was unwilling to see his forces financed locally – that is, by requisitioning and looting, the traditional methods. These *ad hoc* sources of revenue were thus closed to him. The regular taxation system had fallen into disrepair during the five years of civil war, and even after the re-establishment of order, its yields were small; in 1926 the tax revenue was somewhere between $13,000,000 and $16,000,000.[12] This rose to $22,000,000 in 1927, chiefly as a result of reforms in tax collection; a Tax Regulation Committee (Cheng-li shui-wu wei-yüan-hui) was set up.[13] The lucrative gambling tax was tightened up, by confining gambling to government-licensed dens, selective import duties were introduced, and the taxation system streamlined, chiefly by cutting down the number of miscellaneous taxes; but the majority of taxes were still collected inefficiently, and as much as 50 per cent of actual revenue never reached government hands.[14] The burden of taxation on the peasantry was increased through the imposition of land tax supplements (*fu-chia shui*). The peasants of Kuei hsien, for example, who in 1921 had only paid a 3 per cent supplement for police purposes (*ching ping fei*) paid a 50 per cent supplement in 1926, 30 per cent for militia (*t'uan-wu*) and 20 per cent for education. By 1928, the supplement had risen to 90 per cent of the land tax, and was to rise still higher.[15]

The opium tax was a more secure source of income than regular taxation. The opium trade between Yunnan–Kweichow and Canton–Hong Kong continued when most other trade ceased; it was so lucrative that it could bear steep increases in price caused by transit taxes and by the expenditure on guards for the opium convoys (see Fig. 4). Opium was transported by horse and mule caravans to Pose, and then by boat down through the West River system. ' Poseh [*sic*] in west Kwangsi, had its " opium days ", when caravans of hundreds of horses transporting Kweichow and Yunnan opium arrived in town.'[16] But though the trade never dried up, it flourished only when a stable military authority existed to guarantee the passage of shipments from one taxation point to the next; this authority was also the collecting agency for the transit tax – or opium suppression tax, as it was euphemistically called. One of Huang Shao-hsiung's first acts after he gained control of Wuchow in 1923 had been to set up his own Opium Suppression Bureau there – that is, his own opium taxation bureau.

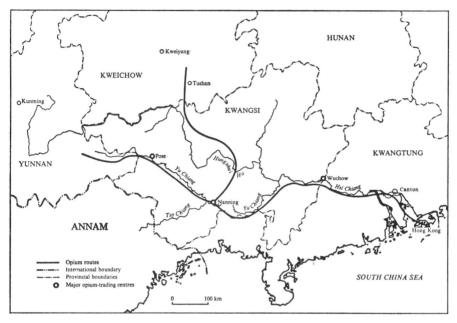

Fig. 4. Opium routes through Kwangsi

The trade through the province grew in proportion to the stability of the province; between 1926 and 1929 it yielded an average of $10,000,000 per annum.[17] Figures for the opium tax yield did not appear in the official provincial budget. This sum was therefore above and beyond the figures for provincial income given above; it can be assumed that most of it was spent directly on military affairs. The Kuomintang was pledged to the suppression of opium smoking in China, and so, technically, was Kwangsi; the opium trade was seldom mentioned publicly – and when it was, it was referred to as the trade in ' special goods ' (*t'e-huo*). For Kwangsi the trade was economically essential, and was recognised as such even by the Kuomintang. In November 1926, Chiang Kai-shek wrote to Huang Shao-hsiung that it would be ' inconvenient ' to reduce the trade in ' special goods ', while the possibility of financial assistance to Kwangsi from Kwangtung remained limited.[18] In 1928, Li Chi-shen stated in an almost sacrificial tone that Kwangtung (then under his control) should not suppress opium consumption, though this was desirable, since suppression would have severe repercussions on the economies of Yunnan, Kweichow and Kwangsi, all of which depended on opium.[19]

In common with other Chinese leaders, the Kwangsi leaders found
the trade in opium rather embarrassing, since they were officially committed to the banning of opium. A few gestures were made; the Kwangsi
Government banned opium smoking in January 1929, set up thirteen
opium suppression offices, and ordered all smokers under forty to give
up smoking within three months.[20] Token arrests of opium dealers were
made, though one such dealer, the former head of Fengshan hsien, was
provided with the opium smoker's paraphernalia in prison.[21] This type
of gesture had no effect on the trade in or the consumption of opium.

Apart from raising revenue, Huang faced the problem of attempting
to stabilise the Kwangsi currency, a prerequisite for the revival of trade.
Hong Kong dollars, Indo-Chinese piastres, Mexican silver dollars, and
Cantonese dollars all circulated within the province, as did traditional
silver ingots and copper cash. Kwangsi had no single provincial currency,
but only a series of virtually worthless paper issues, put out by any warlord powerful enough to force their acceptance; coins in circulation were
usually debased.[22] (The new Kwangsi leaders had themselves indulged in
the production of worthless money: in May 1925 their mint at Kueip'ing
was turning out $200,000 worth of 20 cent coins everyday, which were
60 per cent alloy. They subsequently refused to accept these coins in tax
payment.[23])

Huang now set about trying to remedy this situation. His original
aim was to establish a Kwangsi paper and metal currency which could
be exchanged without difficulty with other neighbouring currencies. To
do this a complete re-issue of paper currency, a new reserve fund to
back the currency, and a purification of the metal currency were needed.
Huang started off with good intentions. In January 1926, all debased
coins were recalled, and new coins were minted from the $6,000,000
worth of pure silver obtained after the old coins were melted down.[24] In
May of the same year, the Kwangsi Bank was set up in Wuchow to
control the paper currency of the province. It issued notes backed
initially by the proceeds ($2,000,000) of a huge consignment of opium
seized near the Yunnan border. This method of acquiring backing Huang
described as 'turning black goods into white silver'.[25]

Huang was anxious at first to try to stamp out currency speculation;
on 1 June 1926 the chairman of the Kweilin Chamber of Commerce was
executed for causing the depreciation of bank notes in his own favour.[26]
But Huang could not keep himself to the narrow path of financial
probity, and was soon seduced by the desire for greater liquid resources.
By 1928, the Kwangsi Bank was being used as a subsidiary provincial
treasury, issuing large amounts of unbacked paper money.[27]

Huang was also concerned to stimulate trade. Kwangsi's external trade had withered after 1921. Cantonese merchants who conducted much of the trade in eastern Kwangsi had left the province when it descended into chaos, to return only when the new leaders restored stability. Their absence, incessant military operations and rampant banditry brought virtually all trade, internal and external (except, as we have noted, the trade in opium), to a halt. Once order was restored, trade quickly picked up; by 1926, total trade, excluding the opium trade and the ' native trade ' (trade in small vessels) had reached something like the proportions of pre-1921 trade. There was, however, a serious imbalance in the trade; imports were almost double exports.[28]

The upturn in trade continued until 1929, although the import surplus rose even higher. Kwangsi's problem was that though it had little to offer in the way of exports, its demands for imported goods were very high. Kwangsi's major exports were agricultural products, livestock, tung oil, firewood, charcoal and minerals. (The province's mineral reserves, as revealed by Ting Wen-chiang's partial survey of the province in 1928, were rich, but had not yet been exploited.[29]) The province's specialities were bizarre, and did not yield a large income: ' the world's supply of star anise is produced here; cassia [cinnamon] is also produced . . . fishing lines made from the intestines of a species of silkworm form a speciality peculiar to this province '.[30] Kwangsi also exported live anteaters, for the delectation of the gourmets of Canton and Hong Kong.[31]

None of these items was particularly valuable as an export commodity, nor was there any immediate possibility of encouraging growth in production. The Kwangsi Government made some attempts to try to boost exports, by organising a trade exhibition of local products at Liuchow,[32] by fostering the planting of tung plantations,[33] and by giving incentives to mining companies, in the form of loans and official sales bureaux.[34] To discourage imports, anti-foreign boycotts received official support, and protectionist import levies were introduced.[35] But none of these measures was sufficient to alter the adverse balance of trade, which was inevitable while Kwangsi was dependent on imports to supply the bulk of her needs in manufactures and semi-manufactures, and to equip her armies.

THE FORMATION OF LINKS
BETWEEN KWANGTUNG AND KWANGSI

Kwangsi had traditionally looked to Kwangtung as her natural, if senior, partner. Huang Shao-hsiung now had to restore good relations between the two provinces, after a long period of division which had left deep scars. On the political level, the recent enmity between the two provinces was replaced by the alliance between the two provinces under the flag of the Kuomintang, an alliance which was cemented by the close personal ties between the Kwangsi leaders and Li Chi-shen, who gained control of Kwangtung with the departure of the Northern Expedition. Huang was now concerned to base the alliance on a firmer foundation; he wanted not an act of political union, a submission of Kwangsi to the Kwangtung of the Kuomintang, but a working relationship between two independent provinces. He was not subsuming Kwangsi's interests within the Kuomintang, but maintaining them as a separate entity, and serving them by allying with Kwangtung. His activities represented not the conversion to a new ideology, but the re-assertion of a traditional relationship.

Kwangtung was prosperous and advanced. Its capital, Canton, was the commercial, political and cultural centre of South China; Kwangsi was poor, backward and uncultured. Its relationship to Kwangtung had always been one-sided; it was variously described as Kwangtung's ' vassal ',[36] its ' step-child ',[37] or, with greater panache, as ' Rome to Kwangtung's Greece '.[38] Only in one respect could Kwangsi match or surpass Kwangtung: in the quality of its fighting men. Over the past century, Kwangsi had developed a tradition of producing tough, aggressive fighters, especially from among the Hakka people settled in the province. These fighters had first made their mark during the Taiping Rebellion, and then in the Sino-French War (1884–5); they had allowed Lu Jung-t'ing to dominate Kwangtung between 1916 and 1921, and they formed virtually the only ' liquid asset ' of the Kwangsi Clique during its whole career up to 1949. Kwangsi's political ties with the Kuomintang were based on the ' export ' of her troops, to take part in the Northern Expedition, and, on numerous occasions, to help in suppressing dissident forces within Kwangtung.[39] Kwangsi troops played a key role in buttressing the domination of Kwangtung by Li Chi-shen. Kwangsi probably received financial aid from Kwangtung, but this aid was a matter of personal arrangement between Huang Shao-hsiung and Li Chi-shen, and was not based on any formal agreement.

As far as political union with Kwangtung was concerned, little formal progress was made or desired. The form of union existed, in the Canton Branch Political Council of the Kuomintang, which technically held sway over Kwangtung and Kwangsi. (This Council was set up in October 1927.) But since the Kuomintang had failed to exert any real authority over its converted warlords, its local political organs in areas controlled by such men had only a paper authority. The important political alliance between Kwangtung and Kwangsi was that between the Kwangsi Clique and Li Chi-shen.

As we have seen, Li Chi-shen had been instrumental in bringing the Kwangsi leaders into the Kuomintang camp. He was a native of Wuchow who had made his career in the Kwangtung Army; his connections with Kwangsi only became marked with the rise to power of the future leaders of the Kwangsi Clique. His political attitudes were almost indistinguishable from those of the Kwangsi leaders – a strong leaning towards regional autonomy, a belief in autocratic rule based on military control, coupled with a desire for modernisation. He shared the Kwangsi Clique's antipathy to Communism, and, later, to Chiang Kai-shek.[40] It can be assumed that some of these attitudes originated with Li Chi-shen, who acted as a paternal figure to the young and inexperienced Kwangsi leaders.

Under his rule, Kwangtung became virtually autonomous; the Kuomintang was preoccupied with affairs in the Yangtse provinces, and with the growing rift within the Party. Li took advantage of this situation to impose his personal and authoritarian rule on Kwangtung. He clamped down heavily on Left-wing activity within the province, turning what had been the seat of revolution into a revolutionary backwater. The purge of Communists in April 1927 was as ferocious in Canton as it had been in Shanghai. But the events of late 1927 (described above, pp. 84–6) shattered Li's independence, and although he managed to re-establish himself, his position from 1928 to 1929 was weaker than it had been before.

In addition, Li began to suffer from his overt connections with the Kwangsi Clique, which aroused native Cantonese hostility. He used Huang Shao-hsiung as his deputy whenever he was out of the province (usually to attend meetings of the Central Executive Committee), calling Huang down from Kwangsi just before his departure; Huang spent eight months between November 1926 and November 1927 in Kwangtung. Huang's always flamboyant presence emphasised Li's connections with Kwangsi and offended Cantonese local chauvinism.

Li acted as the Clique's major spokesman within the Kuomintang, since he was its only member to hold a seat on the Central Executive Committee. The advantages which his position in Kwangtung brought to Kwangsi were substantial, but were less material than psychological. Above all, it meant that for four years, Kwangsi felt itself at ease with its neighbour.

POLITICAL ACTIVITY IN KWANGSI, 1925–1927

The relationship between Kwangtung and Kwangsi was often a one-sided one, with Kwangsi the receiver of influences from Kwangtung.

Kwangsi frequently reflected, on a reduced scale, the pattern of events in Kwangtung. This was particularly true of the political activity which swept Kwangtung in the mid-1920s and overflowed into Kwangsi, pushing up the West River like a tidal wave.

The establishment of a Kuomintang organisation in Kwangsi preceded the official alliance of the two provinces in March 1926. A Party Branch was established at Wuchow in 1924, but it had no connection with the emergent Kwangsi leaders or their troops.[41] A labour federation was formed there at the end of the same year, and by the middle of 1925, membership was compulsory.[42] These labour organisations were set up by activists sent in from Kwangtung, many of whom were Communists; they gradually extended their activities from Wuchow to all the major centres of Kwangsi.[43] A Communist Party Bureau and a branch of the Communist Youth League (Ch'ing nien t'uan) were established in the province in 1925, and worker, peasant, student and women's organisations were set up.[44]

This political activity was outside the range of the military leaders of Kwangsi; they had no functional connection with it. It was limited to the major riverine centres of Kwangsi, and within those centres to the young and the poor; it had gained no foothold among local leaders. When the Kwangsi leaders allied themselves officially to the Kuomintang, they found themselves at the head of an independent growth. Though they were believed by foreigners in the province to have adopted the ' bolshevik code of behaviour ', and to have thrown in their lot with the ' Red government of Canton ',[45] their position at the head of the Kuomintang apparatus was nominal, a situation that was reflected in the first Provincial Executive and Supervisory Committees, set up in January 1926; though Huang Shao-hsiung was chairman of the Executive Committee, a majority of its nine members were Communists or Left-wingers.[46]

For a while, the Kwangsi leaders were prepared to let themselves be carried by the tide, to give their support to the mass movements, in particular to anti-foreign, anti-imperialist and anti-religious agitation.

Pai Ch'ung-hsi was the leading sponsor of the anti-religious movement, which was aimed chiefly against superstitious practices. Pai was not interested in ' spontaneous ' mass action, but in disciplined military operations. Early in 1926 his troops went into action, smashing idols, decapitating statues, and converting temples for use as schools and Party headquarters. In an article entitled ' The Twilight of the Gods ', a Kweilin missionary described the destruction of the idols in a temple which ' formerly housed a realistic model of Hell '.[47] In Chaop'ing hsien, a majority of temples were converted into public schools.[48] In Kuei hsien thirty-two temples were in use as schools, and nine as public build-ings.[49] Many of the soldiers who carried out what they regarded as sacrilege were so disturbed that they prayed for forgiveness to the idols before destroying them[50]; in some areas the iconoclasm actually led to clashes between local inhabitants and troops.[51] Pai's close association with the anti-religious movement may raise the suspicion that his motives were not disinterested, that mixed in with a desire to abolish superstitious practices was Pai's distaste, as a Moslem, for other religions. But his policy was actively supported by Huang Shao-hsiung, though in the case of his local temple, Huang bowed to the wishes of his mother; there the idols were allowed to remain, and Huang stood by his mother's side while she prayed to them.[52]

The anti-foreign demonstrations in the province forced the majority of foreigners to leave the province. The Kwangsi Chinese Christian Promotion Society in Wuchow issued a proclamation stating that: ' The saying that missionaries and doctors are vanguards of the Imperialists proves to be a fact undeniable. Fragrances and stinks must be separa-ted . . .'[53] The anti-foreign movement made no distinction between nationalities; though it had started in response to the Hong Kong strike and boycott, and had therefore been aimed principally against the British, it was now directed impartially against all foreigners. Rex Ray, the Texan ' Cowboy Missionary ', was glad to leave the province, to get away from ' the devil's crowd ', and to return to ' the good old U.S.A. and Texas sunshine '.[54] Only the French Jesuit missionaries, stationed chiefly in the less agitated western parts of the province, stayed at their posts, though they were subjected to constant harassment.[55] Chinese Christians had no escape route. In Kweilin, the business agent of the Southern Baptist Mission was paraded through the streets, wearing a dunce's cap, with fire-crackers exploding at his heels. He was denounced at a series of public meetings, and branded on either cheek with the characters ' *yang nu* ' (foreign slave).[56]

These incidents were minor in comparison to the fury of the anti-foreign movement in other provinces, notably Hunan, but they were serious enough to undermine permanently the position of foreigners in the province. In the ' Wuchow Incident ' (March 1926), the British behaved with characteristic high-handedness, but this was the last occasion on which foreigners dared to behave in this way. (The Incident occurred when a British gunboat, en route to retrieve the body of a British oil salesman murdered by bandits in the Lungchow region, blockaded the port at Wuchow in retaliation for the refusal of the local authorities to provide the boat with pilots.)

Anti-foreign incidents continued sporadically throughout 1927, but

most of them were directed only against property. The force of the movement was spent after the Hong Kong Strike ended in October 1926.

By this time, there had been a recession across the whole spectrum of political activity in the province, and an increasing coldness had developed between the provincial Kuomintang hierarchy and the Communists. As early as April 1926, attempts were made to curb union activity in Kwangsi.[57] Part of the reason for this coldness lay in the fact that control over the local Communist operations had passed from the hands of a conciliatory leader, Ch'en Mien-shu (he was concurrently a member of the Kuomintang Provincial Executive Committee) to the much more radical Huang Jih-k'uei and his Russian adviser.[58] But its roots lay in the attitudes of the Kwangsi leaders; though they tolerated and occasionally encouraged anti-foreign and iconoclastic manifestations, they were opposed to any activities which called for major social reforms. Huang was probably annoyed by student attacks on his appointees in the Wuchow area – his nephew was head of the Provincial Propaganda Training School (Kuang-hsi sheng-li hsüan-ch'uan-yüan yang-ch'eng suo) there; a t'ung-hsiang was head of the Second Middle School (Sheng-li er chung).[59] He was alarmed when workers started to agitate for higher wages, when the mass movements protested against official corruption, and urged an end to the trade in opium. These were social evils which, for all their adherence to the revolutionary ideology of the Kuomintang, the Kwangsi leaders had no intention of reforming. Huang Shao-hsiung wanted well-behaved mass movements which would ignore local evils, and concentrate on attacking foreigners, whose actual importance in Kwangsi was negligible. The foreign community in Kwangsi was tailored to Huang's needs as a butt of mass activity, since it was small, weak, and given to retreating to Hong Kong. The Communists were not prepared to play Huang's game, and were intent on trying to launch a real social revolution. Conflict was inevitable.

From the spring of 1926, Huang started to exert pressure on the mass movements. He did not abandon his radical public façade, but acted through subordinates, usually local police chiefs and army commanders. In Nanning the editor of the Kuo-min jih-pao, Huang Hua-piao, acted as his front man in conducting a campaign against radical students and union members.[60] In July Hsiang-tao chou-pao, the chief Chinese Communist organ, printed a letter which reported repression and reaction in Kwangsi. The letter, and the advice it inspired, gave an indication of the uncertainty of the Kwangsi Communists as to what policy they should follow; they were advised not to respond to persecution by going underground, but to continue to work openly, following the official Communist Party policy of co-operating with the Kuomintang.[61] Their

confusion, and the confusion within the local Kuomintang, which reflected the factionalism developing within the national Kuomintang, played into the hands of Huang Shao-hsiung, who was not confused. The radical camp, divided and without any outstanding leaders, was highly vulnerable to Huang's pressure. The fact that the radical movement was localised, in the main riverine cities, also helped Huang. In much of Kwangsi, political organisations existed still on paper only. In 1926, fifty-one *hsien* party branches reported that there was no work in progress in their branches, this at a time when elsewhere the radical movement was at its height.[62] Huang began overtly to act against the mass movements.[63]

The ineffectiveness of local radicals was revealed most clearly in the case of the peasant movement. Other branches of the mass movements made a better showing, at least in some areas. In Nanning, for example, the Ch'ing nien t'uan (Youth League) was tightly organised along small-cell lines, and published two journals, *Ko-ming chih hua* (Flowers of Revolution) and *Hsüeh chung* (Bell of Blood).[64] But while other provinces organised millions of peasants, only a few thousand peasants were organised in Kwangsi. There were only two *hsien* peasant organisations and only thirty-four at the *hsiang* level, many of which were dominated by politically reactionary gentry and local landlords. Forty Kwangsi men were in training at the Peasant Movement Training Institute in Canton, but there seem to have been few local radicals actually at work on peasant organisation.[65] The head of the Kuomintang provincial peasant department was an elderly *chü-jen*, whose conception of his responsibilities was to abandon his scholar's robe for peasant clothing; he was regarded by Huang Shao-hsiung as naïve and eccentric, and incapable of organising the peasantry.[66]

Some of the ineffectiveness of the radical movement in Kwangsi may be ascribed to the lack of interest shown in backward, isolated Kwangsi by central Communist and radical Kuomintang leaders, who felt that their manpower was better deployed in provinces such as Hunan and Kiangsi. Young activists wanted to be nearer the real centres of mass agitation, in the areas along the advance of the northern expedition. When Huang Shao-hsiung organised the most radical elements in the province into a comfort corps for soldiers fighting at the front, and despatched them to Wuhan, there were no protests.[67]

By the end of 1926, the development of the mass movements in Kwangsi had been arrested. The actual Purge of Communists (Ch'ing-tang) in April 1927 was almost an anti-climax, and was only the final stage of a gradually intensified programme of repression. The number of arrests was not more than a few hundred.[68] Most of the Communist and radical Kuomintang leaders managed to flee the province, though several were captured and executed, including two members of the Kuomintang Provincial Executive Committee.[69]

The second Kuomintang Provincial Executive Committee, which took office shortly after the Purge, had an almost entirely new membership; Huang Shao-hsiung was the only member of the first committee to sit on the second. The mass movements were dead; there were occasional anti-foreign demonstrations, but no opposition to the Kwangsi Clique itself, at least on the surface. The people of Kwangsi retreated into apathy. The upsurge of mass activity in 1925 and 1926 had not been strong enough to challenge the supremacy of the Kwangsi Clique. Only in one area was there serious and sustained opposition to the Kwangsi Clique, in the Chuang area of northwest Kwangsi.

THE CHUANG PEASANT MOVEMENT AND SOVIET

The province of Kwangsi has a high proportion of non-Han minority peoples. In 1958, when the Kwangsi Chuang Autonomous Region was set up, it was estimated that out of a population of 19,000,000, 35 per cent (7,000,000) were Chuang, 58 per cent Han (11,000,000) and the rest members of small minority groups. Similar proportions were found in population figures for the 1930s.[70] The Chuang, with the other minority peoples such as the Miao and the Yao, are the aboriginal inhabitants of Kwangsi. They once occupied the whole of the area later designated as Kwangsi province, but as the Han migrated into the area (from the T'ang dynasty on – see above, p. 25), they were driven up into the hills in the north and west of the province.[71] The majority of the Chuang did not preserve their identity as a separate people, but became sinicised. Only a few, in the remoter areas of the province especially in the Left and Right River Valleys, clung to their Chuang identity and remained outside the control of the provincial authorities. It was among these people that the Chuang Peasant Movement developed in the early 1920s. (The present ' Chuang ' population of the Kwangsi Chuang Autonomous Area presumably consists largely of long-sinicised Chuang.)

Relations between the Han and sinicised Chuang, and the tribal people approached a state of permanent warfare. The minority peoples were desperately poor; they farmed the infertile hill land, while the valley land was in the hands of Han and sinicised Chuang.

In the early 1920s, the sufferings of the minority peoples were exacerbated by the depredations of roving bands of soldiers after the collapse of the provincial government in 1921. In response to this anarchic situation, Wei Pa-ch'ün, the son of a local landlord, started to organise the peasants in Tunglan hsien into self-protection associations.[72]

These first stirrings were soon squashed by the local landlords, and in 1924, Wei was forced to flee. He went to Canton, and studied at the Peasant Movement Training Institute there (later directed by Mao Tse-tung).[73] In 1925, Wei returned to Tunglan, and revived his organisational work; he set up his own peasant training institute.[74] Perhaps because of Wei's training in Canton, the movement was more successful in resisting the attacks made on it by the local authorities, but in spite of his connection with the revolutionary movement, the activity in Tunglan still had the character of incoherent revolt, motivated more by racial, anti-Han feelings than by a desire for social revolution. There was a strong ritual element; oaths were sworn and the blood of chickens drunk ceremonially before engagements with the local militia forces.[75]

During 1925 and 1926, the movement expanded; in January 1926, the *hsien* town of Tunglan was occupied and a revolutionary committee was set up there.[76] Initially, the Kwangsi authorities tried to suppress the movement, but since the policies of organisation of peasant associations and of rent reduction, the main planks of the Tunglan movement, were official Kuomintang policies, Huang Shao-hsiung found it difficult to treat this peasant movement as a rebellion. He was forced to negotiate with Wei.[77] The leader of Huang's negotiating team, Ch'en Mien-shu, a member of the Kuomintang Provincial Executive Committee and a Communist, became *hsien-chang* of Tunglan, and quickly brought Wei and other peasant leaders into the Communist Party.[78] The relationship between Wei and the Communist Party can only be guessed at; there are indications that the Party was unhappy with Wei's work, drawn from frequent references to the need to ' strengthen Party work '. An outsider, Yü Shao-chieh, was made first head of the local Party branch.[79]

By 1927, when the Purge occurred, the Peasant Movement in Tunglan and the surrounding area had grown to such a size that it was able to survive military actions against it, though it was forced to retreat into the hills.[80]

In 1929, after the defeat of the Kwangsi Clique by Nanking, control of the province passed to a group of Leftist officers from Li Tsung-jen's Armies, who had defected to Nanking and precipitated the fall of the Clique. Their defection had been arranged by Yü Tso-po, a prominent Kwangsi Left-winger, who had been forced to leave the province in 1927. Yü's co-operation with Nanking had been sanctioned by the Communist Party, and Communist workers were now sent into the province. They concentrated their efforts on infiltrating the forces of Li Ming-jui (who was already very Left-wing).[81] When the Kwangsi Clique returned to power in the province in October 1929, three regiments formerly under Li Ming-jui's command, now Communist-controlled, retreated towards the Communist-held areas in the northwest of the province.

During his brief period as Governor of Kwangsi, Yü Tso-po had sent supplies to the Peasant Movement in Tunglan, while the local and Central organisations of the CCP had sent cadres to help improve local organisation. When the Communist-led units retreating from Nanning entered the Right River Valley, and took the opium centre of Pose, Wei Pa-ch'ün immediately made connection with them. Teng Hsiao-p'ing, the chief representative of the CCP Central Committee in Kwangsi, arrived in the area shortly before the incoming troops. A Front Committee was set up, of which Teng was secretary.[82]

The capture of Pose provided a rich source of income, the tax on opium in transit through the city. Stocks actually in the town were seized, and only released on payment of a heavy sum in taxation.[83] With the help of this income, and of the experienced cadres drafted into the area, the Peasant Movement was able to expand rapidly; several more *hsien* were brought under its control, and its armed forces were expanded.

On 11 December 1929 (the second anniversary of the Canton Commune) the Right River Soviet was set up; its chairman was Lei Ching-t'ien, a Nanning man.[84] The Soviet soon extended to nine *hsien*. The armed forces in the area were reorganised as the Red Seventh Army, with a strength of about 10,000 men. Chang Yün-i was commander of the Seventh Army, and Teng Hsiao-p'ing was political chief of the Soviet (see Fig. 5).[85]

These men were all recent arrivals. The establishment of the Soviet and of the Seventh Army marked the eclipse of the Chuang in the leadership of the movement. They were now relegated to secondary posts. Wei Pa-ch'ün had no political authority, though he was a regimental commander in the new army. Post-1949 accounts of this period have attempted to give the picture of happy co-operation between Han and Chuang, of altruistic Han coming to help their benighted brothers, but it seems likely that there was a great gulf between the Han outsiders and the local Chuang. The Han were exasperated by the racial motivation of the Chuang, and by their lack of political sophistication. It was useless, for example, to speak to them of the concepts of freedom and equality, for they did not exist in the Chuang language. The only way their meaning could be got across was by physical demonstration: one man riding on another's shoulders equals inequality and repression; two men standing side by side equals equality.[86] Wei Pa-ch'ün had nursed his followers

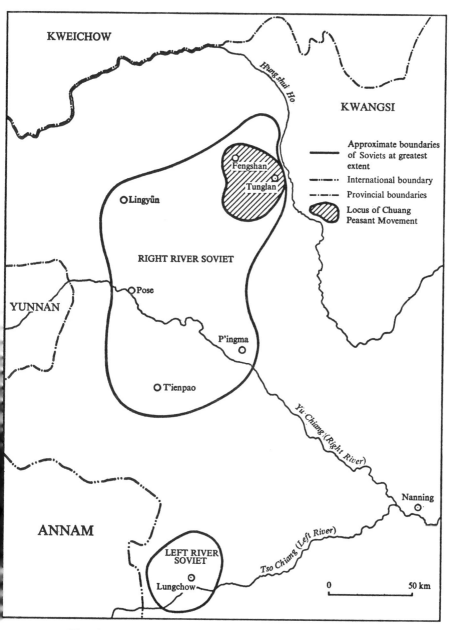

Fig. 5.   Right and Left River Soviets in Kwangsi, early 1930

gradually towards socialism; the new arrivals wanted the pace speeded up; in the process they pushed the Chuang leaders into a back seat.

The establishment of the Soviet in the Pose region did not at first make a great impact on the local population. There was little disturbance. The trade in opium was not curtailed; its revenue was used to issue every officer and man of the new army with twenty silver dollars in monthly pay – a move which may explain the rapid rise in the size of the army, since this was, by local standards, a small fortune.[87] The work of disarming local militia units was carried out very sketchily, an oversight which was to cause great trouble later on. In the rural areas, there was more political activity; land was confiscated, and a start was made at dividing it.[88]

In February 1930, a second Soviet was set up, in the Left River Valley at Lungchow, and the Red Eighth Army was established, numbering between 2,000 and 3,000 men, many of them bandit converts.[89] Initially, the activities of the Soviet were much more violent than those of the Right River Soviet. The French Consulate was sacked, and the Catholic mission attacked, on the suspicion, undoubtedly justified, that the missionaries were harbouring 'bad elements' – local landlords and merchants.[90] Teng Hsiao-p'ing explained the attacks on the French as being inspired by the relations that the Communist movement in Kwangsi had with the Annamite rebels.[91] The Annamite authorities responded by bombing Lungchow and by closing the Kwangsi-Annam border.[92]

The military organisation of the Eighth Army was very shaky, and the army could not resist counter-attacks launched by the re-established Kwangsi Clique. Within two months, the Left River Soviet collapsed, and a few remnants of the Eighth Army made their way across country to join up with the Seventh Army.

The Right River Soviet was more secure. Though it had neglected the problem of crushing local opponents, it had silenced them temporarily, and appeared to be well in charge. Emboldened by its success, the Red Seventh Army decided to expand the area of its control still further. An expedition was launched, which brought not further success, but the beginning of disaster. It revealed two things: first that the Soviet's control was far less secure than it appeared superficially, and second that many of the local minority peoples were just as hostile to Communist Han as they were to anti-Communist Han. As soon as Soviet troops left on their expedition of expansion, the landlords and their militia revived themselves, and, with the help of Yunnanese troops, struck at the Soviet organisations. Pose and other towns in the Right River Valley were lost.[93] And as the Communist forces pushed towards the Kweichow border, they met with hostile reaction from many of the local people. Without local intermediaries and tactful compromise (as the Communists were to find later on the Long March), it was impossible to establish friendly relations with the minority peoples.[94]

With its position badly shaken by the loss of much of its original area of control, the Seventh Army and the remnants of the Soviet were dealt a further crushing blow in the summer of 1930 – this time by the Communist Centre in Shanghai. In August, Teng Hsiao-p'ing, who had been to Shanghai to consult with the CCP Centre, arrived back with instructions (written in June) that the Seventh Army should leave the Soviet area and move to the Central Soviet in Kiangsi.[95] This order was based on the Centre's recent decision, initiated by Li Li-san, to fight for cities, and therefore to centralise all scattered military units. It was an order which was so unrealistic that it was almost insane. To get to Kiangsi, the army would have to march 1,100 kilometres over mountainous terrain, through territory garrisoned by hostile forces. The Soviet area would be left virtually undefended. There was apparently a clash between Wei Pa-ch'ün and Teng Hsiao-p'ing as to whether the order should be obeyed or not, but Teng insisted on its acceptance, and in September, the bulk of the Seventh Army departed.[96] The Seventh did not arrive in Kiangsi until the spring of the following year; their journey was an agonising battle against cold, hunger, rugged terrain and constant enemy harassment, a foretaste of the rigours of the Long March. Only one-third of the men who started reached Kiangsi.[97]

The Soviet area came under attack from forces of the Kwangsi Clique almost immediately after the departure of the Seventh. Tunglan hsien was devastated, but the Soviet administration, along with many of the local inhabitants, retreated into the hills, where they held out for some time. Eventually they were crushed and Wei Pa-ch'ün himself betrayed and executed. His head was displayed throughout the province, a grisly warning to would-be dissidents.[98]

Other leaders of the Kwangsi Communist movement met similarly violent ends. Yü Tso-yü, the commander of the Eighth Red Army, fled to Hong Kong, but was extradited by the British authorities to Canton, where he was executed.[99] Li Ming-jui went with the Seventh Army into Kiangsi, but was executed there, on suspicion of being in league with Wang Ching-wei.[100]

The Kwangsi Soviet could not survive the ineptitude of its local directors, who failed to establish a firm basis for the Soviet, and of the CCP Centre, which removed its only prop. With the collapse of the Soviet came the suppression of the Chuang revolt, their autonomous movement destroyed largely as a result of their association with Communist Han, who had taken over their movement, expanded it to the point where it invited massive retaliation from the provincial authorities, and then left it defenceless. Other minority peoples continued to rise in rebellion – there were Miao risings in 1933 and 1934 [101] – but the Chuang remained dormant until 1949. Nor was there any further Communist activity in Kwangsi until 1949; a skeleton underground organisation was maintained in the major cities, but was never strong enough to organise overt activity.[102]

The activities of the Chuang Peasant Movement had little effect on the rest of Kwangsi. They are interesting chiefly for the light they throw on the relations of the minority peoples with the Han, and because of their connection with contemporary policies of the Communist Centre. For the Kwangsi provincial authorities, they represented only an irritant, which did not interfere with the general process of government. From 1925, the province was militarily secure, and after the suppression of the mass movements, the bulk of the civilian population was under firm control. These were the conditions that Huang Shao-hsiung needed to carry out his plans for the reconstruction of his province. Let us now turn from this long digression to see what Huang was able to achieve.

THE RECONSTRUCTION OF KWANGSI, 1926–1929

The term ' reconstruction ' (chien-she) had a great vogue in the late 1920s and early 1930s. It was a catch-all phrase used to describe the various policies which were instituted (frequently on paper only) in the period after the military consolidation of much of China under the Kuomintang flag. It was mandatory, both for the Central Government at Nanking, and for individual but autonomous areas under the Kuomintang flag, to produce reconstruction schemes, to set out glowing descriptions of the new, reconstructed China that was to emerge from the implementation of the schemes. The ideal of reconstruction had first been outlined by Sun Yat-sen, who produced his Chien-kuo ta-kang (Outline for National Reconstruction) in 1924. It was made up of twenty-five articles, which contained provisions for the work to be undertaken at the various stages of the revolution – military, tutelary and constitutional. The articles recognised that development would be uneven, and that individual areas would move ahead at different speeds. One of their unifying aims was to prepare the way for local self-government, and to provide the economic conditions in which this local self-government could function.[103]

Huang Shao-hsiung's attitude to the question of reconstruction was to adopt the general slogan of reconstruction, without outlining a specific programme, and without paying too close attention to Sun Yat-sen's own proposals, especially for local self-government. According to Sun's Article 7, the province should have moved out of the military period and into the tutelary one as soon as the military settlement of the province was achieved. But although the province set up the organs of civilian tutelary control, such as a Provincial Executive Committee, it remained under military control. There was no attempt to undertake the training in self-government at *hsien* level which Article 8 called for. Kwangsi's reconstruction consisted chiefly in attempts to put the province's economy and administration on a viable footing, to return to the limited level of efficiency and prosperity at which its economy had operated before 1921, and plan for a more auspicious future.

Huang Shao-hsiung propagated ideas on reconstruction energetically. With good will, discipline and outside help (in the form of loans and advice) Huang believed that Kwangsi could soon make enormous strides. There were plans to train large numbers of specialists, to build wooden aeroplanes to open up air links between individual sections of the province, to export huge quantities of tin and tung oil.[104] Many of these schemes had an air of unreality about them. All of them depended, as Huang recognised, on a reduction of the proportion of the provincial income going to the military, and on an improvement in the calibre of administrators.[105] But they began to seem slightly less unrealistic when Kwangsi started to attract outside assistance, in the form of expert guidance rather than financial help.

During Huang Shao-hsiung's rule of the province, from 1926 to 1929, most of the rest of China was seriously affected by warfare. In these areas, there was little chance for specialists to work. A number came to Kwangsi, where conditions were more favourable. Eighty per cent of the experts engaged in reconstruction projects in Kwangsi came from outside the province.[106] In addition to this resident corps, other experts came to Kwangsi on short trips (which were frequently combined with officially-financed tourist trips in the Kweilin region, one of China's most famous scenic spots). In 1928, a large group of experts was sent to the province by the Academia Sinica to initiate a comprehensive programme of scientific survey and research. Kwangsi was chosen for this programme because ' it has for a number of years enjoyed peace and order, and has itself started on a programme of reconstruction and internal development '. The group included meteorologists, biologists, geologists, agricultural and forestry experts, anthropologists, archaeologists, sociologists and economists, most of whom were expected to spend some time in the province.[107] In the same year, an educational seminar was held at Kweilin, to discuss plans for the development of education in the province; 2,000 academics and teachers attended, many of them nationally-known men from outside the province.[108] Ting Wen-chiang, China's best-known geologist, spent ten months in the province, doing the preliminary work for a geological survey of Kwangsi.[109]

The visiting experts were principally concerned with making long-term plans for the development of the province's agriculture, industry and mining, which were slow to show results. The noticeable achievements of Huang's reconstruction schemes were improvement of the superficial fabric of the province, chiefly in the cleaning up of its cities and in the development of roads.

Huang started on a programme of urban improvement, a task which was urgent. Most of Kwangsi's cities were built on the banks of the West River and its tributaries, and were subject to severe flooding, since the level of the river fluctuated enormously according to season. They were crowded, and frequently swept by huge and uncontrollable fires. Over-crowding and slum conditions encouraged the spread of disease; malaria, dysentery, cholera, smallpox, meningitis, typhoid, leprosy, diphtheria and plague (bubonic and pneumonic) were all endemic in Kwangsi.[110] There were frequent epidemics, and though vaccination, the only effective preventive, had been practised in the province from the turn of the century,[111] there were no comprehensive programmes of vaccination. Urban improvements offered some hope of limiting epidemics.

The work of urban improvement was concentrated at Wuchow, the main commercial centre (and the native place of many of Huang's personal followers), at Nanning, the provincial capital, and at Liuchow, at the geographical centre of the province (where Huang had plans for establishing a new capital). Streets were widened, roads surfaced, sewers installed, and water and electricity plants set up.

Road construction moved ahead rapidly. Traditionally, Kwangsi's communications had been water-borne, but river traffic was often very slow, especially on journeys upstream, and was frequently interrupted by changes in water level. The road construction programme was undertaken partly in the interests of aiding trade, but equally importantly to facilitate military movements. The construction of a good road to the Kweichow border was chiefly designed to help the shipment of opium from Kweichow through Kwangsi. The road-building programme was the most successful facet of reconstruction in Kwangsi; by 1928, Kwangsi was listed as having more good roads than any other province in China.[112]

Other aspects of communications development were less successful. The plan for a railway between Kweilin and Hengchow, a spur of the Canton–Wuhan line, was revived, but came to nothing. It was not built until the Anti-Japanese War. Nor was another projected railway, between Lungchow and Nanning, connecting with the line built up to the Chinese-Annam border on the Annamese side, ever built. A tentative survey was made for a line between Szechwan and the sea, but no further progress was made. The main reason was that there was no local capital available for such costly projects. Foreign sources, which had provided the capital for much of China's early railway development, were not prepared to risk capital in ventures which seemed, after the events of the middle 1920s, to be hazardous.

Huang laid stress on the need for industrial development and in 1928 introduced his Industrial Plan. He believed that if Kwangsi could set up some light industrial enterprises, the burden of imports would be eased. He sponsored a scheme to set up small plants, with government capital, though only two or three dozen ever got off the ground.[113] He also tried to raise loan capital from Kwangsi natives living abroad. Very little progress was made; the only factories which opened in Kwangsi between 1926 and 1929 produced items of peripheral importance to the economy – ice, cigarettes, matches etc. – which played little role either in easing Kwangsi's import surplus or in aiding the development of the province.[114]

In the field of education, Huang was slightly more successful. It was clear that though Kwangsi could depend temporarily on outside experts to help in the task of reconstruction, the province would eventually need its own experts. In 1928, Kwangsi University was set up at Wuchow, as a technical training institute which would produce the experts needed for reconstruction. Its first director was Ma Chün-wu (see above, p. 47), who had a high reputation as an educator. The university was Huang's favourite scheme, and he shaped it to suit his own tastes. He felt that the establishment of a university would bestow on him an aura of intellectual respectability; but his university was not to be a place for ' high level vagabonds ' (kao-teng yu-min), a phrase which he implied included anyone not pursuing a course of vocational training. He wanted to train only tools for his reconstruction programme. He had no time for arts courses, and none were offered.[115] The province also established a number of middle schools but it left the question of primary schools to the localities, encouraging them to set up as many as possible, and to locate them in temples. Between 1925 and 1927, over fifty primary schools were set up in Chaop'ing hsien. These were directed by the administration of the hsien city. In Kuei hsien, several hundred schools were set up in the same period.[116] The province's only other educational establishments were a few vocational schools and a military school – a branch of the Whampoa Academy, set up in 1926.[117]

Little attention was paid to the mammoth task of improving agriculture; the prospect of making across-the-board improvements was too daunting, and the Kwangsi authorities contented themselves with setting up an experimental station at Liuchow. This centre, which was staffed by experts from Canton, conducted experiments on crop improvement and animal husbandry. Unfortunately, its schemes were impractical in poverty-stricken Kwangsi. Most peasants could not afford to rebuild their own homes, let alone put up a chicken house which was more costly than an average peasant house.[118] (This type of example can be given of many reconstruction projects, both in Kwangsi and elsewhere; the projects were designed by experts who, however well-meaning, had little idea of what peasants could actually afford. They planned for an ' objective ' situation which was more likely to be found in the foreign countries where they had received their specialist training than in China). The one policy which might have benefited all of Kwangsi's peasants, that of reduction in land rents, which was still official Kuomintang policy, was discontinued in Kwangsi and in the other three provinces under the control of the Kwangsi Clique in 1928.[119] This action can be taken as an example of the shallowness of the Kwangsi leaders' commitment to social reform, and also as an indication of where (at least part of) their political constituency lay – in the landlord class.

Some progress was made in reclamation and in reafforestation (much of the original forest cover of the province had now disappeared, partly because of the slash-and-burn agricultural techniques of the minority peoples). A reclamation area was designated near Liuchow, and the work of land reclamation allocated to disbanded soldiers, each of whom was given ten *mou* of land.[120] This was one of the very few official schemes introduced anywhere in China to cope with the problem created by the huge number of surplus troops in almost every province. The planting of trees was encouraged, partly to combat soil erosion, and partly to provide two valuable exports: tung oil and star anise. This was not a new policy; several plantations had been laid out in 1912 and 1913, each with large capital injections and up to 1,750,000 trees.[121] The Kwangsi Government merely expanded these activities. Tung oil was particularly important. Tung trees were hardy, needed little attention and could be planted on otherwise barren hillsides. Tung oil was an important export for China, and a crucial one for Kwangsi. One Chinese exporter described the importance given to the trade:

' A good many of my countrymen entertain the idea that China Tung Oil is indispensable for foreigners, as if it were bread and butter . . . it is simply beyond their imagination that Tung Oil is only used as a drying agent – they insist on a conception nothing short of meta-physical.' [122]

At Nanning, Huang Shao-hsiung introduced a scheme whereby civil servants were obliged to plant a certain number of the trees. It was while he himself was doing his stint one day in the spring of 1929 that he received the news that Li Chi-shen had been arrested in Nanking, the first move in Chiang Kai-shek's campaign to destroy the Kwangsi Clique.

Li's arrest marked the end of the period of stability in Kwangsi which had allowed Huang Shao-hsiung to carry out his limited reforms. Soon afterwards the province was temporarily lost to the Clique, and Huang never again acted effectively as its chairman.

Huang's rule over Kwangsi was a great improvement over the anarchy which preceded it; it gave the province internal security, a luxury which few other provinces enjoyed at the time. A tentative start was made at economic modernisation, though it was little more than a foundation for the more systematic efforts of the Kwangsi Clique in the 1930s. Huang's efforts might have been more successful if he had not wiped out a large number of the most effective and modern-minded people in the province, in his attacks on Communist and Left-wingers, if he had instead concentrated on wiping out the endemic corruption in business and bureaucratic circles. He made some gestures in this direction, but he made no moves against the people involved in the opium trade, for fear of disrupting the province's major source of revenue, nor did he clean up local administration to any significant degree. Huang was well aware of whom he could afford to offend, and whom not. Commercial and landlord interests were too strongly entrenched, and their support for his political position was too valuable for them to be attacked. He limited himself to homilies on the need for local officials to come close to the people, which were taken for what they were worth – nothing.

Huang's efforts should not be seen as a systematic scheme for modernisation, but rather as a piecemeal, unco-ordinated response to opportunities which presented themselves to his attention. He was enthusiastic for the undertaking, and he made long tours through the province to try to stimulate local work, but his chief function was not to create a ' New Kwangsi ', but to keep the old Kwangsi as a secure base for the Kwangsi Clique. This demanded a stable and efficient military organisation, both in terms of regular forces, and of local militia forces, for whose support he depended on the local elite. His fellow-leaders outside the province did not object to his schemes for reconstruction; they gave the province a reputation for progressiveness, and they encouraged efficiency which strengthened the Clique's base. The detailed administration of the province was left entirely in Huang's hands; he only met Li Tsung-jen once during the period after the start of the northern expedition, Pai Ch'ung-hsi not at all.

Since Huang lacked any ideological or theoretical framework in which to mould his plans, they often took on a patchwork nature, giving the impression sometimes of being decided on whim. He had a penchant for superficial, quickly-realised schemes, which attracted outside attention, rather than for basic reforms. A university was tacked on to a very weak basic education system; an extensive bus service was set up, with palatial bus stations, though few people could afford the fares; sophisticated agricultural experiments were conducted, but the oppressive agricultural system was not reformed; electricity plants were installed, but their output was so low that the lights they powered were weaker than oil lamps.

None of these measures did anything to relieve the chronic poverty of the bulk of Kwangsi's inhabitants, nor did they change its basic economic and social structure. Only the Chuang Peasant Movement, which was anathema to Huang, made any attempt to improve the lot of the peasantry. Elsewhere, the peasants were still governed by the same landlords and local administrators who had ruled before Huang's advent. The only improvement in their position lay in the removal of the constant threat of depradations by bandits and lawless soldiers. This in itself was an improvement, but not sufficient to justify any great hymns of praise.

6
'Kwangsi Empire': the Kwangsi Clique after the Northern Expedition

We have seen the Kwangsi leaders now in several stages of their career – as young officers, as provincial militarists, as members of the Revolutionary Army. We now see them in the briefest and most abortive stage of their career, as rulers of a multi-province bloc. This is the period where they usually enter other accounts of twentieth-century China – as rowdy interlopers, put smartly in their place by Chiang Kai-shek. For the Clique it was almost an aberration, a period when success went to its collective head and made it abandon all caution.

After their retreat to Wuhan, the Kwangsi leaders cut themselves off from Nanking. They concentrated their attention on expanding their control to cover Hunan as well as Hupei; and since Chiang could not prevent the Kwangsi Clique from invading Hunan, he decided to try to abort the attack by giving aid to the Hunanese commanders. 'What appeared to be a struggle between Hupei and Hunan was in fact a disguised battle between Chekiang and Kwangsi ' [1] – a very thinly disguised one. He was unsuccessful; by the end of February, 1928 most of Hunan was in Kwangsi hands.

The Hunan Campaign was holding up the final stage of the Northern Expedition, the push on Peking; Chiang could not launch his troops north with a potentially hostile grouping on his flank. He reached an agreement with Feng Yü-hsiang, whose troops were stationed to the north of Hupei, to bring pressure on the Kwangsi Clique. The Clique could not resist the combined pressure of Feng and Chiang, and agreed to compromise.

Li Chi-shen came north to arrange the Wuhan-Nanking compromise. He extracted from Nanking an undertaking to recognise the autonomy of the four Kwangsi-dominated provinces, to recognise Yunnan and Kweichow as within the Kwangsi sphere of influence, to sever connections with Wang Ching-wei and the Left Kuomintang (whom the Clique especially detested), to move Chang Fa-k'uei's troops into north China, and to waive the right to revenue from Kwangtung; in return the Clique agreed to recognise Nanking's paramount authority, to abstain from threatening its rear, and to send troops on the continued Northern Expedition (these troops to be financed from Nanking).[2]

Li Chi-shen's successful negotiations demonstrated the benefits that the Kwangsi Clique could draw from the loose nature of the Clique's structure, which allowed it to operate simultaneously on several, occasionally conflicting, fronts. Here Li was operating not as an integral member of the Clique, but as a mediator, drawing both on his association with the Kuomintang Centre and on his connections with the Clique; as he was not directly involved in the dissension between Nanking and Wuhan, he could negotiate from the side-lines.

In April 1928 the Northern Expedition got under way again. The First Group Army advanced north up the Tientsin-P'uk'ou Railway, the Second (Feng Yü-hsiang) moved into Chihli and West Shantung, and the Third (Yen Hsi-shan) moved east out of Shansi. The Fourth Group Army (Li Tsung-jen), commanded at the front by Pai Ch'ung'hsi, was kept in general reserve.[3] Peking fell to Yen Hsi-shan on 12 June. Pai Ch'ung-hsi's troops followed Yen's into the city, and quietly began to challenge Yen's forces for control of the Peking-Tientsin area.

At the beginning of July, Li Tsung-jen and Chiang Kai-shek came to Peking, and went with Feng and Yen to Pi Yün Ssu (Temple of the Azure Clouds) in the Western Hills outside Peking, to announce the end of the Northern Expedition to the spirit of Sun Yat-sen, whose body lay in a great silver casket in the temple.

> A dramatic episode marked the impressive memorial rites. . . . Chiang Kai-shek flung himself sobbing upon the casket containing the dead leader's remains, and was led still sobbing from the scene by Feng Yu-siang [sic].[4]

The Northern Expedition was finished. Except for a few areas of resistance, China south of the Great Wall was reunified. But the reunification was superficial; of the four generals at Sun's bier, three were deeply committed to maintaining their regional autonomy. They were within the Kuomintang camp, but not of it.

The failure of the Kwangsi Clique to establish themselves as national leaders at Nanking forced upon its leaders a reassessment of their position, and of the directions in which they could develop. If there was no room for them at the Centre, what should they do and where should they go? Should they drop their pretensions to political involvement and revert to the status of provincial warlords? Or should they submit to the fiat of Nanking and turn themselves into loyal subordinates? The second alternative was out of the question. The Kwangsi leaders had lost what faith they had in the political leadership of the Kuomintang while they had looked on, as bystanders, at the hideous in-fighting of 1927. The only force that the Kwangsi leaders would submit to was superior military force, and this, at the beginning of 1928, Nanking did not possess. The first alternative was equally unacceptable. The Northern Expedition might not have succeeded in absorbing the warlords who flocked to the Kuomintang flag, but it had changed irrevocably the definition of warlordism. It was no longer possible for men who held independent military power to cast themselves simply in the role of regional militarist. The age of *tu-chüns*, of provincial military governors had passed. The impossibility lay not in the degree of control that the Kuomintang was able to exercise, but in the changed political climate. Men who had managed to establish themselves as independent military commanders were usually politically shrewd. Since their survival was predicated on an ability to smell out potential winners, to sense the drift of events (so that they could form the most advantageous alliances) they were quick to throw in their lot with the rising political force, whether in their own part of China, or in the country as a whole. This sensitivity to political movement had led, as we saw in Chapter 4, many warlords to join the Kuomintang side in the early stages of the Northern Expedition. Where this sensitivity was not entirely cynical, where it was linked to at least a modicum of political interest, as was the case with the Kwangsi Clique, the pressure for a continuing involvement with the Kuomintang was overwhelming. There could be no turning back from the formal commitment to the Kuomintang flag.

But this commitment did not mean submission to the Kuomintang Centre at Nanking. For the Kwangsi Clique it meant a manipulation of Kuomintang principles and organisational laws, and a further attempt to find a political liaison with one of the Kuomintang's inner factions; it meant specifically the manipulation of the Branch Political Council system to justify regional autonomy for the Kwangsi Clique, an autonomy dressed in Kuomintang colours.

Branch Political Councils, a concept originally introduced by the Wuhan Government in July 1927 (see above, p. 83) had been established by the Fourth Plenum (January 1928) at Canton, K'aifeng, T'aiyuan and Wuhan; a fifth was set up at Peking after the fall of that city and a sixth, later still, at Mukden. They were, as their siting indicates, a means of recognising the independent administration of Li Chi-shen (Canton), Feng Yü-hsiang (K'aifeng), Yen Hsi-shan (T'aiyuan) and Li Tsung-jen (Wuhan). Nanking hoped that they would be nothing more than a temporary expedient, and that once their Chairmen had been persuaded (or forced) to abandon their autonomy, the Councils would be wound up.[5] The Chairmen thought otherwise; the Councils were for them convenient ways of associating themselves with the Kuomintang without bowing to its authority.

The Kwangsi Clique came to dominate three of these Councils – at Wuhan, Canton and Peking. They used them not as organs of day-to-day administration, but as political mouthpieces, as a means of conferring respectability upon themselves. The Councils gave an aura of political involvement to the essentially militarist behaviour of the Clique. Li Chishen, the most articulate spokesman of the Clique, argued that the Councils were in tune with contemporary political tendencies:

> We are laying the greatest stress upon the regional governments. In Hankow, Canton, Chekiang and elsewhere the Branch Political Councils are being managed with the greatest care. Tried Party men are given the most important positions and very fine work is being done. There regional councils are permanent institutions and are more representative of the Nationalist Movement [than the Nanking Government]. We stress the regional councils because they are in accordance with the political tendency of the time.[6]

Li justified the Councils by an appeal to ' objective ' circumstances; he envisaged a ' co-operation between separate governments (*fen-chih ho-tso*).[7] It was a circular argument. He himself was one of the main contributors to the ' objective ' circumstances which made the establishment of the Councils possible. Without his type of regional powerholding, ' objective ' circumstances would not have demanded regional centres of government.

He was also misleading in speaking of the ' very great care ' with which the Councils were managed. The regional militarists of the Kwangsi Clique were not interested in how they were managed, or in how the Councils themselves managed local affairs. Their concept of regional government was *laissez-faire*. They were not concerned, nor did they have the resources, to set up a Kwangsi ' colonial ' administration. They were prepared to leave the management of local affairs in local hands, making only two provisos: that there should be no local disorder, and that money to finance the Clique's armies should be readily forthcoming.

At Wuhan, the Clique applied its *laissez-faire* concept by appointing as Garrison Commander Hu Tsung-to, a Hupei native who had served in the Kwangsi forces and as Chief Civil Administrator Chang Chih-pen, a Hupei native with connections with the Right-wing Western Hills group of the Kuomintang.[8] The Wuhan authorities were zealous opponents of Communism; during the early part of 1928 executions of Communists took place every day. They were catholic in their dislike of foreigners. Red and White Russians were arrested impartially; the re-established mission schools were banned from using the Bible in their instruction; a strong propaganda campaign was launched against the Japanese.[9] In their social and economic policies, they were unenlightened; their aim was to bludgeon the population into submission, to force it to pay its taxes, not to institute any kind of reform. The memory of the popular upsurge of 1926 and 1927 was still very fresh, and the authorities were frightened of a recrudescence of popular agitation.

In Hunan, the Clique's position was much weaker. Though it dominated the province militarily, and had it hemmed in by Kwangsi forces in Hupei, Kwangtung and Kwangsi, it had to accept, as the price of its otherwise favourable settlement with Nanking, a Nanking appointee, Lu Ti-p'ing, as Governor. Its attitude to local administration therefore became not so much one of *laissez-faire* as of forced uninvolvement.

In Kwangtung, Li Chi-shen was more deeply occupied in local administration; he had already been running the province for two years. His main concern now was to establish better relationships with Hong Kong. While Wuhan railed against Soviet and Japanese imperialism, Li was negotiating with the arch imperialist, Great Britain. His negotiations bore fruit, in the form of an official visit by the governor of the colony to Canton in March 1928. This visit would have been unthinkable at any stage in the past few years, and was the clearest possible indication of the defeat of radicalism in south China.[10]

This divergence of policy towards the Powers by two branches of the Clique again points up the convenience for the Clique of operating from several centres. The divergence became very clear at the time of the Chinan Incident (May 1928): anti-Japanese demonstrations were forbidden at Canton, but were officially encouraged in Wuhan.[11] Wuhan had nothing to lose by pursuing an anti-imperialist policy; as the Clique had found earlier in Kwangsi, it was a useful method of channelling potential mass activity into harmless directions. But Canton, with its large foreign trade, found it expedient to appease the British and Japanese. Because of physical separation, this contradiction did not appear as a basic policy disagreement within the Clique.

In Peking, the third major area (aside from the home province which is discussed in Chapter 5) dominated by the Kwangsi Clique, the situation after the completion of the Northern Expedition was complex. Kwangsi control there was very limited. The nine months that Pai Ch'ung-hsi spent there should have been a time to enhance the reputation he had won on the Northern Expedition; in fact they were empty months. It might have been a chance for Pai to move away from the parochial atmosphere of the Clique. He was in many ways the most gifted of the Clique's leaders, his bearing and his public utterances up to this stage suggested that he felt himself to be an exceptional man, a man with a great future on the national scene, beyond the parameters of regional militarism.

Pai's potential was not realised at Peking; he was unable to make a mark for himself. There were several reasons: he was involved for much of his stay there in a struggle for control with Yen Hsi-shan; he had no existing following, civilian or military, in the north; he found himself in a city undergoing a major political and economic recession, as a result of the transference of the capital to Nanking. He apparently felt uncertain and hesitant in the strange world of the north. His ineffectual-ness left Pai with a reduced sense of himself; he never again appeared as self-confident, as convinced of his worth, as he did during the closing stages of the Northern Expedition.

Pai's struggle with Yen Hsi-shan stemmed from Chiang Kai-chek's attempts to check his unruly military allies by playing them off against each other. Neither Pai nor Yen, nor least of all Feng Yü-hsiang was given paramount authority in the north. Their forces were intermingled, and they were left to undermine each other – a new version of the policy of divide and rule. A furtive struggle between Yen and Pai started immediately after the fall of Peking. Yen found his appointees crowded out by Nanking civilian officials and Kwangsi officers. His appointee as mayor was forced to resign before he had even taken up office.[12] At the end of July, temporarily out-manoeuvred, Yen stumped morosely back to T'aiyuan. But he soon returned. Pai was involved in a campaign in East Hopei to mop up the remnants of Chang Tsung-ch'ang's armies, and in delicate manoeuvres to get Chang Hsüeh-liang into the Kuomin-tang camp.[13] He was also forced to return about a third of the troops he had brought north with him to Wuhan; military threats were developing in Hunan, and there was renewed Communist activity there – P'eng Te-huai rose in rebellion in July 1928.[14] The weakening of his military position, and his preoccupation with the problems of the northeast, was seen by Yen as a cue for a renewed attempt to instal himself in Peking. He returned to the city in September, and stayed there until December, shadow-boxing with Pai. Pai emerged on top temporarily, but his position was slipping; he was losing control over his own troops. So insecure was his position that he tried to make a dignified withdrawal, but he was dissuaded from doing so by emissaries from Nanking, who feared that his departure would strengthen Yen too much.[15] Pai's response was to retreat into hospital.

Pai's tenuous position in Peking allowed him little scope for civilian administration. He attempted to control mass activity in the city, but without much success. After the fall of Peking mass organisations became legal and the people of Peking responded enthusiastically. Union membership jumped from nil to 30,000 in the first month after the Kuomintang occupation. Pai's attempts at curtailing union activity were countermanded from Nanking; some unions even brought their members out on strike – the postal workers in September, and the tram workers in November.[16] Pai in fact controlled neither the civil administration, nor the Branch Political Council, which was made up of senior Kuomintang politicians, and headed by Chang Chi.[17] Kwangsi dominance in Peking was illusory.

Having looked at the way in which the Kwangsi Clique expanded its sphere of control, and at its attitudes towards the administration of the areas under its control, let us look at how the Clique hung together, at what support it had beyond the Clique itself.

The structure of the Clique remained almost unchanged; the vast increase in the territories it controlled did not bring any new men into the top rank of the Clique. Since the Clique depended for its cohesion on the personal relationships between its four leaders, relationships which had been built up slowly, and could survive separation, expansion would have been problematic. The interests which united the Clique – a desire for the expansion of Kwangsi Empire, a militarist attitude towards government, a distrust of mass activity – were shared by the secondary leaders of the Clique. But none of these men had achieved a strong enough individual position to warrant his promotion; none had the independent military command which could force the leaders to accept him as equal. The only secondary leader of the Clique who made a bid for personal power was Hu Tsung-to, the garrison commander of Wuhan. Hu was interested in moving *away* from the Clique, not into its upper echelon. Since his return to his native province, Hupei, he had become disenchanted with the idea of Kwangsi Empire, and was reasserting his Hupei identity and using it to increase his local authority. He thus found himself at odds with the Clique.

The unity of the Clique leadership was the only tie between the various arms of the Kwangsi Empire. There was no systematic plan for the government of the areas controlled by the Clique, no blueprint for future action; each leader acted according to the dictates of the local situation. This lack of overall policy was not surprising. The Kwangsi leaders must have been as startled by the rapid transformation in their fortunes as the Nanking leaders were alarmed by it. They cannot have anticipated, when they finally fought their way to the top in one of China's most backward and poverty-stricken provinces that three years later they would find themselves controlling an empire within an empire,

Fig. 6.   Limits of Kwangsi control, 1928–9

which stretched from 'Chennankuan in the south to Shanhaikuan in the north' (see Fig. 6).[18] The Kuomintang had dreamt for a long while of national control; the other major militarists still holding on to their independence (Feng Yü-hsiang, Yen Hsi-shan, Chang Hsüeh-liang) had all established themselves well before their connection with the Kuomintang, and had joined it from a position of strength. But the Kwangsi leaders had started from a negligible base, the control of a province of little economic or strategic importance, and had carved out their empire fortuitously, amidst the vicissitudes that accompanied the Kuomintang rise to national power. The Kwangsi leaders did not commit their troops to the Northern Expedition to win a Kwangsi Empire. Their principal motivation was their desire to play some part in what they sensed was the most important and forward-looking political and military movement of their time.

But though they may initially have had no thought of extending their own domains, their commitment to the nationalist cause (which ran parallel to but distinct from their regionalist aims) was eroded in the welter of competing groupings within the Kuomintang. As the Kuomintang tore itself apart, unity ceased to have much meaning. The Kwangsi leaders had between themselves a much narrower unity, that of the regional group, founded on common origin, and bonded through common experience and personal connections. This unity was unshakeable, and they were thrown back on to it when the Kuomintang ceased to command their allegiance to national unity.

The supplanting of weak nationalist loyalties by strong regionalist ones did not mean that the Kwangsi Clique came out openly against national unity. This would have been unthinkable in a situation where the nationalist ideology of the Kuomintang had become the new orthodoxy, where the bulk of Chinese who thought about such matters were deeply concerned about China's divisions, and were committed to national reunification as a first stage to resisting foreign encroachment. The Kwangsi leaders continued on paper to plead vociferously for unity. They found their regionalist position embarrassing; they sensed that their position was closer to that of the old warlords than it was to the Kuomintang ideal of a soldier subordinate to civilian authority. To compensate for this divergence between theory and practice, they tried to present themselves as loyal Kuomintang men, devoted to the cause of China's rebirth, practically and progressively working towards this end. They poured out high-flown speeches and telegrams, which, if read independently of other contemporary source material, give the impression of devout nationalism. When they are compared, however, with the rest of the record, they can be seen in two ways: either as evidence of dishonesty and insincerity, or as an indication that these aims were real, but rarefied, that they existed on a plane detached from the questions of day-to-day political and military affairs. It is probably more useful to view them in the second light. The Kwangsi leaders' mode of behaviour, their tacit assumption of a division between long-range goals and short-term advantage, had become axiomatic for the whole of the Kuomintang. Unless one wants to dismiss every Kuomintang leader as a hypocrite (many of them were, which complicates the situation), one must accept that their commitment to higher goals was still real, but that immediate issues had achieved paramount importance.

The political platform of the Clique was defined in reference to other people's positions. Only one of its members, Pai Ch'ung-hsi, pursued an independent line, and that in a direction in which the other Kwangsi leaders could not follow him. Pai took his status as a Moslem, and as one of China's minority peoples, seriously. After the fall of Peking, he called on Nanking to give special aid to the Manchus (Ch'i-min); in November 1928, he became a member of the China Moslem Society (Chung-kuo Hui-chiao hui).[19] In a speech in December, he urged Nanking to give more support to the minority peoples of the Inner Asian border regions. He described the foreign oppression these people were suffering – the Manchus from Japan, the Mongols of Outer Mongolia and the Uighurs and Moslems of Sinkiang from the Soviet Union, the Tibetans from the British – and asked that they be given material aid to help them throw off the foreign yoke.[20] Pai was especially interested in Sinkiang, where there was a large Moslem population. He made numerous proposals for the settlement of disbanded soldiers in the province, to prevent its 'sovietization', and even thought of leading an expedition into the northwest himself, as a new Tso Tsung-t'ang, come to re-establish Central authority on the borders of China.[21]

The political protestations of the Kwangsi Clique could carry little weight on their own. To survive within the Kuomintang framework, the Clique needed political allies, men who were already well-established within the Kuomintang. They found their allies at this stage in the group known as the Party Elders, men such as Wu Chih-hui, Chang Ching-chiang, Li Shih-tseng and Ts'ai Yüan-p'ei. These men had prestigious records within the Kuomintang, but no real authority within the Party structure. They were regarded as old-fashioned and impractical, though their integrity was never questioned; the name 'Party Elders' suggests the honorific position that they held within the Kuomintang. Several of them still kept to the vows of frugality and abstinence which they had made as young anarchists twenty years before. Though they had abandoned anarchism in favour of the Kuomintang, they had not lost their dislike of bureaucratic, centralised government. Li Shih-tseng in particular advocated the devolution of authority, and though what he meant was something very different from the regional military control that the Kwangsi Clique favoured, the Clique took his attitude as a justification of its regionalist power-holding. The Elders were presumably aware of the divergence of interpretation between themselves and the Clique, but they gave it their support, partly because they had no other allies within the Kuomintang, and had been offered no share of power at Nanking, and partly because they approved of the discipline and public frugality of the Kwangsi leaders.[22]

Beyond the Elders, whose influence was entirely within Party circles, the Clique had few civilian allies outside the provinces they controlled. But its political connections were improved in September 1928, when Hu Han-min returned from a self-imposed exile. As one of Sun Yat-sen's earliest followers, Hu's prestige within the Kuomintang was enormous. After his return, he was unable to assume at Nanking the kind of authority he felt he deserved; his actions were circumscribed by those already entrenched there. He became instead the focal point of the Right-wing and, through his links with the Party Elders, also associated with the Kwangsi Clique.

These political connections had little effect on the actual position of the Clique, and on the situation within the areas under its control. As in its earlier association with the Western Hills faction (now sunk from sight), the Clique's political connections were never seen as key determinants in policy making but only as useful window-dressing for a position based on military might. In mid-1928, the Clique ruled four provinces (Hunan, Hupei, Kwangtung, Kwangsi) and three major urban areas (Canton, Wuhan, Peking). It controlled about 350,000 troops, of whom 120,000 were stationed in the south, and 230,000 in Hunan-Hupei and the Peking-Tientsin region.[23] Superficially, this represented a formidable strength, but it was a shaky edifice. The Clique's internal weaknesses were ironic, given the nature of its rise to power: firstly this huge force contained many poorly-amalgamated warlord units; secondly, the Clique's forces were deeply divided on regional lines. They presented the same threat to the Clique that, on a larger scale, the Clique presented to Nanking. Outside Kwangsi, only a minority of the Clique's forces were actually Kwangsi units. Kwangtung was garrisoned almost entirely by Cantonese units, Hunan by Hunanese ones; in both areas local chauvinism was strong, and was reinforced in Kwangtung by a tradition of hostility to Kwangsi. In Peking and in Hupei there were Kwangsi units, but they were outnumbered.

The bulk of the troops with Pai Ch'ung-hsi in Peking were Hunanese, formerly under the control of T'ang Sheng-chih, whom the Clique had taken over after defeating T'ang in late 1927. Three of these Hunanese units were commanded by Kwangsi natives, fellow-students of Pai from Paoting. These men, Li P'in-hsien, Yeh Ch'i and Liao Lei, were regarded by the Clique as loyal; in fact their loyalties were divided, for whatever the closeness of their personal connections with Pai, their own subordinates were Hunanese, and still loyal to T'ang, who was fulminating against the Clique from his exile in Hong Kong [24]; to have followed the Clique against their own men would have been suicidal.

The situation in Hupei paralleled that in Peking, but in reverse; there the problem was not ' foreign ' troops commanded by Kwangsi men, but Kwangsi troops commanded by ' foreigners '. Two of the senior Kwangsi commanders at Wuhan were in fact Hupei natives. Hu Tsung-to and T'ao Chün had served for many years in the Kwangsi Army, and had moved into the Wuhan region with their Kwangsi troops. But once established in Wuhan, their ties with Kwangsi weakened, and they quickly established strong local positions. Li Tsung-jen inadvertently helped them to move in this direction, through his policy of placating local antipathy to ' foreign ' troops by raising up local men, whom he believed would remain loyal to Kwangsi control. He miscalculated. Hu and T'ao became less and less amenable to Kwangsi control, and even discriminated against Kwangsi troops, whom they conveniently regarded as ' guest ' troops, in the distribution of local revenue. Their independent stance was made possible by the fact that both men now controlled substantial numbers of Hupei troops, whose original commanders had been dismissed.[25] The behaviour of Hu and T'ao angered and alienated Kwangsi men formerly of equal rank, men such as Li Ming-jui, Yang Teng-hui, Hsia Wei and Chung Tsu-p'ei. Chung returned to Kwangsi in disgust, but the other three remained in Hupei, a prey in their bitterness to external influences.[26] These influences took the form of secret liaison with Yü Tso-po, a prominent Kwangsi Left-winger, and a bitter opponent of the Clique. Yü was a cousin of Li Ming-jui, and through him he was able to direct the resentment of other Kwangsi officers in Hupei against the Clique leaders.

The make-up of the forces controlled by the Kwangsi Clique in 1928 was this: of the 12 divisions in the Fourth Group Army, only 2 were commanded by Kwangsi natives who had served in the Kwangsi Army; 5 had strong connections with Kwangsi, either as Kwangsi natives commanding Hunanese units, or as Hupei natives commanding Kwangsi troops, but their loyalty was suspect; and 5 had no prior connection with Kwangsi.[27] The senior command positions were in Kwangsi hands: Li

Tsung-jen was Commander-in-chief, Pai Ch'ung-hsi Field Commander. In addition, the Clique controlled the troops of Kwangtung and Kwangsi, which had not been incorporated into the Group Army system. Huang Shao-hsiung's control over troops in Kwangsi was solid, and he had about 5,000 loyal Kwangsi troops in Kwangtung.[28] But command over the rest of Kwangtung's troops, though nominally Li Chi-shen's, was actually in the hands of his subordinates, whose loyalty was to their province, not to the outsider, Li.

This military situation made the Clique extremely vulnerable to betrayal. It was impossible to build up a large military grouping on the basis of provincial loyalty; Kwangsi could not supply the men. Other units had been amalgamated, but they could never be ' converted ', since they did not share the fundamental identification of the Clique – with Kwangsi. These units and their commanders were susceptible to offers to abandon the Clique.

At least one of the Kwangsi leaders was aware of the danger of the situation. At the end of 1928, Huang Shao-hsiung proposed to Li Tsung-jen that the Clique should withdraw its forces from Hupei, and concentrate them nearer Kwangsi, shrinking the area of Kwangsi control, but making it tighter.[29] But by this stage Li was too enthralled by the position he had acquired in Central China to conceive of abandoning it, however compelling the argument. He preferred to try to hold on to as much territory as possible, and dismissed Huang's suggestion.

Kwangsi's shortage of dependable military support was paralleled by an almost complete lack of civilian aides. There was no question of the Clique being able to fill civil posts with capable Kwangsi men; there were almost none. Local men were installed as administrators. The main criterion of selection was that they should be politically Right-wing; their loyalty to the Clique was not important, since they were not intended to exercise any decisive authority, but to remain subordinate to military authority. In Hupei, Li Tsung-jen left civilian government alone; he adopted the foolhardy (for an outsider) slogan ' Hupei for the Hupei natives '.[30] The civil administration of Hunan was entirely in Hunanese hands. In Kwangtung, Li Chi-shen, the Chairman of the Branch Political Council, was at odds with Ch'en Ming-shu, the Provincial Chairman. In Peking, Pai Ch'ung-hsi was unable to exert any authority over local administration, involved as he was in the struggle for military domination with Yen Hsi-shan. Nowhere except in Kwangsi did the Clique control the administration of the areas they dominated militarily.

The economic weakness of these areas provided the final facet of a gloomy picture. All except Kwangsi were traditionally among the more prosperous areas of China. But in 1928, Kwangtung, Hunan and Hupei were still recovering from the disruptions of 1927, a process which was particularly slow in Hunan. There was a serious failure of the autumn harvest in both Hunan and Hupei in 1928, and by the end of the year, there was widespread famine in the two provinces.[31] Peking was suffering from a catastrophic commercial decline, which set in after the transfer of the capital, and of many national and international organisations, to Nanking. Between June and November, 1928 3,500 businesses in the city closed; about a quarter of a million people were destitute.[32] The Peking-Tientsin area was becoming a backwater. The channels connecting Tientsin with the sea were silting up; everything was running down, even the fabric of the cities.[33] Wuhan was still gravely affected by the curtailment of foreign business, which, in the context of officially supported anti-foreign boycotts (especially anti-Japanese) showed little sign of reviving. One hundred thousand people were unemployed in the three Wuhan cities.[34]

Beyond its military, political, administrative and economic weakness, the Clique was strategically ill-placed to resist an attack from Nanking. The main force of the Clique was concentrated at Wuhan, up-river from Nanking. For the defence of Wuhan, a strong naval force was necessary, since an attack would almost certainly be river-borne. Nanking had a much better navy than did Wuhan. Wuhan's connections with the other centres of the Clique were tenuous. Peking and Wuhan were connected only by the thin tentacle of the Peking-Wuhan Railway, large sections of which were not under Kwangsi control. The railway link between Wuhan and Canton was incomplete. The deployment of the Clique's forces was cumbersome, and left very little room for manoeuvre. They were stretched from 'Chenankuan to Shanhaikuan', but they were stretched very thin.

In the face of such palpable weakness, why did Nanking delay its attack on the Clique? Nanking probably feared an alliance of the Clique with either Feng Yü-hsiang or Yen Hsi-shan. But above all Nanking was unwilling to see the fragile unity of China shattered so soon after it had been won. An attack on Wuhan would be an admission that the unification had only been partial, that four provinces under the Kuomintang flag were not under Kuomintang control, that one of the largest military groupings in China was still hostile. The situation was common knowledge, of course, but Nanking did not want to draw attention to it. In order not to admit its own weakness, Nanking had to tolerate the behaviour of the Kwangsi Clique until it could crush it firmly. In March 1929 it felt able to act.

7

The first defeat

We have discussed the Kwangsi Clique during 1928 and the first part of 1929, looking at its structure, its political and military attitudes, and at the nature of its control. This discussion has been punctuated by references to the Central Government at Nanking, and to the Kuomintang. We now move from a regional to a national focus, and look at the position of the Central Government after the end of the Northern Expedition. We shall see how the Kwangsi Clique related to the Centre, and how the Centre disposed of the Clique.

In 1928, the main task before the Central Government was to consolidate its rule over a reunified China. The Kuomintang had turned its back on revolution, and had moved to a conservative position, which looked with mistrust on mass activity.[1] But the hope of sudden transformation which had underlain the lost revolutionary fervour remained, and found expression in torrents of speeches, articles, official plans and conferences, whose themes were unification, modernisation, independence, progress, and national revival. The words which expressed the hope took on a meaning of their own; the leaders of the Kuomintang spoke with passion of their plans for a new China, and felt they had achieved something by their words alone. A delusive and schizophrenic process was under way. Faced with the magnitude of China's problems, her new leaders eschewed the grinding effort that a real solution of these problems demanded, and satisfied themselves with outpourings of words, as if the words themselves contained solutions. A depressing experience for any student of Republican China is to plough through reams of these speeches, conference reports and official plans, most of them blueprints for an almost utopian future, with always the knowledge that the vast majority came to nothing, that the reforms remained on paper.

R. H. Tawney described the reactions of a Westerner confronted with these designs for the future:

A man is interested in some particular line or policy. He is shown a programme of reform more complete than any that will be applied in

129

his own country in the next quarter of a century. He pricks up his ears. Then he inquires what is being done to carry it out. He learns that nothing is being done, that no one is very hopeful that anything will be done, that there is little finance or administrative staff, that the last official concerned in the business was not wholly above suspicion in the matter of money, and that his successor cannot visit the areas which most need attention for fear of being kidnapped.[2]

The fault of the men who played the game of words was not that they were cynical, self-interested men (though many of them were) who were using fine words as a cover for base actions, but that they lacked any compulsion to action, that they no longer felt any driving political commitment. Their original commitment to the Koumintang had been eroded by the strife within the Party, and by the influx into the Party, during and after the Northern Expedition, of men who had never had any commitment, with whom they now had to contend for power. Many of the former bureaucrats of the various Peking Governments had moved to Nanking, where their administrative skills gave them the entrée to important governmental posts. The ideology of the Kuomintang had ceased to provide either a unifying force, or a spur to action. A framework of legal sanctions was established, which should have had the effect of obliging China's new leaders to put aside individual and factional interests, but they carried little force. In a fluid society, social sanctions to 'upright behaviour' and devotion to duty were unclear, and therefore weak. There was no leader strong enough to rise above the factionalism within the Party and the nation. Chiang Kai-shek's position depended on his consummate ability to manoeuvre and manipulate within this factional framework, rather than on moral dominance or popular charisma.[3]

The Kuomintang's inability to launch itself into new endeavours, its political and social confusion, and its preoccupation with distant goals rather than immediate concerns impeded the imposition of its authority over its major military allies, Feng Yü-hsiang, Yen Hsi-shan, Chang Hsüeh-liang and the Kwangsi Clique. It gave them a breathing space in which to consolidate their regional power-holding. The Kuomintang had defeated China's warlords, only to find that two-thirds of China provinces nominally under its control were controlled by 'Kuomintang warlords'. (I prefer this term, though it appears at first sight contradictory, to James Sheridan's 'residual warlords'.[4] These men combined a pattern of behaviour which differed in few respects from earlier warlord behaviour with some commitment to Kuomintang ideology. An interesting question is whether the same term could be applied to Chiang Kai-shek.) These 'Kuomintang warlords' were prepared to accept, to some degree, the ideology of the Kuomintang, but not its authority. They were not prepared to hand over regional control to ' national ' leaders who asked for their submission, but not for their participation in the administration of a reunified China. They clung to their military independence, as the only means of securing for themselves a voice in China's affairs, regional or national.

When Chiang failed to persuade them to submit, he was left with no alternative but to fight them. If unity could not be achieved by mutual agreement, he would achieve it by force. In the spring of 1929, the Kwangsi Clique, the most vulnerable of the regional groupings, was crushed. During the following year, Feng Yü-hsiang and Yen Hsi-shan were defeated. The most glaring abuses of national disunity were removed, but the more fundamental abuse, the gulf between words and action, between policies and their implementation, remained. The traditionalist, righteous tenor of the Kuomintang's attacks on the ' bandits ' and ' rebels ' encouraged a self-satisfied feeling of rightness, and distracted attention from the superficiality of these conquests, which had destroyed the most visible manifestations of disunity, but not its roots.

In his memoirs, a prominent Kuomintang politician, Chou Fo-hai lamented the lost chances of the Kuomintang:

If, after the memorial service [to Sun Yat-sen] in the Western Hills in July, 1928, everyone had buried themselves with one heart and one spirit in the [work of] rehabilitation and reconstruction, how could the battles of spring 1929 at Wuhan, and of winter 1929 in Honan have occurred? How could the large-scale fighting of 1929 in Central China Plain have happened? In this fighting, the extent of the losses in men and matériel was staggering. If there had not been these repeated civil wars, how could the communists have gone on the rampage, and called forth successive years of military operations to suppress them? [5]

But the Kuomintang in 1928 suffered from a mass of internal conflicts and lacked any common will to resolve them. The opportunities offered in the crucial period after the reunification were wasted; everyone supported the *ideals* of unification, of social, economic, political and military reform, but in an atmosphere of mutual suspicion and factional enmity, no one was prepared to do anything concrete about them.

THE QUESTION OF DISBANDMENT

In July 1928, after they had announced victory to Sun Yat-sen's spirit, the four Group Army Commanders met in closed session at T'angshan, near Peking, to discuss the future of their armies. The following day a communiqué was issued which recognised the supreme authority of the Military Committee over all four Group Armies, and called for the establishment of a Disbandment Committee, for the reorganisation of Kuomintang forces into 60 divisions (as opposed to the 176 divisions, divided between 50 armies which then existed),[6] for the reduction of overall troop numbers to about 500,000 and for the smooth reintegration of disbanded men into civilian life. In the interim before the Disbandment Committee could start working, Group Army Commanders were to be responsible for disbandment in their own armies, and were to reduce their troops by between 30 per cent and 50 per cent within six months. An order forbidding further recruitment was issued on 9 July.[7]

The number of troops in China at this stage was somewhere in the region of 2,000,000, of which well over 1,000,000 were under the Kuomintang flag.[8] In terms of the area and population of China, this figure was not excessive, but 'given economic backwardness, the protracted warfare, the decline in production, and the sufferings of the people [China] could not bear the burden of support for these great numbers of troops '.[9] The bulk of these troops was not financed from Nanking; some had still not accepted even nominal Kuomintang control (namely, Chang Hsüeh-liang); others in the three areas controlled by the Second, Third and Fourth Group Armies, and in the outlying provinces, were financed locally. But while they were no financial burden on Nanking, Nanking also received no revenue from the provinces they controlled. Only Chekiang, Kiangsu, Anhwei, Kiangsi and Fukien, garrisoned by the First Group Army, made contributions to the National Treasury, and only the first two made reliable payments. In a speech to the Disbandment Committee in January 1929, T. V. Soong, the Minister of Finance, described the situation in other provinces:

> The national revenue for such provinces as Hunan, Hupei, Kwangtung, Kwangsi, Shensi, Kansu, Honan, Shansi and Suiyuan, not to mention those from the Three Eastern Provinces, Szechwan, Yunnan and Kweichow, are entirely appropriated by the localities mentioned. In the provinces of Hopei, Shantung and Fukien the revenue officials are at least commissioned by the Central Government, but in other provinces they are appointed by local and military authorities, and most of them even fail to render accounts.[10]

Autonomous military control meant autonomous financial control. From its limited revenue, Nanking had to support not only the First Group Army, but also the apparatus of the National Government. How limited this revenue was is indicated by Soong's calculations of the optimum revenue of the National Government from the provinces: 45

per cent of this revenue would be contributed by the four provinces under the control of the Kwangsi Clique – Hunan, Hupei, Kwangtung and Kwangsi; in fact they contributed nothing.[11] One reason for the abortion of many of the Kuomintang's schemes for reconstruction and rehabilitation becomes apparent: there was no money for them.

It was also clear that the proportion of military spending to civilian spending (then running at roughly 80 per cent : 20 per cent) would have to be adjusted if the Government was to have any funds for new policies. This could be most easily achieved by reducing the number of troops. Just as the National Government was hamstrung by the demands of military expenditure on its meagre revenues, so were the areas controlled by the other Group Armies. Feng Yü-hsiang imposed enormous taxes on his provinces to support his forces; the over-taxation helped to reduce many of their inhabitants to starvation.[12] Yen Hsi-shan brought financial chaos to Shansi, by diverting so much of the provincial revenue for military purposes that the provincial administration had to be financed by unbacked paper currency.[13] Kwangsi levied constant surcharges on the land tax, most of which went for military support.

There was no opposition to the general principle of disbandment; the broad outline of the T'angshan Communiqué was ratified at the Fifth Plenum of the Kuomintang Central Executive Committee meeting at Nanking in August. A certain amount of voluntary disbandment took place. Desertion was common, and the slowing of recruitment, which prevented the replacement of deserters, soon cut numbers. The armies were pruned of their least valuable men – opium smokers, old men and boys, troops incorporated from the worst of the warlord armies. Untrustworthy units were completely disbanded. The First Group Army contained large numbers of such undesirables, and early reported large numbers of demobilisations.[14] In Kwangtung, Li Chi-shen disbanded several units commanded by rivals.[15] The Fourth Group Army reduced the size of several units of non-Kwangsi origin, and disbanded others *in toto*.[16] Huang Shao-hsiung in Kwangsi demobilised 20,000 men, and set them to road building and land reclamation.[17] (This figure, published by Huang himself, was 25 per cent higher than the *total* number of men under his command in 1926. It indicates the very rapid growth in army numbers between 1926 and 1928; even after disbanding this large number, Huang still retained a considerable force.) Demobilisation was carried out in conjunction with the reorganisation of all Kuomintang troops into divisions, usually accomplished by substituting the title *shih* for *chün*. This process was completed by the end of November, by which time 340,000 men had been disbanded.[18] Very few of them were reincorporated into civilian life. For many of them, especially those disbanded away from native areas, leaving the army meant entering destitution.

The process of disbandment went no further. By January 1929, when the Disbandment Conference opened, it was clear that hopes of widespread troop reductions were unfounded. Dead wood had been trimmed, but there were still, according to Ho Ying-ch'in, the Chief of Staff, at least 1,600,000 troops in China (900,000 in the four Group Armies); and while the First Group Army (Nanking), with 240,000 men, was the largest single Group Army, it was considerably smaller than the combined forces of the Kwangsi Clique (Fourth Group Army and Kwangtung–Kwangsi troops) which numbered 350,000.[19] There were deep divisions between the four Group Army commanders as to the ultimate balance of strength between their forces, and a common suspicion held by Feng Yü-hsiang, Yen Hsi-shan and Li Tsung-jen that Chiang Kai-shek was trying to reduce their forces at the expense of their parity with his.[20] Chiang's appeal to his allies to disband more rapidly, entitled ' My Hopes for the Disbandment Committee ' gave some indication, by its beseeching tone, of how fragile the unity between the Kuomintang militarists was. He called upon them to abandon selfish ambitions, and independent power, and to follow instead the examples of Japan and Turkey in uniting under Central leadership. He made polite concessions to regional independence by speaking with approval of the federal systems of the United States and Germany, but he stressed that these systems worked only because the Central Government retained control over *military* and foreign policy.[21] He appealed to the patriotism of his fellow-commanders, and called for their loyalty to the Centre, an appeal which might have been more emotive if these men had not regarded the ' Centre ' as the power-base of a rival military force. They were unmoved; they would not disband further, nor would they surrender their regional authority.

It was clear that voluntary disbandment had failed, that the regional militarists were firmly entrenched, and that they would only surrender to superior force. This situation carried the corollary that China's other internal problems could not be solved: ' putting the army in order was the first step to putting finances in order; if nothing was done about finances, there was no point in talking about People's Livelihood, or Reconstruction '.[22]

' Disbandment ' remained current in Chinese military life only to the extent that the term remained in use as a part of the name of military headquarters (in a purely formal change of nomenclature, the title of Group Army was abandoned in favour of ' Disbandment Area Headquarters ', after the Disbandment Conference); these headquarters were increasingly concerned, not with disbandment, but with waging civil war. The plan to reduce the armed forces was scrapped. The civil war swelled the strength of the army to over 200 divisions of heterogeneous troops, and the only reductions were those affected by casualties as thousands of men perished in internecine war.[23]

THE FIFTH PLENUM

The moves towards military centralisation and rationalisation after the Northern Expedition failed, because no one wanted them to succeed (except the millions of Chinese who suffered from the existence of swollen armies). Moves towards political unity were equally unsuccessful. There were numerous factions within the Party, chief of which were factions centred around Chiang Kai-shek (Kan-pu P'ai); the Re-organisation Faction (Kai-tsu P'ai), led by Wang Ching-wei; the Revivalist Faction (Fu-hsing P'ai), led by Hu Han-min and the Party Elders' Faction (Yüan Lao P'ai). The divisions between these factions were clearly revealed at the Fifth Plenum of the Central Executive Committee, held in August 1928 to re-establish political harmony. The greatest depth of enmity existed between Wang's faction, the ' Left-Kuomintang ', and the factions on the Right, Hu's faction and the Party Elders. Of the many clashes at the Plenum, the struggle between these two groups over the question of the Branch Political Council system was one of the bitterest. (Other major issues raised at the Plenum which we shall not discuss here, were the programme for the Period of Tutelage, the constitution, the role of the Party, and the question of mass movements.)

The Branch Political Councils had been set up as a rationalisation of regional control during the closing stages of the Northern Expedition. They had considerable powers for the execution of civil and Party authority in the areas assigned to them, which corresponded to the areas ruled by the Group Armies, and were in effect the civilian and political arms of these armies. Their actions were defined within the framework of Kuomintang policy, but they were completely independent of the Centre. With the exception of the Peking Council, their Chairmen were Regional Commanders – Li Tsung-jen at Wuhan, Feng Yü-hsiang at K'aifeng, Yen Hsi-shan at T'aiyuan and Li Chi-shen at Canton. Yen and Feng appear to have attached little importance to them, presumably because they were content to rule without even the semblance of official sanction, but Li Tsung-jen and Li Chi-shen, who had made earlier, deeper commitments to the Kuomintang, felt the need for official clothing for their independence, and valued the Councils.

The Reorganisationists campaigned at the Plenum for the abolition of the Councils, which they regarded not only as anti-pathetic to the realisation of real unity, but also as threats to Party ascendancy over the military. Chiang Kai-shek, their recent enemy, shared their dislike of regional autonomy, and entered an uneasy and brief alliance with them, whose aim was the winding up of the Councils.[24] They were opposed by Li Chi-shen (the only member of the Kwangsi Clique entitled to attend the Plenum) and by the Party Elders. Li claimed, disingenuously, that the Councils represented no threat to the Centre, but were essential in a country as vast as China if there was to be effective government.[25] The Elders, who were wary of over-centralisation and the development of a bureaucratic, detached mode of government, supported him to the extent of walking out of the Plenum when a decision to dissolve the Councils seemed imminent. Eventually a compromise was reached, by which the Councils would be allowed to continue in existence until the end of 1928, but with increased Central involvement within the areas they controlled.[26]

This walk-out was only one of the many that occurred during the course of the Plenum, which took on a farcical aspect.[27] If the leaders of the Kuomintang could not even stay together in one room, what hope had they of solving China's problems? These problems were to a large extent ignored; they served only as foci for factional struggles. When the Plenum was over, Chiang Kai-shek and the majority of the delegates retired from Nanking. Chiang went into the hospital in Shanghai for treatment of a 'severe toothache', and then on to Fenghua, his native place. Li Tsung-jen was in a neighbouring room at the hospital, being treated for eye trouble (possibly a recurrence of trouble from an old facial wound).[28] Li Chi-shen went off to scenic Mokan Shan with some of the Party Elders. Only Feng Yü-hsiang stayed in Nanking, providing a spectacle for the inhabitants and an embarrassment for the sybaritic Nanking officials with his ostentatious frugality.[29] The decision to abolish the Branch Political Councils by the end of the year was not a knock-out for the fortunes of the regional militarists, but it was a defeat on points. The Kwangsi Clique, at Wuhan, was the most directly threatened by Nanking's determination to stamp out military regionalism. In terms of military power, the Clique was vulnerable; in terms of political support, it was defenceless. The hostility between Nanking and Wuhan increased throughout the period from the summer of 1928 to the spring of 1929, in spite of efforts, chiefly by the Party Elders, to bring about a rapprochement.

It was becoming apparent that the Kwangsi Clique was losing its sense of proportion, and that overweening ambition had replaced calm calculation in forming Clique policy. The Clique was planning even further extensions of its authority.

The Clique's ambitions lay towards the other southwestern provinces, which they hoped to bring into a defensive alliance, dominated by Kwangtung and Kwangsi. The 'enemy' against whom the provinces needed defence was not specified; the proposed alliance was in fact an attempt to extend regional autonomy, under the Kwangsi Clique, to encompass the whole of southwest China. In September 1928, a five-province meeting to discuss matters of 'common defence' (Wu-sheng lien-fang hui-i) was held at Liuchow, Kwangsi.[30] This kind of activity was almost completely divorced from any connection with Kuomintang ideology; it had, however, a strong similarity with the manoeuvrings of large warlords before the victory of the Kuomintang.

The Clique, which had been at pains to give the impression that it was close to the ideology of the Kuomintang, began to show itself openly contemptuous of the Kuomintang. This gradual shift from superficial acceptance to open contempt was important, for it indicated that the Clique was feeling confident enough to stand entirely on its own. Though this confidence was misplaced, it gave an idea of the depth of penetration within the Clique's leaders of independent, regionalist attitudes. Li Tsung-jen in Wuhan manifested such attitudes most clearly. Huang Shao-hsiung was dubious about the over-extension of Kwangsi power from north to south, but not about the idea of extending the base area in the south. Pai Ch'ung-hsi in the north was in no position to undertake similar enterprises.

An example of the Clique's casualness towards Kuomintang opinion was its involvement in the Shanghai Opium Scandal, which erupted in December 1929. Officially the Kuomintang had pledged itself to the eradication of the opium traffic in China (though unofficially it continued to draw a considerable revenue from opium monopolies, and from Opium Suppression taxes – that is, the tax on opium in transit).[31] The Conference for the Suppression of Opium met at Nanking in November, and passed sweeping resolutions on the banning of opium trading and smoking. At the end of the same month, the Shanghai Municipal Police discovered a consignment of 20,000 ounces of opium being off-loaded, at night and under military guard, from a steamer just in from Wuhan. The police tried to seize the opium, but were stopped by the guards, who claimed that the opium was ' official ' and was consigned to the Shanghai Garrison Commander, Hsiung Shih-hui, an old colleague of the Kwangsi Clique. They then rushed off with the opium into the French Concession.

The matter might have ended there, if the Shanghai Police Commissioner had not raised it with the newly-established Opium Suppression Commission in Nanking. A good deal of publicity was given to the case; no one doubted that the Kwangsi Clique had been caught selling opium in Shanghai to raise money for arms shipments. Public protest was loud, and a team went to Shanghai to investigate. But before it could start work, an official clamp-down on investigation and public comment was imposed. The Police Commissioner was dismissed, the Chairman of the Opium Suppression Commission and the Mayor of Shanghai resigned. The case was never resolved, nor were any of the high-ranking officials and officers involved censured. Only a few minor smugglers were prosecuted.

The case badly strained the progressive, reformist image of the Kuomintang; the provisions of the Kuomintang's policy on the suppression of opium had been blatantly disregarded within days of their being laid down. The stigma of old-style warlord practice was attached to the Kwangsi Clique, as consignees of the opium, but also to Nanking, where the clamp-down on investigation had originated.[32]

THE NANKING-KWANGSI CLASH

After the unsatisfactory conclusion of the Disbandment Conference in January 1929, a clash between the Nanking Government and its independent militarist allies was widely expected. To live up to its claim to have reunified China, to put its finances on a sound footing, and to convince foreign governments with which it was negotiating for the revision of unequal treaties that it was something distinct from the ' National ' Governments of the Warlord Period, Nanking had to discipline its errant allies, whose open independence made mockery of its claim to national sovereignty. The Kwangsi Clique was the obvious first target, because it was strategically a sitting duck, and because its recent behaviour had branded it as anti-pathetic to the new China that was to emerge after the northern expedition. The political ineptitude of its leaders had led them to press their policies of aggrandisement in the face of mounting hostility, at Nanking, and in the areas under Kwangsi control. ' The warlords of the Kwangsi Clique were quite unaware that Heaven was angry and the people murmuring in resentment, and simply continued with their plans to extend their sphere of power.'[33] Nanking did not even have to seek a specific pretext for attacking the Clique; the Clique provided one by flouting Central authority so outrageously that the Centre was forced to act.

In February 1929 the Wuhan Branch Political Council issued an order dismissing Lu Ti-p'ing as Chairman of Hunan, and followed the order by forcibly evicting Lu from Ch'angsha, the Hunan provincial capital. The issue involved in Lu's dismissal was a crucial one: the control of Hunan revenues. These revenues were a vital part of the total revenue of Wuhan; if they were lost, the whole position of the Kwangsi Clique at Wuhan would be placed in jeopardy. The Council gave as its reason for dismissing Lu that he had not been remitting this revenue to Wuhan.[34] What Lu had been doing with the money is unclear; Wuhan believed that he had simply been retaining it in Hunan; it is also possible that he had been sending money to Nanking, which, as national capital, had technically the first claim on ' national ' taxation. Wuhan suspected that Nanking was sending Lu arms and ammunition to help him to rise against the Kwangsi Clique. Nanking protested immediately against Wuhan's action, which controverted the amended regulations of the Branch Political Councils (passed in August 1928) and claimed that Wuhan had dismissed Lu just to prevent him from remitting ' national ' tax revenue to Nanking.[35]

Lu's dismissal, apart from being illegal, was also rash, for Chiang Kai-shek was now in a position to counter such a strident challenge to Nanking's authority. He was in the process of squeezing out opposition-ist political groupings, notably the Left Kuomintang. The mass move-ments were moribund. His plans for the improvement of the quality of his military forces seemed feasible, especially after the arrival (at the end of 1928) of a group of German military advisers, who, in addition to laying the foundations of a better army, gave Chiang valuable strategic and tactical advice.[36] Chiang was making headway, too, in his relations with the Powers, many of whom now accepted his government as the National Government.

Chiang's pre-eminence at Nanking suggested that the holders of regional power should assert their independence tactfully. The Wuhan leaders acted instead arrogantly and defiantly. The leaders of the Kwangsi Clique subsequently tried to claim that they had not in fact initiated Lu's dismissal, and that they had been deceived by their sub-ordinates.[37] This seems unlikely. Though Li Tsung-jen was not in Wuhan when the order was issued, his hurried, nocturnal departure from Nanking two days after Lu's dismissal, and his defence of Wuhan's actions from the security of a hospital bed in the French Concession at Shanghai, suggests that he was involved in them.[38]

Chiang's preparations for war with Wuhan were virtually complete. A propaganda campaign against the Kwangsi Clique was organised.[39] Heavy concentrations of troops had been built up in Anhwei and Kiangsi. By the middle of March, Nanking had at least 150,000 men facing only 60,000 Wuhan troops.[40] Chiang's private 'diplomatic' overtures had secured promises of (temporary) support from Feng Yü-hsiang and Yen Hsi-shan, and of defection from many of the Kwangsi Clique's subordinates. These negotiations must have taken some time to complete, and were probably well advanced by the time of the Hunan affair.

Wuhan and Nanking were squared off for battle. But before fighting broke out, there was a hiatus while feverish negotiations for a settlement took place. The Party Elders, acting as political brokers, tried to assuage Chiang, and to get the Kwangsi leaders to retract. A commission was set up to investigate the Hunan affair, a commission whose composition suggested that it would not be hostile to the Kwangsi Clique (Li Tsung-jen, Li Chi-shen, Ts'ai Yüan-p'ei – a Party Elder – and Ho Ying-ch'in – immediate subordinate of Chiang, but briefly associated with the Clique in 1927).[41] Li Tsung-jen and Pai Ch'ung-hsi made official gestures of conciliation, but refused to go to Nanking; both men had retired to hospital beds, Li in Shanghai, Pai in Peking.[42] Li Chi-shen, however, came north to participate in the work of the commission, his personal safety guaranteed by the Party Elders.[43] He apparently believed that he would be able to repeat his mediation of the year before, when he had helped to prevent a clash between Wuhan and Nanking. Li Tsung-jen was less sanguine. The day before Li Chi-shen arrived in Shanghai, he resigned all his posts.[44]

He was right in thinking that the fate of the Kwangsi Clique was sealed. Massive defections from the Clique confirmed it immediately In Hunan, Wuhan's appointee to succeed Lu Ti-p'ing, Ho Chien, resigned after a few days in office, declaring that the divisions within China would 'deeply wound the Tsung-li's [Sun Yat-sen] spirit in Heaven'.[45] In Peking, Pai Ch'ung-hsi's subordinates deserted him in favour of their former Commander, T'ang Sheng-chih. (Pai had been in retreat already for over a month, in hospital and in a villa in the Western Hills, and had transferred control to a subordinate, in recognition of his impotence.) T'ang was actually in north China, and with the help of $2,500,000 presumably supplied from Nanking, had regained the allegiance of his former subordinates.[46] Pai escaped from Peking thanks to the dual loyalty of some of these men; the Kwangsi natives among them could not resist T'ang's return, but they made sure that their fellow-provincial should escape.[47] He made his way south by boat, evading arrest off Shanghai by hiding in a wardrobe, and reached Kwangsi early in April. It was an ignominious return for a hero of the Northern Expedition.[48]

Further defections were prepared, but were not revealed until fighting started. In Kwangtung, Li Chi-shen's immediate subordinates, the

Cantonese Generals Ch'en Chi-t'ang and Ch'en Ming-shu, had pledged themselves to Nanking. In Hupei, the defections of the Kwangsi Commanders Li Ming-jui and Yang Teng-hui were assured. The methods used to induce these two men to defect did not involve financial or strategic inducements, but played on familial and political ties. The agent of their defection was Yü Tso-po, Li Ming-jui's cousin, and one of the leading Left-wing figures from Kwangsi. Chiang Kai-shek's agents approached the exiled Yü in Hong Kong, and persuaded him to cooperate in the destruction of his old enemies, the Kwangsi Clique leaders. Acting through a go-between, he persuaded his cousin and his cousin's sworn-brother, Yang Teng-hui, to defect once the fighting began.[49]

Nanking's preparations were complete, an attack up the Yangtse was expected daily, and yet the hiatus continued. For a while it even seemed possible that Li Chi-shen and the Party Elders would manage to work out a negotiated settlement. But just as the Elders had concluded that they had succeeded in ' transmuting a large affair into a small one, and a small one into nothing ' [50] Li Chi-shen was arrested, and accused of plotting against the Nanking Government.

His arrest caused a sensation, especially among the delegates to the Third Kuomintang Congress, which had opened in Nanking a few days earlier. Li's imprisonment was not arduous; he was put under house-arrest at T'angshan Hot Springs, along with one of the Elders who had guaranteed his safety. His body-guard, ' Two-Gun ' Cohen was promised by Sun Fo (then Minister of Communications) that his employer would not be harmed:

> You must surely know that two of my venerable colleagues have guaranteed with their lives that General Li would be safe in Nanking. The senior of these has already honoured his pledge. He made the customary preparations for self-destruction, and warned General Chiang that unless he was allowed to share Li Chai-sum's [sic] imprisonment, he would commit suicide within the hour. He is now incarcerated with your chief.[51]

After Li's arrest, developments followed swiftly. On 26 March, the Third Congress dismissed Li Tsung-jen, Li Chi-shen and Pai Ch'ung-hsi from all their posts, and expelled them from the Kuomintang for life. An official declaration of war on the Kwangsi Clique was made, followed by a detailed denunciation (T'ao-fa Kuei-hsi hsüan-ch'uan ta-kang), which accused the Clique of having shattered the unity of the nation and the authority of the Kuomintang; particular abuse was heaped upon Pai Ch'ung-hsi, who was characterised as the evil genius of the Clique.[52] Chiang Kai-shek denounced the Clique as feudal regionalists, selfish, secretive and opportunist. His detailed charges accused them of having joined the Kuomintang only to further their private aims; of having been in touch, during the Northern Expedition, with the Kuomintang's enemies, chiefly Sun Ch'uan-fang; of having systematically looted Nanking in the second half of 1927; of having tried to sow disaffection among the Group Army commanders; of having disregarded the regulations on disbandment and on the Branch Political Councils; of having tried to form an anti-Nanking alliance in the southwest; and of being crude, primitive, old-fashioned and a disgrace to China.[53]

Having delivered himself of this blast, Chiang ordered the advance on Wuhan, which was taken on 5 April.

The speed of collapse confirmed the weakness of the position of the Kwangsi Clique in central and north China. It also indicated a great improvement in Nanking's military capacity. Although Nanking's naval superiority, which made any riverine positions indefensible, was probably the key element in its military success, the performance of its infantry, which advanced by forced marches, was impressive. Much of the credit for Nanking's strategic superiority went to the German military adviser, Colonel Bauer, who drew up the detailed plan of attack.[54] It was his first and last service for Nanking. Bauer's reward was to catch smallpox in Wuhan of which he died.[55]

With the loss of Wuhan, the great edifice of Kwangsi power came tumbling down. The Clique lost all its territories outside Kwangsi – Kwangtung had by now declared against Kwangsi – and the bulk of its troops, retaining only those under Huang Shao-hsiung. At the beginning of April, Li Tsung-jen and Pai Ch'ung-hsi, now shorn of all authority, generals without armies, met Huang at his home near Wuchow. It was the first time that they had been in Kwangsi since they left for the Northern Expedition three years before. Instead of returning in triumph, they returned as refugees. They were seething with anger and frustration at their defeat, and with humiliation at its ease. Huang Shao-hsiung was less agitated; he had not been translated from a petty regional figure to an important national one, and he was less than sympathetic to his colleagues' distress. The unity between the three men became taut and uneasy.

Huang had come to regard Kwangsi as his private domain, and had shown genuine, if erratic, interest in improving it. Li and Pai had regarded Huang as their bailiff, whose job was to keep Kwangsi quiet and secure, and periodically to give military support to the Clique's larger interests, to supply new recruits for the armies in the north and to send financial aid to them. This work he had carried out in comparative obscurity, without attracting the fame of Li and Pai. Now his defeated colleagues returned home, brought down by their over-weaning ambitions for territorial conquest, which he had opposed. (See above, p. 127.) Nor had this ambition disappeared with defeat; it continued to mar the judgment of Li and Pai. Their aim was to counter-attack as swiftly as possible, and to try to recapture Wuhan.

Huang understood the realities of the situation much more clearly. He saw that the Clique's large-scale regionalism had been defeated, and its extended area of control, which had been developed more by accident than design, could not be regained by a military expedition. He believed that the Clique's only hope now was to return to a narrower regional control, that of the single province of Kwangsi, and that it should seek an agreement along these lines with Nanking. He was also opposed to committing the remaining forces of the Clique – his own troops – to any extra-provincial adventure.

His realistic approach aroused suspicion and anger in Li and Pai, a suspicion that he might have sold out to Nanking. There was an open breakdown in co-operation between the three men; there had been major disagreements before, but this was the first time that they came into the open.[56]

The split expressed itself in the reactions to the proposals for a peaceful settlement which the Kwangsi leaders now received from Kwangtung and from Nanking. There was apparently no intention to attack Kwangsi. Nanking was already involved with an impending clash with Feng Yü-hsiang,[57] and with trouble over the Chinese Eastern Railway. The Cantonese were not concerned to launch a punitive expedition against Kwangsi, which would be expensive and time-consuming, but only to rid Kwangtung of Kwangsi influence. Kwangtung offered a settlement to Kwangsi along these lines, with the added incentive of an undertaking to continue to pay Kwangsi a military subsidy, and to purchase opium exported from Kwangsi.[58] Nanking was less conciliatory, but still not menacing. It limited itself to ' advice ' to the Kwangsi leaders to surrender, admit their faults and go abroad to improve themselves.[59]

Li and Pai refused to accept this advice. They fired off a fierce demand for the release of Li Chi-shen, and for the restoration of their good names. Under duress, Huang Shao-hsiung added his signature; the alternative would have been an immediate split.[60] Though there were to be no negotiations with Nanking, Huang kept in touch with Canton, hoping still that he could reach a peaceful settlement with the province which could most directly threaten Kwangsi.[61]

Li and Pai were in a reckless mood, however. It was almost inconceivable to them that they could have lost so much so easily, that they could be branded as traitors and bandits, and expelled from the Party. Their pride was deeply wounded, they could not wear the stigma of bandit lightly. (Though this was simply a traditional term for ' enemy ', it meant that the Kwangsi leaders had been stripped of all their coveted respectability.) They decided to launch out again, using the remaining troops of the Clique – Huang Shao-hsiung's.[62]

This decision was a further source of grievance to Huang. Li and Pai, having lost enormous numbers of troops, were preparing to put his troops at risk in what he regarded as a hopeless attempt to set up a multi-province bloc in south China, of the type they had just lost. He knew that the casual opportunities which had come to the Clique during the course of the Northern Expedition would not be repeated, and that an impetuous attack would lead to disaster. But Huang, still the circum-spect provincial militarist, could not prevail over two outraged large-regionalists, whose pride had been pricked, and whose indignation drove them to make an attempt, however reckless, to reassert their position as regional chiefs.

Faced with Kwangsi's intransigence, Nanking decided to attack, using not Nanking forces, which were preparing for war with Feng Yü-hsiang, but those of Kwangsi's neighbours, the main thrust to come from Hunan and Kwangtung, with flanking attacks from Yunnan, Kweichow and Szechwan. On 4 May, Huang Shao-hsiung, who had tried to the last moment to settle the question peacefully, was dismissed as Chairman of Kwangsi. The following day, Kwangsi forces already pressing into Kwangtung clashed with Cantonese forces.

The Kwangsi Clique adopted as the new nomenclature of their forces the title of Hu-Tang Chiu-Kuo Chün (Protect the Party, Save the Country Army), a choice which suggested that they still saw themselves in a Kuomintang context. That they, Party parvenus and now Party traitors, should cast themselves in the role of Party protectors was almost ludicrous; but they were unwilling to abandon all semblance of political motivation, and their new title provided this. The same title was adopted a few weeks later by Feng Yü-hsiang, though whether this was by pre-arrangement with Kwangsi is not clear.[63] Nanking accused the Kwangsi Clique and Feng of being in league, but the distance between the two groupings prevented the formation of any co-operation, even if any was intended. The Kwangsi Clique was in any case feeling bitter towards Feng; his temporary understanding with Nanking in March had been a key factor in their defeat in Central China.

The Kwangsi drive down the West River was at first so successful that Canton was threatened. Confusion and panic in the city were increased when bombs fell on the Bund. The bombing was at first blamed on the Kwangsi Airforce (which did not exist) but turned out to be the work of inexperienced Cantonese pilots, trying to bomb vessels believed to be pro-Kwangsi lying off the Bund.[64] But the Kwangsi forces were soon thrown back; Hunanese forces started to attack into north Kwangsi. The Kwangtung front was reinforced with the troops of Li Ming-jui and Yang Teng-hui, which had been transferred south from Wuhan by sea, and they took Wuchow on 6 June. Li was appointed Disbandment Commissioner (that is, chief military commander) for Kwangsi, and Yü Tso-po Provincial Chairman.[65]

Huang Shao-hsiung and Pai Ch'ung-hsi fled from Kwangsi through Lungchow, and made their way to Hong Kong where Li Tsung-jen had been for some time, trying to muster support for Kwangsi. They had now lost even their base.

Their flight, and the fighting which preceded it, brought Kwangsi close to the despairing chaos through which it had passed between the fall of Lu Jung-t'ing and the rise of the Kwangsi Clique. The currency collapsed, trade and commerce were dislocated, and civil government broke down. Huang was reminded of Lu as he and Pai fled, along the same route that Lu had used eight years before.[66]

THE AFTERMATH OF DEFEAT

A few years later, when Li Tsung-jen and Pai Ch'ung-hsi were again established as overlords of Kwangsi, Li made a speech which, perhaps unwittingly, described his career to 1929:

> Since the [foundation of] the Republic the majority of senior officers have received an education, and some have also received higher education. But they have still not been able to nurture the pure and lofty characters [which would encourage them] to go out and strive for the nation. The result is that we are still sunk in the chaos of warlordism; the nation's peril increases daily, and society becomes increasingly disturbed. What is the reason for this? It is entirely due to the lack of psychological reconstruction, to the pervasiveness of self-seeking. . . When they [the senior officers] started out, though they wanted to work for the nation, they found themselves in a corrupt environment, surrounded by an atmosphere of self-seeking, tainted and misled. They could not resist it.[67]

Four years of control of Kwangsi, and three years of participation in national affairs had brought out similarities between the Clique and traditional warlords which had been less obvious when they had defeated one of these men, Lu Jung-t'ing, in 1924. The similarities expressed themselves in a series of negative attributes: lack of political conviction, lack of social responsibility, lack of allegiance to a higher authority, lack of respect for civilian rule. In trying to carve out a Kwangsi Empire, they had repeated Lu's errors.

The manner of their rise to power in Kwangsi, in the context of warlord struggles, had assured that these negative attributes would be latent in the leaders of the Kwangsi Clique. This was the school in which they had been brought up. But in 1926, the possibility had existed that they would realise a different potential, and become servants of the revolution. Two paths had lain open to them: to stay in Kwangsi, as provincial warlords, or to join in the great enterprise to reunify and revolutionise China. They had kept a foot in both camps. Huang Shao-hsiung had remained in Kwangsi as a provincial ruler, though of a more enlightened type than Lu Jung-t'ing. He had shown greater interest in provincial administration, and in modernisation. He had moved forward from the position of provincial warlord.

By contrast, Li and Pai, operating on a wider plane, had moved backwards, in terms of their political commitment, and their concern for national unification. The characteristics of local chauvinism, self-aggrandisement and authoritarian, militarist rule, latent in them from their early careers, had been accentuated during their careers in the Kuomintang armies. An orthodox interpretation, Kuomintang or Communist, would attribute this process to their basic veniality. But it can also be argued that it was a reaction to the failure of the Kuomintang to create in China a hostile atmosphere for the retention and development of independent military control, that is, the Kuomintang's failure to make the Kwangsi Clique and the numerous other converted warlords submit to civilian, Party rule. They were possibly willing to do this in 1926. But by this time the Kuomintang itself had turned against civilian rule, and had emerged, in 1928, as a military-dominated government; political or ideological sanctions had ceased to have any compulsion, not least because the Kuomintang itself had downgraded them. Operating in these circumstances, the Kwangsi leaders reverted to a pattern of behaviour where only military force counted, and where only a regional military base provided security.

Some of the military men of the Clique's generation managed the transformation from petty warlord to military servant of a political party, but not under the Kuomintang. Chu Te and Ho Lung are two examples. Chu's case is especially remarkable, since his career as a warlord had corrupted him very deeply, and had led him amongst other things, to opium smoking. A combination of accident and personal potential led Chu into the Communist Party; he rose above his background. Li and Pai went another way. The possibilities for transformation within them were not developed. The conditions they encountered encouraged them to slip back into warlord practices, as did many of their fellow-converts.

In the end, the Kuomintang, having failed to remould its warlord allies, was forced to continue the anti-warlord wars officially ended with the completion of the Northern Expedition, and to crush its erstwhile converts. In the process, Chiang Kai-shek established himself as absolute master of the Kuomintang, its government and its armies. He consolidated Kuomintang control over much of China; it was not again threatened by large-scale regional independence.

But this did not mean that local autonomy was outlawed. Large-scale regional independence was replaced by provincial independence. Numerous provinces remained outside the sphere of effective Nanking control. They offered little threat to Nanking, since they were governed as individual units by local men who had little interest in expansion. But they contradicted Nanking's claims to rule over a unified China. They also made Nanking's tasks of eradicating Communist strongholds, and of resisting Japanese encroachment, virtually impossible.

8

Back to the province

The defeat of 1929 seemed to have completely destroyed the Kwangsi Clique. Of its leaders, three were in exile, and one in prison. Its armed forces were dispersed and transferred to the command of other men; all the territories held by the Clique, including the home province, were lost. This seemed total defeat, but it was not. Two factors intervened to allow the Clique to recoup its position to the extent that it regained the base from which it had started its expansionist activities in 1926. The first factor, which created conditions of extreme instability in Kwangsi, was the inability of the men appointed by Nanking to administer the province. The reason for this we shall outline below. The second was the cohesion, not just of the Clique's leaders, but of the second level within the Clique.

We now need to define what we mean by the Kwangsi Clique, to discuss the structure of the Clique, and to see how and why it stuck together. Until now, we have usually meant by the Clique its four leaders – Li Tsung-jen, Huang Shao-hsiung, Pai Ch'ung-hsi, and Li Chi-shen – four men who co-operated on a basis of near equality; each controlled his own subordinates, each directed his own area of interest without major intervention from the others. They met very seldom, and never formulated any specific programme by which all were bound. They co-operated with each other in the interest of their native province, in the interest of the nation and the Kuomintang, and in their own personal interest: together they amounted to something; on their own they would have been insignificant. There was some friction between them, in areas where their personal interests seemed to conflict – namely, between Li Tsung-jen and Huang Shao-hsiung (see above, p. 54) – but potential divisions were usually overcome by mutual checks and balances.

The structure of the Clique at this early stage (and later on) was informal. There was no formal, ordered hierarchy; indeed, as far as the members of the Clique were concerned, there was no Clique – 'Kwangsi Clique' was a term used of them, not by them. Nevertheless, there was an organisation which had an unwritten hierarchy, and its informality and looseness made it no less real. Its members understood how it worked, and worked within this understanding.

We shall look now not simply at the leadership of the Clique but also at the very important second level of the Clique, a large group of men who remained loyal to the Clique leadership for all or large parts of their careers. These men, mostly army officers, were just as important to the Clique as were its leaders. Their loyalty determined whether the Clique held together or not, their application on its behalf determined the success of its policies. It is difficult to say precisely who was a member of the second level of the Clique. I have chosen to look only at men who reached high positions (Brigade Commander, Head of Provincial Government Department, etc.) at some stage in their career, though the hierarchy of the Clique extended much lower. It is also difficult to define the relative standing of individuals. For this reason I have referred to anyone associated with the Clique but not in the clearly-defined leadership as a member of the second level, a loose and unsatisfactory term, but the best that can be done with existing evidence.

There is also a problem of defining who belonged to the Clique at any given stage; the Clique existed as a more or less distinct entity for 25 years (1925–49), during which there was movement into and out of it. I have divided this period into three – 1925–9, 1930–6, 1936–49. Of these three the middle period is the crucial one for determining who was a member of the Clique, for in that period membership involved an element of choice. Before 1929, there was usually no choice for young men who had started on a career within Kwangsi before the Clique emerged; the only possibility of advancement for them was within the Clique's loose framework. In the third period the Clique's teeth had been drawn, and it had ceased to operate as an independent organisation; most of its members found themselves working for a higher authority – the Central Government. But in the middle period there was a real alternative: to stay with the Clique, or to switch allegiance to the Central Government. (The alternative was probably loaded in material terms, since it was the practice of the Central Government to offer material incentives to potential defectors.) There is a remarkable continuity in the membership of the second level, the reasons for which we shall discuss below.

We shall now look at this second level of leaders, at their background, their pattern of recruitment into the Clique, the nature of their ties to the Clique. I have attempted a rough tabulation of the members of the Clique (see Appendix I); the criteria used for inclusion are length of service (usually covering at least two of the three periods of their service) and importance of service (usually rising to the kind of rank indicated above).

Background. Little is known of the early life of members of the second level of the Clique; but since many of its military members shared the same education as the leaders of the Clique, in the Kuang-hsi lu-chün hsiao-hsüeh (Kwangsi Military Elementary School) and the Paoting Military Academy, many of them probably had similar social backgrounds to the Clique leaders – families which were not prosperous, but which had some pretensions to education, families which were not wealthy enough to send their sons abroad or to one of the main centres of China for their education, but still wanted them to have some kind of modern education. Certainly none of the Clique's second level were men of bandit origins, as were many of the previous generation of Kwangsi soldiers. They were modern-minded soldiers, with some idea of developments beyond Kwangsi. For those who graduated from Paoting there was a possibility of service beyond Kwangsi, which several men who were associated with the Clique in the second and third stages of its existence took – Yeh Ch'i, Liao Lei, and Li P'in-hsien all went into the Hunan Army.

Even less is known of the background of the civilian associates of the Clique. Most of them had a modern education, usually outside Kwangsi; this is all that can be said with certainty about them. Very few were survivors from the Imperial administration.

Almost all the men, either civilians or soldiers, were of the same age or younger than the Clique leaders.

Recruitment. The bulk of the military members of the second level of the Clique became associated with it by accident rather than choice, many of them through the fact that they served in the Kwangsi Model Battalion with the later leaders of the Clique, and then went on to become the direct subordinates of one of the four leaders. Some joined the Clique in the second period, after their careers in other parts of China had come to a halt. Civilian associates were drawn into the Clique either because they were already working in Kwangsi when the Clique came to power, or because they wished to go back to their native province.

It is difficult to work out how important personal ties were either in recruiting men into the Clique or in retaining their loyalty once they were in. Communist sources list personal factions within the Clique, and have no difficulty in assigning virtually all the Clique's members to one or other of the leaders.[1] There are cases of short- and long-term associations between individual leaders and followers – namely, Li Tsung-jen's with Huang Chung-yüeh, a civilian adviser who worked with Li for almost thirty years. But there are no clear and lasting lines of personal association within the Clique; by contrast there are many cases where individuals seem to have switched allegiances from one leader to another, without apparently harming their positions within the larger Clique. There is some indication that place of origin (and therefore dialect) operated as a close tie between a leader and members of the second level; Huang Shao-hsiung, for example, seems to have had a large number of close followers from his own home, Jung hsien. The bulk of the Clique's military followers came from one of two areas: the larger Kweilin area, including Kweilin, Hsingan, Kuanyang, Yangshuo, P'inglo, Kungch'eng, Ch'uanchou, Lip'u and slightly further away Liuchow; and the larger area around Jung hsien – Yulin, Peiliu, Ts'enhsi, Luchu'an, Ts'angwu, Wuchow, Li hsien, Kueip'ing, Kuei hsien and Popai. But these regional distinctions were not absolute, and never amounted to regional cliques within cliques. Of all the leaders Huang Shao-hsiung seems to have been the most prone to call on regional ties, and on familial ties in recruiting supporters (see above, p. 100); but even in his case the ties proved tenuous; very few of the men he had raised up went with him when he left Kwangsi, and could no longer guarantee them jobs. Those who left him – men such as Hsia Wei and Wu T'ing-yang, both fellow-natives – were not affected in their careers by losing his patronage.

In the first stage of its operation, from 1925 to 1929, the Clique may to some extent be seen as an example of Andrew Nathan's ' linked Clique ', a structure whose members are recruited individually and sequentially by one leader, who then co-operates for mutual benefit with other leaders, without ever incorporating the individual hierarchies into a single body. This type of Clique is a flexible, informal organisation, held together not by any political programme or organisation, but by the relationship of its members to the leader; without the leader, the Clique cannot survive.[2] Not enough information is available to document such a structure in the case of the Kwangsi Clique, to demonstrate close hierarchies of association between individual leaders and members of the second level. Individual leaders clearly had their own subordinates who were personally loyal to them, but not all the associates of the Clique ' belonged ' to one of the leaders. Even in the first stage of its operation, we cannot see personal ties as absolute determinants of Clique membership. When we get to the second period, they seem still less crucial. We see then some men switching allegiance without great difficulty, and many others operating without any apparent personal ties. Those who left the Clique at the end of the first period went not because their leader had died politically, but for other reasons: Yü Tso-po and Li Ming-jui because they had joined the Communist side; Hu

Tsung-to and T'ao Chün because they had abandoned the Clique in favour of careers in their native province, Hupei; and Yang Teng-hui and Lü Huan-yen because they changed sides so many times in the confused fighting of 1929 that they played themselves off the board. Huang Shao-hsiung's supporters in fact survived his political demise.

Few of the civilian members of the Clique were personally bound to any one leader. The most prominent civilian adherents – Ma Chün-wu, Lei Pei-hung and Lei Yin – had such high stature as individuals that they were beholden to no one. Nor was there any indication that the military men who joined the Clique at the start of the second period – Yeh Ch'i, Li P'in-hsien and Liao Lei – were attached to any particular leader.

There were distinct strands within the Clique in the second period associated with individual leaders, but they represented functional rather than personal ties. Pai Ch'ung-hsi was close to the modern-minded, professional soldiers in the Kwangsi Army and Militia, Li Tsung-jen to the slightly more conservative officers, and to the rural leaders, Huang Hsü-ch'u to commercial leaders, government officials and local officials. These strands of affiliation were not mutually hostile; they represented different functional interests, not conflicting personal interests. The strands were closely entwined together, and were not a source of instability to the Clique.

It seems difficult then to see the cohesion of the Kwangsi Clique simply in terms of the hierarchical personal connections which are the principal cement of Nathan's linked Clique. What then induced the remarkable cohesion which the Kwangsi Clique demonstrated? Why, in 1929, when its leaders were exiled and penniless, did the second level wait for their return, instead of setting up on their own or defecting to Nanking? We shall look at some of the cohesive elements.

PROVINCIAL IDENTITY

The sense of provincial identity within Kwangsi was very strong, created by the isolation of Kwangsi, by its sense of being disparaged by other provinces, and by its history of rebellion against Central authority. There was a sense of solidarity of fellow-provincials against the rest. The Kwangsi Clique had disposed of all its major rivals within the province, leaving no alternative focus for provincial loyalty. Kwangsi provincial identity as a positive force exercised a strong cementing influence on the members of the Clique. As a negative attribute, it also prevented their detachment from the Clique. Members of the Clique knew that in a situation where they had to compete with Chekiang and Kiangsu natives – as they would if they put themselves under the umbrella of Nanking – they would come off badly, for no one else shared their high opinion of the worth of Kwangsi men. Their most secure future lay with a continuing association with Kwangsi – and therefore with the Kwangsi Clique.

Provincial identity was not an overwhelming concern; it did not prevent Yü Tso-po and Li Ming-jui from breaking with the Clique when they found a higher, ideological identity.

MILITARY SERVICE PATTERNS

For the military members of the second level of the Clique, their involvement in the Kwangsi military apparatus was an important incentive for remaining within the Clique. Each of the major military forces within China (in 1929 the four Group Armies) had its own career structure. There was little possibility that men from one career structure would be incorporated into another. The prospects for officers who left one group were dismal: mercenary service, service at a lower rank elsewhere, or retirement. Even if they managed to continue their careers elsewhere, they would be commanding men with whom they had no ties, units raised in other parts of China, whose personal loyalty to them would be negligible. There was no possibility of taking one's troops with one; the days of wandering ' guest ' armies had passed.

COMMON INTERESTS WITHIN THE CLIQUE
AS A WHOLE

There was a community of interest between the Clique leaders and its second level, which was not associated with personal ties to one man. It was based on similar social and educational backgrounds, a common faith in the military way, and shared political views which were authoritarian but not opposed to change and improvement. This community of interest should not be over-stressed, though it did exert some influence on the cohesion of the Clique. Men who understood each other and were basically in sympathy with each other's large but vague aims were likely to stay together. It is within this context that ideological questions should be seen. The Kwangsi Clique had no separate ideological position of its own. When it spoke of ideological commitment, it spoke of its own modified version of the ideology of the Kuomintang, which it regarded as the new orthodoxy of China. Since there was an assumption of ideological commonality across all China, it could not be a feature which distinguished the Kwangsi Clique from other groupings, and therefore not a source of particular identification with the Clique for its members.

LEVELLING WITH THE SECOND LEVEL
OF THE CLIQUE

This explains both why the second level of the Clique remained loyal to the leaders, and why no member of the second level challenged the leaders for supremacy over the Clique when they were down. Before 1929 there was a clear distinction between the leaders and the second level. Even with the greatly-expanded area of the Clique's operation, no members of the second echelon were brought into the first. The nearest approach to such an elevation was the preferment that Li Tsung-jen gave to the Hupei natives Hu Tsung-to and T'ao Chün at Wuhan, which aroused strong resentment and opposition from other members of the second echelon (see above, p. 126). Though many of the members of the second level were able men, technically capable of assuming leading roles, there was too little differentiation between them to provide for the elevation of one above the others. Individual members of the second level may have wanted to advance themselves at the cost of others, but where there was no existing distinction of sufficient magnitude, and where no special opportunity occurred which would have placed one at advantage over the others, they were forced to accept each other's equality, and, in 1929, to wait for leadership for the return of the original leaders.

MERCENARY INTERESTS

It is usual to regard the connections between militarists and their subordinates as essentially those of self-interest and materialism – that is, mercenary relations. As James Sheridan describes these relationships, ' the hierarchies of loyalty came to be based less and less on ethical considerations and more and more on mercenary ones; service was increasingly conditioned on expectations of reward '.[3] The importance of self-interest in maintaining the cohesion of the Clique cannot be denied, though it operated in a more subtle way than that described above. The second level of the Kwangsi Clique were not simply selling themselves to the highest bidder – indeed in 1929 and 1930 the leaders of the Kwangsi Clique could not bid at all, though Nanking could. But outside their connection with the Kwangsi Clique, it was probable that the members of the second level of the Kwangsi Clique would find their material rewards very uncertain. Even if they sold out to Nanking, their careers and therefore their rewards would probably be short-term and problematic, and would amount at best to posts of little real influence. This was what Huang Shao-hsiung found when he left the Kwangsi fold; he occupied a series of posts with prestige but little real influence.[4] There was little possibility of Kwangsi men re-establishing themselves where others, with well-established connections, were already entrenched – that is, in the world of Nanking. A long involvement with the Kwangsi Clique necessitated a continuing involvement, not for the size of reward, but for any reward at all.

COERCIVE TIES

The possibility that the second level of the Clique was bound to its leadership by coercive ties must be rejected, for the simple reason that in 1929 when the ties of the Clique were most tried, the leaders had no force to bring to bear on their subordinates.

All these reasons for cohesion do not suggest that the possibility of factional fighting within the Clique was absent. The framework for factionalism existed. But the importance of stability within Kwangsi, if the province was to resist its many external enemies, the community of interest between the leaders of the Clique and the second level, the perception that unity was more productive than in-fighting, showed the Clique members that the continued cohesion of the Clique offered them much more than dissension, that it gave them a possibility for a continued career, with its rewards, which disunity did not. The experience of 1929 and 1930 showed this cohesion operating in practice.

Let us now look at the background against which the Kwangsi leaders reasserted their authority. After their flight in April 1929, control of the province passed to the cousins, Yü Tso-po (Provincial Chairman) and Li Ming-jui (Disbandment Commissioner/Military Commander). Yü and Li were already Left-wing, and Yü was close to the Communist Party; his return to Kwangsi had been sanctioned by the Communist organisation in Hong Kong.[5] Their main concern after their assumption of power in Kwangsi was to foster a leftward movement within the province. Political activity in the province surged up, Communist workers were sent into the province from Hong Kong and Canton, intensive political training was started in some units of the armies, especially those of Li Ming-jui. Their connection with the Communist Party was not their ony external political connection. Though their appointments were from Nanking, they were involved in complicated negotiations with Wang Ching-wei's oppositionist Reorganisation faction of the Kuomintang, to help find Wang a base in south China from which to attack Nanking. The only significant result of their dealings with Wang was a break with Nanking, in the early autumn of 1929.

Their preoccupation with national matters prevented them from establishing any real control over the former subordinates of the Kwangsi Clique, who soon began establishing independent zones of control within the province. Yü and Li were deposed, by army commanders who had technically declared for Nanking, but were in fact preparing for the return of the leaders of the Kwangsi Clique. Li, Pai, and Huang slipped back into the province, and by the end of November were again in control. Yü and Li moved into the west of the province, where the Chuang–Communist movement had expanded during the confusion of the past months, and where the Right River Soviet was established in December (see above, p. 104).

The Kwangsi Clique was now back in the position it had held before the start of the Northern Expedition – military controllers of a single province, provincial warlords. But they were not yet ready to accept this reduced role. They regarded their eclipse as temporary; they were not persuaded that their role on the national stage was ended. They were determined to try and recoup their position as commanders of a large regional grouping. Their plans for renewed expansion involved them once again in a temporary alliance with a faction of the Kuomintang; after their alliance with the Right-wing Western Hills faction in 1927, and with the conservative Elders faction in 1928, they now formed an alliance with the Left-wing Reorganisation faction. If anything could underline the political opportunism (always within a broad Kuomintang framework) of the Clique, it was their ability to form alliances across the whole range of political positions within the Kuomintang. The only common feature of these alliances was that they were all founded on an antipathy to Chiang Kai-shek.

Wang had his political prestige to offer the Clique, plus military backing, in the form of Chang Fa-k'uei, who arrived in Kwangsi with his army at the end of 1929.[6] Together, the forces of Chang and the Kwangsi Clique drove into Kwangtung, Chang's troops with the aim of re-establishing Wang Ching-wei there, the Kwangsi forces with the aim of extending Kwangsi dominion. The expedition was poorly conceived and hastily planned; after some initial successes, the Chang–Kwangsi troops were driven back in disarray.[7]

The failure to restore the authority of the Kwangsi Clique beyond the borders of Kwangsi did not deter the Clique's leaders from another attempt. They could still not accept that they *had* lost their status as leaders of a large regional domain, they still clung tenaciously to the belief that they could re-establish themselves. Their mood was one of bitterness and desire for revenge; they were desperately eager to push out from Kwangsi, towards central China. In the spring of 1930, they allied themselves with a conglomeration of Chiang Kai-shek's enemies, who were organising a movement of opposition to Nanking in north China, Yen Hsi-shan, Feng Yü-hsiang and Wang Ching-wei. Its aim was to establish a new government at Peking, to prepare for which the Enlarged Congress of the Kuomintang was held there in July (K'uo-ta hui-i). This political move was linked with a series of attacks on Nanking: Yen and Feng from the north, the Kwangsi Clique and Chang Fa-k'uei from the south. By the end of the year, they had all been defeated. Yen and the Kwangsi Clique managed to cling on to control of a single province, but Feng's career as a militarist ended. The alliance which at first sight seemed impressive and threatening had no stronger tie than opposition to Chiang Kai-shek; there was no common aim, other than to see his downfall. All the leading figures involved in the warfare of 1930, and in the Enlarged Congress were fighting to recoup their *individual* positions; they had all been at odds with and allied with each other several times over the past three years. These alliances, whether *pro* or *anti*, had been founded only on temporary convenience; none had lasted and the present alliance proved no more durable. Chiang Kai-shek was now all-powerful in central China; he was thus able to crush this many-headed but leaderless uprising, though not without bloody fighting.

The fighting was most severe in the north; in the south, bad management and over ambition quickly led to disaster for the Kwangsi–Chang Fa-k'uei forces attacking north through Hunan. The Field Commanders, Chang and Pai Ch'ung-hsi, the ablest tacticians in the Kuomintang Armies, made, in their haste, two cardinal strategic errors: they failed to defend either their flank or their rear. A flanking attack by Chang's former subordinate, Ts'ai T'ing-k'ai, cut off the head of the army from its reinforcements.[8] At the same time (July 1930) an attack from Yunnan into Kwangsi penetrated as far as the provincial capital, Nanning, which was besieged.[9] Chang and Pai were forced to withdraw to Kwangsi, but were not able to prevent most of southeastern Kwangsi from falling into Cantonese hands.[10] Hunanese troops occupied the northern section of the province, leaving the Kwangsi forces controlling only a small area in the middle of the province. The Clique was, once again, *in extremis* (*ssu-mien Ch'u-ke*).[11]

For Huang Shao-hsiung, this third defeat in little over a year was too much. He had been angered by the refusal of the other leaders of the Clique to come to terms with Nanking and Canton after their defeat in April 1929; the reckless attacks into Kwangtung and Hunan, in December 1929 and in the early summer of 1930 increased his anger, and led to an open breach. He resigned as Chairman of Kwangsi, dissociated himself from the anti-Nanking enterprise, and left Kwangsi.

His association with the Kwangsi Clique was at an end. He now moved over to the Nanking side, and was rewarded with a series of high administrative posts (he was Minister of the Interior, 1932–5; Chairman of Chekiang, 1939–46). The break between Huang and the Clique was not absolute; Huang remained on terms of personal friendship with the other leaders, and occasionally visited Kwangsi; his protégés within the province were not dismissed. He himself saw his departure as the outcome of irreconcilable policy disagreements, not as the outcome of personal enmity [12] (though where he drew the line between the two he did not say). This was the only serious split that occurred in the top rank of the Clique throughout its long career, and it was less a defection than a parting of ways. Huang was succeeded in the top rank by another Huang (but no relative), Huang Hsü-ch'u.

The crushing defeat of 1930 forced upon Li Tsung-jen and Pai Ch'ung-hsi the realisation that they must now forget about re-establishing themselves as overlords of several provinces. Their military strength, weakened by a string of defeats, was only sufficient to allow them to control Kwangsi. Their defeat in the Yangtze Valley, followed by the defeats of Feng Yü-hsiang and Yen Hsi-shan in north China, had strengthened Nanking's authority to the point where Chiang no longer feared attacks by dissident militarists. His focus of attention shifted from the enemies within his own Party to the Communists in Kiangsi. (His preoccupation with his ' allies ' had allowed the Communists a valuable breathing space in which to strengthen their base in Kiangsi.)[13] Regional independence persisted, but typically only within a single province and in peripheral provinces. Shansi, Shantung, Szechwan, Kweichow, Yunnan, Kwangsi, and Kwangtung were all independent of Nanking for the greater part of the period until the outbreak of the Anti-Japanese War. The rulers of these provinces accepted that the day of multi-province blocs had passed, and that they must limit their activities. In some provinces – notably Kwangsi and Shansi, whose affairs have been described by Donald Gillin in his book *Warlord* – this reduction in scale intensified the interest of the local rulers in their own province. The Kwangsi leaders put one career behind them and embarked upon another; they abandoned the vision of Kwangsi Empire, and made plans for a new Kwangsi.

These plans, which were lumped together under the name of the Kwangsi Reconstruction Movement, required first that Kwangsi stabilise relations with its neighbours, that Kwangsi move from inviting attacks by these neighbours to forming alliances or at least non-aggression pacts with them.

Relations with Kwangsi's foreign neighbour, the French colony of

Annam, were easily restored to a friendly basis. Early in 1931, Huang Hsü-ch'u, the Provincial Chairman, and Li P'in-hsien, the Chief-of-staff, paid an official visit to the colonial Governor-general, and assured him of their desire for friendship between their province and Annam. Given the minimal nature of relations between Kwangsi and Annam, distant amiability was all that was needed.[14] Kwangsi's key neighbour was Kwangtung; the continuing hostility between the two provinces was seriously affecting Kwangsi's communications with the outside world, depressing trade and undermining the provincial economy. Short of complete economic collapse, a rapprochement between the two provinces was essential (as it had been for the emergent Clique in 1925).

A return to good relations could not be achieved simply by willing it. Inter-provincial alliances were typically based on common interest, economic or political, or on a balance of strength between two provinces, as between Yunnan and Kwangsi. The two provinces were often at odds over the opium trade between Yunnan and Canton, which passed through Kwangsi. The Yunnanese objected to the heavy taxation which opium was subjected to on its journey through Kwangsi. In periods when the provincial authorities in Kwangsi were well established, the Yunnanese had to accept this situation; when, however, Kwangsi was weak, the Yunnanese would invade Kwangsi, to extend Yunnanese control of the opium routes. This they did in 1924, 1926, 1929 and 1930. Kwangsi could easily stabilise its relations with Yunnan by maintaining a strong body of troops in the Yunnan border region. With Kwangtung, however, the relationship was more complicated. Short of actual Kwangsi military occupation, the only guarantee of stable relations was an alliance based on common cause. In seeking better relations with Kwangtung, the Kwangsi leaders looked for a suitable issue on which to base a formal alliance; from this formal alliance, other practical arrangements would follow.

An occasion for rapprochement between the two provinces presented itself in February 1931. Hu Han-min, the Chairman of the Legislative Yuan, was arrested in Nanking for his opposition to the promulgation of the Provisional Constitution.[15] Hu's arrest caused an upsurge of opposition to Nanking in Canton, where Hu's influence was strong, and led to the establishment of an Extraordinary Committee (of the Central Executive and Supervisory Committees of the Kuomintang) in Canton, made up of Cantonese members of the Central Committees, with other anti-Chiang politicians and militarists.[16] An alliance of southwestern provinces was formed, in which Kwangsi participated, and in the summer of 1931, a short-lived expedition was launched north towards Nanking. With Canton taking up a position of strong hostility to Nanking,

Kwangsi had a cause around which to build a new alliance with Kwang-tung. In the first part of May, the relationship between the two provinces changed suddenly from enmity to friendship.

The Extraordinary Committee set up a government made up of Cantonese politicians of all shades of political opinion, from the Left-Kuomintang Wang Ching-wei to the Right-wing Tsou Lu to the conservative T'ang Shao-yi and Hsü Chung-chih, and including the defeated regional militarists Li Tsung-jen and T'ang Sheng-chih. It was never more than a paper government. Real power at Canton remained with Ch'en Chi-t'ang, the local military chief. It was in the same embarrassing position that Sun Yat-sen had been in several times when he tried to establish an independent base at Canton – independent of the National Government, but not of the local military leaders. Ch'en Chi-t'ang proved unwilling to take advice, and when, after the Mukden Incident (September 1931), national opinion swung strongly in favour of renewed national unity, the politicians at Canton accepted Nanking's offer of reconciliation. (This offer involved Chiang Kai-shek's temporary retirement, from December 1931 to March 1932.)

Southern independence continued after the departure of the politicians. Kwangtung and Kwangsi, still friends, were openly defiant of Nanking; Yunnan and Kweichow maintained a *de facto* independence. In December 1931 three organs were set up in Canton: the Southwest Executive Branch of the Central Executive Committee (Chung-yang chih-hsing wei-yüan-hui hsi-nan chih-hsing pu); the Southwest Political Council of the National Government (Kuo-min cheng-fu hsi-nan cheng-wu wei-yüan-hui) and the Southwest Military Branch Council of the National Government (Kuo-min cheng-fu hsi-nan chün-shih fen-hui). These organs claimed for themselves a dubious legality, based on the manipulation of resolutions of the Fourth Congress of the Kuomintang. They represented on paper the five provinces of Kwangtung, Kwangsi, Yunnan, Kweichow, and Fukien, but had authority only over the first two. Even there, they played no part in the internal affairs of either province; they operated only as organs of opposition to Nanking.[17] Their only political prestige came from the presence of Hu Han-min, who was allowed to leave Nanking at the end of 1931, and returned to the south. All three councils were dominated by the military – Ch'en Chi-t'ang and the Kwangsi leaders – who had no intention of seeing them operate as active, independent units.

The main function of the Councils was to give some semblance of political respectability to autonomous provincial governments. The leaders of Kwangtung and Kwangsi could not reconcile the fact and the form of provincial independence. While they had no intention of surrendering *control* to any higher body, they needed still to maintain the concept of a higher authority, with the province as a subordinate unit. They viewed the idea of complete provincial independence with distaste; to be a petty provincial militarist was undesirable; to clothe one's actual independence with ' national ' forms made provincial autonomy comfortable.

The principal production of these bodies over the next few years were verbal assaults on Nanking, usually self-righteous attacks on Nanking's failure to resist Japanese advances. These verbal attacks were never extended into physical ones, even when opportunities for alliances with other anti-Nanking forces presented themselves, as in the Fukien Rebellion of 1933. The southern leaders had no intention of provoking hostilities with Nanking; they realised that they were unlikely to succeed. (There was no danger of an attack from Nanking, heavily committed against the Communists in Kiangsi; the Communists in fact acted as a buffer between Nanking and the independent Southwest.)

With the re-establishment of friendly relations with Kwangtung, Kwangsi was secured against attack from the quarter traditionally most dangerous to her. But this security did not permit the Kwangsi Clique to plan offensive operations outside the province. The Clique now accepted that, beyond its association with the new organisations in Canton, its operations would be confined to the single province of Kwangsi. What was needed now was a concrete, practical formula for the government of this province, one which would not only manage the province well, but also give some lustre to the tarnished image of the Clique. By espousing apparently progressive measures of reform and reconstruction, the Clique felt that it might establish on a small-scale a viable alternative to Nanking. The Clique hoped to win itself a reputation not as the enemy of the Kuomintang, but as one of the leading upholders of the ideals of Sun Yat-sen. Having failed to establish physical dominion, the Kwangsi Clique was now trying to claim a political dominion, not one which would involve the formation of a new party, but one in which the ideals of Sun would be ' truly observed '. Improbably, the Clique began to claim for itself the mantle of ' true heir '. It was improbable for the Kwangsi Clique to do this, given its recent record; the action in itself was characteristic of non-Communist movements of opposition to Nanking, which often justified their opposition in terms of an attempt to uphold Sun's will against its perverters in Nanking.

This new departure required for the first time that the Clique outline specific policies; its leaders could no longer follow their earlier practice of making adjustments to the turn of national events, with the guiding principle of extending Kwangsi power. They were no longer operating on a fluid national scene, but on a stable Kwangsi one, and their former behaviour was no longer relevant. They adopted a scheme for authoritarian reform, for the military, political, economic and cultural reconstruction of Kwangsi.

It required also that the Clique take on a slightly more formal organisational structure. The two levels – leadership and second level – remained distinct, but the cohesion between the two, and the co-operation within levels became closer. The members of the Clique met frequently; much of their activity centred on the provincial capital at Nanning. The physical separation of the earlier period, which had led to the evolution of different policies in different areas, was gone. It was no longer sensible for each leader to concern himself with all facets of government, so they worked out a system under which they shared responsibility for planning and for policy-formation, but divided responsibility for implementation. Li Tsung-jen was responsible for external relations and for the generation of popular support within the province; as such his position was most conspicuous to the outside world, he was often in Canton and Hong Kong, and he was frequently regarded as the outright ruler of the Clique. In fact, Pai Ch'ung-hsi, who directed the Kwangsi army and militia, exerted as much, if not more, influence both within the province and in Canton, Huang Hsü-ch'u, as a newcomer, was less influential; his responsibility was for the civil administration of Kwangsi.

There were occasional references outside Kwangsi to splits within the Clique, and to disharmony between Li and Pai. If these existed, they did not surface. The two men had been associated for a long time, they had shared the fortunes and misfortunes of the Clique, their personal ambitions had been fulfilled and then shattered. They seemed in no mood now to break with each other; a co-operative relationship was still the easiest and most fruitful in which they could operate.

The Kwangsi Clique emerged from the anguish of 1929 and 1930 with its unity enhanced, with a stronger sense of cohesion than before. Its leadership was unchallenged, its second level closely loyal yet not servile. Its identity was firmly militarist and regionalist, a definition which would apparently qualify the Clique for the title of ' warlord ', but which, as we shall see below, could also be turned into something more positive.

9

Reconstruction

The Kwangsi Reconstruction Movement, which got under way in late 1931, drew its inspiration from the Kuomintang's ideal of creating a New China out of the reunified China. Sun Yat-sen had embodied the ideal in his *Fundamentals of National Reconstruction (Chien-kuo ta-kang)*, a long document, published in 1924. It was broken down into four parts: the first part outlined general revolutionary principles, the next contained provisions for reconstruction in the military period: the third dealt with the Period of Tutelage; and the fourth with the Constitutional Period. The document concentrated chiefly on the question of local self-government, and on the means by which the population would be trained to achieve this. Characteristically, it was a blend of generalities, of specific requirements and of immoderate optimism.[1]

After 1928, the Kuomintang and the National Government started to make plans for the implementation of Sun's *Fundamentals*. A National Reconstruction Commission was set up, and, in 1931, a National Economic Council, which was to supervise the financing and planning of reconstruction work. There were numerous lower-level reconstruction committees. The term reconstruction came to be used not only for official enterprises, but also for smaller, often private endeavours, such as the Ting hsien educational experiment, and the Tsoup'ing rural reform movement. Reconstruction quickly became a catch-all term used to describe any attempt to introduce change, whether this meant the establishment of a model *hsien*, the building of roads, the setting up of a factory, or the outlining of a large economic plan. Its usage became as loose as such terms as ' modernisation ' or ' Westernisation '. This loose-ness created serious problems; different people were doing different things, all under the same general rubric. Some were politically pro-gressive, and were attempting to move towards popular participation; others were authoritarian. Some were serious; others never got their plans beyond the paper they were written on. Some worked within an official framework; others were independent. Some tried to adhere to

Sun's *Fundamentals*; others ignored it. Most of the myriad schemes introduced under the general heading of reconstruction suffered from two defects: lack of funds, and lack of direct relation to the technical beneficiaries – the common people. These defects tended to mean that reconstruction projects spent far longer in the planning stage than in the implementation stage, if indeed they ever got that far:

> ' The ancients said that to cure a seven-year illness, a medicine which took three years to work was needed. Now one may say that a five-year plan for reconstruction needs five years of calculation, investigation and research.' [2]

The most serious defect of the officially-sponsored programmes of reconstruction, was that they never occupied a high priority in the National Government's general policy.[3] The Government was still preoccupied with military affairs, with the Communists in Kiangsi, and with the growing Japanese threat. At the same time, the composition of its political and military constituency made Nanking unwilling to press reconstruction measures which would offend important sections of this constituency. Major rural reforms, for example, would antagonise many of Nanking's military supporters, who were closely tied to the existing rural elite. The fear of such opposition from influential supporters caused Nanking to soft-pedal many of its reconstruction projects.

Whatever the weakness of the National Reconstruction Movement in its implementation, as a slogan the term reconstruction exercised a great pull. The use of the term became mandatory for anyone concerned to present an image of change. This was undoubtedly the reason why the Kwangsi leaders chose to use it to describe their ventures after 1931.[4]

The general tone of the Kwangsi Reconstruction Movement was authoritarian and spartan, its policies reflecting the military backgrounds of the Kwangsi leaders. In theory these policies were cast within the general framework of Sun Yat-sen's Three People's Principles and of his *Fundamentals of National Reconstruction*. In practice, the vagueness of the Principles and of the *Fundamentals* gave wide scope for their modification to suit the particular circumstances of Kwangsi, and to conform with the personal ideas of the province's leaders. There was no question of Kwangsi ever adopting any other ideological framework, or of creating one of her own. The Clique's long connection with the Kuomintang, and the acceptance (if often token) of Sun's ideals in most parts of China, encouraged a continuing adherence to an ideology which was broad enough to allow many interpretations. Kwangsi regarded the Kuomintang ideology as the most practical one: ' Our feelings towards the highest political lines were that communism was untrustworthy, capitalism was unworkable, and consequently only the Three Principles of the People were suitable.'[5] This qualified endorsement indicates something less than revolutionary ardour; the simplistic categorisation of the three ideologies is a telling revelation of the ideological naïveté of the Kwangsi leaders. They were much clearer about the ' isms ' they rejected – individualism, anarchism, utilitarianism, romanticism, communism – than about those they supported.[6]

Though the Kwangsi leaders considered themselves as within the broad framework of the Kuomintang, they cited other influences, and considered other alternatives. Pat Ch'ung-hsi cited with respect ideas of Darwin, Kropotkin and Kuan-tzu;[7] Li Tsung-jen mentioned Confucius and Gibbon.[8] Their interest was not in a general theory, but in individual facets which supported specific positions held by the Clique leaders. Li cited Confucius and Gibbon, for example, to bolster his belief that learning through experience, through individual study, was just as important as formal learning, and that the most important attribute of the intelligent man was a questioning mind. This idea obviously had attraction for a man of little formal education. It is unlikely that either Li or Pai had any systematic knowledge of the foreign theories they cited. This was the great age of ' isms ' in China. Any idea which seemed remotely relevant to China's situation was taken up somewhere; it was essential for anyone with pretensions to political or intellectual sophistication to have a stock of foreign names to quote.

It is safe to assume that the influence of the Western ideas cited above was negligible. Another Western influence was, however, important: the conservative revolution of Fascism. Mussolini's ideas of the corporate state, of national regeneration coupled with dictatorial rule, of fierce opposition to Communism and of directed mass mobilisation struck chords in the Kwangsi leaders. In the early 1930s, Fascist influence was apparent in Kwangsi. A French missionary reported in 1934 that

' It seems certain that while the word of command is to rely in the main on the principles given by the Founder of the Republic in his Triple Demism [Three People's Principles], the mode of execution of the plan is based on Italian Fascism. The Fascist doctrine is in fact frequently presented in the government journal at Nanking, and a long exposé of this doctrine, its aims and its methods is laid out in a booklet of about a hundred pages on sale in all the modern bookshops. . .'[9]

Li Tsung-jen and Pai Ch'ung-hsi both sent personal followers to Europe, to study Italian and German Fascism.[10] (This interest in Fascism put them at variance with the intellectual leader of the Kuomintang in south China, Hu Han-min, who attacked Fascism as a debased political theory, quite contrary to Sun Yat-sen's beliefs.[11])

Fascist influence on policy formation in Kwangsi is difficult to document. Much of the official justification and explanation of Kwangsi policy in the early 1930s did not appear in print until the late 1930s. In the interim, the Italian annexation of Abyssinia (1935) and the formation of the Axis Alliance between the European Fascist countries and Japan caused a revulsion against Fascist ideology (if not its tactics) in China, and it became impossible to refer to it favourably. But in the early 1930s, in Kwangsi and in other parts of China, the influence of Italian Fascism was strongly felt. The desire to build a strong nation in China appeared to correspond with what was happening in Italy and Germany, ' countries which many believe to have achieved " national revival " by means of authoritarian rule in the teeth of economic depression, communism and international opposition '.[12]

There was one further external influence on Kwangsi and 'ts Reconstruction Movement, that of the independent reconstruction enterprises being undertaken elsewhere in China – the Ting hsien Mass Education Experiment, the Tsoup'ing Rural Reconstruction Research Institute and others. Most of these enterprises were small, never encompassing more than a few *hsien*, and were directed by intellectuals who wanted to put their theories for the regeneration of China into practice, to serve as an example for others.

Kwangsi was particularly influenced by two experiments. From the Honan Village Government College, run by P'eng Yü-t'ing in Chenp'ing hsien, Honan, Kwangsi borrowed much of the structural framework of its Rural Reconstruction Movement (see below, p. 168). From the Tsoup'ing experiment, Kwangsi borrowed an intellectual respectability for its own efforts. The Tsoup'ing experiment was directed by a Kwangsi native (long resident in Peking), Liang Shu-ming, who had served during the late 1920s as head of the Kwangtung-Kwangsi Reconstruction Committee; he was thus a man with whom the Kwangsi leaders felt some affinity. Liang was a sophisticated thinker; his movement had an intellectual foundation, and an intellectual leadership, which the Kwangsi leaders could not emulate. They shared his basic premise, that China must be reborn from the bottom upwards, that salvation lay not in Communist class struggle, nor in Kuomintang attempts to impose solutions from above, but in organising and reconstructing rural society, in educating the peasantry, and in integrating the leadership and the led, the intellectuals and the masses. Liang's influence on the Kwangsi Movement was not direct; his specific proposals were not adopted. But his ideas, and the wide coverage that they were given in the non-Kuomintang press, provided Kwangsi with a useful cross reference, and an intellectual grounding which Kwangsi could not match.[13]

These experiments, which got under way before the Kwangsi Reconstruction Movement, provided standards against which to plan Kwangsi's policies. Their influence on Kwangsi must be inferred; the Kwangsi Movement was essentially a local movement, and was intent on doing things the Kwangsi way. Little credit was given to outside influence, particularly to outside Chinese influence.

The Reconstruction Movement depended for much of its popular support on the highly-developed provincial particularism of the province. The moving force of the Movement was 'Greater Kwangsi-ism' (Ta Kuang-hsi chu-i) or 'local patriotism' (l'amour de la petite patrie).[14] This was a force which the Kwangsi leaders did not have to create; it existed already, an intangible but potentially powerful force for mobilisation. In a province whose heroes had all been soldiers, it was closely associated with the military, a fact which made it easy for an essentially military government to foster. Under the Clique's leadership, Kwangsi provincialism was encouraged, in a spate of speeches and articles which extolled the peculiar virtues of the province: militancy, discipline, energy, adaptability – virtues which in some cases existed more in the minds of the Kwangsi leaders than in reality. One very real characteristic of Kwangsi – poverty – was turned into a virtue in much the same way that the state of ' poverty and blankness ' became a virtue for the Communist Party; poverty was a good starting-point for new programmes – there was nothing to destroy.

STRUCTURE OF THE RECONSTRUCTION MOVEMENT

The Kwangsi leaders based their programme for reconstruction on the *Kwangsi Reconstruction Programme* (*Kuang-hsi chien-she kang-ling*), issued in 1934.[15] This document, which claimed to be entirely guided by Sun's Three People's Principles, in fact controverted some of Sun's specific provisions. It spoke of self-government at the provincial level, not, as Sun had, at the *hsien* level. The ' present stage ' of the revolution was described as ' a national revolution against imperialism and feudalism ' [16]; no mention was made of Sun's Tutelary Period, which China had technically entered in 1928. The *Programme* outlined a tripartite policy for the administration of reconstruction work, the Policy of Three-fold Self-Reliance (*San tzu cheng-ts'e*). The first part, Self-defence, was linked loosely to Sun's first Principle, Nationalism (*Min-tsu chu-i*); Kwangsi would defend itself so that it could work for reconstruction, and thus, eventually, for the restoration of China. Sun's Nationalism did not mean defending provincial autonomy. The second part, Self-government, proposed first that Kwangsi would be a self-governing province, and second that all administrative measures would be based on the ' will of the people '. This was a long way from Sun's second Principle of Democracy (*Min-ch'üan chu-i*); there were no specific provisions, as there were in Sun's outline for National Reconstruction, for a mechanism for movement towards local self-government. The third part, economic Self-sufficiency, was the least divergent, being fairly closely based on Sun's third Principle, People's Livelihood (*Min-sheng chu-i*). The document laid out a series of specific programmes in the fields of economic, political and cultural reconstruction. A militia system was envisaged as the key unit of organisation; the provincial bureaucracy was to be cleaned up; agricultural and industrial innovation was planned; the system of land holding was to be regulated; military and civilian education was to be expanded. These proposals became the basis of reconstruction work in Kwangsi.

The *Reconstruction Programme* and its dependent policy, the *San-tzu cheng-ts'e*, were an amalgam of Sun's ideas and the Clique leaders' own ideas. The Kwangsi leaders were not concerned that in some respects (periodisation and level of self-government), their ideas directly controverted Sun's, nor that some of their ideas, notably the militia system, were nowhere mentioned by Sun. The *San-tzu cheng-ts'e* seems in fact to have been more a modification of the system introduced by P'eng Yü-t'ing in Chenp'ing, Honan, than of the Three People's Principles. P'eng had developed a policy of Self-defence, Self-government and Self-enrichment (*Tzu-wei, Tzu-chih, Tzu-fu*); he had also used the militia system as an organisational framework. P'eng's three policies were themselves ' developments ' of the Three People's Principles; the Kwangsi leaders went one stage further, in effect one stage further away from Sun's principles.[17] In spite of these departures, and in spite of the fact that Kwangsi's independence offended against Sun's most fundamental ideal of national unity, Huang Hsü-ch'u felt able to claim that Kwangsi's policies were ' completely in accord with the principles laid down by the *Kuo-fu* (Sun Yat-sen) and also absolutely without contradiction in relation to actual conditions '.[18]

At the provincial level, there was a separation between military and civilian functions; the provincial government financed the army – the practice of local requisitioning was abandoned – but had no control over it. At lower levels, however, military and civilian elements were closely integrated, through the militia system.[19] The regular army was reorganised and contracted to between 20,000 and 30,000 men. Kwangsi no longer needed offensive forces. Pai Ch'ung-hsi, now in command of all regular forces within the province, concentrated on modernising and retraining Kwangsi's reduced number of troops; he eventually created probably one of the best fighting forces in Republican China.[20] The troops were known collectively as the Fourth Group Army (in 1931 the Clique had re-assumed the nomenclature granted to its forces in 1928); there were two individual armies, the Seventh and Fifteenth.

Strenuous efforts were made to recruit men for the army systematically, through conscription levies, rather than through a haphazard assembly of recruits. The aim was to secure through the levies men who would volunteer for military service, men who would serve out of a feeling of public duty, rather than as mercenaries. These hopes proved at first illusory. Conscription levies were first held in 1934, but not more than two-fifths of the recruits obtained were volunteers.[21] There was considerable corruption: wealthy families bought their sons out, controverting the official system of selection of non-volunteers by lot.[22] But the conscription system had so much to recommend it that the military authorities persisted with it. Men who were obtained through this system could be smoothly re-integrated into civilian life after their two-year service; the quality of recruits could be kept high; and by presenting conscription as the lot of the dutiful citizen, the authorities provided themselves with an excellent pretext for paying low wages to serving soldiers.

Overall expenditure on the army was reduced, since Kwangsi troops were not involved in any major campaigns, but it still ate up a large proportion of Kwangsi's slender resources. The army, like the rest of the province, had adopted a policy of self-sufficiency, and this meant that costly programmes for developing Kwangsi's munitions supply had to be set up. In 1934, $1,000,000 was earmarked for the establishment of provincial arsenals; German munitions experts were employed at the Nanning Arsenal, the largest in the province.[23] Foreign advisers were also used to establish a small air force; English instructors trained Kwangsi pilots at Liuchow, Japanese and Italian sources supplied planes.[24]

The new army bore little resemblance to earlier provincial armies. The movement towards a professional, disciplined army, initiated by the Kwangsi leaders before they left the province in 1926, but interrupted by the mushrooming of their forces during the northern expedition, was finally implemented.

' It seems that they [the soldiers] have little to borrow from the past. Manoeuvres and exercises are conducted according to the most modern principles, tanks and rapid-firing cannons are used in parallel with aeroplanes, marches are cadenced to the rhythm of patriotic songs, discipline is in force from top to bottom of the scale; still better, a politeness, refined in the case of the officers, probably enforced among the men, but politeness nevertheless, leaves far behind it the crudities of . . . a time still close.'[25]

This new spirit was one facet of the militarisation of the province, of an installation of military values throughout the province, of the establishment of the army as an example to the civilian world, which became one of the most striking features of the new Kwangsi. We shall return to this below.

The provincial government was reorganised and streamlined alongside the province's military structure. In 1934, all branches of the provincial government were incorporated into a single office, the Combined Government Office (Kuang-hsi sheng cheng-fu ho-shu), administered by a provincial government Committee whose chairman was Huang Hsü-ch'u.[26] The Committee was made up exclusively of civilians (though some had previously held military posts), and included men with long administrative experience: Huang Chung-yüeh in financial administration, Li Jen-jen and Li P'in-hsien in educational affairs, Wu T'ing-yang in reconstruction work. Several of its members served concurrently on the provincial Kuomintang Executive Committee. The government was responsible for the economic affairs of the province, for large-scale reconstruction enterprises, for financial affairs (taxation, currency regulation, banking, etc.) and for middle and higher education. Its policies were determined by the principles outlined in the San tzu cheng-ts'e, though they related less to the principle of Self-defence than to those of Self-government and Self-sufficiency. The government was not the paramount authority of the province; this role was exercised by the military chiefs (that is, by Li Tsung-jen and Pai Ch'ung-hsi), thought they seem to have allowed Huang a degree of autonomy in his administration. Their main concern was with the regular army, and with the militia system, which came to operate, at the local level, as the major unit of control and organisation.

THE MILITIA SYSTEM

The Kwangsi Militia (Min-t'uan) was the basic organisational framework of the Kwangsi Reconstruction Movement. At its inception, it was a loose association of militia units of a traditional nature, raised in response to the chaos which descended on the province after the defeats of the Kwangsi Clique in 1929 and 1930. It was subsequently transformed into an organisation of general mobilisation, whose functions were not only local defence, but also economic, political and social reconstruction.

The establishment of militia units was a traditional response to instability. Militia units were raised either by government authorities, to supplement inadequate regular troops, or by leaders of individual localities, as a means of self-protection when official protection failed. Kwangsi had long experience of these types of organisation. In the period immediately before the outbreak of the Taiping Rebellion, many *hsien* had organised their own forces as a protection against bandits and river pirates, in face of the failure of the provincial authorities to quell these disruptive elements.[27] As Philip Kuhn has shown in his study of late Ch'ing militia organisation, militia units could be used in several ways. In some cases, where government authority still carried weight, the official sanctioning of militia organisation led to a downward extension of government authority, to the creation of ' a peripheral branch of the state bureaucracy itself '.[28] In other cases, the militia system became an organised expression of customary gentry functions, in a situation where government control had become so remote and so ineffective that a more clearly-defined pattern of local administration was needed than that provided informally by local gentry.[29] In Kwangsi, militia organisation was a permanent feature of local life; most *hsien* had regularly maintained militia units from at least the Tao-Kuang Period (1821–51). The head of the militia was often the *hsien* magistrate, or, after 1911, the *hsien-chang*.[30]

There are several general characteristics of militia units which explain both why the Kwangsi Clique chose to use them as the basis for its reconstruction programme, and why the militia system took the form that it did. First of all, militia units were generally raised by existing local elites, and served as a means of entrenching their authority; they tended to rely on existing social and economic sanctions for their smooth functioning, and were thus politically conservative forces. Secondly, they remained essentially local organisations; the loyalty of militia men was always to their locality, not to any higher sphere. Thirdly, they were financed locally, and represented for provincial authorities a cheap way of ensuring local order. Fourthly, they were not fully military organisations; militia men still performed their civilian functions when conditions allowed, and did not regard themselves as regular soldiers.[31]

What the Kwangsi Clique did after 1931 was to organise existing but unco-ordinated militia units into a coherent, province-wide structure. In a situation where their own regular army units had been so weakened by defection and defeat that they could no longer maintain local order, the Clique gave official sanction and an encompassing organisation to the established guardians of local order. What they were doing differed little at first from the actions of nineteenth-century provincial officials, though it went beyond the sanctioning of individual units to the establishment of a provincial organisation. The militia was regarded as an off-shoot of the provincial military structure (except for the period 1932–3, it was directly controlled by the provincial military establishment – see Appendix IV).[32]

Until 1933, the militia functioned simply as a para-military organisation, with no duties beyond those of local control. Its structure was very simple: each *hsien* was ordered to train four corps of 90 men each for full-time militia service; 12 regional militia commands were established within the province. The militia was financed by the *hsien* authorities and armed by local requisitioning of private weapons. By the end of 1931, about 50,000 militia men were in service.[33] All able-bodied men between the age of 18 and 45 were eligible for service, and recruits were obtained by conscription. The focus of organisation was the *hsien* town; men were sent there for training, and despatched from there for specfic operations.[34]

The militia handled the maintenance of local order, and the suppression of minor banditry, while the regular forces eradicated serious resistance, especially in the area of northwest Kwangsi formerly controlled by the Right River Soviet. In spite of the opposition of many of its participants, militia men who were forcibly drafted into the service,[35] the system was so successful in restoring local order, and in controlling the local population, that the Kwangsi leaders decided to extend its scope, and to use it as the vehicle for wider mass organisation and for the implementation of the Clique's economic, social and political policies. This extension meant that the Clique was putting into an organised framework many of the functions which local militia organisations had subsumed to themselves from the late Ch'ing on, leaving their implementation in local hands, but returning their overall direction to the provincial level. The Clique was not prepared to see the activities of the militia continue under the direction of conservative local gentry; its intention was to standardise these activities, to dress them up with a veneer of modernisation and popular participation.

The new militia system involved a comprehensive division of the population not unlike the *pao-chia* system. Ten households (*hu*) constituted one *chia*, ten *chia*, one village, ten villages, one *hsiang* and so on. Each village was expected to maintain one militia reserve unit (*hou pei tui*), each *hsiang* a large regular militia unit (*ta tui*).[36] All able-bodied men were trained on a rota system, first for a brief period of full-time service, in a large unit, and then for a much longer part-time period, in the reserve units. The reserve units formed a huge pool from which the regular militia units could be supplemented in emergency, and from which men could be drafted into the regular army.

The new system involved important modifications of the earlier one. First of all, the focus of training shifted from the *hsien* towns to the rural areas, making the break with civilian life for militia members less severe. Secondly, although the primary purpose of training remained local defence, instruction in political and economic affairs was given, and attempts were made to give some basic education. Thirdly, the provincial authorities now bore a greater degree of responsibility for the financing of the militia; the province budgeted between three and four million *yüan* for militia expenditure.[37] Compensation was given to wage-earners during their period of full-time training; this group constituted, however, only a small percentage of militia men, for peasants were considered to be self-employed, and were expected to give their services voluntarily, thus removing what the Kwangsi leaders conveniently regarded as the mercenary stigma of traditional militia systems.[38]

The basis of the militia system were the village and the *hsiang* units, but units were also set up in schools and in government offices. No one was exempt from militia training, except the sick, the criminal and members of vital professions.[39] In terms of numbers of men trained, the system was very successful. By 1935, the Kwangsi authorities claimed that over 45,000 men had been trained.[40] A single *hsien* (Liuchiang hsien) reported that it had organised 96 reserve units of about 90 men each, of which 24 were fully trained.[41]

The system was also successful in maintaining local order, and in ridding the peasantry of the scourge of banditry, which had previously exerted a heavy toll. Most peasants welcomed a system which, however demanding, protected them from the unpredictable and devastating attacks of bandits. Bandits ceased to be a problem after about 1934. In Kuei hsien, a key communications centre which had traditionally been a focus of bandit activity, the local militia organisation was so successful in subduing banditry that it was able to replace the local garrison of the regular army, which was closed down. Since the local militia had as weapons only 231 rifles (of eight different makes, most of them antique) and 35 pistols, its authority must have been moral rather than physical.[42]

This new system was a departure from traditional systems, where militia units had protected the interests of the local elite against disruption from bandits and from the local population itself. It was not only a province-wide organisation, it also had an over-riding political, social and economic programme, and a commitment to the welfare of the people. As applied to the militia the *San-tzu cheng-ts'e* meant, in

Pai Ch'ung-hsi's words, that ' politically [the people], should be able to govern themselves; economically, they should be able to be self-sufficient; militarily, they should be able to defend themselves '.[43] The aim of the leaders of the Kwangsi Clique was to secure the organised participation of the people in the defence of the province, and in its political, economic and social reconstruction. Technically, this partici-pation was the first step towards local self-government, but this goal was kept well in the future. It was quite clear that militia training ' would not permit of the immediate achievement of local self-government [though] it tends by its training to create the conditions which will bring self-government nearer realisation '.[44]

The Clique accepted the concept of self-government only on their own terms: participation without rights. Its leaders convinced themselves that while low-level organisation and mobilisation were essential for the unification of the province, the people were not yet sophisticated enough to be entrusted with any self-government.[45] They thought in terms of a disciplined, directed mass voluntarism, involving the enthusiastic but controlled participation of the people in projects designated by the militia authorities. As originators of these projects and policies, the Clique leaders presented themselves as men of the people, slightly home-spun, straightforward and dedicated; they made much of the fact that their own origins were humble, and claimed to understand the problems and desires of the common man. They emphasised practicality, and insisted on action. They hoped to avoid the problems which they felt had hampered the reconstruction projects sponsored by the National Government – over-planning, bureaucratic administration, tardiness in implementation. Their system would be rough and ready, but it would at least do something.

We must now ask several questions: were the Kwangsi leaders serious in their intention of reconstructing Kwangsi? Did they achieve even part of what they set out to do? Did the Reconstruction Movement follow the lines of its programme? These questions cannot be answered fully. Much of the source material on which answers must be based is biased – it consists of the reports put out by the Kwangsi Clique itself. But there are other rich sources which supplement this material. Firstly, there are several comprehensive and apparently frank (because they are frequently critical) surveys of the Kwangsi economy and society, com-piled under official auspices but by independent experts. Chief of these is Ch'ien Chia-chü's *Kuang-hsi sheng ching-chi kai-k'uang*; Ch'ien was a nationally-known economist and sociologist, with radical leanings. Another important study is *Kuang-hsi sheng nung-ts'un tiao-ch'a*.

Secondly, there are numerous eye-witness reports on Kwangsi's Reconstruction Movement, some from missionaries long resident in the province, others from prominent intellectuals such as Hu Shih and Liang Shu-ming, who visited Kwangsi once its reconstruction projects had started to gain attention. Thirdly, there are numbers of detailed reports on individual *hsien*; there are traditional *hsien* gazetteers for several *hsien* (the last of which was published in 1940), and there is also a compilation which covers all of Kwangsi's 94 *hsien* – *Kuang-hsi ko hsien kai-k'uang*.

The apparent openness of the Clique to independent reports provides part of the answer to the first question we asked above: were the Kwangsi leaders serious in their plans for reconstruction? The fact that they were confident enough to seek the help of outsiders who might be critical suggests that they were. The size and complexity of the reconstruction enterprise, and in particular of the militia system, suggest also a considerable degree of commitment. Part of the commitment came from a desire to improve their province for its own sake. An equally compelling motive was to show up Nanking. If poor, remote Kwangsi could successfully reconstruct and modernise itself, then the failure of other provinces to do as much would reflect badly on the Central Government at Nanking. Kwangsi's bitterness towards Nanking did not disappear after defeat; it continued to fester, and to provide Kwangsi with a nagging spur to action. Since the Kwangsi Clique could no longer attack Nanking physically, it decided to attack through propaganda, and through doing what Nanking claimed to be doing, only better.

ADMINISTRATORS

Let us look at the men who administered the Reconstruction Movement, for the calibre of these men and the way in which they were used were crucial to the work of reconstruction. At the provincial level, there was an emphasis on reforming and remoulding existing officials; the provincial government was streamlined, and all its work channelled through one Combined Government Office. Its civil servants were subjected to a para-military discipline; their working day was divided into periods by bells, they wore a grey uniform (very similar to the military uniform, except that it carried no marks of rank), they were subjected to regular examination.[46] These reforms were designed to make the provincial government operate more smoothly. At the same time, its tasks were reduced. The provincial government was concerned only with financial and economic affairs, with the upper levels of education, and with major reconstruction projects. General policy formulation, relations with other provinces and defence affairs were the responsibility of the military, and of the leaders of the Kwangsi Clique. At the other end of the scale, many of the functions normally carried out by the provincial government were transferred to the *hsien* governments, and to the militia system. At this level, Kwangsi made a radical departure from traditional patterns of administration both in terms of the men who staffed local government organisations, and in the scope and nature of their duties. This departure was forced upon the Clique leaders partly because of the enlarged scope of their plans, and partly because of their dissatisfaction with existing local government.

The chief activities of local government and of the militia system were to be in local defence, in basic education and in local administration. These activities were to be carried on in parallel, at the *hsien* level, at the *hsiang* level and at the village/street level. Other activities such as the inauguration of communal and co-operative schemes for re-afforestation, for laying out plantations, for establishing public granaries, for instruction in agricultural method were envisaged. Each locality was to provide men as required for *corvée* labour. Censuses were to be taken, and land registered.

All these undertakings required a huge bureaucracy to staff them; three distinct posts had to be filled at each level, in 94 *hsien*, 2,464 *hsiang* and 25,000 village/street units. It was inconceivable that Kwangsi could supply enough competent men to fill each of these posts. The solution was very simple: a system known as *San-wei i-t'i* (Three in One) was introduced, which provided that at each level, one man should concurrently occupy three posts; the *hsien-ch.ang* was also militia chief and education chief; the village head was also school principal and militia head. The man would have his office in the village school (usually in a converted temple or ancestral hall) which would also be the community centre (*ts'un kung suo*) and militia headquarters. Government-run institutes were set up to train these men, for a period varying between six and eighteen months, depending on previous educational experience.[47] The 'shoe-string approach' (*ch'iung tso-fa*) was supposed to give local officials sufficient authority to dominate existing local leaders. The headship of the *hsien*, *hsiang* or village provided local authority, the educational post supplied a salary, allowing men without private means to perform the functions traditionally exercised by the unsalaried, but amply rewarded, gentry.[48] This system made the militia an integral part of local government; the masses would be drawn simultaneously into the militia, basic education and local government.

What the Kwangsi Clique was talking about was a new breed of local leaders. The Clique had lost confidence in the local gentry and intended to curtail its political and administrative authority, if not its economic power. They had come to regard much of the gentry as reactionary, opposed to any change, concerned only with its own interests. They were angered by gentry opposition to the new militia system. The Clique intended to place local administration in the hands of young, educated, modern-minded men, and remove it from old-fashioned, middle-aged and elderly local gentry.

An examination of the age, origin and education of *hsien-chang* reveals major differences between the system in force until about 1933 and its successor. The new *hsien-chang* in 1934 were no longer natives of the *hsien* they served in; not one of 94 was serving in his native *hsien*. All but four were Kwangsi natives, and many were serving in *hsien* near their native place, but they had no direct ties with the specific locality. Most of them were young; 78 were under 45, 44 under 35. The majority were well educated; 59 had higher education of some type, another 12 were military school graduates. They also had considerable experience: 45 had some kind of military experience, usually not as line officers but in military administration or supply; 40 had worked for the provincial government; 37 had held some education post; 14 had been newspaper editors; 47 had already served as *hsien-chang*. Many of them were obviously 'new men', trained in modern schools, with a modern conception of their function. Their range was probably still limited; only 20 had actually served outside Kwangsi, and their modern-mindedness has therefore to be seen in relation to Kwangsi, not to China as a whole.[49] The Clique was trying to create a new type of local official, and to re-establish a modified law of avoidance, which would prevent the intimate association of gentry and *hsien-chang*. At levels below the *hsien*, however, the Clique expressly intended to use local men, though once again, education and a modern-minded attitude were given emphasis.

It was not expected that these reforms would be achieved easily. The Clique was well aware of the hostility which they would arouse in the local gentry, and in some of the serving *hsien-chang*, particularly when they were coupled with an attempt to clean up local administration. In 1933, 20 former *hsien-chang* were in Nanning gaol, atoning for corrupt activities.[50] Two years later, 20 *hsien-chang* posts were unfilled, because their incumbents had been dismissed for corruption or incompetence.[51] The most serious threat however came from the clash between the new men and the established local elite:

' To carry out a new type of government using new men required great determination. . . The large numbers of young men graduating from the militia cadre schools and returning to fill posts were breaking the rice bowls of the old militia commanders and local gentry. As they also concurrently held the post of basic school head, they deprived the gentry of their monopoly over education, which they considered to be their independent right. What is more, since they conscripted troops and corvée labour for the government, they inconvenienced the local landlords who held local wealth and power. Not long after the new government was implemented, these young men came into opposition with the landlords and gentry, in a struggle between old and new.'

They were subjected to abuse, and in some cases the local population was incited to rise against them.[52]

There was a contradiction in the Clique's determination to curtail the power of the gentry: the Clique might want to remove the gentry's political authority, but it was not interested in changing the economic structure of rural life, in reducing the economic power of the gentry, on which their other activities rested. In some cases the contradiction became a negation; a survey of Ssuen hsien in 1934 revealed that changes were entirely superficial (*huang t'ang pu huan yao*), and that local landlords and bandits continued to control the *hsien*.[53]

Superficially, the policy of replacing old men with new worked; the sight of local officials in simple home-spun grey clothing astonished and impressed visitors from other parts of China, who were used to seeing local officials in silk gowns or western dress, both of which were banned in Kwangsi.[54] Local officials were technically subject to regular inspection, and to periodic examinations of competency; heavy fines and punishments were laid down for malefactors, and were certainly administered occasionally. A French missionary report of 1934 noted a great improvement in the calibre of local officials, and the disappearance of the utterly incompetent or venal; officials were constrained to accept a simple and disciplined life, with meagre financial rewards: ' no luxury, no waste, only an *aurea mediocritas* [golden mean] with the satisfaction that the accomplishment of one's duty gives, helped by a convinced patriotism '.[55]

One element was lacking in the prescription for the new type of local official – any reference to their political commitment to the ideals of the Kuomintang, indeed of any provision for local Party work. While the Kwangsi Clique claimed to be implementing the true spirit of Sun Yat-sen's principles, actual Party organisation was put into cold storage. The Party was out of touch with the Kuomintang headquarters in Nanking, and was controlled directly by the Clique, which expected it to play only a minimal role in propaganda work and political training.[56] Party membership in the province fell off drastically; in 1934 there were only 5,671 members in the province, a decrease of 95 per cent over the very high (and probably padded) figure for 1926 (128,394).[57] There were Party branches in only 29 of 94 *hsien*. In several *hsien*, Party branches had actually been closed down.[58] Kwangsi, which had claimed 23 per cent of national Party membership in 1926, only had 1·7 per cent in 1934. Only 21 Kwangsi *hsien-chang* in 1934 had ever held any Party position, at any level.[59] The Kwangsi Clique attached no importance to formal Party organisation; possibly they feared that a Party organisation might become independent, might look towards Nanking. In any event, they saw no contradiction in claiming to represent the highest form of Kuomintang activity while restricting the actual operation of the Party.

ORGANISATIONAL ACHIEVEMENTS OF THE MILITIA SYSTEM

We now turn to look at what the new system of local government actually achieved, in the fields of local defence, local administration and basic education. Although the militia system was intended to embrace both the urban and the rural areas, we shall look mainly at the rural areas, for it was here that the main impact of the new system was felt. During the first period of reconstruction in Kwangsi, under Huang Shao-hsiung (1926-9), the main emphasis had been on cleaning up the urban areas. These were the most conspicuous areas, and the areas which demanded most urgent attention. It had become the practice of would-be modernisers to concentrate their efforts in the urban areas, and this practice was still continued over much of China. Tearing down a few slums, widening a few roads, forcing coolies to wear shirts – these were seen as an adequate demonstration of progressiveness, of a will to modernity. But the Kwangsi leaders, in an overwhelmingly agrarian province, had begun to appreciate that if their province was to be fundamentally changed, this process had to start from the rural areas. This feeling lay behind their attempts to rid the local gentry of some of its authority, to instal a new breed of men as *hsien-chang*, and to establish the militia system as a mechanism of local organisation.

The level of government operation was lowered. Traditionally, the arm of the provincial authority had not penetrated below the *hsien*; the gentry had handled the administration of local affairs in a quasi-official way. Now the Kwangsi leaders aimed to extend their administration to the village level, to penetrate Kwangsi society from top to bottom.

The change that they hoped for could not be a fundamental one, for they had no intention of fomenting rural revolution, of overthrowing established patterns of land tenure, of curtailing usury. Without these basic reforms, their reforms, which centred on the involvement of local government in the life of the peasantry, could never be more than superficial. It must be said, however, that they went beyond anything else that was happening in Republican China, where only in a few isolated pockets were any official or private attempts being made to change rural China. To see what effect their programmes had on rural Kwangsi, we must first look at the actual conditions of Kwangsi's peasants.

In Kwangsi, the percentage of poor peasants was very high – 72·1 per cent; only 6·6 per cent of the rural population was classed as rich peasants or landlords.[60] The system of tenancy was less well-established in Kwangsi than in other areas. About 44 per cent of peasants farmed only land they owned themselves and another 25 per cent owned some land and rented the rest. The rate of tenancy varied across the province – it was much higher near the Kwangtung border, and lower in the remote areas of the province where there was still plenty of untilled land – but across the province an upward drift in the rate of tenancy, running at 1 or 2 per cent a year, was evident. In general the size of land holdings was small; 41 per cent of the rural population farmed five *mou* or less, a land holding inadequate to keep a family.[61] Twenty-five per cent of peasant families had no water buffalo, the essential draught animal for rice cultivation.[62] Rents were usually paid in kind, and often ran to half the produce of the land rented.[63] Most of the cottage industries on which the peasants depended to supplement their income from grain production were declining; the import of foreign yarn had wiped out the rural spinning industry, except in remote areas. Weaving was still widespread, but usually only provided for the needs of an individual family, and not for the market.[64] Many farmers produced coarse cane sugar, but since they lacked the machinery to refine it, they were at the mercy of the local refineries, which skimmed off what profit there was in the business.[65]

There were few agricultural labourers (that is, landless peasants) in any given area; instead casual labour was supplied in Kwangsi by itinerant workers, both male and female, who put themselves up for hire at regular markets. Employers were particularly anxious to hire women, who were as strong as men, worked as hard as them, but ate less and received lower pay.[66] In remote areas near the Kweichow border, slavery still persisted. The slaves were usually outsiders, children of refugee families, though local children were also sold into short-term servitude.[67]

These conditions indicate a very severe and chronic agricultural crisis; they were compounded by heavy taxation, and by the burden of usury. At least 40 per cent of the peasantry were heavily indebted, some in the form of mortgages on their land, some in loans in cash and kind. The average rate of interest for cash loans across the province was 29 per cent per annum, 4 per cent per month.[68] Persistent indebtedness and lack of working capital forced peasants to sell their crops in advance, when prices were 30 per cent to 40 per cent below those after the harvest.[69] Most of the loans were made by landlords; since they could get such a high return on capital from usury, they were unwilling to invest surplus capital in agricultural development. Usury thus not only kept the peasantry indebted, but also hampered rural improvement.

The Kwangsi peasant was in a critically weak position, was indeed scarcely able to keep his head above water. What effect did the proposals of the Kwangsi Clique for a new system of rural administration, and for the militia system, have on the overall condition of the peasantry? The answer is probably very little. The provincial authorities did, as we have seen, inform themselves fully on the plight of the peasantry, but their unwillingness to foster rural upheaval – the militia system was designed in part to prevent this – kept them from anything but palliative reforms. An order was made to hold rents at 37 per cent of the crop, but there is no evidence that it was ever implemented.[70] The provincial government simplified the taxation system, but did not reduce the demands on the rural sector. In 1933, local tax supplements in Kuei hsien (paid by all peasant proprietors and many tenants) amounted to 200 per cent of the tax itself.[71] Although the provincial government had undertaken to finance the militia system, it did this by imposing tax supplements to pay for specific items of 'reconstruction expenditure'. In Kuei hsien in 1933, these were: education – 60 per cent; self-government – 50 per cent; public granary – 50 per cent; establishment of bank – 30 per cent; road construction – 20 per cent.[72]

What then did the militia system achieve? First of all, it gave to the province internal stability, and protected the rural areas from the depradations of banditry. Secondly, it promoted a para-military atmosphere of discipline and duty. Thirdly, it introduced a series of co-operative schemes at the local level, such as re-afforestation, communal ploughing, the planting of oil-bearing trees, the establishment of granaries and fish ponds; the aim of these schemes was not, however, to benefit the peasants engaged in them, but to raise money to pay the salary of the local official (village head/school head/militia head).[73] Fourthly, it administered land registration and censuses, in preparation for local self-government, though both these tasks were carried out with such inefficiency that the results were virtually useless.[74] The militia system played an important part in population control, by preventing free movement; individuals were obliged to register in the militia, and were not allowed to leave the areas in which they were registered.[75]

The single most striking achievement of the militia system was its educational work. The basic education movement, launched in 1933, and administered as an integral part of the militia system, called for compulsory education for children between 6 and 12, and for part-time instruction for illiterate adults. Large numbers of basic schools were set up in villages and streets, to give children and adults the rudiments of education, to train them for eventual participation in local government, and to instil a national consciousness. Though the programme can never have achieved universal education, it seems to have had considerable success. A Communist attack on the Kwangsi Clique admitted that education had penetrated even the most backward areas of the province, though the form of education offered was seen only as an attempt to 'traduce the intellectuals and dupe the people'.[76] The schools were usually very simple, often in converted temples or ancestral halls (which they shared with the village office and the militia headquarters); no attention was paid to the external trappings of education; children often came to school barefoot. Education was not free, but payment in kind, rather than in cash was accepted.[77] The aim was to provide quantity, not quality; the standard of instruction was probably very low, but the opportunity of education was given to many who would otherwise been ineligible through poverty. The programme appealed to the universal desire for education, as the only hope of an escape from misery.

If the militia system provided some benefits for the peasantry, in assuring local order, and in giving a modicum of education, it demanded much from them. On top of their existing economic burdens, which it did not alleviate, were placed heavy demands in extra taxation and in time. It was not a game (*hao-wan ti tung-hsi*).[78] Whether one regards it as an attempt to turn the province into a vast military camp, as some of its detractors did, or as a painfully partial attempt to reform rural China, is unimportant. What it represented was the only large-scale undertaking in Republican China (outside the Communist-held areas) that paid any attention to the rural areas. It represented a realisation on the part of the leaders of the Kwangsi Clique that something had to be done about the bulk of China's population, a realisation that was manifestly lacking in the areas under the control of the Central Government. That 'something' consisted less of basic reform than of control through organisation, with a dose of education and a few minor reforms thrown in to sugar the pill.

Let us look now at the larger operations of the Clique, at the activities of the provincial government, and in particular at the reasons why Kwangsi came to be known briefly as a 'model province'.

In 1934 and 1935, Kwangsi began to attract attention as a place where attempts were seriously being made to implement the ideals of reconstruction. Large numbers of articles about Kwangsi appeared in the independent press – in such highly-respected and widely-circulated journals as *Tung-fang tsa-chih, Tu-li p'ing-lun, Kuo-wen chou-pao* and in foreign language journals (published chiefly in Shanghai) – *China Weekly Review, China Critic, People's Tribune.* All of these journals catered to the independent elements in Chinese society, and all were deeply concerned about the question of reconstruction: they published regular reports on reconstruction, and articles on any schemes which seemed innovative. The paucity of such schemes in parts of China controlled by Nanking, coupled with the fact that most of these journals were at odds with Nanking, led to a concentration on such schemes as the Ting hsien Mass Education Experiment, the Tsoup'ing Rural Experiment, and from about 1933 on, the Reconstruction Movement in Kwangsi. Large numbers of journalists visited Kwangsi on extended tours, and most returned with glowing accounts of their visits.

What most impressed the visitors was not the backwoods schemes of modernisation which Kwangsi was undertaking, but the new spirit which they felt within the province, which caused one observer to refer to the province as a ' New Sparta '.[79] This spartan spirit was a product of the heavy infusion of the military spirit into the province, of which the militia system was the chief vehicle. It was also the effect of the strenuous attempts to banish shows of wealth by the Kwangsi leaders and officials. While many official organisations were housed in grandoise modern buildings, running the architectural gamut from classical revival to Spanish-American (most of which were probably started under Huang Shao-hsiung's flamboyant rule), their staffs, dressed in solemn grey uniforms, as befitted the new self-restraint and discipline, seemed out of place in them.

In the true Spartan mould, the provincial authorities prescribed a heavy dosage of competitive sports, both Chinese and Western. Tennis, football, basketball, swimming, traditional boxing and short-sword fighting were all encouraged and given great publicity. The Kwangsi leaders frequently attended sports meetings, to underline their official approval.

The militarisation (*chün-tui hua*) of Kwangsi grew out of the attempts of the Kwangsi leaders to incorporate the army into civilian life, both through the militia system, and through a new policy for which Pai Ch'ung-hsi took chief responsibility, known as the *San-yü cheng-ts'e.* The original motive behind this ' militarisation ' was undoubtedly a strategic one, a move to secure local peace in Kwangsi, and to protect Kwangsi from invasion. But the success of this work prompted the Kwangsi leaders to embark on much more ambitious schemes to impose the disciplined, frugal life of the soldier upon the whole population. The Kwangsi leaders never wavered in their devotion to the military way of life; they believed it to be a high calling, a calling which needed to be established in its own right. They battled against the traditionally low status of the soldier, demanding an abandonment of the old slogan ' *hao t'ieh pu tang ting, hao jen pu tang ping* ' (good iron is not used for nails, good men are not used for soldiers). They felt the need to present the soldier not as the rapacious, unruly brute that the people of Kwangsi knew, but as a public-spirited, self-disciplined, self-denying member of society. They promoted an image of the soldier which drew strongly on foreign influences, but which they also linked to historical precedents within China (and which was also strikingly similar to the image of the Communist soldier).

The first step towards promoting the army as a model for civilian life was the establishment of strong discipline within the army itself. As we saw above, one of the first moves of the Kwangsi Clique after their enforced retreat into Kwangsi was to tighten up the structure of the army, to reduce its numbers, and to clean up its ranks. This work was directed by Pai Ch'ung-hsi, and he did it with great thoroughness. In 1932, for example, he had an officer who had been caught converting army funds to his private use publicly shot, at a military parade in Nanning.[80]

The second stage was to get the militia system going, to bring the military and the people into intimate contact at the basic level. The third stage was to implement the *San-yü cheng-ts'e*. The three elements of this policy involved the militia training of all able-bodied men (*yü ping yü t'uan*), the military training of students (*yü chiang yü hsüeh*) and the raising of troops through conscription rather than through financial inducement (*yü mu yü cheng*). Pai claimed a vague and all-encompassing historical precedent for this policy; it was, he said, the kind of system which had prevailed in traditional China, until the Sung had demoted the military to a subordinate and despised position in Chinese society.[81] There were no historians to argue with him. He wanted to return to the golden age of the past, to establish the professional dignity of the soldier, to set his worth beside, or even above, the literary man.

The scheme of giving military training to students grew out of the anti-intellectual prejudices of the Kwangsi leaders. (The student-training scheme had also a practical aim – to create potential officers and militia leaders.) Li Tsung-jen expressed this anti-intellectual prejudice when he described most students as flabby in mind and body; military training, he said, would give them backbone. He and Pai criticised students and intellectuals for their inactivity in the defence of the nation, for their tendency to satisfy their outrage at the nation's shame in speeches, instead of in action.[82] Li and Pai wanted to eradicate the disdain for the military, which had kept the educated and privileged away from the army; enforced military training would have this effect, and would purge the students of romantic and impractical attitudes, of such ' perverse habits ' as playing violins and flutes.[83]

The atmosphere at Kwangsi University, the main showplace of student military training, was austere and puritanical; all students wore military uniforms (without military insignia), and lived a life of extreme discipline; there were no ' frivolous ' subjects, such as literature, on the curriculum.[84] The students were organised into military units, and trained by regular officers; they were obliged to do physical labour, both around the university during term, and on farms during vacations. This kind of physical labour would not, as an outside commentator noted, have been seen in any other university in China.[85] It fitted Pai Ch'ung-hsi's belief that intellectuals were corrupted by the softness of urban life: ' Many people, especially intellectuals, regard rural life as intolerable, and gather together in the cities, with the result that the villages are tragically on the verge of collapse.' [86]

Within a short space of time, certainly by 1934, the province had taken on a superficial air of military discipline and purpose. Li, Pai and Huang Hsü-ch'u set the style, living apparently frugal and disciplined lives. There is no solid evidence that they used their positions to amass personal fortunes, as one might expect of men in their positions. None of them deposited large fortunes outside China, as did many Kuomintang military and political figures, nor do Communist attacks accuse them of enriching themselves. Their lead was followed by lower officers and officials; the impression was given of a happy integration of the leaders with the masses. As one chauvinistic westerner remarked:

> It would be difficult to describe the cordial spirit that exists between the officials and people in this oriental province. To say the least, it resembles the relations between the rulers and the ruled in the best governed states in the occident.[87]

The Kwangsi leaders were anxious to create an impression of closeness to the masses, of a paternalistic concern for the welfare of the people, of an attempt to push their province, through the adoption of military standards, towards modernisation.

The puritanism of the Kwangsi leaders also found expression in policies of social reform which were similar to the policies of the New Life Movement (which was not launched until 1935, when such policies were well established in Kwangsi). Women's skirts and men's trousers had to cover the knee, women's sleeves the elbow.[88] Prostitution, gambling and opium smoking were regulated, and their operations were confined to certain areas under official supervision, out of bounds to soldiers and civil servants [89]; they were not banned, because they brought in lucrative tax income. Extravagant social behaviour was frowned upon.[90] In 1933, a list of regulations for 'the improvement of social customs' (Kai-liang feng-su kuei-lü) was published, which admonished the people to refrain from extravagance at weddings, funerals and births. Wedding presents were not to exceed 160 yüan in value, and were to be Chinese products (kuo-huo). Marriage below the age of eighteen for men and sixteen for girls was forbidden. The populace was ordered not to consult witches, wizards or any upholders of superstitious practices.[91] Paradoxically, the attack on superstition coincided with ascription of supernatural powers to the house-fly and the mosquito. Gaudy posters used in a public-health campaign showed braves battling against a ferocious tiger and a loathsome serpent; on the tiger's back was the character for 'fly', on the snake's, that for 'mosquito'.[92]

The campaign against popular religion, begun in the 1920s, was continued with great enthusiasm. Many temples were closed down, to the delight of the French missionaries in the province, who believed that the Kwangsi people would turn towards Catholicism rather than live without religion. For the first time in over 50 years of pastoral work, large numbers of converts were made; the destruction of a large temple in Nanning coincided with the construction of a new chapel there.[93] For the first time the missionaries' charitable work received official approval. Under the patronage of the beautiful Madame Li Tsung-jen, a forceful personality who saw herself in the same mould as Madame Chiang Kai-shek, fulfilling the same wifely role as adviser and alter ego, charitable works became fashionable.[94] There was a marked reduction in officially-sponsored hostility to foreigners, with one important exception: the Japanese. Though Japanese advisers were being used to help train the new air force, they had to be kept well out of sight. Publicly, the Kwangsi leaders kept up a strident anti-Japanese campaign.

The new atmosphere in Kwangsi restored the military reputation of the province, which had plummeted after the defeats of 1929 and 1930; it was tested in 1934, when Communist troops passed through the northern part of the province, at the start of the Long March. They were pursued by large numbers of Nanking troops, with whom the Kwangsi authorities were principally concerned; the entry of Nanking troops into the province would eradicate Kwangsi's autonomy. Two-thirds of Kwangsi's regular troops were sent into the area, supplemented by 200,000 local militia men.[95] The Kwangsi leaders were determined to get the Communist forces out of Kwangsi as quickly as possible. Pai Ch'ung-hsi opened up a corridor across the edge of the province, cleared the local population from it, and destroyed food supplies within it. He used guile to convince the local population, when they returned, that the Communists were really bandits: fire-raisers, masquerading as Communists, committed acts of arson in the wake of the Communist forces. His tactics were successful: 'on the one hand the Red Army had nowhere to lodge and nothing to eat; on the other hand, the local people suspected the Red Army as fire-raisers, and therefore showed hatred towards the Red Army'.[96] The Communist forces took only seventeen days to cross Kwangsi, and suffered heavy casualties.

There is no indication that the Kwangsi Clique co-operated tactically with Nanking forces, though Nanking later claimed that they did.[97] Kwangsi wanted only to keep out of any major involvement, either with the Communist troops, or with the Nanking pursuers. They acted against the Communists, but only to keep them moving – out of Kwangsi.[98]

We have now examined the fields of reconstruction in Kwangsi which fell under two of the three sections of the *San tzu cheng-ts'e*, that is, military reform and the militarisation of the province, and the reform of local administration. We shall now look at the third section, that of *tzu chi*, economic self-sufficiency.

The main concern of the Kwangsi authorities in the field of economic reconstruction was to ensure Kwangsi's economic independence. The provincial authorities were handicapped by the province's poverty, by the depressed economic situation in China and abroad, and by the fluctuating rates of exchange between Kwangsi's currency and Chinese and foreign currencies.[99] Kwangsi's economy – except for isolated sectors in the remoter areas of the province – was dominated from outside, chiefly by Canton and Hong Kong. Kwangsi's exports consisted of livestock, grain and perishable products for the Canton market, and of tung oil for the international market. The market prices of most of these products were moving downwards (partly due to the world depression), and Kwangsi's markets were contracting.[100] Total external trade was declining, and there were large numbers of business failures in the main commercial centres of Kwangsi.[101] Trade figures for 1933 at Wuchow and Nanning were well below those for 1928, the last year in which figures were not affected by internal disruption.[102] Kwangsi started her plans for economic reconstruction in the teeth of a severe trade recession which affected not only Kwangsi, but the whole of southwest China.

As trade declined, Cantonese merchants, who dominated the trade of the province, began to remove themselves and their capital from the province. (Cantonese merchants controlled 23 out of 24 banks in

Wuchow; only 19 per cent of the businesses in that city were actually owned by Kwangsi natives.[103]) By 1935, the population of Wuchow, the economic hub of the province, had shrunk to half the figure of 120,000 which it reached at the peak of its prosperity.[104]

The currency situation was very precarious. Kwangsi was suffering a heavy outflow of silver; in some areas of the province, silver had virtually disappeared from circulation. Even more seriously, as far as the bulk of the population was concerned, the value of copper cash (determined in relation to silver), the main means of exchange, was falling. In many areas, the value of copper cash had halved over the ten years up to 1933.[105] The provincial bank issued paper currency, but fell quickly into the trap of issuing unbacked notes; in 1934, $6,600,000 worth of paper currency was issued, in 1936 between $40 and $60,000,000.[106] These un-backed notes only increased the general monetary instability of the pro-vince, forcing prices within the province up, and increasing the impover-ishment of the population.[107] At the same time, the decline in trade put many people out of work, especially in the riverine areas; in 1933, for example, about ten per cent of the working population of Kuei hsien, an important trade centre between Nanning and Wuchow, was un-employed.[108] The cost of living was rising fairly rapidly, and many people were falling into destitution, becoming vagrants (yu-min).

This was a grim background against which to launch a programme of economic reconstruction; since many of the factors that contributed to it were outside the control of the Kwangsi authorities, the provincial government directed its attention to trying to improve what was within its control, and in particular to trying to balance the adverse trading situation. Tariffs and controls were placed on imports, local industries were developed to provide import-substitutes, and exports encouraged: a heavy programme of road building was undertaken to improve com-munications.[109]

The general economic policy governing the provincial government's actions seems to have been a rough and ready combination of private enterprise and government control. None of the Kwangsi leaders knew much about economics, nor were they interested in economic theory. They patched together snippets from traditional Chinese theory and practice, from current Western thought and from current practice within China. This theoretical weakness gave their economic policy a rather haphazard air. In other fields of reconstruction, the Kwangsi leaders had attempted to evolve a theoretical framework of their own; but economic theory was too much for them. They compensated to some extent by making use of modern economic techniques; the Statistical

Bureau of the provincial government functioned well, and large-scale economic reports were compiled.

To regulate imports, and to check the quality of exports, a trade bureau was set up at Wuchow. Various imports, chiefly luxury goods, were banned altogether; imports of goods which could be manufactured locally, such as cotton cloth, were discouraged.[110] One category of imports virtually disappeared: the boycott of Japanese goods, instituted after the Mukden Incident, was almost watertight.[111] These kinds of import restrictions could not be pushed too far; Kwangsi had a 700-mile frontier with Kwangtung, and heavily-taxed goods could be easily smuggled.[112]

To provide local import-substitutes, the provincial government adopted a dual policy of encouraging private enterprise through tax concessions, and of injecting government capital into wholly or partially government-owned enterprises. A number of factories and workshops were set up, to supplement existing private enterprises, but their scale of operation was very small, and their output can have had little effect on import figures. Even at Wuchow, the commercial centre of the province, industry was in its infancy.[113] In 1935, there were only 65 factories in the province, 54 privately-owned and 11 government-owned. Kwangsi had no paper mill, and only one tannery.[114]

There was no surplus capital in private hands within the province to finance industrial development. Landlords preferred to invest capital in lucrative usury, merchants were doing so badly that they had no surplus. Attempts were made to obtain investment capital from Kwangsi natives living outside the province, but there is no evidence that this scheme yielded significant investments.[115] Foreign investment was equally difficult to obtain:

' the provision of foreign capital for sound schemes is the principal requirement of this area [Kwangtung and Kwangsi], but the present [1935] world unrest, the lack of clearly defined and realisable security, and the spirit of economic nationalism and high taxation in China, do not at present dispose financial interests to engage in schemes involving long credits.' [116]

The development of exports centred on tung oil and mining products. Tung oil usually accounted for about 30 per cent of Kwangsi's exports, and plans were now made to turn the province into the ' land of tung ' (*t'ung chih kuo*). In 1933, every able-bodied man was ordered to plant ten tung saplings per annum, and special committees were set up in every *hsien* to supervise the work.[117] This kind of project was a long-term one, and could not be expected to produce rapid success. As far as minerals were concerned, Kwangsi possessed good deposits of tin and manganese, and thanks to the work of Ting Wen-chiang in the late 1920s (see above, p. 110), the provincial government was well informed on the location and potential of mineral resources. The main problem was to find methods of exploiting them commercially. This the Kwangsi Government left to private mining companies, controlling the industry only through the licensing of concessionaires.[118]

None of these activities had much effect on the adverse balance of trade. The import surplus was reduced from the point, in 1933, where it ran at three times the province's exports,[119] but Kwangsi was not able to bring its trade into balance, nor to halt the outflow of money from the province to pay for imports. With its trade out of balance, the province's hope of economic self-sufficiency remained a dream.

Another aspect of government economic activity was taxation reform, a reform which consisted not of reducing taxation, but of simplifying the means by which it was collected. Many petty taxes were abolished; systems of direct tax collection replaced tax farming; local taxation offices (*hsien*) were put under the provincial office.[120] These reforms secured a rise in provincial income every year until 1937, a rise that was partly accounted for by increased efficiency in collection, but also by an increasing burden of taxation. But, except in 1934, the rise in income did not keep pace with the rise in expenditure.[121]

In 1934, the provincial budget was balanced for almost the first time in living memory. This achievement was due not to improved financial management, but to the enormous rise in the income from ' opium suppression fines ' (the tax on opium in transit), as normal traffic, disrupted by the warfare within Kwangsi, resumed. Kwangsi also managed to attract much of the traffic in opium which during Kwangsi rule at Wuhan had passed through that city; opium taxation at Wuhan declined by almost 50 per cent between 1929 and 1933.[122]

The Kwangsi Government was dependent on opium income; 50 per cent of the annual provincial revenue was derived from opium taxation.[123] The government tried to keep down opium consumption within the province, and very little opium was grown, but taxing the transit trade in opium was another matter. The commercial prosperity of the province, limited as it was, depended on the opium trade, in which a large proportion of private businesses were involved.[124] The government participated in the trade, besides taxing it; opium caravans coming from Kweichow, where 70 per cent of transit opium originated, were guarded by Kwangsi troops; from Wuchow to Canton they were often conveyed in Kwangsi gunboats. The same treatment was given to consignments from Yunnan.[125] The opium caravans were enormous; it was quite common for caravans of 2,000 horses to arrive at Pose, the trans-shipment point for the West River system from Yunnan.[126] The Kwangsi authorities built a good motor road up to the Kweichow border, nominally as a reconstruction scheme, but clearly to ease the transport of opium. On this road in 1935, a French missionary saw a heavily-guarded convoy of 25 lorries, carrying many tons of opium.[127]

Kweichow was virtually a commercial dependency of Kwangsi, and ultimately of Kwangtung. But when Nanking troops occupied the province in their pursuit of the Communists on the Long March, Kweichow was forced to switch allegiance. Opium from Kweichow again flowed out to the north, through Hunan to Wuhan.[128] Kwangsi revenue from opium taxation declined sharply, precipitating a financial crisis within the province.[129]

This development confirmed the opinion of H. G. W. Woodhead, the editor of the *China Year Book*, that regional independence in southwest China depended to a great extent on the opium revenues available to regional militarists:

> It is difficult to see how disbandment will ever become practicable until the Szechwan, Yunnan, Kweichow and Kwangsi militarists have been deprived of this source of revenue. They are able to obstruct or defy the Central Government only because they are in a position to maintain their armies out of this illicit source of revenue. Deprived of this source of income, they would have to conform to the wishes of the National Government.[130]

The Kwangsi leaders apparently felt no moral repugnance about their opium trading; the trade was carried on quite openly. Only one concession was made to propriety: opium was referred to officially as 'special goods' or 'mountain goods'; it did not appear as a regular item on budget sheets, and to balance the omission, military expenditure was also omitted.

The crisis precipitated by the loss of opium revenue after 1935 is an indication of the fundamental instability of the Kwangsi economic situation. The disproportionate dependence on opium income, and the equally disproportionate expenditure on the military, created a highly precarious situation.

The only really successful aspect of economic reconstruction in Kwangsi was the road-building programme. The work started by Huang Shao-hsiung between 1926 and 1929 was continued: in 1933, Kwangsi had more roads than any province except Shantung and Kwangtung.[131] The main function of road building was not in fact to help trade; Kwangsi still had very few motor vehicles, petrol was imported and expensive, and most of Kwangsi's exports were bulky primary products which could not bear heavy transportation costs.[132] There seem to have been three main reasons for the massive road-building programme. The first was to provide work for disbanded soldiers and for the unemployed, to prevent them from becoming bandits; road workers did their work 'voluntarily' or under *corvée* regulation, receiving food and lodging, but no pay. The second reason was strategic, to allow the swift and simple transportation of troops throughout the province; a good road network made it possible to centralise troop concentrations, and eliminate many small garrisons. The third reason was to help opium traffic. Good roads were built up to the Kweichow border, and between Pose and Nanning. The population of the province benefited very little from the new road system; though many of them laboured in the construction of the roads, they were not allowed to use their wheelbarrows on them; since this was the vehicle most widely used by the peasantry, they were effectively debarred from transporting goods on the new roads.[133]

The government had plans for the development of other more modern forms of communication, such as railways and aviation. But little progress was made. A prestige airline was established in 1934, to link the major cities of Kwangsi with Canton, but its operations were limited. There was no railway construction until after the start of the Anti-Japanese War, when the link between Kweilin and Hengchow (Hunan) was finally constructed, after twenty years of planning.

The schemes of economic reconstruction scarcely scratched the surface of Kwangsi's misery. There was no attempt to eradicate the real evils which oppressed the bulk of Kwangsi's population – the land tenure system, and the widespread practice of usury. The taxation burden was made heavier rather than lighter. Economic self-sufficiency was not achieved. The province continued to depend on opium for the bulk of its revenue.

The provincial government was involved in other aspects of reconstruction work besides the economic. It directed middle and upper education, and was also responsible for major experimental reconstruction projects.

In education, the government put a heavy stress on practical and vocational training, to produce the technicians and managers for the future development of reconstruction work. But Kwangsi had neither the money nor the trained teachers to administer a very large programme. There was an enormous imbalance between the basic level of education and the upper levels: in 1933 there were only 577 university and technical school students and 14,533 middle school students to 650,000 primary school children.[134] This imbalance was potentially dangerous, for it meant that there was no possibility of fulfilling the expectations which many children in the primary system might have of getting further education.

In the experimental area, the government sponsored schemes of re-afforestation, irrigation, veterinary work and local co-operatives. A small co-operative was set up near Nanning to demonstrate how a co-opera-tive association could help the peasantry. It seems to have worked principally as a loan society, though it probably also fostered co-operative labour, a practice which was already well established. It was not a success; very few peasants joined, and there was an ever present danger that it would be taken over by the local gentry, whose preroga-tives as usurers the scheme tried to pre-empt.[135]

The government's major experimental schemes were in agriculture; several experimental stations were set up, the largest of which was at Liuchow. The station covered 100,000 *mou*, and its principal function was to demonstrate reclamation techniques, in the hope that it would stimulate a larger movement to open up the huge area of undeveloped land in Kwangsi.[136] The experiment attracted attention, but was not a great success. Many of the peasants drafted into the area departed, and the director, Wu T'ing-yang, was eventually forced to resign, accused of overspending and overbearing behaviour.[137]

Looked at in the worst light, the provincial government's attempts at reconstruction between 1931 and 1936 appear as a string of half-baked and predoomed schemes. Looked at in their best light (as the Kwangsi leaders were not afraid to view them) they represent an attempt to introduce change, which struggled unsuccessfully against adverse cir-cumstances. The truth is somewhere in the middle: that the govern-ment leaders were interested in change; that they did not know how to go about it in the most practicable way; that their determination not to unleash a social revolution prevented them from making any funda-mental changes. They were well-meaning men, looking to the future, but still held firmly by the past.

10

The second defeat

During the first half of the 1930s, the Kwangsi Clique ruled the province of Kwangsi as an autonomous unit. Its leaders allowed no external interference in the affairs of their province, either from the National Government at Nanking, or from their neighbours. Their attitude towards their neighbours, especially towards Yunnan and Kweichow, was proprietorial – the Clique was the strongest single political and military entity in southwest China – but it did not involve the extension of Kwangsi control over them. The Kwangsi Clique had rejected the idea of Kwangsi expansion; its leaders turned from the overweaning desire to expand the Clique's area of control to an attempt to administer the limited area of Kwangsi in a constructive way.

They did not reject national and nationalist concerns. There were two strands to their policies: Self-defence meant the protection of Kwangsi from threats by the Central forces, *and* the creation of a base for the protection of China against foreign invasion; Self-government meant the autonomous administration of Kwangsi province *and* the start at local self-government throughout the nation; economic Self-sufficiency meant the establishment of an independent economy in Kwangsi *and* a step towards national economic reconstruction. When Pai Ch'ung-hsi said that ' the reconstruction of Kwangsi serves as the basis for the restoration of the Chinese people ',[1] and that ' reconstructing Kwangsi is the means, restoring China the end '[2] what he was saying was that he thought Kwangsi had found a means of rationalising the apparently contradictory commitment to both the region and the nation. The Kwangsi leaders still felt themselves to be nationalists; but nationalism was a remote and rarefied ideal, a distant vision of a strong, rich, united China. As regional rulers, the Kwangsi leaders were confronted with problems which nationalism could not speak to: regional defence, local administration, local economic revival. To cope with these problems, the Kwangsi leaders created a series of programmes designed to meet the specific needs of their province; to apply them, they fostered a sense of

194

provincial distinctiveness and provincial unity. Out of existing, incoherent provincialism, the Kwangsi leaders created a positive provincialism, founded on an historical image of the province as warlike
and courageous, tough and spartan.

There is apparently a contradiction here: how could men who thought
themselves to be nationalists commit themselves to the enhancement
of regionalism? What they believed they were doing was putting regionalism at the service of nationalism. They established the ultimate centrality of nationalism, and made regionalism its correlative, the first
stage on the road to national revival. The strong China of the future
would be constructed on a series of strong provinces. Regionalism and
nationalism became mutually supportive, not mutually contradictory.
Since the strong nation would develop from its strong regions, regionalism became the servant of nationalism, ' the basis for the restoration of
the Chinese people '. And nationalism in the future justified regionalism
in the present, the means towards the end. The Kwangsi leaders tried to
find a position in which both the demands of independent military
power-holding and of the principles of the Kuomintang were satisfied.
They refused to see themselves as enemies of the nation, or as fundamental offenders against the new orthodoxy of the Kuomintang.

The ideology of the Kuomintang had established itself as the new
political and intellectual orthodoxy, and was given at least lip-service
even by those who had no intention of implementing its policies. It part-
filled a yawning gap in the Chinese polity – the absence, after the collapse
of the Ch'ing Dynasty, of an all-encompassing ideology. The limitations
of this new ideology were so vast that a comparison with the lost Confucian orthodoxy seems incongruous – it lacked cohesion, it had no
established core of devotees, it lacked an organisational framework, its
principles were vague – but it still provided a focal point for political
commitment, a commitment without which the Kwangsi leaders, for
example, could not function. Their specific political and economic principles were ill-formulated, a hotch-potch of ideas drawn from whatever
sources presented themselves, or caught the attention of the Clique and
its advisers. An adherence to the ideology of the Kuomintang gave
coherence to confusion, provided an umbrella for uncertainty.

The strength of the new orthodoxy is underlined by the fate of the
survivors of the old, Confucian order in the Japanese puppet governments in north China. Looked at in the most charitable light, these
elderly, conservative men were following ' the old Chinese tradition of
giving more or less disinterested service to whomsoever happened to be
in power at any given time '.[3] They were completely ineffective, partly
because they were puppets, and were allowed no real authority by their

masters; partly because they were held in contempt by many Chinese under their jurisdiction just because they were puppets; but also because they represented an order that was dead. The Japanese were eventually forced to operate through a puppet Kuomintang Government. Even with complete military control, they could not revive the old order, but had to use at least the form of the new.

The independence of Kwangsi and of other provinces during the early 1930s seriously weakened the National Government at Nanking, as it was intended to. In physical terms, it undermined Nanking's claims to govern a reunited China, and it made Nanking's moves against other internal enemies more difficult. In political terms, it helped to confuse still further the ideology of the Kuomintang. It also showed up the weakness of many of Nanking's economic and social programmes; by displaying a province which, though poor, was reasonably well administered and was embarked upon a programme of reconstruction, Kwangsi provided a parallel standard against which to measure Nanking's progress towards these goals. The independent provinces never represented a threat to Nanking's stability; they were no longer expansionist, nor did they inspire other provinces more closely linked to Nanking to attempt to establish their own autonomy. But they were more than pinpricks; they were a constant reminder of the limited nature of Nanking's control, and, in the case of Kwangsi, of Nanking's slow progress towards reconstruction.

Nanking could not prevent the continuation of Kwangsi's independence by military means; through the early 1930s it was preoccupied with the Communists in Kiangsi, with more threatening military blocs in north China, and with the Japanese encroachment. The southwestern provinces equally were not concerned to challenge Nanking; they were content to remain within their independent satrapies. They no longer had the capacity to attack the well-established Nanking Government. After the collapse of the independent government in Canton in 1930, the southwestern generals stopped giving support indiscriminately to any anti-Nanking movements. Neither Kwangtung nor Kwangsi gave support to the Fukien Revolt (1933), though such support was widely anticipated, not least by the leaders of the Revolt, one of whom was Li Chi-shen, formerly a member of the Kwangsi Clique.[4] The Southwest Political Council was maintained as an organ of opposition to Nanking, and issued a stream of bitter denunciations of the Nanking Government, but its denunciations took no practical form. The southwestern leaders refused numerous peace overtures from Nanking, but they also refused to co-operate with anti-Nanking elements where there was no specific interest of their own involved.

This stalemate persisted until 1935. In that year the situation changed. Nanking extended its authority deep into south and southwest China, by ousting the Communists from Kiangsi, and by gaining control over Kweichow and Yunnan as its forces pursued the fleeing Communist forces. The independent leaders of Kwangtung and Kwangsi found themselves encircled by Nanking troops. This encirclement had a catastrophic effect on the Kwangsi economy; Kweichow opium no longer passed through the province, but went north through Wuhan; Kwangsi's income was halved. In Kwangtung, Ch'en Chi-t'ang's position was threatened by the loss of support of many of his subordinates, who began to move towards Nanking. Ch'en's rule in Kwangtung had brought unusual prosperity to the province, but he had alienated many of his followers by allowing too many of the fruits of this prosperity to pass into the hands of his family and friends.[5]

By late 1935, Nanking had an overwhelming military force facing Kwangtung and Kwangsi; between 400,000 and 600,000 troops were massed in a great arc stretching through Fukien, Kiangsi, Hunan, Kweichow and Yunnan. Against these, Kwangtung and Kwangsi could only muster between 270,000 and 300,000 men.[6] Under this military threat, there were signs that the hardline of resistance to Nanking was weakening. The Southwest Political Council sent a group of representatives to the Fifth Congress of the Kuomintang (November 1935), its first open participation in Kuomintang affairs for some years. The Kwangsi leaders received the newly appointed (by Nanking) Governor of Kweichow, Wu Chung-hsin, in Kwangsi, on his way to Kweichow after the Congress, and took him on a tour through the province. Wu had been Pai Ch'ung-hsi's Chief-of-Staff in Peking in 1928, and his appointment to Kweichow was undoubtedly made partly in the hope that this personal tie would help to bring about a settlement with the Kwangsi Clique.[7]

At the same time the southwestern leaders were preparing for war. In May 1936, Hu Han-min, the chief political opponent of Nanking in the south, died, and his death stimulated an upsurge of anti-Nanking and anti-Japanese sentiment. The southwestern leaders used this revival of popular concern to launch a massive anti-Japanese campaign, which was by association a campaign against the weakness of Nanking's resistance to Japan.[8] In May 1936, Kwangtung and Kwangsi forces were reorganised as the Anti-Japanese National Salvation Army (K'ang-Jih chiu-kuo chün), commanded by Ch'en Chi-t'ang, Li Tsung-jen and Pai Ch'ung-hsi.[9] Ts'ai T'ing-k'ai, the hero of the 1931 resistance to Japan in Shanghai, was persuaded to return from exile in Hong Kong to lend his prestige to the army.[10] On 1 June, an official campaign was launched (the *Liu-i yün-tung*); a battery of telegrams was issued, calling for resistance to

Japan, and troops moved north into Hunan, ostensibly on their way to fight the Japanese in north China.[11] The independent generals of southwest China took their last stand as regionalists – on a nationalist plank.

The campaign collapsed almost immediately. Many Cantonese leaders defected to Nanking, according to prearranged (and frequently prepaid) arrangements with Nanking. Early in July, Ch'en Chi-t'ang fled to Hong Kong, his career in Kwangtung in ruins, but his retirement handsomely provided for by a fortune stowed away against such disaster.[12]

The Cantonese collapse ended the anti-Japanese anti-Nanking campaign, and brought Kwangtung under Nanking control, but it did not bring Kwangsi to heel. Kwangsi forces were withdrawn into the province to prepare for siege. The whole province was mobilised, all able-bodied men were drafted for military service. Transport was requisitioned by the military; civilians fled the towns, fearing bombing; there were constant air-raid alerts. The Kwangsi currency slumped, and the provincial government started printing notes to subsidise the army; the Kwangsi economy teetered on the edge of collapse.[13] A ' National ' Government was set up at Nanning, with Li Chi-shen as Chairman; Ts'ai T'ing-k'ai's Nineteenth Route Army was reformed in Kwangsi; Kwangsi officers and men swore blood oaths to defend the province to the last.[14]

But the tide was turning against Kwangsi. Chiang Kai-shek presented himself in a light of statesmanlike magnanimity, and flew to Canton to continue negotiations for a peaceful settlement. The Japanese pleasure at China's obvious disunity created pressure for a settlement, which was enhanced by their reaction to an incident at Pakhoi, in southwestern Kwangtung. The only Japanese in that city, a medicine dealer, was murdered by troops of the Nineteenth Route Army; in retaliation, Japanese gunboats moved into Pakhoi harbour, and for a while seemed about to use the Incident as a pretext for aggression in that area. The Incident was settled at the end of September, but by that stage the threatening Japanese behaviour, and the realisation that it evoked of the weakness of a disunited China, had forced the Kwangsi leaders to move towards settlement with Nanking. This would be a patriotic act; continued resistance to Nanking could only be construed as selfish blindness to China's danger.

Early in September, a settlement was reached; the terms were not harsh; Li Chi-shen was ordered abroad, Pai Ch'ung-hsi to Nanking [15]; Li Tsung-jen was permitted to remain in Kwangsi, as Pacification Commissioner; Huang Hsü-ch'u remained as Chairman of Kwangsi, but was ordered to accept Nanking appointees to key financial posts. Nanking agreed to make an immediate draft of $3,000,000 to ease the financial crisis in Kwangsi. A reduction in the size of the Kwangsi Army was ordered, but Nanking troops were withdrawn from the Kwangsi borders.[16]

For the second time, the Kwangsi Clique had succumbed to Nanking, though its defeat in 1936 was far less shattering than that of 1929. The Clique retained a reduced control over Kwangsi province; its internal policies were not changed. The policies of reconstruction initiated in the early 1930s continued to be implemented, in many cases with greater success than in the earlier period. The militia expanded enormously, especially after the start of the Anti-Japanese War. The War brought an economic boom to the province, as industries displaced from Occupied China moved to the south.

Personally, the Kwangsi leaders emerged from the confrontation with Nanking with their reputations enhanced. Kwangsi's open call for resistance to Japan won widespread support from patriotic organisations, whether justified or not.

> Whatever may have been the motives of the South-West leaders in their anti-Japanese propaganda, the fact remains that they have unleashed a flood of patriotic passion throughout their own provinces, and have gained themselves wide-spread sympathy among the patriotic elements of the nation.[17]

Li Tsung-jen and Pai Ch'ung-hsi went on to enhance these reputations still further during the Anti-Japanese War.

THE RECONSTRUCTION MOVEMENT – A COMPARATIVE EXAMINATION

How much was the Kwangsi Reconstruction Movement representative of reconstruction projects elsewhere in China, during the decade from 1928 to 1937? The National Government laid numerous plans for reconstruction; several other independent provinces, notably Shansi and Kwangtung, launched their own movements; there were numerous small-scale experiments, such as the Ting hsien mass education experiment, and the Tsoup'ing experiment.

In the absence of detailed studies of the parts of China controlled by the Nanking Government, direct comparison with Nanking-sponsored reconstruction projects is difficult. We may look at two general works, both of which are sympathetic to the Nanking Government; the first is a contemporary account, George Taylor's *The Reconstruction Movement in China* (1936), the second a recent study, *The Strenuous Decade,* edited by Paul Sih. Both list large numbers of projects which the National Government and its agencies initiated, and present an impressive display of *intention*. Neither of them, however, can point to many concrete achievements. Taylor's book, published just before the outbreak of war with Japan, was still optimistic; Sih's can only blame the lack of demonstrable achievement on the Japanese invasion. If sympathetic sources are hard put to paint a glowing picture of Nanking's reconstruction work, then Nanking's achievements were probably very limited. We may ascribe this poverty of achievement to a variety of factors: failure to establish unified authority over the whole of China; foreign pressure and invasion; preoccupation with eradicating Communism; the lack of a solid ideological commitment to social change; lack of political unity; lack of positive leadership. These factors combined to block the progress of reconstruction work in Nanking's China. In comparison to Nanking's achievements then, Kwangsi's must rate well, however small they were.

We are presented with different problems in comparing the Kwangsi Reconstruction Movement with the small-scale reconstruction enterprises: here the question of scale makes comparison difficult. The Ting hsien and Tsoup'ing experiments, and the various small experiments directed by Nanking, operated within a limited sphere, usually that of a single *hsien*. They were concerned only with implementing specific schemes, not with administering a large area, as was the Kwangsi Clique. Some of their schemes paralleled work that was going on in Kwangsi – mass education is one example – but while such schemes represented the main focus of endeavour, for Kwangsi they were only part of a much larger programme.

Our most useful comparisons can be made with another single province experiment, that of Yen Hsi-shan's Shansi. Donald Gillin's illuminating study of Yen provides the information on which a comparison may be made. There are great dissimilarities between the two provinces – Shansi was more involved with other provinces than was Kwangsi; it was considerably more developed commercially and industrially; Yen had controlled the province for a much longer period – but there are also important similarities. Both provinces were administered by men who depended for their authority on military control. Both were hostile to Nanking. Both had a strongly developed sense of provincial identity. Both embarked on major programmes of reconstruction – Shansi's was the Ten Year Plan for Reconstruction (*Shan-hsi sheng cheng-fu shih-nien chien-she chi-hua*), which was principally concerned with the economy of the province.[18]

Let us look at the points of comparison between the two provinces and their leaders, taking first of all the question of political attitudes and ideological direction. Both Yen and the Kwangsi Clique were military men, as were the bulk of their immediate supporters. Both were influenced by the ideology of the Kuomintang, and formulated their policies within its broad framework, not so much on the basis of political conviction as on a recognition that this was the new orthodoxy. Both were eclectic in their secondary ideological borrowings from Chinese and Western sources. Both were practical and disciplinarian, trusting military methods and suspicious of intellectual solutions. But these similarities were outweighed by differences. First of all, Yen was more influenced by foreign ideas than were the Kwangsi leaders. Though he was anti-Communist, he had a profound respect for the Soviet Union, and for its achievements in modernising Russia.[19] He was also attracted by the authoritarian Fascist movements in Europe. Secondly, Yen was much less committed to the idea of revival through militarisation than were the Kwangsi leaders. He relied for local control on an omni-present police force, rather than on combining local control with militarisation through the militia system, as the Kwangsi Clique did.[20] Yen was anxious to secure mass participation in his projects, but he set up no mechanism to channel and direct such participation. Thirdly, Yen's political attitudes were less clearly formulated than were those of the Kwangsi Clique. He was not concerned, as the Kwangsi leaders were, to establish himself as a respectable political figure on the national scene. He was preoccupied, in a narrower way than was the Kwangsi Clique, with the affairs of his own province.

This narrower provincialism stemmed from Yen's long administration of Shansi; he was accustomed to considering only the affairs of the province, and, periodically, the expansion of Shansi control to other provinces. He had never had more than a peripheral relationship to political developments within China. His main focus of interest, for twenty years, had been Shansi. His attitude stemmed also from the fact that his position as provincial overlord was much more vulnerable than that of the Kwangsi Clique. Shansi was much more susceptible to Nanking economic pressure, surrounded as it was by Nanking-controlled provinces. Kwangsi's economy was linked to Kwangtung, which was also independent of Nanking. Japanese influence in Shansi was strong, and although Yen frequently took up a public stance of opposition to Japan, he could not resist Japanese pressure; indeed he sometimes found it convenient to co-operate, particularly in the economic sphere.[21]

These external pressures meant that Yen did not share the Kwangsi's leaders' feelings of local omnipotence. The Kwangsi leaders had absolute local control, and were anxious to exert this control in every sphere of provincial life. They had virtually no organised local opposition to contend with. This gave them the leeway, which Yen did not have, to develop any programmes they liked.

The aims of the Kwangsi movement were overtly political, and centred around the ideal of popular organisation, and the establishment of Kwangsi as a bastion of Kuomintang ideology. They were strengthening Kwangsi to strengthen China. Yen on the other hand was primarily concerned with developing Shansi's economy for Shansi's benefit, and for the benefit of himself and his immediate subordinates. Yen was continuing, in modified form, the type of provincial rule which he had already exerted for twenty years. The Kwangsi leaders were approaching the problems of provincial administration for the first time. They were provincialists, but provincialists of a new type, who were not exclusively concerned with their own province, but saw it as part of a larger whole, the nation.

THE KWANGSI CLIQUE – A GENERAL VIEW

We must now try to piece together a general view of the Kwangsi Clique, and set it in its historical context. We must examine the tortuous relationship between form and reality which characterised its career.

The most striking feature of the Clique's general attitudes was its mixture of certainty and confusion. The Clique was very certain about the desirability of discipline, a military style of life, of authoritarian attitudes towards government, but uncertain about ideological direction, about its relationship to the Kuomintang, about its attitude to political and social problems at the local level. This confusion and uncertainty was not confined to the Kwangsi Clique; it was the key source of the ideological confusion and disjointed experimentation of the whole Kuomintang period. The Kuomintang started its political career by severing its ties with the past, by aiming at the future, in which an ill-defined new China would emerge. But the Kuomintang's advent to power in the late 1920s involved the loss of much of its revolutionary ambition. The government which emerged in 1928 was elitist, it had turned its back on mass activity, and on basic economic and social reform. It was essentially a conservative administration, conserving its position against the population directly under its control, against internal enemies, both militarist and Communist, and against alien invaders. It lost its thrust towards the future, it ceased to have any sense of historical progress.

The Kwangsi leaders participated closely in this process. They played an important role, in 1927 and 1928, in the crushing of the mass movements, and in the stamping out of social reform. Later on, back in Kwangsi, they remained firmly committed to authoritarianism, they went in horror of undirected mass activity. But they had not lost all vision of the future. They were not backward-looking conservatives, for they were well aware that the Confucian past was dead. It was a past for which they had no deep-seated affection; it had brought nothing but suffering, either to their province or to their own families. They were conscious of the past, and they referred frequently to historical precedent, but their choice of examples differed diametrically from those of the conservatives at Nanking. While Chiang Kai-shek extolled Tseng Kuo-fan as the man who had tried to save China from internal collapse, the Kwangsi leaders regarded him as a traitor. Their heroes were the Taipings, the rebels who had tried to overthrow the system. Memorials were erected to Taiping leaders, the provincial government sponsored the research of Taiping scholars, and published their work.[22] This interest was dictated in part by local chauvinism, by the fact that the Taiping Rebellion had started in Kwangsi, by the fact that Kwangsi had produced very few other prominent historical figures. But it went beyond a desire to extol the peculiar virtues of Kwangsi's history. Pai Ch'ung-hsi saw the Taipings as a progressive force, whose wholly admirable desire to change China had foundered on their inability to achieve internal unity, and on major strategic errors.[23] Pai sought in the Taipings, and in much earlier pre-Sung historical precedents, examples of China's glorious military tradition, a tradition which he believed had been swamped, with disastrous consequences, by the civilian, scholarly tradition. He saw China's revival in terms of a revival of the disciplined, military approach to China's problems.

This conviction of the rightness of the military way could not be more than a means to an end; the end itself still had to be formulated, and this was where the Kwangsi leaders started to slip into confusion, to feel the lack of perspective on the future. Their confusion led them to take up an ill-formulated ideological position: on the one hand they kept themselves within the broad framework of the Kuomintang ideology, which they accepted as the new orthodoxy; on the other hand they borrowed eclectically from social and political theories, Chinese and foreign; and in the third place they reacted pragmatically to the changing conditions of the moment. They had no systematic ideological position, above all they had no clear view of where they were going, beyond their determination to drag Kwangsi into the present. Their dilemma was very much like that of Yen Hsi-shan in Shansi, who believed he had drawn together the 'best features of militarism, nationalism, anarchism, democracy, capitalism, communism, individualism, imperialism, universalism, paternalism and utopianism'.[24] This eclecticism was not, as Jerome Ch'en has pointed out, a symptom of ideological chicanery, but of the lack of an overriding ideological direction which bedevilled all those concerned in the 1930s with 'what was to be done' in China, a dilemma that was only solved when the Communists, with their clear sense of historical direction, came to power.[25]

What then did the Kwangsi Clique feel it was doing? Why did it embark upon a scheme for reconstruction, for provincial development? There was no physical pressure upon it to do so – after it had re-established its hold over the province (by about 1932) its control was absolute, and could resist any internal or external pressure. Nanking left Kwangsi alone, the people of Kwangsi were concerned not with schemes of development, but simply with staying alive. They had to be roused from political apathy by the Clique; there was no question of the Clique's responding to popular pressure. The Reconstruction Movement was inspired from the top, from the leaders of the Clique.

There were probably two main inspirations behind the Clique's policies of reconstruction. The first was a 'national' one, a concern to implement Sun Yat-sen's designs for reconstruction in the period after the establishment of Kuomintang authority. In this sense the Kwangsi leaders saw themselves as leaders of national development, as attempting to move their province along the path prescribed by the *Kuo Fu*. They were putting themselves in harmony with the new orthodoxy, moving, however imperfectly, towards the new China. They had some sense of the nation's future, though as we have seen, it was a very confused sense, and it contained no clear goals.

The second inspiration was a local one, a self-conscious form of regionalism. They were attempting to develop Kwangsi for its own sake, not as a unit outside the national framework, but as a part of the nation independent of the National Government. Their regionalism contained no hint of secession, but it did contain a strong feeling of the province as a distinct entity. The Kwangsi leaders were concerned to build up their province's historical consciousness, to establish its special characteristics, to present it, to itself and to China, as a unique and valuable area. They were not claiming a Kwangsi monopoly of such attributes; there was an assumption that any province could do the same, given the will. What their self-conscious regionalism involved was an attempt to provide a practical framework for political, economic and social activity, more concrete than the amorphous national framework, a framework which was geared to local conditions, which was easily understood by the populace.

This high-sounding definition is reduced immediately when we remember that the self-conscious regionalism of the Kwangsi Clique emerged only *after* its ambition to dominate a multi-province region had been crushed, that the Clique's provincial control depended not on the leadership of aroused provincial sentiment, but on military control. Nevertheless, the impulse to improve the province must be seen as the key reason why the Kwangsi Clique moved beyond simple provincial control to the initiation of a provincial Reconstruction Movement.

It may also be seen as a partial explanation of the divergence between form and reality which characterised many of the individual facets of reconstruction. The Kwangsi Clique managed to formulate detailed *forms* for the reconstruction of the province; it seldom managed to make the form reality, at least in a complete sense. There were objective reasons for this failure, chief of which were the poverty of the province and the shortness of time available before the loss of independence in 1936. Most of the schemes by which the Clique's leaders hoped to establish themselves as saviours of Kwangsi were long-term, needing for their implementation a prolonged period of peace and freedom from external intervention. As it turned out, they had at most five years, during which they were never isolated from external influences. With the possibility of realisation in the future, but their desire to salvage their province in the present, form became more important to the Clique's leaders than its realisation. Lack of achievement in one field never prevented them from formulating new schemes for others, even where these were dependent on the first. They did not view their schemes for reconstruction as following a progressive pattern; their guidelines for reconstruction provided an over-arching unity, but no provisions for the stages of implementation. Though they made progress in several fields, notably in the organisation of the population under the militia system, there was no feeling that failure vitiated the programme. What mattered was that they had set out the form, not that they had made it work. Form itself came to be regarded as achievement, of which the reality, in the cases where it did emerge, was simply a confirmation.

THE DECLINE OF THE CLIQUE

The loss of provincial autonomy in 1936 meant the end of the Kwangsi Clique as an independent regional Clique. Nanking did not take over the province – Huang Hsü-ch'u remained Provincial Chairman until 1949 – nor did it break down Kwangsi regionalism. But Kwangsi was integrated into the national system, especially on the economic and financial level. The Kwangsi leaders were not punished for their long resistance to central authority, chiefly because the Central Government lacked the means to punish them. There could be no question, in 1936, with the Japanese threat growing more ominous by the day, of a punitive expedition against Kwangsi.

Within a year, China was at war with Japan, and the Kwangsi leaders moved from being ardent opponents of the National Government to being amongst its defenders against Japanese invasion. Li Tsung-jen was made Director of the Fifth War Zone and Pai Ch'ung-hsi became Director of Military Training for the National Army, and Deputy Chief-of-staff to Ho Ying-ch'in. Chiang Kai-shek still did not trust the Kwangsi generals; Pai had no front command, in spite of his reputation of one of China's foremost tacticians. He, like Chang Fa-k'uei, the only general whose military reputation rivalled Pai's, was kept in nominally authoritative but practically powerless positions for most of the war. Li Tsung-jen was allowed some actual command, but after his victory at T'aierch'uang (1938) (an improbable victory, won with inferior troops against overwhelming Japanese forces, which came in the middle of a series of shattering Chinese defeats), he, too, was put in cold storage, and spent the rest of the war fretting in inactivity and powerlessness.

Kwangsi troops, under subordinate commanders, played a more active role in the war. The Kwangsi Armies were expanded, from the reservoir of trained men created by the militia system, and were sent north to fight in central China, where they acquitted themselves well – far better than the majority of troops under Nanking's command. Kwangsi troops in the Tapieh Shan (Anhwei–Hupei border region) kept up semi-guerrilla resistance to the Japanese throughout the war.

Kwangsi province itself was radically changed by the war. The province was not finally occupied by the Japanese until 1944, and as one of the last remaining areas of Free China, it was inundated with refugees. Refugee intellectuals and students poured into the province, creating a new atmosphere of intellectual and political activity. Huang Hsü-ch'u tolerated and even encouraged their work, and established for himself a progressive reputation. The province underwent rapid economic development; manufacturing enterprises, which the Kwangsi Clique had struggled unsuccessfully to establish in the early 1930s, mushroomed. The province became, briefly, one of Free China's major economic support areas. (This rapid development backfired after the war, when there was a sudden and devastating economic recession.[26]) For seven years, the province was scarcely touched by the larger war, and prospered. When the war moved into Kwangsi, however, it suffered horribly; during the Japanese invasion, at least 100,000 people were killed, houses were burnt in huge numbers, draught animals slaughtered, factories and public buildings destroyed, and the province's communications shattered.[27]

The Kwangsi Clique ceased to exist as a functioning unit after 1936. It continued to act as a focus of loyalty for Kwangsi men serving outside the province, and as a source of low-keyed opposition to Chiang Kai-shek. But it represented no threat to the Centre, and superficially, relations between the Clique leaders and Chiang Kai-shek were friendly. (Pai Ch'ung-hsi was editor of a panegyric to Chiang, *Wei-ta ti Chiang Chu-hsi*, published in 1946.)

The new closeness proved illusory. Behind the scenes, hideous and confused wrangling went on, of a complexity which defies untangling. Chiang still did not trust the Kwangsi generals; he still preferred to keep real authority in his own hands, or in the hands of close personal subordinates. Li Tsung-jen was sent off to Peking, where he held the prestigious but powerless position of Head of the Generalissimo's Headquarters. He again found himself isolated and inactive. Pai held the nominally important position of Minister of Defence, but was in fact powerless. All major military decisions were made by Chiang.

In the years before the Communist conquest of the Mainland, the Kwangsi leaders drew away from the Centre again. They did this not as regional overlords, but by acting as a focus for some of the discontent within Kuomintang military circles. Of the ten or so regional military groupings associated with Nanking (from Kwangtung, Kwangsi, Yunnan, Szechwan–Sikang, Manchuria, the Northwest, Shansi, Shensi–Kansu, Ninghsia and Hunan), the Kwangsi group was still the most powerful and the most cohesive.[28] With Ho Ying-ch'in, a general who had long been close to Chiang, but was no longer trusted, Pai and Li formed a loose anti-Chiang grouping which was known as the White Fox Alliance (a pun on the three men's surnames).[29] Li Tsung-jen in fact began to emerge as a possible alternative to Chiang. In May 1948 he stood for the office of Vice-president, running against Chiang's nominee, Sun Fo. The election was fought bitterly and dirtily. Li won not so much because he had wide support, though he presented an attractive image of bluff honesty, but because many Kuomintang leaders were now opposed to Chiang. As Tso Shun-sheng, then Mayor of Shanghai, put it: Although we had ulterior motives for supporting Li, we felt we were still representing the will of the people who were genuinely for him.'[30]

In January 1949, Communist forces took Peking. In the face of this loss, and of rapidly-declining confidence in his ability to win the war, both in Chinese and foreign circles, Chiang Kai-shek resigned. Li Tsung-jen became Acting President.

Li tried to reach a negotiated settlement with the Communists, and in this he had the support of many non-Communist Chinese.[31] But the Communists were now in much too powerful a position to contemplate anything but outright victory; the terms that they demanded for a peaceful settlement amounted to total surrender on the Kuomintang side, and Li rejected them.[32] The only major outcome of Li's attempts at negotiations was that several of the members of his negotiating team stayed in Peking – including Li Chi-shen and Huang Shao-hsiung – and came out for the Communists.

If the Communists were not interested in negotiating, Chiang Kai-shek was even less so. He had apparently decided by this stage to retire to Taiwan. He was especially anxious that Li Tsung-jen should have no success as Acting President, either militarily or diplomatically. Personal hostility appeared to outweigh his desire to defend China. He ensured that Li was in a position of extreme weakness:

> 'what Nationalist troops remained were commanded by officers who still took orders from the Generalissimo. The currency was becoming daily more valueless, and what metal or other liquid assets the government possessed had been taken to Formosa under the Generalissimo's orders.' [33]

Li was left alone in Nanking, powerless and isolated. In April, when Communist forces crossed the Yangtse, he retreated, passing through a series of temporary capitals, as Communist forces swept over China. Eventually he flew to the United States. Pai Ch'ung-hsi, in command of the Wuhan region, tried to put up a last ditch defence against the Communists, but defections from his subordinates made his task impossible. By the end of the year, all of south China was in Communist hands. Pai fled to Taiwan. Large sections of the Kwangsi Army fled into French Indo-China, where they were disarmed by the French, and, much later, dispatched to Taiwan. A few of the civilian associates of the Kwangsi Clique chose to stay in China, but they were men who had always been well to the left of the main political line of the Clique.

The Kwangsi Clique finally broke up. The mainland was lost and with it the province. The Clique's leaders were scattered: Li Tsung-jen in New Jersey, Pai Ch'ung-hsi in Taipei, Huang Hsü-ch'u in Hong Kong, Li Chi-shen and Huang Shao-hsiung on the mainland. All were powerless, the only task before them to write their memoirs. Li Tsung-jen participated in the Columbia Oral History Project, and, with the help and guidance of T. K. Tong, a four-volume autobiography was compiled. No memoir has yet been published for Pai Ch'ung-hsi; Huang Hsü-ch'u contributed an inexhaustible stream of articles on the Clique to the Hong Kong journal, *Ch'un Ch'iu*. Huang Shao-hsiung and Li Chi-shen published nothing after 1949, though Huang had previously published his ghost-written (by his secretary Li Tse-min) autobiography, *Wu-shih hui-i*. Li Chi-shen and Huang Shao-hsiung held various posts on the mainland – Li was Chairman of the Revolutionary Committee of the Kuomintang until his death in 1959 – but it may be assumed that these posts were nominal. In 1957, Huang, along with several other former militarists, was denounced as a rightist. In Taiwan, Pai Ch'ung-hsi was allowed no authority. He died in 1967. In Hong Kong, Huang Hsü-ch'u was active in organising and helping former associates of the Clique, but this was social rather than political work. Li Tsung-jen in the USA dabbled in anti-Chiang machinations, but soon abandoned his efforts, realising probably the futility of attacking a man who was safely ensconced on Taiwan. surrounded by his most intimate friends and advisers.

Within a few years of the Communist accession to power, the Kwangsi Clique and its leaders had faded out of sight. But in 1965 there was an unexpected postcript; Li Tsung-jen returned in secret to Peking, to be welcomed home with a blaze of publicity. He was old and homesick; fifteen years in New Jersey had not reconciled him to exile. His chronically sick wife had lost faith in Western doctors and believed that her illness might be cured by Chinese doctors.

According to one rather petty-minded source, the ' servant problem ' in Englewood Cliffs was a major source of discontent to Li and his wife, though whether they thought that China would be better in this respect was not mentioned.[34] These reasons, combined with an official guarantee of their safety sent to them before they left the USA, were sufficient to explain their return. But what were Peking's motives in bringing Li Tsung-jen, a bitter enemy of Communism, the former Public Enemy Number 2 (after Chiang Kai-shek), back to China? To the Chinese public, he was either forgotten or unknown, as were many of the former Kuomintang figures who were brought out to welcome him – Huang Shao-hsiung, Hsiung K'o-wu (Szechwan militarist and Kuomintang leader), Chiang Kuang-nai and Ts'ai T'ing-k'ai (Cantonese militarists and anti-Japanese heroes), Lu Han (Yunnan militarist), Li Jen-jen (civilian associate of the Kwangsi Clique), Shao Li-tzu (leading Kuomintang politician), Fu Tso-i (subordinate of Feng Yü-hsiang). Even P'u Yi, the former Emperor, was wheeled out to receive Li.[35] Peking's chief reason was brought out in the speeches of welcome made to Li by Mao Tse-tung, who gave him a special audience, and Chou En-lai: it was to encourage the return to China of people who feared that their association with the Kuomintang might prejudice their position if they came home. Li's return was presented as a patriotic gesture, as the natural action of a true Chinese. If he, the former Acting President of Kuomintang China, could return safely, who could not? Mao told Li that ' we will welcome all those who have fled abroad and want to return; when they return we shall treat them all correctly '.[36]

Li's public treatment immediately after his return continued the theme of patriotism triumphant over political differences. Whatever evil deeds the black sheep had committed would be obliterated in the warm embrace of the mother country. During his triumphal tour of China, and even on his visit to Kwangsi, there were no recriminations, no public criticism. At his reception in Nanning, Li apologised to the people of Kwangsi for his crimes as ruler of Kwangsi, but in a perfunctory and *pro forma* way.[37]

If Peking was embarking on a programme to draw back potentially useful exiles, it was aborted almost immediately by the start of the Cultural Revolution. The upheaval of years that followed deterred others from following Li's example. But it did not affect Li's personal position. While leading Communist figures were falling into disgrace, Li survived. His name always appeared at the end of the shrinking lists of Communist leaders at official functions – ' . . . and *Mr* Li Tsung-jen '.

Li saw men who had once been his bitter opponents, whom he had fought on the battle-field, fall victims to the turmoil in the upper echelons of the Communist leadership. If he felt the irony of the demise of men such as Chu Teh and Teng Hsiao-p'ing, it was not apparent in his last public utterance, his official letter of farewell, published after his death in January 1969. At the end, it was not Li Tsung-jen the Kwangsi regionalist or Li Tsung-jen the Kuomintang militarist that counted, but Li Tsung-jen the patriot: ' In this glorious period, I feel most profoundly that to be a part of the Chinese people is an incomparable glory.' [38]

11

Conclusion

We return to the major theme of this study, the relationship between regionalism and nationalism. Was the Kwangsi Clique regionalist or nationalist? A chronological examination of the Clique's career suggests that it was both – by turns. Until 1925, the Clique was absorbed in regional concerns; from 1926 to 1929 it was active in national politics; from 1930 to 1936 it was limited to the region; from 1937 to 1945 it was committed to the struggle to preserve the nation. This tortuous process gives the impression that the Clique was caught between two magnetic poles, drawn strongly to one until the current was reversed and it was pulled in the opposite direction. This impression is misleading. The Kwangsi Clique was both regionalist and nationalist – at the same time. The Clique's leaders functioned in the indistinct but real framework of layered loyalties which we have described above (see p. 194). Their ideal was to work for the region and the nation, to put the region at the service of the nation. Their practice departed from this ideal, departed some times so far that it seemed to negate the ideal. In an unstable national situation, they were continually responding to changing situations, which might accentuate their national commitment (for example, the start of the Northern Expedition) or erode it (for example, the later stages of the Expedition). Their regionalism might weaken when they were most deeply committed to the nation, but it was enhanced by the imperfect nature of the reunification in 1928. While regional power-holding persisted, the Clique needed to keep tight hold over its own region to survive (for example, its rapid withdrawal from Nanking at the end of 1927 when Kwangsi was threatened).

The gulf between the ideal and actual behaviour indicated a major divorce between theory and practice; the Kwangsi leaders talked one way and acted another. But the divorce was not absolute. However imperfectly, the Kwangsi leaders were concerned with national issues; they were never, except for a brief period in 1928 and 1929, entirely concerned with the creation and maintenance of regional power-hold-

211

ing. They tried to reconcile the two pressures of regionalism and nationalism, to arrange them in a hierarchy in which nationalism, in theory at any rate, took pride of place. The fatal irony of this layered loyalty was that the persistence of regionalism undercut nationalism, the nationalism of national unity.

The Clique leaders were never precise about what they meant by nationalism; their adherence to it depended on its being potent but imprecise, not closely linked to specific political and social policies. If nationalism were made precise, if it were linked to concrete policies, their adherence to it would become problematic, for their independence of action, permitted by their regional power-holding, would be circumscribed by their higher commitment.

Their uncertainty about the precise meaning of nationalism was only one facet of their general ideological uncertainty. Though they recognised the importance of ideological commitment and the need for a higher allegiance as a *sine qua non* for China's revival, they were not sophisticated thinkers. They inhabited the world of ideological gropers, not of ideological positivists. They were incapable of adopting or inventing coherent, complete ideological positions which might offer solutions to China's problems.

Their gropings were not out of character with their period. Political and intellectual historians of Republican China tend to look at sophisticated intellectuals when they are examining ideological questions, at people who could write coherently and cogently, and to assume that these people were crucial to the formulation of ideological positions. In a sense they were, at least as initiators of ideological debate. But they had no monopoly of ideological questions, nor did their sophistication deter the less sophisticated but politically powerful from trying to come up with their solutions – which often, as with the Kwangsi Clique, amounted to an eclectic borrowing from a wide range of ' isms ', with the dominant contributor to the brew the ideology of the Kuomintang.

Some people adopted ideological positions which fell outside either of the main strands of modern social and political thought – Communist and Kuomintang – but failed because they could not translate their theories into practice. This was the fate of the Christian movement in China, of experiments such as Liang Shu-ming's Rural Reconstruction Movement. And though others tried one ideological salvation after another, working through the great ' solutions ' of the world and discarding them one after another, they usually ended up in one or other of the major camps, if they did not withdraw completely. For those who were not Communists in the period up to the Anti-Japanese War, the camp was usually the Kuomintang camp. The Kuomintang was accepted as the new orthodoxy, but as an ideological umbrella rather than as a straight and narrow path. Many continued their gropings under this umbrella, sometimes half-heartedly, usually with the proviso that they might interpret any tenet of the Kuomintang to their own satisfaction, given that they had the independence of the Centre necessary for this kind of behaviour. The very vagueness of the Kuomintang's ideological positions allowed this modification and manipulation; it became the Kuomintang's worst enemy, for it created conflict within the Kuomintang, and protracted and ultimately vitiated any Kuomintang solution to China's problems. It also allowed for interesting experimentation, of which the Kwangsi Clique's attempts at reconstruction was an example.

The Kwangsi Clique was not a gang of blinkered warlords. Its members were often confused, and sometimes devious, but they were not charlatans. They were convinced militarists, who realised the limitations of militarism, and perceived the need to find a solution to China's problems which combined military and political strands. Their commitment to the military way usually took precedence over their commitment to political solutions – they were not politicians in uniform – but it never became an end in itself. It always needed the justification of commitment to a higher political and ideological end.

This study was not intended as an eulogy of the Kwangsi Clique – a ludicrous enterprise which would be a travesty of historical accuracy. Few of the Clique's former members have been interested in white-washing their past behaviour. They might not feel obliged to apologise for it, as Li Tsung-jen did when he returned to China, but neither would they make great claims for it. Their achievements were relative at best, in comparison to Nanking's; they would not stand comparison with the achievements of the Communist rulers of Kwangsi after 1949. They were tentative efforts at reform and reconstruction, hampered always by a veto on social upheaval and by a nagging involvement with affairs beyond their direct control.

In this study, we have looked at the workings of regionalism and nationalism, at their interaction and their antagonism. We have tried to understand how regionalism could rise above crude regional protectionism, and associate itself with nationalism. As the regionalists of traditional China were always drawn back to the Centre, so the regionalists of the 1920s and 1930s were drawn to something beyond their small world, to a higher ideological allegiance, to a force which could fill the vacuum left by the collapse of the old order. The only candidate for this post was nationalism. To be concerned with China's problems in the 1920s and

1930s did not mean that one could not be a regionalist – it meant that one had to combine one's regionalism with nationalism. That this combination denied the fulfilment of nationalism, that it prevented the blooming of an ideology, linked to nationalism, which would replace the lost Confucian order, was a problem which China's regionalists would not face. They might claim to serve nationalism through regionalism; they could not deny regionalism to serve the nation.

Appendices

Appendix I. Members of the second level of the leadership of the Kwangsi Clique *

Name	Place of birth	School[1]	College	1st unit[2]	Type of Service[3]	Association with Clique leader[4]			
						LTR	HSH	PCH	HHC
Chang Jen-min	Liuchow	KHLCHH	Paoting	KHMFY	M	123	—	—	—
Chang Kan	—	KHLCHH	Paoting	KHMFY	M	—	—	123	—
Ch'en Hsiung	Jung hsien	KHLCHH	Paoting	KHMFY	M	—	—	1	2
Ch'eng Ssu-yüan	P'ingyang	—	—	—	P/A	3	—	12	—
Ch'iu Chang-wei	—	—	—	—	S	23	—	—	—
Chou Tsu-huang	Kweilin	—	Paoting	Hunan	M	—	—	—	—
Chu Chao-sen	Jung hsien	Law school	—	—	S/A	—	1	—	2
Chung Tsu-p'ei	Kungch'eng	KHLCHH	—	Kwangsi	A	—	1	—	—
Hsia Wei	Jung hsien	KHLCHH	Paoting	KHMFY	M	—	1	23	—
Hsü Chi-ming	—	KHLCHH	Paoting	KHMFY	M	—	—	—	—
Hu Tsung-to †	Hupei	—	Paoting	—	M	—	—	—	—
Huang Chen-kuo	Liuchow	—	Paoting	—		—	—	—	—
Huang Chi	Kweilin	—	Wisconsin	—	S/A	—	—	—	—
Huang Chung-chin	Nanning	—	—	—	S/A	—	1	—	23
Huang Chung-yüeh	Kweilin	Law school	—	—	S/A	123	—	—	—
Huang Hsü-ch'u	Jung hsien	KHLCHH	Peking	KHMFY	M/A	1	—	—	—
Huang P'u-hsin	Ho hsien	—	France	—	M	—	—	—	—

* This list is imprecise; many details of individual careers are missing, especially of the non-military members of the Clique. Connections with individual leaders are very difficult to ascribe accurately; many of them are simply guesses, based on closeness of service and attitudes.

† Indicates person who broke with Clique at some stage.

Notes

[1] School: KHLCHH – Kuang-hsi lü-chun hsiao-hsüeh (Kwangsi Military Elementary School).

[2] 1st unit of service (military): KHMFY – Kuang-hsi mo-fan ying (Kwangsi Model Battalion).

[3] Type of service: M – military; S – specialist (education, agriculture, etc.); P – political; A – administrative, governmental.

[4] Association with Clique leader: LTR – Li Tsung-jen; HSH – Huang Shao-hsiung; PCH – Pai Ch'ung-hsi; HHC – Huang Hsü-ch'u. Numbers indicate period of association: 1 – pre-1929; 2 – 1930–6; 3 – 1937–49.

Appendix I—continued

Name	Place of birth	School	College	1st unit	Type of Service	Association with Clique leader			
						LTR	HSH	PCH	HHC
Huang Shao-hsiung	Jung hsien	KHLCHH	Paoting	KHMFY	M/A	—	—	—	—
Huang T'ung-chiu	—	—	—	—	P/A	—	—	—	—
Lei Pei-hung	Nanning	—	Harvard	—	S/A	—	—	—	—
Lei Yin	Nanning	—	Japan	—	P/A	—	—	—	—
Li Ch'ao-fang	Kueip'ing	KHLCHH	Paoting	Kwangsi	M	—	—	—	—
Li Jen-jen	Kweilin	Military school	—	Kwangsi	S/A	—	—	—	—
Li Ming-jui †	Peiliu	—	—	Kwangsi	M	23	—	—	—
Li P'in-hsien	Ts'angwu	KHLCHH	Paoting	Hunan	M	—	—	—	—
Li Tsung-jen	Kweilin	KHLCHH	—	Kwangtung	M/A	—	—	—	—
Liang Ch'ao-chi	Peiliu	KHLCHH	Paoting	KHMFY	M	—	—	—	—
Liang Han-sung	P'ingyang	KHLCHH	Paoting	—	M	—	—	—	—
Liao Lei	Luch'uan	KHLCHH	Paoting	Hunan	M	—	—	—	23
Lin Mo	Kwangtung	—	Japan	Kwangsi	S/A	—	—	—	—
Lu Ching-ts'un	Kweilin	—	Paoting	Kwangsi	M	2	1	—	—
Lü Huan-yen †	Luch'uan	KHLCHH	Paoting	Kwangsi	M	—	—	—	—
Ma Chün-wu	Kweilin	—	Berlin	—	S/P	—	—	—	—
Meng Chih	—	KHLCHH	—	Kwangsi	M	—	—	—	—
Pai Ch'ung-hsi	Kweilin	KHLCHH	Paoting	KHMFY	M	—	1	—	—
P'an Chu-chi	Jung hsien	—	Wisconsin	—	P/A	12	—	—	—
P'an Yi-chih	—	—	—	—	P	—	—	2	—
T'an Lien-fang	Liuchow	KHLCHH	Paoting	Kwangsi	M	23	—	—	—
T'ao Chün †	Hupei	—	Kwangtung	—	M	—	—	—	—
Wang Kung-tu	Yungfu	—	Moscow	—	P	—	—	—	—
Wei Keng-t'ang	Jung hsien	—	—	Kwangsi	A/S	—	1	—	—
Wei Yün-sung	Jung hsien	Kwangsi	—	Kwangsi	M	2	—	—	—
Wei Yung-ch'eng	Lungchow	—	—	—	P/A	—	—	2	—
Wu T'ing-yang	Jung hsien	Kwangsi	—	—	M/A	—	1	—	—
Yang Teng-hui †	Shanglin	—	—	Kwangsi	M	—	—	—	—
Yeh Ch'i	Jung hsien	KHLCHH	Paoting	Hunan	M	—	—	—	—
Yü Chih-fang	—	KHLCHH	Paoting	KHMFY	M	—	—	—	—
Yü Tso-po †	Peiliu	—	Paoting	KHMFY	M/P	—	—	—	—

Appendix II. *Kwangsi's militarists at period of maximum intra-provincial confusion, 1922/3* *

Militarist	Area of control	Personal background	Number of troops
Chang Chün-ju	Pingyüan	—	2–3,000
Ch'en T'ien-t'ai	Wuhsüan	—	2–3,000
Ho Chung-ch'üan	Jung hsien	—	2–3,000
Li Pai-yün	West of Lungchow	—	2,000
Li Tsung-jen	Yülin	Military school	2,000
Liang Hua-t'ang	Kweilin	—	2,000
Lin Chün-t'ing	Kweichow border	Illiterate	1,000
Liu Chen-huan	Nanning	Provincial army	7–8,000
Liu Ch'üan-chung	Kueip'ing	—	2–3,000
Liu Jih-fu	Pose	Provincial army	3–4,000
Lu Fu-hsiang	Wuming	Illiterate	3 regiments
Lu Yün-kao	East of Nanning	Illiterate	3,000
Meng Jen-chien	Lungshan–Hsinch'eng	Hsiu-ts'ai	2,000
Shen Hung-ying	Northeast Kwangsi	Bandit	20,000
T'an Hao-ch'ing	Lungchow	Bandit	2,000
Wei Chao-lung	Laip'in	—	2–3,000

* Lu Jung-t'ing was out of the province at this time, in temporary retirement.
Sources. Much of this information is drawn from 'Li Tsung-jen Autobiography', Ch. 10, p. 6. Other information comes from a wide variety of sources.

Appendix III. Militarist conversions to the Kuomintang during 1926 *

Militarist	Place of origin	Kuomintang nomenclature	Conversion date	Troop strength
Cheng Ch'ien	Hunan	6th Army	January	—
Li Tsung-jen	Kwangsi	7th Army	March	15,000
T'ang Sheng-chih	Hunan	8th Army	April	20/30,000
Ho Lung	Hunan	1st Independent Brigade	May	—
Ho Yao-tsu	Hunan	2nd Independent Brigade	July	—
Wang T'ien-p'ei	Kweichow	10th Army	July	12,000
Fang Pen-jen	Kiangsi	11th Army	August	6,000?
P'eng Han-chang	Kweichow	9th Army	August	—
Lai Shih-heng	Kiangsi	14th Army	August	15,000
Jen Ying-chih	Hupei	12th Army	September	8,000
Fan Chung-hsiu	Hupei	13th Army	September	10,000
Liu Tso-lung	Hupei	15th Army	September	10,000
Ts'ao Wan-shun	Fukien	17th Army	October	18,000
Hsia Ch'ao	Chekiang	18th Army	October	—
Yang Sen	Szechwan	20th Army	October	10,000?
Fan Shih-sheng	Yunnan	16th Army	November	20,000
Liu Hsiang	Szechwan	21st Army	November	—
Lai Hsin-hui	Szechwan	22nd Army	November	—
Liu Ch'eng-chih	Szechwan	23rd Army	—	—
Liu Wen-hui	Szechwan	24th Army	November	—
Ch'en Yi	Chekiang	26th Army	December	6,000
Teng Hsi-hou	Szechwan	28th Army	December	—
T'ien Sung-yao	Szechwan	29th Army	December	5,000
Wei Yi-san	Fengtien	30th Army	December	—

* This is not an exhaustive list; it serves only to give some indication of the magnitude of militarist conversions to the Kuomintang. Some of the commanders were soon dismissed (namely, Peng Han-chang in February 1927, and Wang T'ien-p'ei in August), but many of them managed to retain control of their armies and of their regions. Many of the militarists arranged to defect to the Kuomintang well before they actually declared for it, hence the disjunction in army numbering.

Note

[1] The first five armies of the Kuomintang were set up in August 1925, commanded by Chiang Kai-shek (later Ho Ying-ch'in), T'an Yen-k'ai, Chu P'ei-te, Li Chi-shen and Li Fu-lin.

Appendix IV. *Kwangsi militia organisation, 1934*

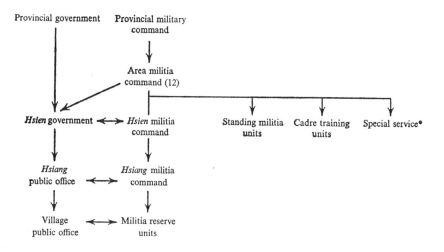

* *T'e-wu pan* – The Special Service – performed intelligence duties.
Source. Kuang-hsi chien-she chi-p'ing, p. 180.

A chronology of events in China, 1911-1936, with particular reference to Kwangsi and the Kwangsi Clique

1911	September	Kwangsi declares independence of throne.
1916	March	Kwangsi declares independence of Yüan Shih-k'ai, as part of Hu-kuo Movement.
	July	Lu Jung-t'ing gains control of Kwangtung.
1917	April	Lu named Commissioner of Liang Kuang after trip to Peking.
	June	Start of Hu-fa Movement. Kwangtung and Kwangsi declare independence.
	August	Military government set up in Canton, Sun Yat-sen head.
1918	May	Sun driven out of Canton.
1919	—	Miao rising in northwest Kwangsi.
1920	October	Kwangsi forces driven from Kwangtung – Li Tsung-jen establishing himself in Yülin area.
	November	Sun Yet-sen returns to Canton.
1921	April/May	Kwangsi attack into Kwangtung.
	June	Cantonese counter-attack and occupation of Kwangsi.
	November	Sun Yat-sen preparing northern expedition, in Kweilin.
1922	—	Large-scale Chuang-Yao rising in Kwangsi.
	April	Cantonese troops withdraw from Kwangsi.
	June	Autonomous Army (Tzu-chih chün) formed in Kwangsi.
	August	Ch'en Chiung-ming drives Sun Yat-sen out of Kwangtung – Huang Shao-hsiung joins Li Tsung-jen in Yülin.
1923	January	Sun Yat-sen re-establishes himself at Canton with aid of Kwangsi–Yunnan militarists, including Shen Hung-ying.
	April	Shen breaks with Sun.
	July	Huang Shao-hsiung takes Wuchow from Shen, with Cantonese help.
	November	Li Tsung-jen and Huang Shao-hsiung take Kuei hsien.
1924	January	1st Congress of Kuomintang.
	April	Lu Jung-t'ing besieged at Kweilin by Shen Hung-ying.
	June	Li and Huang take Nanning.
	July	Li and Huang establish joint headquarters at Nanning.
	August	In alliance with Shen Yung-ying, Li and Huang take Liuchow. Lu Jung-t'ing driven out of Kwangsi.
	November	Kuomintang names Li Tsung-jen Rehabilitation Commissioner of Kwangsi, Huang Shao-hsiung his deputy.
1925	February	Li and Huang defeat Shen Hung-ying.
	March	After death of Sun Yat-sen, T'ang Chi-yao proclaims himself Grand Marshal – Yunnanese troops take Nanning.
	June	Kwangsi–Yunnan troops ousted from Canton.
	July	Li and Huang recapture Nanning. Kwangsi reunified – National Government set up in Canton.
	August	Kuomintang troops reorganised in five armies.

1925	September	Office of civil government set up in Kwangsi, Huang Shao-hsiung head.
	November	Kwangsi troops move into Nanlu area of Kwangtung, to help Kuomintang in reunification of Kwangtung.
1926	January	2nd Congress of Kuomintang–Wuchow Meeting, to discuss Kwangtung–Kwangsi alliance.
	March	Act of Unification between Kwangtung and Kwangsi – Part of Kwangsi forces reorganised as Seventh Army – SS *Chung-Shan* Incident.
	April	T'ang Sheng-chih declares for Kuomintang – Northern troops attacking into Hunan.
	May	Kwangsi troops move into Hunan.
	June	Chiang Kai-shek named Commander-in-chief for northern expedition – Provincial government set up in Kwangsi.
	July	Official start of northern expedition – Fall of Ch'angsha.
	August	Feng Yü-hsiang declares for Kuomintang–Yunnanese attack into Kwangsi repulsed.
	September	Peasant rising in Tunglan hsien, Kwangsi – Hankow, Hanyang, fall to Kuomintang forces.
	October	Start of Kuomintang Campaign into Kiangsi.
	December	Fall of Wuch'ang – Kuomintang Government moves to Wuhan: Chiang Kai-shek sets up rival government at Nanch'ang.
1927	March	Fall of Shanghai – Nanking Incident.
	April	Purge of Communists in Shanghai, Canton, Kwangsi–Chiang Kai-shek sets up government in Nanking.
	May	Continuation of northern expedition from Wuhan and Nanking.
	June	Feng Yü-hsiang declares for Nanking.
	July	Wuhan comes out against Communists – Northern forces start counter-attack on Nanking.
	August	Nanch'ang Rising – Chiang Kai-shek resigns.
	September	Establishment of Special Committee at Nanking – Branch Political Council set up at Wuhan – Chang Fa-k'uei leads troops back to Kwangtung.
	October	Branch Political Council set up in Canton.
	November	Kwangsi forces from Nanking drive T'ang Sheng-chih from Wuhan – *Coup* against Huang Shao-hsiung in Canton.
	December	Canton Commune – Reassertion of Kwangsi control in Kwangtung in putting down Communist rising – Collapse of Special Committee – Kwangsi leaders move to Wuhan.
1928	January	Chiang Kai-shek returns to power in Nanking – Kwangsi extends power into Hunan from Wuhan.
	February	Kuomintang forces reorganised into four Group Armies – Branch Political Councils established at Wuhan, K'aifeng and T'aiyuan.
	March	Reconciliation between Wuhan (Kwangsi) and Nanking.
	April	Northern Expedition gets under way again.
	May	Chinan Incident.
	June	Fall of Peking – Start of Period of Tutelage – Branch Political Council set up in Peking.
	July	T'angshan Meeting.
	August	Fifth Plenum of Central Executive Committee of Kuomintang.
	November	Shanghai opium scandal – Kwangsi leaders implicated.
	December	Kwangsi Reconstruction Conference – Chang Hsüeh-liang declares for Kuomintang.

1929	January	Disbandment Conference.
	February	Wuhan dismisses Lu Ti-p'ing as Chairman of Hunan.
	March	Nanking impeaches Wuhan Branch Political Council – Pai Ch'ung-hsi leaves Peking secretly – Li Chi-shen arrested in Nanking: he, Pai and Li Tsung-jen dismissed from all posts – Branch Political Councils dissolved.
	April	Kwangsi Clique loses Wuhan, Hunan and Hupei.
	May	Kwangsi forces attack into Kwangtung from Kwangsi.
	June	Cantonese counter-attack – Kwangsi leaders flee from province.
	August	Nanking names Yü Tso-po Chairman of Kwangsi, Li Ming-jui Disbandment Commissioner.
	September	Chang Fa-k'uei rebels against Nanking.
	October	Yü and Li defy Nanking, dismissed from posts.
	November	Kwangsi Clique regains control of Kwangsi.
	December	Right River Soviet established at Pose – Unsuccessful attack of Kwangsi forces into Kwangtung.
1930	February	Left River Soviet established at Lungchow.
	March	Left River Soviet collapses.
	June	Kwangsi forces attack into Hunan – Yunnan forces attack into Kwangsi.
	August	Expanded Conference (*K'uo-ta hui-i*) meets Peking.
	September	Right River Soviet crushed – First organisation of Kwangsi Militia.
	October	Huang Shao-hsiung breaks with Kwangsi Clique.
1931	February	Hu Han-min arrested in Nanking.
	March	Alliance of southwestern provinces formed in Canton.
	April	Troops from Kwangsi Soviets reach Kiangsi.
	May	Extraordinary meeting of Kuomintang Executive and Supervisory Committees opens in Canton.
	June	National Government set up in Canton – Cantonese forces leave Kwangsi.
	July	New provincial government set up in Kwangsi.
	November	Rapprochement between Nanking and politicians in Canton.
	December	Southwest Executive Bureau of Central Executive Committee of Kuomintang, Southwest Political Council and Southwest Military Branch Council set up in Canton.
1932	—	Mass education movement launched in Kwangsi.
1933	—	Yao rising in northern Kwangsi.
	November	Fukien Rebellion.
1934	January	Combined Government Office set up in Kwangsi.
	March	Promulgation of Kwangsi Outline for Reconstruction.
	December	Communist troops on Long March cross edge of Kwangsi.
1935	January	Kuomintang troops gain control of Kweichow.
1936	May	Death of Hu Han-min.
	June	June 6th Movement (*Liu-i yün-tung*) launched in Kwangtung and Kwangsi.
	July	Cantonese generals go over to Nanking – Fall of Ch'en Chi-t'ang.
	August	Independent government set up in Kwangsi.
	September	Pakhoi Incident.
		Kwangsi–Nanking settlement.

Notes

Abbreviations

BSME	*Bulletin de la Société des Missions-Etrangères de Paris*
CKCSYKHCS	*Chung-kuo chien-she yü Kuang-hsi chien-she*
Compte rendu	*Compte rendu des travaux de la Société des Missions-Etrangères de Paris*
CYB	*China Year Book*
KHHHKMTL	*Kuang-hsi Hsin-hai ko-ming tzu-liao*
KHKMHIL	*Kuang-hsi ko-ming hui-i lu*
KMWH	*Ko-ming wen-hsien*
KWCP	*Kuo-wen chou-pao*
NCH	*North China Herald*
TCSSNCKCSS	*Tsui-chin san-shih-nien Chung-kuo chün-shih shih*
TFTC	*Tung-fang tsa-chih*

Introduction

[1] Wang Tsao-shih, *Chung-kuo wen-t'i ti fen-hsi* (Shanghai, 1935), pp. 48–9.

[2] J. E. Spencer, 'On Regionalism in China', *Journal of Geography*, XLVI, I, No. 4 (1947), 123–36.

[3] Jean Chesneaux, 'The Federalist Movement in China, 1930–1933', in Jack Gray (ed.), *Modern China's Search for a Political Form* (London, 1969), p. 96.

[4] Ho P'ing-ti, *Chung-kuo hui-kuan shih-lun* (Taipei, 1966), pp. 40–53. After 1911, *hui-kuan* were commonly known as *t'ung-hsiang-hui*.

[5] Rupert Vance, 'The Regional Concept as a Tool for Social Research', in Merrill Jensen (ed.), *Regionalism in America* (Madison, 1951), p. 123.

[6] 'Li Tsung-jen Autobiography', Ch. 5, p. 4. Unpublished manuscript, deposited in the Butler Library, Columbia University.

[7] Ho P'ing-ti, *Chung-kuo hui-kuan shih-lun.* Ho notes that the existence of such organisations tended to break down regionalism, rather than reinforcing it, since in a limited way it exposed Chinese of different regions to each other.

[8] Joseph Levenson, 'The Province, the Nation and the World: the Problem of Chinese Identity', in Albert Feuerwerker, Rhoads Murphey and Mary Wright (eds.), *Approaches to Modern Chinese History* (Berkeley, 1967), p. 276.

[9] This poem, by T'ao Hsing-chih, was dictated to me from memory by Jerome Ch'en.

[10] George Sokolsky, *The Tinder Box of Asia* (New York, 1932), p. 53.

[11] James Sheridan, *Chinese Warlord: The Career of Feng Yü-hsiang* (Stanford, 1966); Donald Gillin, *Warlord: Yen Hsi-shan in Shansi Province, 1911–1949* (Princeton, 1967); Winston Hsieh, 'The Ideas and Ideals of a Warlord: Ch'en Chiung-ming (1878–1933)', *Harvard Papers on China*, XVI (1962), 198–244; Jerome Ch'en, 'Defining Chinese Warlords and Their Factions', *Bulletin of*

223

the *School of Oriental and African Studies*, XXXI (1968), 563–600; Andrew Nathan, 'Factionalism in Chinese Politics', paper presented to the 1971 Annual Meeting of the American Political Science Association.

[12] Ch'en, 'Defining Chinese Warlords', p. 579.

[13] Sheridan, *Chinese Warlord*, pp. 16–30.

[14] See Nathan, 'Factionalism'. Odoric Wou compares the structure of warlord cliques to that of the Chinese lineage organisation. See Odoric Y. K. Wou, 'A Chinese "Warlord" Faction: the Chihli Clique, 1918–1924', in Andrew Cordier (ed.), *Columbia Essays in International Affairs*, Vol. III (New York, 1967), pp. 249–74.

[15] Ch'en, 'Defining Chinese Warlords', p. 568. See also Robert North, *Kuomintang and Chinese Communist Elites* (Stanford, 1952), pp. 55–61, for a discussion of the social origins of later militarists.

[16] *Kuo-min-tang chou-k'an*, 7 (1924), 4.

[17] *China Weekly Review*, 28 June 1930, p. 150.

[18] Franz Michael, 'Regionalism in Nineteenth-Century China', introduction to Stanley Spector, *Li Hung-chang and the Huai Army* (Princeton, 1964), p. xxi; and *ibid.*, p. 171.

[19] Hsieh Pao-chao, *The Government of China, 1644–1911* (Baltimore, 1925), p. 296.

[20] Mary Wright, review of Spector, *Li Hung-chang*, in *Journal of Asian Studies*, XXV, No. 2 (1966), 332. Hereafter cited as *JAS*.

[21] John Fincher, 'Political Provincialism and the National Revolution', in Mary Wright (ed.), *China in Revolution: The First Phase* (New Haven, 1968), pp. 185–226.

[22] Chesneaux, 'The Federalist Movement', pp. 104–5.

[23] Ch'en, 'Defining Chinese Warlords', p. 570.

[24] Sheridan, *Chinese Warlord*, pp. 14–15.

[25] Edgar Snow, *Far Eastern Front* (New York, 1934), p. 295.

[26] Paul Linebarger, *The China of Chiang Kai-shek* (Boston, 1941), p. 99.

[27] Levenson, 'The Province, the Nation and the World', p. 270.

[28] For a discussion of the genesis of mass nationalism, see Chalmers Johnson, *Peasant Nationalism and the Rise of Communist Power* (Stanford, 1963).

[29] Some commentators have tried to define regional cliques within the Communist leadership. One, with a vivid imagination, defined a 'Hunan Clique', led by Mao Tse-tung, P'eng Te-huai and Liu Shao-ch'i. Shih Pu-chih, 'Kuo-chun ti-wu-tzu wei-ch'ao yü Chung-kung t'u-wei', *Ch'un-ch'iu*, 164 (16 July 1957), 13–14. With the benefit of hindsight, this particular alliance seems highly improbable, but this is not to say that regional affinity has not been important in forming links in Communist China.

[30] *BBC, Summary of World Broadcasts*, FE/2983/B/11. Translation of broadcast editorial from *Che-chiang jih-pao*, 13 March 1969.

Chapter 1

[1] Anon., *Trois mois au Kouangsi* (Paris, 1906), p. iv. Hereafter cited by title.

[2] H. McAleavy, *The Black Flags in Vietnam* (London, 1968), pp. 98–9.

[3] J. L. Buck, *Land Utilisation in China* (Shanghai, 1937), p. 82.

[4] Chi Ch'ao-ting, *Key Economic Areas in Chinese History* (London, 1936), p. 30.

[5] H. J. Wiens, *Han Chinese Expansion in South China* (Hampden, Connecticut, 1967), pp. 132, 144. Ch'in troops dug a canal between the headwaters of the Li River in Kwangsi and the Hsiang River in Hunan, to speed communications with Central China. See Joseph Needham, *Science and Civilisation in China*, Vol. IV (Cambridge, 1961), Pt 3, pp. 299–306. Two thousand years later, the canal served the Taipings for troop and supply transport. Laai Yi-faai, 'The River Strategy of the Taipings', *Oriens*, V, No. 2 (1952), 306.

[6] Wiens, *Han Chinese Expansion*, pp. 201–6.

[7] Liu Chieh, 'Kuang-hsi liang ta hsi-p'ai min-tsu ti you-lai chi ch'i yen chin', *Kuang-hsi t'ung-chih-kuan kuan-k'an* (Kweilin, January 1948).

[8] In 1820, Kwangsi's population was 7,429,120. Ho P'ing-ti, *Studies on the Population of China* (Cambridge, Mass., 1959), p. 56.

[9] Laai Yi-faai, 'The Use of Maps in Social Research', *Geographical Review*, LII (1962), 96.

[10] Wiens, *Han Chinese Expansion*, p. 187.

[11] Laai Yi-faai, 'The Part Played by the Pirates of Kwangtung and Kwangsi Provinces in the Taiping Insurrection', unpublished Ph.D. dissertation, University of California, 1950, pp. 92–107.

[12] *Ibid.*, pp. 113–22.

[13] For discussions of the Taiping Rebellion, see Franz Michael, *The Taiping Rebellion* (Seattle, 1966), Teng Ssu-yu, *New Light on the History of the Taiping Rebellion* (Cambridge, Mass., 1950).

[14] For a full discussion of these rebellious movements, see Hsieh Hsing-yao, *T'ai-p'ing t'ien-kuo ch'ien-hou Kuang-hsi ti fan-Ch'ing yün-tung* (Peking, 1950), pp. 1–25. See also Vassili Iliouchetchkine, 'Les sociétés secrètes et les sectes herétiques en Chine au milieu de XIXe siècle', in Jean Chesneaux, Feiling Davis and Nguyen Nguyet Ho (eds.), *Mouvements populaires et sociétés secrètes en Chine au XIX et XX siècles* (Paris, 1970), pp. 117–32.

[15] Kwangsi gazetteers are full of descriptions of such revolts. See for example *Kuei hsien chih* (Kuei hsien, 1935; reprinted Taipei, 1967), p. 161.

[16] See Lai Hsin-hsia, 'Shih lun Ch'ing Kuang-hsü mo-nien ti Kuang-hsi jen-min ta ch'i-i', *Li-shih yen-chiu*, 11 (1957), 57–77; and Kuang-hsi shao-shu min-tsu she-hui li-shih tiao-ch'a tsu, *Kuang-hsi Hsin-hai ko-ming tzu-liao* (Nanning, 1960), p. 12. Hereafter cited as *KHHHKMTL*.

[17] For a full description of this rebellion, see Lai Hsin-hsia, 'Shih lun Ch'ing Kuang-hsü mo-nien ti Kuang-hsi jen-min ta ch'i-i'.

[18] Ts'en was the son of the Governor-general of Yunnan and Kweichow at the time of the Sino-French War (1875), Ts'en Yü-ying, a violent xenophobe. The family's reputation for anti-foreignism was enhanced in 1900, when Ts'en Ch'un-hsüan escorted the Empress Dowager to Sian after foreign troops occupied Peking. See Ts'en Yü-ying's biography in A. Hummel, *Eminent Chinese of the Ch'ing Dynasty* (Washington, D.C., 1943), Vol. II, pp. 743–6; and Ts'en Ch'un-hsüan, *Lo-chai man-pi* (Peking, 1933; reprinted Taipei, 1962), pp. 11–12.

[19] *KHHHKMTL*, pp. 7, 11.

[20] For accounts of Liu Yung-fu's career, see Ella Laffay, 'La formation d'un rebelle: Liu Yong-fu et la création de l'armée des pavillons noirs', in Chesneaux *et al.*, *Mouvements populaires*, pp. 248–66; and McAleavy, *The Black Flags*.

[21] Lai Yen-yü, *Kuang-hsi i-lan* (Nanning, 1935), 'Kwangsi in Brief', p. 2.

[22] Lai Hsin-hsia, 'Shih lun Ch'ing Kuang-hsü mo-nien ti Kuang-hsi jen-min ta ch'i-i', pp. 75–7.

[23] A different version of the French failure to develop trade is given in a British source: 'The French are neither as capable as pioneers, nor as competent to fill lonely outposts as Albion's bulldog breed' – W. Burton, *The French Stranglehold on Yunnan* (Shanghai, 1933), p. 7. The French expressed some interest in Kwangsi's mineral deposits, and under official Chinese direction, there was some prospecting. Some of the deposits were deceptive; good quality coal 'discovered' near the Kwangtung border turned out to be Cardiff coal arranged judiciously over a worthless seam. *Trois mois au Kouangsi*, p. 129.

[24] J. Dautremer, 'Yunnan et Kouangsi, frontières indo-chinoises', *Bulletin de l'Association amicale Franco-Chinoise*, I, No. 5 (1909), 284.

[25] A. Baudrit, *Bétail humain : rapt, vente et infanticide dans l'Indochine et dans la Chine du sud* (Saigon, 1942), p. 20.

[26] Joseph Cuenot, *Au pays des pavillons noirs* (Hong Kong, 1925), p. 5.

[27] *Compte rendu des travaux de la Société des Missions-Etrangères de Paris, 1921* (Paris, 1922), p. 78. Hereafter cited as *Compte rendu.*

[28] *Bulletin de la Société des Missions-Etrangères de Paris*, 110 (February 1931), 95. Hereafter cited as *BSME.*

[29] Cuenot, *Au pays des pavillons noirs*, p. 137.

[30] *Compte rendu, 1920* (Paris, 1921), p. 44.

[31] Feng Ho-fa (ed.), *Chung-kuo nung-ts'un ching-chi tzu-liao, hsü-pien* (Shanghai, 1935), pp. 305–6.

[32] *KHHHKMTL*, pp. 2–5.

[33] H. Schriffrin, *Sun Yat-sen and the Origins of the Chinese Revolution* (Berkeley, 1968), p. 217.

[34] Huang Hsü-ch'u, ' Ts'an-chia Hsin-hai ko-ming Liu-chou tu-li ti hui-i ', *Ch'un-ch'iu*, 66 (1 April 1960), 7–8.

[35] T'ao Chü-yin, *Pei-yang chün-fa t'ung-chih shih-ch'i shih-hua* (Peking, 1957), Vol. I, p. 68.

[36] For discussions of the revolutionary movement in Kwangsi, see Chung-kuo jen-min cheng-chih hsieh-shang hui-i ch'üan-kuo wei-yüan-hui, Wen-shih tzu-liao yen-chin wei-yüan-hui (ed.), *Hsin-hai ko-ming hui-i-lu* (Peking, 1962), Vol. II, pp. 430–540. The same source gives details of Lu Jung-t'ing's connections with bandits and secret societies: see pp. 506–11.

[37] For details of the relations between Lu and other Kwangsi military figures, see Chin T'ien-jung, ' Hsi-nan lao-chiang Liu Chen-huan chuan-chi ', *Ch'un-ch'iu*, 166 (1 June 1964), 3–4; and Li Mo-hsing, ' Hsin-hai ko-ming tsai Liu-chou ', *Chin-tai shih tzu-liao*, 2, No. 19 (1958), 48.

[38] T'ao Chü-yin, *Chin-tai i-wen* (Shanghai, 1945), p. 58.

[39] *Idem, Pei-yang chün-fa*, Vol. II, p. 175.

[40] Ts'en Ch'un-hsüan, *Lo-chai man-pi*, pp. 10–11.

[41] Hsiao Yüan (pseud.), ' Chi Lu Jung-t'ing ', *Kuo-wen chou-pao*, XIII, No. 12 (30 March 1936), 28. Hereafter cited as *KWCP.*

[42] For a full description of the anti-Yüan Shih-k'ai Movement, see Jerome Ch'en, *Yuan Shih-k'ai* (London, 1961).

[43] Wen Kung-chih, *Tsui-chin san-shih-nien Chung-kuo chün-shih shih* (Shanghai, 1930; reprinted Taipei, 1962), Vol. III, pp. 48–9. Hereafter cited as *TCSSNCKCSS.*

[44] *Chao-p'ing hsien chih* (Chaop'ing, 1934; reprinted Taipei, 1967), pp. 99ff.

[45] Lu spent most of his time at his palatial home near Nanning; the magnitude of his responsibilities as ruler of two provinces seems to have stunned him into inactivity.

[46] T'ao Chü-yin, *Pei-yang chün-fa*, Vol. III, p. 105.

[47] Huang Hsü-ch'u, ' Ts'an-chia Hsin-hai ko-ming Liu-chou tu-li ti hui-i ', p. 8. Lu commanded the largest single body of troops in Kwangtung, but had only minimal control over Cantonese units, over the provincial guard and over Yunnanese troops which remained in Kwangsi after the Hu Kuo Movement. *TCSSNCKCSS*, Vol. II, p. 337.

[48] T'ao Chü-yin, *Pei-yang chün-fa*, Vol. III, p. 171.

[49] Sun Yat-sen was so enraged by Lu's negotiations with Peking that he ordered gunboats loyal to himself to bombard the headquarters of the Kwangtung *tu-chün*. Ts'en Ch'un-hsüan, *Lo-chai man-pi*, pp. 14, 19.

[50] Li Chien-nung, *The Political History of China, 1840–1928* (New York, 1956), p. 388.

[51] *Hua-tzu jih-pao*, 27 April 1918.

[52] T'ao Chü-yin, *Pei-yang chün-fa*, Vol. V, pp. 193–204.

[53] Huang Shao-hsiung, *Wu-shih hui-i* (Shanghai, 1945), p. 45.

Chapter 2

[1] Jerome Ch'en, review of Donald Gillin, *Warlord*, in *Bulletin of the School of Oriental and African Studies*, XXXI, No. 1 (1968), 180–1.

[2] Several of Huang Shao-hsiung's relatives held minor posts as *hsien-chang*, school principal, etc. See N. Fierce, 'Kuo-min cheng-fu chih-hsia ti Kuang-hsi', *Hsiang-tao chou-pao*, 165 (28 July 1926), 1,651.

[3] The main sources for Li Tsung-jen's early life are *Li Tsung-ssu-ling tsui-chin yen-chiang chi* (Nanning, 1935), and 'Li Tsung-jen Autobiography'. Similar accounts are given in Feng Chü-p'ei, *K'ang-chan chung ti ti-wu lu-chün* (Hankow, 1938) pp. 82–91, and in Li Tsung-jen et al., *Kuang-hsi chih chien-she* (Kweilin, 1939), pp. 12–20.

[4] *KHHHKMTL*, p. 4.

[5] The principal account of Huang Shao-hsiung's early life is given in his autobiography, *Wu-shih hui-i*. The work was ghosted for Huang by his secretary, Li Tse-min.

[6] Huang Hsü-ch'u has given an account of his early life in *Wo ti mu-ch'in* (Hong Kong, 1969). There are also brief accounts in Chou Ch'üan, *Kuei-hsi chieh-p'ou* (Hong Kong, 1949), p. 34, and in Huang Hsü-ch'u, 'Ts'an-chia Hsin-hai ko-ming Liu-chou tu-li ti hui-i', *Ch'un-ch'iu*, 66 (1 April 1960), 7.

[7] Brief accounts of Pai Ch'ung-hsi's early life are given in T. S. Ch'en, 'General Pai, Chinese Patriot', *Asia*, XLII, No. 12 (December 1942), 715; Chang Kuo-p'ing, *Pai Ch'ung-hsi chiang-chün chuan* (Hankow, 1938), pp. 1–2; Feng Chü-p'ei, *K'ang-chan chung ti ti-wu lu-chün*, p. 92; and Hsiang Yü (*pseud.*), 'Pai Ch'ung-hsi ts'ao-ch'i chueh-ch'i Kuang-hsi ti ching-wei', *I-wen chih*, 16 (1 June 1961), 20.

[8] For information on the Kwangsi Military Elementary School, see Huang Shao-hsiung, *Wu-shih hui-i*, pp. 11–30; Hsiang Yü 'Pai Ch'ung-hsi ts'ao-ch'i chueh-ch'i Kuang-hsi ti ching-wei'; and 'Li Tsung-jen Autobiography', Ch. 3. In 1912 the name of the school was changed to Kwangsi Short Course Military Elementary School (Kuang-hsi lu-chün su-ch'eng hsiao-hsüeh).

[9] R. L. Powell, *The Rise of Chinese Military Power* (Princeton, 1955), pp. 290, 299.

[10] *KHHHKMTL*, p. 271.

[11] The leader of the student group was Chao Heng-t'i, then a teacher in a Kweilin school and one of the leading revolutionary activists within the province. Chao later became one of the chief adherents of the Federalist Movement in the 1920s. *KHHHKMTL*, p. 274.

[12] Yüan's attitude to the academy was coloured by his quarrels with the previous head of the academy, Chiang Pai-li, over the amount of money that the academy should receive. When Chiang failed to get what he wanted, he assembled his cadets, made an impassioned speech, then drew a revolver and shot himself, crying that he would rather die than see his work destroyed for lack of funds. He did not die; he was only slightly wounded, well enough to woo his nurse, whom he married after he left hospital. Ts'ao Chü-jen, *Chiang Pai-li p'ing-chuan* (Hong Kong, 1963), pp. 9–11.

[13] C. M. Wilbur and Julie L. Y. How, *Documents on Communism, Nationalism and Soviet Advisors in China, 1918–1927* (New York, 1956), pp. 393, 411, 418. Paoting graduates who rose to high positions within the Kuomintang military hierarchy included: T'ang Sheng-chih, Ch'en Ming-shu, Chiang Kuang-nai, Ho Chien, Chang Fa-k'uei, Liu Shih, Ch'en Ch'eng, Miao Pei-nan, Ch'ien Ta-chün, Liu Hsing, Mao Ping-wen and Hsü Ching-t'ang. Chiang Kai-shek was at the academy before 1911, earlier than most of the men listed above.

[14] Ma Hsiao-chün, 'Kuang-hsi ko-ming-chün fa-yüan chi-lüeh', *Chuan-chi wen-hsüeh*, VIII, No. 1 (January–June 1966), 38.

[15] For information on the Model Battalion, see Huang Shao-hsiung, *Wu-shih hui-i*, pp. 36–8; Ma Hsiao-chün, 'Kuang-hsi ko-ming-chün' pp. 38–9; Hsiang

Yü, ' Pai Ch'ung-hsi ts'ao-ch'i chueh-ch'i ', pp. 20–1; and Kao T'ung, ' Lun Li Tsung-jen Huang Shao-hsiung ch'i-chia chen-shih ', *Ch'un-ch'iu*, 72 (1 July 1960), 12.

16 Huang Shao-hsiung, *Wu-shih hui-i*, p. 36.

17 For details of Li Tsung-jen's career after 1911, see his ' Autobiography ', Chs. 4–8; and *Li Tsung-ssu-ling tsui-chin yen-chiang chi*, pp. 7–11.

18 Another prominent military figure who started his career as a physical-training instructor is Chu Te. His first post after the completion of his formal education was a PT instructor in a middle school. The reaction of his parents, illiterate peasants, to the news that their son was going to teach PT gives some indication of the low status of such work:

'The effect of my confession was terrifying.... First there was a long silence, then my father asked what physical training meant. When I explained, he shouted out, saying that the whole family had worked for twelve long years to educate one son to save them from starvation, only to be told that he intended to teach boys to throw their arms and legs around. Coolies could do that, he shouted in violent bitterness.'

Agnes Smedley, *The Great Road* (London, 1958), p. 76.

Chapter 3

1 *Hua-tzu jih-pao*, 13 January 1923.

2 *Ching pao*, 25 February 1925, in Hatano Ken'ichi, *Gendai Shihna no kiroku* (n.p., n.d.), February 1925, p. 181.

3 *KHHHKMTL*, p. 262.

4 *Yin-hang yüeh-K'an*, September 1924, in Hatano Ken'ichi, *Gendai Shihna no kiroku*, October 1924. These figures are useful only in giving a general impression of the financial situation. These, like many other contemporary figures, are simply quoted in terms of undifferentiated *yüan*, without indicating the value of the money in relation to other currencies.

5 *Chinese Economic Bulletin*, I, No. 6 (June 1927).

6 Chang Yu-i (ed.), *Chung-kuo chin-tai nung-yeh shih tzu-liao*, Vol. II (Peking, 1957), p. 623; and O. Edmund Clubb, *The Opium Traffic in China* (Hankow, 1934), report of U.S. Consul at Hankow, p. 25.

7 *Ping-cheng shih-pao*, 8 March 1924. Pose had formerly been an important transshipment salt centre.

8 Sun always laid plans to move out of Kwangtung as soon as he established a toe-hold there. Theoretically his plans for northern expeditions were the embodiment of his ambition to reunify China. In practice, they usually reflected his difficulty in asserting his independence of his local military supporters, and his desire therefore to reduce their authority over him by extending the scope of action.

9 Cuenot, *Au pays des pavillons noirs*, p. 51.

10 *Ibid.*, p. 69.

11 *BSME*, 3 (March 1922), 107.

12 Huang Hsü-ch'u, ' T'an tao Ma Chün-wu ch'u Kuei cheng hsiang ching ', *Ch'un-chi*, 85 (16 January 1961), 8.

13 Cuenot, *Au pays des pavillons noirs*, p. 52.

14 Ch'ien Chia-chü *et al.*, *Kuang-hsi sheng ching-chi kai-k'uang* (Shanghai, 1936), p. 226.

15 *BSME*, 3 (March 1922), 240.

16 On his journey out of Kwangsi, Ma's boat was attacked by soldiers under Li Tsung-jen's command, and his concubine was killed. Huang Shao-hsiung, *Wu-shih hui-i*, p. 52.

17 Huang Hsü-ch'u, ' Pa-kuei i-wang lu, 18 ', *Ch'un-ch'iu*, 170 (1 August 1964), 17.

18 *KHHHKMTL*, p. 257. The two largest units were those of Shen Hung-ying in northeast Kwangsi and Lu Jung-t'ing in west Kwangsi.

[19] These seven *hsien* were the five *hsien* of Yulin chou, plus Kuei hsien and Jung hsien.

[20] ' Li Tsung-jen Autobiography ', Ch. 11, p. 8.

[21] *Ibid.*, Ch. 10, p. 10.

[22] Paradoxically, Shen had just helped Sun return to Canton. His defection from Sun so soon afterwards was unexpected but not without precedent in the murky waters of Kwangtung warlord politics in which Sun was then dabbling.

[23] Huang Shao-hsiung, *Wu-shih hui-i*, p. 62. After his defeat, Shen was without a base for almost a year. He and his army wandered around the Kwangtung–Hunan–Kiangsi border region until Shen was reconciled with Sun Yat-sen early in 1924. Sun supplied him with money and arms, enabling him to re-establish himself in the Kweilin region. Ting Wen-chiang, ' Kuang-tung chün-shih chi ', *Chin-tai shih tzu-liao*, 3 (1958), 51–3, and *Tung-fang tsa-chih*, XXI, No. 13 (1924), 3. Hereafter cited as *TFTC.*

[24] Mao Ssu-ch'eng, *Min-kuo shih-wu-nien i-ch'ien chih Chiang Chieh-shih hsien-sheng* (Shanghai, 1936), p. 201.

[25] Huang Shao-hsiung, *Wu-shih hui-i*, p. 52.

[26] *Ibid.*, p. 62.

[27] *KHHHKMTI.*, p. 258, and Yang Yi-t'ang, *Teng Yen-ta hsien-sheng i-chu* (Hong Kong, 1949), p. 8.

[28] ' Li Tsung-jen Autobiography ', Ch. 12, p. 12.

[29] *North China Herald*, 21 July 1923. Hereafter cited as *NCH.*

[30] Huang Shao-hsiung, *Wu-shih hui-i*, p. 71.

[31] *Ibid.*, p. 72. Previously connections between the two areas had been by land; now they were linked by water, and contact was much closer. The risk of misunderstanding through poor communications was reduced.

[32] *NCH*, 21 June 1924, p. 447.

[33] *South China Morning Post*, 21 July 1924, p. 10.

[34] *Ibid.*

[35] Rex Ray, *Cowboy Missionary in Kwangsi* (Nashville, Tenn., 1964), p. 18.

[36] ' Li Tsung-jen Autobiography ', Ch. 12, p. 7; Huang Shao-hsiung, *Wu-shih hui-i*, pp. 88–90.

[37] ' Li Tsung-jen Battle Collection ', Vol. I, Ch. 1, n.p. This collection of military documents, battle orders, maps, etc., is on microfilm in the East Asian Library, Columbia University.

[38] *Nan-yang shang-pao*, 30 June 1924, p. 8.

[39] *BSME*, 32 (August 1924), 532.

[40] Mao Ssu-ch'eng *Min-kuo shih-wu-nien i-ch'ien*, p. 353.

[41] Huang Shao-hsiung, *Wu-shih hui-i*, p. 81. Li's banner was the character ' Li ' in red on a black background, Huang's the character ' Huang ' in red on a white background.

[42] ' Li Tsung-jen Autobiography ', Ch. 12, p. 2.

[43] *Nan-yang shang-pao*, 30 June 1924.

[44] *NCH*, 17 January 1925, p. 87. Lu's troops in the Kweilin region were driven into Hunan, and amalgamated into the Hunan Army. *TCSSNCKCSS*, Vol. II, p. 346. Lu retired to Soochow and lived there quietly until 1927, when his home was confiscated by the occupying Kuomintang forces. *NCH*, 2 April 1927, p. 4.

[45] Huang Shao-hsiung illustrated the differences between himself and Pai by describing their chess game, in which one or other was always disastrously defeated: ' He always used encircling tactics and always enjoyed breaking through the enemy defences, I was in the habit of using rush attacks, searching out the enemy's weak points.' Huang Shao-hsiung, *Wu-shih hui-i*, p. 101.

[46] Huang Hsü-ch'u, ' Pai-kuei i-wang lu, 20 ', *Ch'un-ch'iu*, 172 (1 September 1964), 18.

[47] Lo Chia-lun, *Kuo-fu nien-p'u ch'u-kao* (Taipei, 1959), p. 705.

[48] Mao Ssu-ch'eng, *Min-kuo shih-wu-nien i-ch'ien*, p. 357.

49 The Kuomintang's decision to support Li and Huang was taken against strenuous opposition by the Kwangsi generals in Canton. So great was their antipathy that they tried to assassinate Huang when he arrived in Canton. Huang Shao-hsiung, *Wu-shih hui-i*, pp. 78–80.

50 While Huang was in Canton, a disastrous fire, probably started at the instigation of the Kwangsi generals in Canton, destroyed a third of Wuchow, Huang's stronghold. *China Weekly Review*, 3 January 1925, p. 140.

51 Superficially, the Federalist Movement was much stronger in south China than was the Kuomintang. It was strong in Hunan and Yunnan, and in those parts of Kwangtung controlled by Ch'en Chiung-ming.

52 ' Li Tsung-jen Autobiography ', Ch. 13, p. 7.

53 *KHHHKMTL*, p. 264.

54 *BSME*, 42 (June 1925), 369.

55 *NCH*, 2 May 1925, p. 198.

56 Casualties in this last campaign for the unification of Kwangsi were very heavy. Three thousand men died in one of the battles for Liuchow; Yunnanese troops besieged in Nanning died like flies; the extraordinary insanitariness of their living conditions contributed to the heavy death toll. *BSME*, 43 (July 1925), 435.

57 Kao T'ung, ' Li Tsung-jen Huang Shoa-hsiung ch'i-chia chen-shih ', *Ch'un-ch'iu*, 73 (16 July 1960), 12.

58 *Shan-hou hui-i kung-pao*, 1 (February 1925), 317.

59 Lo Chia-lun (ed.), *Ko-ming wen-hsien* (Taipei, 1953–   ), Vol. XI, p. 300. Hereafter cited as *KMWH*.

60 Huang Shao-hsiung, *Wu-shih hui-i*, pp. 113–14.

61 *KMWH*, Vol. XX, p. 3911.

62 Chang Kuo-p'ing, *Pai Ch'ung-hsi chiang-chün chuan*, p. 4; and Kuei K'o (*pseud.*), ' Li Tsung-jen shih-lüeh ', *Hsien-tai shih-liao*, III (Shanghai, 1934–35), 91.

63 *China Weekly Review*, 6 December 1924, p. 28; 29 August 1925, p. 280; and 26 September 1925, p. 353.

64 *NCH*, 25 July 1925, p. 46; and 5 September 1925, p. 295.

65 Jean Chesneaux, *Le mouvement ouvrier en Chine* (Paris, 1962), p. 418; and *Les syndicats chinois* (Paris, 1965), pp. 35–6.

66 *Compte rendu, 1925* (Paris, 1926), p. 775. Some foreign residents even saw T'ang Chi-yao as their saviour from bolshevism. *China Weekly Review*, 4 April 1925, p. 146.

67 ' On February 25th . . . there was a big procession, in Nanning itself, of the bolshevik elements of the city. While passing in front of the mission, the military governor Huoang Tchao Hiung [*sic*], who was at the head of the procession, began himself to storm " down with French Imperialism ". And the crowd chorused after him.' *BSME*, 52 (April 1926), 85.

68 Chung-ku Kuo-min-tang chung-yang chih-hsing wei-yüan-hui, *Chung-kuo Kuo-min-tang ti-er-tz'u tai-piao ta-hui hsüan-yen chi chüeh-i an* (Canton, 1926), p. 85.

69 Huang Shao-hsiung, *Wu-shih hui-i*, pp. 75–7.

70 Li Tsung-jen and Huang Shao-hsiung were elected alternate members of the Central Supervisory Committee at the Second Congress in January 1926. *Ibid.*, p. 122.

71 C. Martin Wilbur, ' Military Separatism and the Process of Reunification under the Nationalist Regime, 1922–1937 ', in Ho P'ing-ti and Tang Tsou (ed.), *China in Crisis* (Chicago, 1968), Vol. I, pp. 203–63.

72 Li Tsung-jen had not been in Kwangtung since he was forced to flee from the province five years before. He did not go to Canton until after the alliance was signed. Huang Shao-hsiung, *Wu-shih hui-i*, p. 126.

73 Chang Ch'i-yün, *Tang-shih kai-yao* (Taipei, 1951–52), Vol. II, p. 486ff.

⁷⁴ 'Li Tsung-jen Battle Collection', Vol. II, p. 1. (See note 37 above.) In January, Wang Ching-wei had promised the Kwangsi leaders financial aid if they would put some of their troops at the Kuomintang's disposal, but there is no evidence that this commitment was honoured. *Hua-tzu jih-pao*, 3 February 1926.

⁷⁵ Li Ang, *Hung-se wu-t'ai* (Chungking, 1942), p. 8.

⁷⁶ *KMWH*, Vol. XX, p. 3916.

⁷⁷ For a discussion of the SS *Chung-Shan* Incident, see Wilbur, 'Military Separatism', p. 238, and Wu T'ien-wei, 'Chiang Kai-shek's March Twentieth Coup d'Etat of 1926', *JAS*, XXVII (1968), 585–602.

⁷⁸ Kwangsi Party membership of 128,394 for October 1926 represented a gain of 377 per cent over the previous figure. Li Tsung-huang, *Chung-kuo Kuo-min-tang tang-shih* (Nanking, 1935), p. 443.

⁷⁹ Hu Hua, *Chung-kuo hsin min-chu chu-i ko-ming shih* (Peking, 1950), p. 78.

⁸⁰ *TFTC*, XXV, No. 16 (24 August 1926), 185.

Chapter 4

¹ For a fuller description of the Kuomintang in 1926, see Wilbur, 'Military Separatism'.

² A detailed account of the Northern Expedition is given in Chang Tzu-sheng, *Kuo-min ko-ming chün Pei-fa chan-cheng shih* (Shanghai, 1933). See also Wilbur, 'Military Separatism'.

³ Wu Hsiang-hsiang, 'Ju-lai-fo yü T'ang Sheng-chih', *Chuan-chi wen-hsüeh*, VIII, No. 3 (1966), 15.

⁴ *Ibid.*, p. 16.

⁵ For a biography of Yeh Ch'i, see Kuang-hsi sheng cheng-fu t'ung-chi ch'u, *Ku-chin Kuang-hsi lü-Kuei jen-ming chien* (Kweilin, 1934), p. 89.

⁶ See Yin Shih, *Li-Chiang kuan-hsi yü Chung-kuo* (Hong Kong, 1954). Yin Shih is the pseudonym of Li Tsung-jen's secretary, Ch'eng Ssu-yüan.

⁷ Mao Ssu-ch'eng, *Min-kuo shih-wu-nien i-ch'ien*, p. 616; and Yin Shih, *Li-Chiang kuan-hsi yü Chung-kuo*, p. 14. Rumours that Yeh was in Wuchow to negotiate T'ang's entry into the Kuomintang were published while the Wuchow Conference between Kuomintang and Kwangsi leaders was still in session. *KWCP*, III, No. 3 (24 January 1926), t'a-shih, p. 1.

⁸ Mao Ssu-ch'eng, *Min-kuo shih-wu-nien i-ch'ien*, p. 616.

⁹ Wilbur and How, *Documents on Communism*, p. 368; and Ts'ao Chü-jen, *Chiang Pai-li p'ing-chuan*, pp. 23–4. On 24 May Chiang Kai-shek saw representatives from Kiangsi, Kweichow and Honan about possible future alliances. Mao Ssu-ch'eng, *Min-kuo shih-wu-nien i-chien*, p. 670.

¹⁰ *KWCP*, III, No. 33 (29 August 1926), ta-shih, p. 3.

¹¹ Literally 'protect the frontiers and pacify the people'. It suggested the limited aim only of establishing absolute military control over the province.

¹² *TFTC*, XXIII, No. 6 (25 March 1926), 1; *KWCP*, III No. 11 (28 March 1926), 36; No. 12 (4 April 1926), 31; and No. 14 (18 April 1926), 29. Wu P'ei-fu's main stronghold was Wuch'ang; he was Hunan's most powerful neighbour, and his neutrality was essential if T'ang were to gain control of Hunan.

¹³ Pai Ch'ung-hsi and Ch'en Ming-shu, former classmates of T'ang at Paoting, were sent to see him in late March, to check on his loyalty. He assured them that he was committed to the Kuomintang. *KWCP*, III, No. 14 (18 April 1926), 29.

¹⁴ *Ch'en pao*, 15 May 1926, in Hatano Ken'ichi, *Gendai Shihna no kiroku*, May 1926, p. 207.

¹⁵ Yin Shih, *Li-Chiang kuan-hsi yü Chung-kuo*, p. 14; and *NCH*, 30 January 1926, p. 186.

¹⁶ Mao Ssu-ch'eng, *Min-kuo shih-wu-nien i-chien*, p. 665.

¹⁷ *KWCP*, III, No. 17 (9 May 1926), 26 and No. 18 (16 May 1926), 31–2. The threat to Kwangsi from Hunan was strong enough to have impelled the Kwangsi

leaders to advance their troops without sanction from Canton, and they seem
to have been moving into Hunan before official orders arrived. 'Li Tsung-jen
Autobiography ', Ch. 15, p. 2; and *Yi-shih pao*, 7 May 1926, in Hatano Ken'ichi,
Gendai Shihna no kiroku, May 1926, p. 96.

18 Wu T'ien-wei, 'Chiang Kai-shek's March Twentieth Coup d'Etat of 1926 ',
p. 590; and Louis Fischer, *The Soviets in World Affairs* (London, 1930), pp.
661–3.

19 Mao Ssu-ch'eng, *Min-kuo shih-wu-nien i-ch'ien*, p. 668. The expedition was not
officially launched until July.

20 *TFTC*, XXIII, No. 15 (10 August 1926), 28.

21 Alice T. Hobart, *Within the Walls of Nanking* (London, 1928), p. 58.

22 Harold Isaacs, *The Tragedy of the Chinese Revolution* (2nd revised ed., New
York, 1966), pp. 113–21; and Jean Chesneaux, *The Chinese Labor Movement*
(Stanford, 1968), pp. 319–44.

23 Wilbur and How, *Documents on Communism*, p. 411.

24 Feng's forces had been holding Wu P'ei-fu's forces at Nank'ou Pass outside
Peking since April, after Wu had ousted Feng from Peking. The stubborn
defence of Nank'ou is one of the most celebrated military exploits of the
Republican period. It was coincidentally a great help to the Kuomintang
(before Feng's actual alliance with it) because it kept Wu tied up, and allowed
the Kuomintang time to make its own advance from the south – Sheridan,
Chinese Warlord, pp. 190–3.

25 *KMWH*, Vol. XII, pp. 91–5 contains details of the T'ang-Li plan and of Chiang
Kai-shek's plan.

26 Wilbur and How, *Documents on Communism*, p. 393.

27 Chiang Tsung-t'ung yen-lun hui-pien pien-chi wei-yüan-hui, *Chiang Tsung-
t'ung yen-lun hui-pien* (Taipei, 1956), Vol. VIII, pp. 229ff.

28 Kuo Mo-jo, *Pei-fa t'u-tz'u* (Shanghai, 1947), p. 39.

29 *NCH*, 11 September 1926, p. 485. The first arrivals at Wuch'ang were a detachment of cooks from the Fourth Army, who arrived at the walls of the city
before the gates were closed, well ahead of the main body of troops. ' Li Tsung-
jen Autobiography ', Ch. 19, p. 6.

30 *KMWH*, Vol. XII, p. 129.

31 Wilbur and How, *Documents on Communism*, p. 418. Teruni was chief Soviet
adviser to the General Political Department of the National Revolutionary
Army.

32 Kuo Mo-jo, *Pei-fa t'u-tz'u*, p. 128.

33 H. O. Chapman, *The Chinese Revolution, 1926/7* (London, 1928), p. 2.

34 M. N. Roy, *Revolution and Counter-revolution in China* (Calcutta, 1946), p.
403.

35 Kuo Mo-jo, *Pei-fa t'u-tz'u*, p. 141.

36 *NCH*, 11 September 1926, p. 485.

37 *Yi-shih pao*, 5 August 1926, in Hatano Ken'ichi, *Gendai Shihna no kiroku*,
August 1926, p. 57; and *TFTC*, XXIII, No. 20 (25 October 1926), 131.

38 The Kuomintang maintained the valuable opium trade which passed through
Wuhan. An Opium Suppression Bureau was set up as soon as the three cities
passed into Kuomintang control, not to prevent the smoking and sale of opium,
but to ensure that the profits from the trade went into the Kuomintang coffers.
See Clubb, *Opium Traffic in China*, p. 122.

39 Huang Shao-hsiung, *Wu-shih hui-i*, p. 127; and Mao Ssu-ch'eng, *Min-kuo
shih-wu-nien i-ch'ien*, pp. 672, 711.

40 *Ch'en pao*, 4 August 1926, in Hatano Ken'ichi, *Gendai Shihna no kiroku*,
August 1926, p. 49; and *NCH*, 14 August 1926, p. 295.

41 *TFTC*, XXV, No. 15 (10 August 1928), 27.

42 The number of Kuomintang troops increased from 100,000 in July 1926 (a figure which already included several recently-converted warlord units) to 260,000 in December of the same year. Wilbur and How, *Documents on Communism*, pp. 381–2. This figure did not include the forces of Feng Yü-hsiang.

43 Conrad Brandt, *Stalin's Failure in China* (Cambridge, Mass., 1958), p. 89. Political work was actively pursued only in three of the original six armies of the National Revolutionary Army, the Second, the Fourth and the Sixth. The First Army lost its political commissar, Chou En-lai, after the *Chung-shan* Incident, and political work was never revived there. Hu Hua, *Chung-kuo hsin min-chu chu-i ko-ming shih*, p. 78.

44 *KWCP*, IV, No. 34 (4 September 1926), ta-shih, p. 1.

45 George Sokolosky, 'The Kuomintang', *China Year Book* (1928), p. 1,350. Hereafter cited as *CYB*.

46 *TFTC*, XXIII, No. 16 (24 August 1926), 185.

47 *Yi-shih pao*, 19 March 1927, in Hatano Ken'ichi, *Gendai Shihna no kiroku*, March 1927, pp. 260–1.

48 The fall of the Shanghai–Nanking region has been described in detail elsewhere. See Brandt, *Stalin's Failure in China*, and Isaacs, *Tragedy of the Chinese Revolution*.

49 *NCH*, 26 March 1927, p. 488; and 2 April 1927, p. 7.

50 Huang Shao-hsiung, *Wu-shih hui-i*, p. 125.

51 Mao Ssu-ch'eng, *Min kuo shih-wu-nien i-ch'ien*, p. 978. This man's name appears in Chinese as Lung-ko-wa. He may be Roman Voytsekhovich Longva. See Vera Vladimirovna Vishryakova-Akimova, *Two Years in Revolutionary China, 1925–1927*, translated by Stephen Levine (Cambridge, Mass., 1971), p. 44.

52 *Ibid.*, p. 140; and Li Tsung-jen, *Li Tsung-ssu-ling tsui-chin yen-chiang chi*, p. 32. F. F. Liu, an associate of the Kwangsi Clique, states that 'Li and Pai shared a soldier's suspicion for the motives of the Communist International in China', but this cryptic statement does not take us much further in understanding the hostility of the Kwangsi leaders to Communism. F. F. Liu, *A Military History of Modern China* (Princeton, 1956), p. 47.

53 Isaacs, *Tragedy of the Chinese Revolution*, p. 144.

54 Arthur Ransome, *The Chinese Puzzle* (London, 1927), p. 112; and *NCH*, 23 April 1927, p. 142.

55 Chiang Yung-ching, *Pao-lo-ting yü Wu-han cheng-ch'üan* (Taipei, 1963), p. 158.

56 *Ch'en pao*, 29 March 1927, in Hatano Ken'ichi, *Gendai Shihna no kiroku*, March 1927, p. 376.

57 Isaacs, *Tragedy of the Chinese Revolution*, p. 173.

58 Chang Kuo-p'ing, *Pai Ch'ung-hsi chiang-chün chuan*, p. 21.

59 *Ibid.*, p. 23. Agnes Smedley tells the same story in *The Great Road*, p. 191, but refers only to 'a Kwangsi unit' as Chou's rescuers, not to Pai Ch'ung-hsi.

60 Isaacs, *Tragedy of the Chinese Revolution*, p. 146; and Liu, *Military History of Modern China*, p. 47. Huang Shao-hsiung, as the titular head of the Seventh Army's political bureau, made a special trip to the army headquarters to direct the Purge there. Huang Shao-hsiung, *Wu-shih hui-i*, p. 182.

61 See Chapter 5 for details of the Communist movement in Kwangsi.

62 *NCH*, 30 April 1927, p. 159.

63 *TFTC*, XXIV, No. 6 (10 February 1927), 111.

64 There were very few Kwangsi natives holding influential positions within the Kuomintang. The Kwangsi leaders had no contact with Kan Nai-kuang, the only major practising politician from Kwangsi. Ma Chün-wu, formerly a close associate of Sun Yat-sen, who was later close to the Kwangsi Clique, was in temporary retirement.

⁶⁵ *KWCP*, IV, No. 16 (1 May 1927), *jih-chi*. Nanking's military strength was considerably below that of Wuhan – 35,000 troops to Wuhan's 65,000. Fischer, *Travels in China*, p. 668. Cheng Ch'ien, commander of the Sixth Army, had switched his allegiance after his army was blamed, unfairly as he felt, for the Nanking Incident.

⁶⁶ Sheridan, *Chinese Warlord*, pp. 228–32.

⁶⁷ *KWCP*, IV, No. 32 (21 August 1927), *jih-chi*; and No. 49 (18 December 1927), *ta-shih*, p. 1. See also Anatole Kotenev, *New Lamps for Old* (Shanghai, 1931), p. 281. Feng Yü-hsiang claims that the execution of Wang T'ien-p'ei had a profound effect on the attitude of Li Tsung-jen and Pai Ch'ung-hsi towards Chiang; they were shocked by the arbitrariness of the action, and came to mistrust Chiang, possibly fearing similar treatment for themselves. Feng Yü-hsiang, *Feng Yü-hsiang hu-i lu* (Shanghai, 1949), p. 5.

⁶⁸ The spirit of Chang's troops had been crushed by the battering they received in the advance north, and by the immediate ceding of the territory they had won to Feng Yü-hsiang. They were withdrawn to the Yangtse, deeply disillusioned, and wanting only to return to Kwangtung. Ts'ai T'ing-k'ai, *Ts'ai T'ing-k'ai tzu-chuan* (Hong Kong, 1946), pp. 212–14.

⁶⁹ 'Huang Shao-hsiung shu Yüeh pien ching-kuo', in 'Liang-tu Kuang-chou shih-pien yü Chung-yang chih-chien ta-hui', p. 8; in *KWCP*, IV, No. 49 (18 December 1927).

⁷⁰ *NCH*, 20 August 1927, p. 311; and *Ch'en pao*, 17 August 1927, in Hatano Ken'ichi, *Gendai Shihna no kiroku*, August 1927, p. 226.

⁷¹ On 8 August, Li Tsung-jen's name appeared at the head of a list of prominent Nanking figures who sent a telegram to Wuhan calling for rapprochement. Tang Leang-li, *The Inner History of the Chinese Revolution* (London, 1930), p. 290.

⁷² *NCH*, 13 August 1927, p. 266.

⁷³ *Ch'en pao*, 24 August 1927, in Hatano, Ken'ichi, *Gendai Shihna no kiroku*, August 1927, p. 215. Li Chi-shen in Kwangtung had been refusing Chiang's orders for some time. *NCH*, 30 July 1927, p. 190.

⁷⁴ Lei Hsiao-ts'en, *San-shih-nien tung-luan Chung-kuo* (Hong Kong, 1955), p. 89.

⁷⁵ *TFTC*, XXIV, No. 20 (25 October 1927), 107; and Chapman, *The Chinese Revolution*, p. 239.

⁷⁶ Gustav Amann, *Chiang Kai-shek und die Regierung der Kuomintang in China* (Berlin, 1936), p. 36.

⁷⁷ Chang Ching-chiang, Hu Han-min, Wu Chih-hui, Li Shih-tseng and Ts'ai Yüan-p'ei all went to Shanghai with Chiang.

⁷⁸ Large numbers of recently-converted Chekiang troops defected back to Sun Ch'uan-fang. Once Sun's attack had been driven off, they rejoined the Kuomintang side. This kind of switching, though defensible to the Chekiang commanders on their own terms, was too flagrant to go unnoticed, and Chou Feng-chih, the senior commander, was forced to resign. *TFTC*, XXIV, No. 23 (10 December 1927), 136; and *KMWH*, Vol. XVI, p. 843.

⁷⁹ Tsou Lu, *Hui-ku lu* (Chungking, 1943), p. 193; and Lei Hsiao-ts'en, *San-shih-nien tung-luan Chung-kuo*, p. 76. The Western Hills group had split with the Kuomintang over the question of Communist participation in the Kuomintang.

⁸⁰ Tsou Lu, *Hui-ku lu*, pp. 200–2; and *KWCP*, IV, No. 37 (25 September 1927), *ta-shih*, p. 1.

⁸¹ *KMWH*, Vol. XVI, p. 2,846.

⁸² Tsou Lu, *Hui-ku lu*, p. 207; and Tang Leang-li, *Inner History of the Chinese Revolution*, p. 303.

⁸³ Chang Chi, *Chang P'u-ch'üan hsien-sheng ch'üan-chi* (Taipei, 1952), p. 98.

⁸⁴ *Huang pao*, 18 August 1927, in Hatano Ken'ichi, *Gendai Shihna no kiroku*, August 1927, p. 249.

⁸⁵ Amann, *Chiang Kai-shek*, p. 45.

[86] Ikeda Iriye, *After Imperialism* (Cambridge, Mass., 1965), pp. 148–58.

[87] *Ch'en pao*, 24 August 1927, in Hatano Ken'ichi, *Gendai Shihna no kiroku*, August 1927, p. 328; and *NCH*, 3 September 1927, p. 389.

[88] *KWCP*, IV, No. 23 (2 October 1927), *ta-shih*, p. 2.

[89] 'T'ang Sheng-chih yü ko fang-mien chih kuan-hsi', pp. 2–4, in *KWCP*, IV, No. 42 (30 October 1927). Wang Ching-wei was briefly chairman of the Wuhan Branch Political Council, but left for Canton in October.

[90] *KMWH*, Vol. XVII, p. 3,028; and *Ch'en pao*, 19 November 1927, in Hatano, Ken'ichi, *Gendai Shihna no kiroku*, November 1927, p. 259.

[91] *NCH*, 26 November 1927, p. 358. Li had been making generous contributions to the Kwangsi leaders in Nanking, which did not endear him to the Cantonese taxpayers. Huang Shao-hsiung, *Wu-shih hui-i*, p. 181; and *NCH*, 10 December 1927, p. 440.

[92] Huang's arrival in Canton was in contravention of an understanding which Li Chi-shen had reached with Wang Ching-wei, and gave fuel to rumours that the Kwangsi leaders were planning a *coup* against Wang and Chang Fa-k'uei. Tang Leang-li, *Inner History of the Chinese Revolution*, p. 311; and *NCH*, 3 December 1927, p. 397.

[93] Even though he was on the run, Huang Shao-hsiung rejoiced in the publicity which the events in Canton brought him, transforming him (at last) from a minor figure to one 'famous throughout the land'. Huang Shao-hsiung, *Wu-shih hui-i*, p. 194.

[94] Donald Gillin, review of Sheridan, *Chinese Warlord*, in *JAS*, XXVI, No. 3 (1967), 473.

[95] *KWCP*, IV, No. 48 (11 December 1927), *ta-shih*, p. 1.

[96] *Yi-shih pao*, 19 November 1927, in Hatano, Ken'ichi, *Gendai Shihna no kiroku*, November 1927, p. 261.

[97] *KMWH*, Vol. XVI, pp. 2,875–9.

[98] The fighting to secure Kwangtung was marked by 'tragic, painful and shameful' battles between Kwangsi troops and those of Chang Fa-k'uei – the same troops which had refused to fight each other in July. Huang Shao-hsiung, *Wu-shih hui-i*, p. 196.

[99] *NCH*, 7 January 1928, p. 1.

[100] Amann, *Chiang Kai-shek*, p. 47.

[101] *NCH*, 10 December 1927, p. 437.

[102] Yin Shih, *Li-Chiang kuan-hsi yü Chung-kuo*, p. 35.

Chapter 5

[1] Huang Shao-hsiung, *Wu-shih hui-i*, pp. 126–7.

[2] *Ibid.*, pp. 133–4.

[3] The Provincial Assembly was the lineal descendant of the Assembly set up in 1910 at the behest of the Ch'ing Government. It had never exercised any real political or administrative authority.

[4] Huang Shao-hsiung, *Wu-shih hui-i*, p. 130.

[5] *Ibid.*, p. 188.

[6] *NCH*, 4 December 1926, p. 444. *Chao-p'ing hsien chih* gives details of anti-bandit campaigns in a single *hsien*.

[7] Reports of major bandit activity are found in *NCH*, 11 February 1928, p. 217; and 20 October 1928, p. 190. See also *BSME*, 61 (January 1927), 52; 69 (September 1927), 569; and 78 (June 1928), 370.

[8] Wu had formed an alliance with T'ang Chi-yao of Yunnan and with Liu Chen-huan, a displaced Kwangsi warlord, to try and launch an attack in the Kuomintang rear. *Ch'en Pao*, 29 September 1926, in Hatano Ken'ichi, *Gendai Shihna no Kiroku*, September 1926, pp. 362–5.

[9] The first figure, 15,000, appears in a report on Kwangsi written in 1928: Kuang Hsiao-an, 'Chien-she hua ti Kuang-hsi pt 1', *KWCP*, V, No. 43 (4 November

1928), 3. The second figure, 20,000, is for a slightly earlier date and appears in *CYB* (1928), p. 1,296. It is probably more realistic than the first.

10 Huang Shao-hsiung, *Wu-shih hui-i*, p. 127; and Hsü Pi-hsü (ed.), *Kuang-hsi chien-she chi-p'ing* (n.p., 1935), p. 57. Hereafter cited by title.

11 Kuang Hsiao-an, ' Chien-she hua ti kuang-hsi pt 1 ', *KWCP*, V, No. 43 (4 November 1928), p. 1.

12 *Ibid.*, p. 8. The currency cited in the source is unspecified *yüan*. The sums listed are therefore only rough indications, not accurate amounts.

13 *Kuang-hsi ko-ming chün pan-yüeh k'an*, 2 (July 1926), 67; and Huang Shao-hsiung, *Wu-shih hui-i*, p. 149.

14 Huang Hsü-ch'u, ' Pa-kuei i-wang lu, 26 ', *Ch'un-ch'iu*, 178 (1 December 1964), 15.

15 *Kuei hsien chih*, pp. 491ff.

16 Clubb, *The Opium Traffic in China*, p. 37.

17 Huang Hsü-ch'u, ' Pa-kuei i-wang lu, 26 '.

18 Mao Ssu-ch'eng, *Min-kuo shih-wu-nien i-ch'ien*, p. 922.

19 *NCH*, 1 December 1928, p. 350.

20 *KWCP*, VI, No. 2 (13 January 1929), *jih-chi*.

21 Kuang-hsi chün-ch'u cheng-chih pu, *Kuang-hsi ko-ming hui-i lu* (Nanning, 1959), p. 65. Hereafter cited as *KHKMHIL*.

22 Ch'ien Chia-chü *et al.*, *Kuang-hsi sheng ching-chi kai-k'uang*, p. 171.

23 *NCH*, 16 May 1925, p. 276; and *BSME*, 52 (April 1925), 249.

24 Huang Shao-hsiung, *Wu-shih hui-i*, p. 132; and Ch'ien Chia-chü *et al.*, *Kuang-hsi sheng ching-chi kai-kuang*, p. 171.

25 Huang Shao-hsiung, *Wu-shih hui-i*, p. 133.

26 *NCH*, 3 July 1926, p. 5.

27 Ch'ien Chia-chü *et al.*, Kuang-hsi sheng ching-chi kai-kuang, p. 172.

28 *Ibid.*, p. 226. See also Maritime Customs figures for the three treaty ports of Wuchow, Nanning and Lunchow printed annually in the *CYB*.

29 Charlotte Furth, *Ting Wen-chiang : Science and China's New Culture* (Cambridge, Mass., 1970), pp. 192–4.

30 George Sokolsky, *China* (Shanghai, 1920), p. 11.

31 *NCH*, 23 February 1929, p. 39.

32 *Ibid.*, 17 March 1928, p. 429.

33 Exports of tung oil were boosted by the upheavals in Hunan in 1927 and 1928. Exports from Kweichow which normally went through Hunan were diverted through Wuchow, making Kwangsi's export figures artificially high. Ch'ien Chia-chü *et al.*, *Kuang-hsi sheng ching-chi kai-kuang*, p. 9.

34 Kuang Hsiao-an, ' Chien-she hua ti Kuang-hsi pt 2 ', *KWCP*, VI, No. 44 (11 November 1928), 4.

35 Huang Shao-hsiung, *Wu-shih hui-i*, p. 154.

36 *NCH*, 25 June 1927, p. 429.

37 Dieter Schulze, *Das politisch-geographisches Kräfterverhältnis zwischen den drei chinesischen sudwest Provinzen* (Heidelberg, 1940), p. 137.

38 Kuang Hsiao-an, ' Chien-she hua ti Kuang-hsi pt 3 ', *KWCP*, VI, No. 45 (18 November 1928), 5.

39 Kwangsi troops fought in Kwangtung on the following occasions: in 1925 in the North River and Nanlu areas, against warlord remnants; in 1927 in the East River area and in the North River area, against Communist troops; and at the end of the same year in the Canton area.

40 Li was known in the foreign press by the (approving) sobriquet of ' Kwangtung's Mussolini '. *NCH*, 3 September 1927, p. 397.

41 Huang Shao-hsiung, *Wu-shih hui-i*, pp. 167–9; and Huang Hsü-ch'u, ' Pa-kuei i-wang lu, 27 ', *Ch'un-ch'iu*, 179 (16 December 1964), 16.

42 *China Weekly Review*, 6 December 1924, p. 8; and *NCH*, 26 September 1925, p. 92.

[43] Shih Hua (*pseud.*), 'Kuang-hsi Kung-chan-tang chih kuo-ch'ü chi hsien-tai', *Hsien-tai shih-liao*, II, 316–18.

[44] *KHKMHIL*, p. 150; and Yang Chia-ming, *Min-kuo shih-wu-nien hsüeh-sheng yün-tung* (Shanghai, 1927), p. 96.

[45] *BSME*, 48 (December 1925), 775; and *NCH*, 30 January 1926, p. 186.

[46] Huang Shao-hsiung, *Wu-shih hui-i*, p. 169.

[47] *NCH*, 23 January 1926, p. 144.

[48] *Chao-p'ing hsien chih*, p. 40.

[49] *Kuei hsien chih*, pp. 411–18.

[50] Huang Hsü-ch'u, 'Pa-kuei i-wang lu, 25', *Ch'un-ch'iu*, 177 (16 November 1964), 15.

[51] *NCH*, 15 January 1927, p. 62.

[52] Huang Shao-hsiung, *Wu-shih hui-i*, pp. 135–6.

[53] *South China Morning Post*, 12 April 1926, pp. 46, 49.

[54] Ray, *Cowboy Missionary in Kwangsi*, pp. 30–1.

[55] *BSME*, 56 (August 1926), 511.

[56] *NCH*, 17 April 1926, p. 105.

[57] *Ibid.*, 1 May 1926, p. 198.

[58] Shih Hua 'Kuang-hsi Kung-chan-tang chih kuo-ch'ü chi hsien-tai', p. 318.

[59] N. Fierce, 'Kuo-min cheng-fu chih hsia ti Kuang-hsi', *Hsiang-tao chou-pao*, IV, No. 165 (7 August 1926), 1,652.

[60] *KHKHMIL*, p. 151.

[61] Fierce, 'Kuo-min Cheng-fu chih hsia ti Kuang-hsi', p. 1,651.

[62] *Kuang-hsi ko-ming chün pan-yüeh k'an*, 2 (July 1926), 46.

[63] In one incident, Huang refused to halt the press-ganging of coolies to act as porters for the army. Huang Shao-hsiung, *Wu-shih hui-i*, p. 171. In another, the police at Wuchow were permitted to open fire on striking workers. Li Yün-han, *Ts'ung jung-kung tao ch'ing-tang* (Taipei, 1966), p. 659.

[64] Mu Wen-hua,, 'Hui-i Kung-chan-chu-i ch'ing-nien t'uan tsai Nan-ning ti tou-cheng', *Hung-ch'i p'iao*, VI, 23.

[65] Jen-min ch'u-pan she, *Ti-i-tz'u kuo-nei ko-ming chan-cheng shih-ch'i ti-nung-min yün-tung* (Peking, 1953), p. 436. Even these few organisations were usually very small. The Liuchiang hsien organisation had only eighty members in 1927. *Liu-chiang hsien chih* (Liuchiang, 1937; reprinted Taipei, 1967), p. 37.

[66] Huang Shao-hsiung, *Wu-shih hui-i*, p. 172.

[67] *Ibid.*, p. 173.

[68] The highest figure, 200 arrests, is given in *KHKMHIL*, p. 158.

[69] Li Yün-han, *Ts'ung jung-kung tao ch'ing-tang*, p. 660. The executed members of the Executive Committee were Liang Liu-tu and Huang Chih-chih; Lei Pei-t'ao, a member of the Provincial Supervisory Committee, was also executed. His brother, Lei Pei-hung, fled the province, but returned in the 1930s to work with the Kwangsi Clique.

[70] For 1958 figure, see Kuang-hsi chuang-tsu tzu-chih-ch'ü ch'ou-pei wei-yüan-hui *Kuang-hsi chuang-tsu tzu-chih ch'ü* (Peking, 1958), p. 43. For earlier figures, see P'ang Tun-chih, *Kuang-hsi she-hui t'e chih* (Hong Kong, 1950), p. 20.

[71] Wiens, *Han Chinese Expansion*, p. 144.

[72] Wei's family was probably sinicised Chuang. His parents died when he was quite young, he sold his patrimony and went travelling through south China. In 1916 he went home to Tunglan and organised a small band of men to support the Hu Kuo Movement. This band was amalgamated into a regular army unit, whose commander sent Wei to study at the Kweichow Military Academy. He graduated in 1919, and then travelled to Szechwan and Kwangtung. In 1922 he finally returned to Tunglan. See Chu Chung-yü (ed.), *Wei Pa-ch'ün* (Peking, 1960), pp. 9–12.

[73] Kuang-hsi sheng-cheng-fu t'ung-chi ch'u, *Ku-chin Kuang-hsi lü-Kuei jen-ming chien*, p. 43.

[74] Chang Yu-i (ed.), *Chung-kuo chin-tai nung-yeh shih tzu-liao*, II, p. 275.

[75] *KHKMHIL*, p. 95. Such practices were still used during the anti-Japanese War by Chuang guerillas. See Kuang-hsi chuang-tsu wen-hsüeh shih-pien chi-shih *Kuang-hsi chuang-tsu wen-hsüeh* (Nanning, 1961), p. 282. Hereafter cited by title.

[76] Li Yün-han, *Ts'ung jung-kung tao ch'ing-tang*, p. 659; and Hsieh Fu-min, 'Chuang-tsu jen-min yu-hsiu er-tzu Wei Pa-ch'ün', *Hung-ch'i p'iao-p'iao*, V, 55.

[77] Huang Shao-hsiung, *Wu-shih hui-i*, p. 319.

[78] Shih Hua, 'Kuang-hsi Kung-chan-tang chih kuo-ch'ü chi hsien-tai', p. 319.

[79] *KHKMHIL*, p. 151.

[80] Hsieh Fu-min, 'Chuang-tsu jen-min yu-hsiu er-tzu Wei Pa-ch'ün', p. 56.

[81] K'ung Ch'u, *Wo yü hung chün* (Hong Kong, 1955), pp. 168, 171. K'ung was a Communist until his defection from the Party in 1934. He was sent to Kwangsi in 1929 by the Party Centre to help organise the Kwangsi soviets. See also *KHKMHIL*, p. 121.

[82] *Min-tsu t'uan-chieh*, 7 (1961), 13.

[83] *China Weekly Review*, 22 March 1930, p. 130.

[84] *Min-tsu t'uan-chieh*, 7 (1961), 16.

[85] Hsieh Fu-min, 'Chuang-tsu jen min yu-hsiu er-tzu Wei Pa-ch'ün', p. 60; and *KHKMHIL*, p. 12. Teng was acting directly under the CCP Centre in Shanghai. His task was complicated by the fact that communications between Shanghai and Kwangsi took up to forty days.

[86] *Kuang-hsi chuang-tsu wen-hsüeh*, p. 288.

[87] *KHKMHIL*, p. 25; and *China Weekly Review*, 22 March 1930, p. 130.

[88] *KHKMHIL*, pp. 11, 14.

[89] *Ibid.*, pp. 125, 136.

[90] *Ibid.*, pp. 127, 137–8. See also *BSME*, 100 (April 1930), 240.

[91] Edgar Snow, *Random Notes on Red China* (Cambridge, Mass., 1957), p. 137. The Annamite rising was the famous and violent mutiny of the Yen Bay garrison, one of the first manifestations of the Vietnamese nationalist movement. It was not a Communist-led rising, and I have found little evidence of a direct link between it and the activity over the border in Kwangsi.

[92] Huang Shao-hsiung, *Wu-shih hui-i*, p. 138.

[93] K'ung Ch'u, *Wo yü hung chün*, p. 202.

[94] *KHKMHIL*, p. 22. See Dick Wilson, *The Long March* (London, 1971), pp. 136–50, for a description of Communist relations with the Lolo and other tribal peoples during the Long March.

[95] K'ung Ch'u, *Wo yü hung chün*, p. 196.

[96] *Ibid.*, pp. 198–9.

[97] *Ibid.*, p. 262.

[98] Hsieh Fu-min, 'Chuang-tsu jen-min yu-hsiu er-tzu Wei Pa-ch'ün', p. 61; and P'ang Tun-chih, *Ch'ing-suan Kuei-hsi* (Canton, 1950), p. 14.

[99] Shih Hua, 'Kuang-hsi Kung-chan-tang chih kuo ch'ü chi hsien-tai', p. 322.

[100] K'ung Ch'u, *Wo yü hung chün*, p. 242. Of the survivors of the Kwangsi Soviets, Teng Hsiao-p'ing's career is well known. Chang Yün-i was Deputy Commander of the New Fourth Army during the Anti-Japanese War; from 1949–58 he was Chairman of Kwangsi.

[101] Feng Ho-fa (ed.), *Chung-kuo nung-ts'un ching-chi tzu-liao, hsü pien*, p. 1,018; and *Kuang-hsi chih chien-she*, p. 513.

[102] Shih Hua, 'Kuang-hsi Kung-chan-tang chih kuo ch'ü chi hsien-tai'.

[103] Chang Ch'i-yün, *Chung-hua min-kuo shih-kang* (Taipei, 1954), Vol. I, pp. 284–321.

[104] Kuang Hsiao-an, ' Chien-she hua ti Kuang-hsi pt 1 ', *KWCP*, V, No. 43, 1–9; *ibid.*, pt 2, *KWCP*, V, No. 44, 1–4.

[105] There was a serious shortage of modern-minded men to help Huang carry out his new schemes. The first Provincial Director of Finance resigned because Huang refused to support his demand for the reinstatement of Confucian rites. Huang Shao-hsiung, *Wu-shih hui-i*, p. 131.

[106] Kuang Hsiao-an, ' Chien-she hua ti Kuang-hsi pt 3 ', *KWCP*, V, No. 45, 5.

[107] *CYB* (1929/30), p. 532.

[108] Kuang Hsiao-an, ' Chien-she hua ti Kuang-hsi pt 3 ', *KWCP*, V. No. 45, 5.

[109] Furth, *Ting Wen-chiang*, pp. 192–4. See also *Ting ku-tsung-pan Wen-chiang shih-shih nien chou-nien chi-nien k'an*, in *Chung-yang yen-chiu yüan yüan-k'an*, III (Taipei, 1956), 72.

[110] *Kuang-hsi chih chien-she*, p. 248.

[111] *Trois mois au Kouangsi*, p. 123. Other methods of preventing the spread of disease were tried. In 1928, during a cholera outbreak at Nanning, a campaign was launched against vermin. Three dollars an ounce was paid for dead flies, a lesser sum for dead rats, on a scale varying according to the size of the rats. *BSME*, 68 (August 1927), 513.

[112] *CYB* (1929/30), pp. 436–44.

[113] Kuang Hsiao-an, ' Chien-she hua-ti Kuang-hsi pt 2 ', *KWCP*, V, No. 44, 2.

[114] Ch'ien Chia-chü *et al.*, *Kuang-hsi sheng ching-chi kai-k'uang*, p. 4.

[115] Kuang Hsiao-an, ' Chien-she hua ti Kuang-hsi pt 3 ', *KWCP*, V. No. 45, 2.

[116] *Chao-p'ing hsien chih*, p. 76; *Kuei hsien chih*, p. 559.

[117] *Kuang-hsi ko-ming chün pan-yüeh k'an*, 2 (July 1926), 72.

[118] Kuang Hsiao-an, ' Chien-she hua ti Kuang-hsi pt 3 ', *KWCP*, V, No. 45, p. 2.

[119] Huang Shao-hsiung, *Wu-shih hui-i*, p. 180.

[120] *KWCP*, V, No. 35 (9 September 1928), *jih-chi.*

[121] Feng Ho-fa (ed.), *Chung-kuo nung-ts'un ching-chi tzu-liao, hsü pien*, p. 354.

[122] C. C. Chang, *China Tung Oil and Its Future* (Hong Kong, 1940), p. 2.

Chapter 6

[1] *Yi shih pao*, 7 January 1928, in Hatano Ken'ichi, *Gendai Shihna no kiroku*, January 1928, pp. 50–1.

[2] *KWCP*, V, No. 12 (1 April 1928), *ta-shih*, pp. 1–2; and *Ch'en pao*, 4 March in Hatano Ken'ichi, *Gendai Shihna no kiroku*, March 1928, p. 59; 14 March, p. 185; 20 March, p. 266.

[3] Four Group Armies were set up by the Fourth Plenum of the Kuomintang Central Executive Committee (February 1928); their size and regional holdings corresponded to the armies and territories controlled by Nanking, Feng Yü-hsiang, Yen Hsi-shan and the Kwangsi Clique.

[4] *Manchester Guardian*, 7 July 1928, p. 16.

[5] Immediately after the fall of Peking, the Fifth Plenum (July 1928) decided to close the Councils by the end of the year. The date for their closure was later put back to March 1929.

[6] *NCH*, 21 April 1928, p. 90.

[7] *KWCP*, V, No. 3 (15 January 1928), *ta-shih*, p. 6.

[8] Chang Chih-pen was a minor Kuomintang politician who had been expelled from the Party because of his association with the Western Hills group.

[9] *NCH*, 18 February 1928, p. 248.

[10] *Ibid.*, 17 March 1928, p. 425.

[11] *Ibid.*, 19 May 1928; p. 264; and 26 May, p. 314, 324.

[12] *Ching pao*, 13 July 1928, in Hatano Ken'ichi, *Gendai Shihna no kiroku*, July 1928, p. 176.

[13] Negotiations with Chang for his entry into the Kuomintang camp began immediately after the assassination of his father Chang Tso-lin, broke down

after his withdrawal into Manchuria and did not start again until October. They culminated in his attachment to the Kuomintang in December.

14 Until his rebellion, P'eng was a brigadier in the Hunan Army. See Jerome Ch'en, *Mao and the Chinese Revolution* (London, 1965), p. 149.

15 *TFTC*, XXV, No. 24 (25 December 1928), 121. Pai made several further attempts to get his resignation accepted, each time without success.

16 *Chiang pao*, 6 July 1928, in Hatano Ken'ichi, *Gendai Shihna no kiroku*, July 1928, p. 88. These were the ' yellow unions ', officially sanctioned by Nanking.

17 Chang Chi, *Chang P'u-ch'üan hsien-sheng chüan-chi*, p. 245. Chang had previously been associated with the Kwangsi Clique on the Special Committee. With him on the Peking Council was Li Shih-tseng, a Party Elder. The Council gave no real representation to the leaders of the underground organisation in Peking, which had existed before the Kuomintang took the city. This under-representation caused considerable local bitterness.

18 Wen Shih (*pseud.*), ' Ti ch'i chun ti mo-lo yü Li-Pai ti hsia-ch'ang ', *Ch'un-ch'iu*, 12 (1 January 1958), 3. *Chennankuan* is the pass between Kwangsi and Annam, *Shanhaikuan* the pass between Hopei and Manchuria. Pai Ch'ung-hsi was proud of the fact that *his* Kwangsi troops had got further than the Taiping troops, who had only got to Tientsin. Hsien Yün (*pseud.*), ' Li Pai shih tsen-yang t'ao-hui tao Kuang-hsi ' *Ch'un-ch'iu*, 65 (16 March 1960), 3.

19 *TFTC*, XXV, No. 21 (10 November 1928), 146; and 24 (25 December 1928), 121.

20 *Shih-chieh jih-pao*, 21 December 1928, in Hatano Ken'ichi, *Gendai Shihna no kiroku*, December 1928, p. 298.

21 *Ching pao*, 24 November 1928, in *ibid.*, November 1928, pp. 315–18. Tso Tsung-t'ang suppressed the Moslem Risings in the northwest in the late 1860s and early 1870s. For Pai's plans to go there, see *Chung-yang chou pao*, 23 (12 November 1928), 5; and 30 (31 December 1928), 8. Sinkiang had been ruled since 1912 by Yang Tseng-hsin who had kept the province independent of Chinese administration, and had kept friendly but autonomous relations with the Soviet Union. Yang declared for the Kuomintang in June 1928, but was assassinated shortly afterwards. His successor, Chin Shu-jen, was more openly pro-Soviet. See A. S. Whiting, *Sinkiang : Pawn or Pivot?* (Ann Arbor, 1958), pp. 8–12.

22 The Kwangsi leaders were at pains to present themselves as plain-living men, uncorrupted by their positions of authority, though Huang Shao-hsiung personally records that when he was almost kidnapped in 1927, his wife, who *was* caught, used the $10,000 and the quantity of jewellery she had with her to buy herself out, Huang Shao-hsiung, *Wu-shih hui-i*, p. 195. A dubious source claims that Li Chi-shen led a private life of great luxury and dissipation. Ya Yen (*pseud.*), ' Li Chi-shen chih Yüeh shih ', in *Hsien-tai shih-liao*, III, 85–91.

23 *KMWH*, Vol. XXV, pp. 24–5.

24 *NCH*, 26 May 1928, p. 318.

25 Huang Hsü-ch'u, ' Pa-kuei i-wang lu, pt 31 ', *Ch'un-ch'iu*, 183 (25 February 1965), 12.

26 Yin Shih, *Li-Chiang kuan-hsi yü Chung-kuo*, p. 39.

27 *Chung-yang chou-pao*, 25 (26 November 1928), 4; and 29 (24 December 1928), 3.

28 *NCH*, 22 December 1928, p. 478.

29 Huang Hsü-ch'u, ' Pa-kuei i-wang lu, pt 31 '.

30 Yin Shih, *Li-Chiang kuan-hsi yü Chung-kuo*. Li Tsung-jen was Chairman of the Wuhan Branch Political Council, but he seldom attended its meetings. The Council was run by Chang Chih-pen, the Deputy Chairman, Hu Tsung-to and Chang Hua-fu, Chief of Staff of the Fourth Group Army; all three were Hupei natives. Between July and October 1928, Li did not attend a single meeting of the Council. See *Wu-han cheng-chih fen-hui yüeh-pao* (July–October 1928), *hui-i lu*.

31 *NCH*, 10 November 1928, p. 478.

32 *Ibid.*, 3 November 1928, p. 196; and 10 November, p. 217.

33 *Ching pao*, 12 December 1928, in Hatano Ken'ichi, *Gendai Shihna no kiroku*, December 1928, pp. 173–5. One of the worst examples of the physical decline of Peking was the felling of trees in the park around the Temple of Heaven. These trees were planted in intricate patterns, connected with the ceremonial function of the Temple.

34 *NCH*, 1 December 1928, p. 480.

Chapter 7

1 See Patrick Cavendish, ' The " New China " of the Kuomintang ', in Gray (ed.), *Modern China's Search for a Political Form*, pp. 138–86, for an excellent description of the process by which the Kuomintang moved away from radicalism.

2 R. H. Tawney, quoted in ' The National Government as Viewed by an English Professor ', *China Weekly Review*, 20 June 1931, p. 86.

3 John K. Fairbank has ascribed Chiang's success at staying at the top of the Kuomintang pile in part to his ability ' to perform the traditional juggling act, to keep regional warlords or politicians in a framework of personal politics practically devoid of ideology '. See his introduction to North, *Kuomintang and Chinese Communist Elites*, p. vii.

4 See Sheridan, *Chinese Warlord*, pp. 14–16, for an illuminating discussion of warlordism after 1928, what he calls ' residual warlordism '.

5 *Ch'en Kung-po Chou Fo-hai hui-i lu ho-pien* (Hong Kong, 1967), pp. 209–10.

6 *KWCP*, V, No. 28 (22 July 1928), *ta-shih*, p. 3.

7 *Ibid.*, 27 (15 July 1928), *ta-shih*, p. 3; and *TFTC*, XXV, No. 17 (10 September, 1928), 126.

8 See Sheridan, *Chinese Warlord*, p. 243, for a detailed discussion of troop strengths. Estimates of troop numbers were very vague; they ranged as high as 2,200,000. *TFTC*, XXV, No. 17 (10 September 1928), 125.

9 *TCSSNCKCSS*, Vol. II, p. 473.

10 Soong's speech is quoted in H. F. Macnair, *China in Revolution* (Chicago, 1930), p. 160. The Central Government exercised no administrative authority in the provinces which were not making remittances to it, as was demonstrated by the fact that when the Civil Government Conference (*Min-cheng hui-i*) was convened in December 1928, only five provinces – Chekiang, Anhwei, Kiangsu, Kiangsi and Fukien – were represented. *TFTC*, XXVI, No. 3 (10 February 1929), 140.

11 T. V. Soong, ' Chüeh-ting chün-fei t'ung-i ts'ai-cheng chih t'i-an ', *KWCP*, VI, No. 6 (22 February 1929), *ta-shih*, p. 6.

12 Sheridan, *Chinese Warlord*, p. 248.

13 Gillin, *Warlord*, pp. 109–10.

14 *Chung-yang chou-pao*, 17 (1 October 1928), 4.

15 Li was chiefly concerned to dispose of units which had been associated with Chang Fa-k'uei, and with out-and-out warlord units, such as those of Li-Fu-lin. *KWCP*, V, No. 27 (15 July 1928), *ta-shih*, p. 4.

16 Details of the reorganisation of units of the Fourth Group Army are given in *Chung-yang chou-pao*, 25 (26 November 1928), 6. In July and August, two Hunanese units were forcibly disbanded. See *TFTC*, XXV, No. 18 (25 September 1928), 125; and *TCSSNCKCSS*, Vol. II, p. 450.

17 *KWCP*, V, No. 43 (5 November 1928), *ta-shih*, p. 3.

18 *Chung-yang chou-pao*, 17 (1 October 1928), 4; and 25 (26 November 1928), 8.

19 Early in 1929, the Fourth Group Army had 230,000 men; there were also 120,000 troops in Kwangtung and Kwangsi. See Ho Ying-ch'in, ' Ch'uan-kuo chün-shu ching-kuo ', in *KMWH*, Vol. XXIV, pp. 24–5.

20 See Li Tsung-jen, *Li Tsung-ssu-ling tsui-chin yen-chiang chi*, p. 45; and *Feng Yü-hsiang hui-i lu*, p. 10, p. 12. Liu discusses the suspicion between Yen, Feng and Li and Chiang in his *Military History of Modern China*, p. 73.

21 Chiang Chieh-shih, 'Kuan-yü kuo-chün pien-ch'ien wei-yüan-hui chih hsi wang', *KMWH*, Vol. XXIV, pp. 3–15.

22 Chang Ch'i-yün, *Tang-shih kai-yao*, Vol. II, p. 695.

23 Liu, *Military History of Modern China*, p. 74.

24 Tang Leang-li, *Inner History of the Chinese Revolution*, p. 344.

25 'Ti-wu-tz'u chung-yang chih-hsing wei-yüan-hui ch'üan-t'i ta-hui chi, 2 ', *KWCP*, V, No. 33 (26 August 1928), 6.

26 *Ibid.* At the end of December, the time-limit on the Councils was extended to March 1929.

27 Those who walked out went straight to Shanghai. Chiang Kai-shek spent a good part of the Plenum going back and forth to Shanghai trying to persuade absentees to return to Nanking to make up a quorum.

28 Li had been wounded in action in Kwangtung in 1916. Recurrence of trouble from this wound was the pretext for many visits to hospital during Li's later career, especially at times when the Kwangsi Clique found itself temporarily embarrassed. It was Li's equivalent of Chiang Kai-shek's toothache, Wang Ching-wei's diabetes, Yen Hsi-shan's heart trouble and Feng Yu-hsiang's stomach upsets, maladies which tended to strike them down when the political situation made a temporary retirement advisable.

29 *KWCP*, V, No. 33 (26 August 1928), *ta-shih*, p. 1; and 34 (2 September 1928), *ta-shih*, p. 2. See also Sheridan, *Chinese Warlord*, p. 244.

30 *NCH*, 13 October 1928, p. 49; and *Ching pao*, 24 November, in Hatano Ken'ichi, *Gendai Shihna no kiroku*, November 1928, p. 327.

31 Clubb, *Opium Traffic in China*, pp. 29–31.

32 Accounts of the Opium Scandal are found in Tang Leang-li, *Inner History of the Chinese Revolution*, p. 354; *KWCP*, V, No. 47 (2 December 1928), *ta-shih*, p. 1; and 48 (9 December 1928), *ta-shih*, pp. 7–8 and *jih-chi*. See also *NCH*, 1 December 1928, p. 345; 8 December, p. 396; 15 December, p. 430; and 22 December, p. 480.

33 Kuei K'o (*pseud.*), 'Li Tsung-jen shih lüeh', *Hsien-tai shih-liao*, III, 94.

34 *KWCP*, VI, No. 8 (18 March 1929), *ta-shih*, p. 1.

35 *Hsin-ch'en pao*, 2 April 1929, in Hatano Ken'ichi, *Gendai Shihna no kiroku*, April 1929, p. 30. Another possible explanation was that Lu had refused to share Hunanese provincial revenues with Hunan commanders with whom he was on bad terms. For an account of the complex relationships between Hunanese commanders, see Wu Hsiang-hsiang, *Ho Chien ti i-sheng* (Taipei, 1964), p. 240.

36 Liu, *Military History of Modern China*, pp. 61–3.

37 Chang Kuo-p'ing, *Pai Ch'ung-hsi chiang-chün chuan*, p. 37. A distinction was made between the leadership of the Kwangsi Clique and the men on the spot in Wuhan, the Hupei Generals Hu Sung-to and T'ao Chün.

38 Huang Hsü-ch'u, 'Pa-kuei i-wang lu, 31 ', *Ch'un-ch'iu*, 183 (26 February 1962), 13.

39 Chou Fo-hai, *Sheng-shuai yüeh-chin hua ts'ang-sang* (Hong Kong, 1956), p. 5.

40 *Hsin-ch'en pao*, 27 March 1929, in Hatano, Ken'ichi, *Gendai Shihna no kiroku*, March 1929, pp. 356–60.

41 *KWCP*, VI, No. 8 (8 March 1929), *ta-shih*, p. 3.

42 *Ibid.*, 9 (15 March 1929), *ta-shih*, p. 2; and *NCH*, 9 March 1929, p. 390.

43 'Military Operations in 1928 ', *CYB* (1929/30), p. 732.

44 *Hsin-ch'en pao*, 10 March 1929, in Hatano, Ken'ichi, *Gendai Shihna kiroku*, March 1929, p. 133.

45 After the defeat of the Kwangsi Clique. Ho was appointed Chairman of Hunan, a post he held until 1937. Wu Hsiang-hsiang, *ho Chien ti i-sheng*.

[46] Ts'ao Chü-jen, *Chiang Pai-li p'ing-chuan* (Hong Kong, 1963), p. 29.

[47] *Ibid.* Three of them, Li P'in-hsien, Liao Lei and Yeh Ch'i subsequently left T'ang Sheng-shih and returned to Kwangsi, where they were closely associated with the Kwangsi Clique.

[48] For accounts of Pai's escape from Peking, see Chang Kuo-p'ing *Pai Ch'ung-hsi chiang-chun chuan*, p. 39; Yin Shih, *Li-Chiang kuan-hsi yü Chung-kuo*, p. 40; and Huang Shao-hsiung, *Wu-shih hui-i*, p. 133.

[49] K'ung Ch'u, *Wo yü hung-chün* (Hong Kong, 1955), p. 165; and Yin Shih, *Li-Chiang kuan-hsi yü Chung-kuo*, pp. 39–40.

[50] *KWCP*, VI No. 11 (29 March 1929), *ta-shih*, pp. 1–2.

[51] Maurice Cohen and Charles Drage, *Two Gun Cohen* (London, 1954), p. 202.

[52] *Hsin-ch'en pao*, 2 April 1929, in Hatano Ken'ichi, *Gendai Shihna no kiroku*, April 1929, pp. 31–3.

[53] *Shang-hai hsin-wen pao*, March 1929, *ibid.*, pp. 62–9.

[54] Bauer had been chief of operations to Field-Marshal Ludendorff during the First World War. He arrived in China at the end of 1927, and took over the post vacated by the Russian military adviser Galin, as adviser to Chiang Kai-shek. In 1928 a further group of German advisers arrived. Liu, *Military History of Modern China*, p. 62.

[55] *NCH*, 13 April 1929, p. 51.

[56] Huang Shao-hsiung, *Wu-shih hui-i*, p. 198.

[57] Sheridan, *Chinese Warlord*, pp. 253–4. The speed of the Kwangsi collapse allowed Nanking to push on quickly with an attack on Feng.

[58] *KWCP*, VI, No. 14 (19 April, 1929), *ta-shih*, p. 3.

[59] Huang Hsü-ch'u, ' Pa-kuei i-wang lu, 32 ', *Ch'un-ch'iu*, 185 (26 March 1965), 19.

[60] Huang Shao-hsiung, *Wu-shih hui-i*.

[61] *TFTC*, XXVI, No. 12 (25 June 1929), 138.

[62] *Ibid.*, 11 (10 June 1929), 118.

[63] Huang Shao-hsiung, *Wu-shih hui-i*, p. 199; and Sheridan, *Chinese Warlord*, p. 260.

[64] *Hsin-ch'en pao*, 11 May 1929, in Hatano, Ken'ichi, *Gendai Shihna no kiroku*, May 1929, p. 148.

[65] Huang Hsü-ch'u, ' Pa-kuei i-wang lu, 31 ', *Ch'un-ch'iu*, 184 (1 March 1965), 20.

[66] Huang Shao-hsiung, *Wu-shih hui-i*.

[67] Li Tsung-jen, *Li Tsung-ssu-ling tsui-chin yen-chiang chi*, p. 2.

Chapter 8

[1] Chou Ch'üan, *Kuei-hsi chieh-p'ou*, pp. 26–31; and P'ang Tun-chih, *Ch'ing-suan Kuei-hsi*, pp. 12–15.

[2] See Andrew Nathan's paper, ' Factionalism in Chinese Politics: The Case of the Cultural Revolution ', delivered at the American Political Science Association Annual Meeting, January 1971, for an original and exciting discussion of factional politics and clique formation in Republican and Communist China. The analysis given here is much cruder than Mr Nathan's. It does not attempt to generalise about the structure of the cliques in general, only to explain the workings of the Kwangsi Clique.

[3] Sheridan, *Chinese Warlord*, p. 17.

[4] Lai Yen-yü, *Kuang-hsi i-lan*, ' Biographical sketches of Kwangsimen ', p. 17.

[5] K'ung Ch'u, *Wo yü hung-chün*, p. 165.

[6] Chang, still loyal to Wang Ching-wei, was trying to repeat his southward drive of 1927, to win a base for Wang.

[7] Huang Shao-hsiung, *Wu-shih hui-i*, p. 207.

[8] *Ts'ai T'ing-k'ai tzu-chuan*, pp. 260–5.

9 Yin Shih, *Li-Chiang kuan-hsi yü Chung-kuo*, pp. 48–9. Nanning and several other cities along the West River were bombed by Cantonese planes. *KHHHKMTL*, p. 266; and *Kuei hsien chih*, p. 1229.

10 After this setback, the alliance between Chang and the Kwangsi Clique collapsed. Chang went abroad and his troops were incorporated into the Kwangtung Army. Chang Kuo-p'ing, *Pai Ch'ung-hsi chiang-chün chuan*, pp. 46–8.

11 Yin Shih, *Li-Chiang kuan-hsi yü Chung-kuo*.

12 Huang Shao-hsiung, *Wu-shih hui-i*, pp. 214–19.

13 Mao Tse-tung, ' Hsing huo liao yuan ', *Mao Tse-tung hsüan-chi* (Peking, 1952), Vol. I, p. 108.

14 Lai Yen-yü, ' Frontier Defence ', p. 51.

15 Chang Kuo-p'ing, *Pai Ch'ung-hsi chiang-chün chuan*, p. 60 .

16 Many of the participants had taken part in the Expanded Conference (*K'uo-ta hui-i*) of the Kuomintang in Peking the year before.Ho Shao-ch'iung *et. al.* (ed), *Ch'en Chi-t'ang hsien-sheng chi-nien chi* (Hong Kong, 1957), p. 75.

17 *KWCP*, IX, No. 6 (2 January 1932), *fu-lu*, pp. 2–3.

Chapter 9

1 Tsou Lu, *Chung-kuo Kuo-min-tang shih-kao* (Canton, 1938; reprinted Taipei, 1965), pp. 648–51.

2 Yung Ni, ' Chien-she yü chi-hua ', *Tu-li p'ing-lun*, 5 (19 June 1932), 9.

3 A recent volume edited by Paul K. T. Sih, *The Strenuous Decade* (New York, 1970) contains exhaustive and laudatory descriptions of the progress made in various fields of reconstruction between 1927 and 1928, but gives less an impression of ' strenuous effort ' than of patchy and limited achievement. In the two crucial fields of rural reconstruction and education, some of the most impressive projects cited were not sponsored by the National Government, but by private groups. The proportion of national income devoted to rural reconstruction was tiny: 0·2 per cent in 1931/2, 3·9 per cent in 1934/5. See Franklin Ho, *Rural Economic Reconstruction in China* (Honolulu, 1936), p. 56.

4 In Shansi, for example, Yen Hsi-shan used the term in the title of Shansi's official plan – Shansi Province Ten Year Reconstruction Programme. See Gillin, *Warlord*, p. 128.

5 Huang Hsü-ch'u, *Chung-kuo chien-she yü Kuang-hsi chien-she* (Kweilin, 1939), p. 2. Hereafter cited as *CKCSYKHCS*.

6 *Ibid.*, p. 203.

7 *Ibid.*, p. 226.

8 *Kuang-hsi chih chien-she*, p. 53.

9 *BSME*, 149 (May, 1934), 310.

10 P'ang Tun-chih, *Ch'ing-suan Kuei-hsi*, p. 18. Pai Ch'ung-hsi consistently attacked Fascist Italy's aggressive foreign policies. See Huang Heng, ' Kuang-hsi chih min-t'uan chi ch'i i-i ', *KWCP*, XI, No. 17 (30 April 1934), 4.

11 Hu Han-min, ' Lun suo-wei fa-hsi-ssu-t'i ', *San-min chu-i yüeh-k'an*, I, No. 4 (15 May 1933), 2.

12 George E. Taylor, *The Reconstruction Movement in China* (London, 1936), p. 35. Pai Ch'ung-hsi also cited the example of Kemal Ataturk, the leader of Turkey's struggle for national independence, and an authoritarian reformer.

13 For a discussion of Liang's ideas, see his *Chung-kuo min-tsu tzu-chiu yün-tung tsui-hou chüeh-wu* (Shanghai, 1936); and Lyman P. Van Slyke, ' Liang Sou-ming and the Rural Reconstruction Movement ', *JAS* XVIII, No. 4 (August 1959), 457–74.

14 Hu Lin, *Kuang-hsi yin-hsiang chi* (Nanning, 1935), p. 44. Hereafter cited by title. See also *BSME*, 149 (May 1934), 316.

15 For the full text of the *Kwangsi Reconstruction Programme*, see Kuang-hsi-sheng tang-cheng-chün lien-hsi hui-i, *Kuang-hsi chien-she kang-ling* (n.p., n.d.).

16 *Kuang-hsi chih chien-she*, p. 1.
17 For an account of P'eng Yü-t'ing's work see Li Tsung-huang, *Chung-kuo ti-fang tzu-chih ts'ung-lun* (Taipei, 1954), pp. 187–90; and Liang Shu-ming, *Chung-kuo min-tsu tzu-chin yün-tung tsui-hou chüeh-wu*, pp. 331–40.
18 *CKCSYKHCS*, p. 199.
19 The general headquarters of the Kwangsi Army sent its appointees to each of the local militia commands. See *San-min chu-i yüeh-k'an*, V, No. 2 (25 February 1935), 96.
20 Evans Carlson, *The Chinese Army* (New York, 1940), p. 31. Carlson, writing much later, described the Kwangsi troops as ' the best of the provincial forces '.
21 Li Po-sheng, ' How Kwangsi Trains Troops ', *People's Tribune*, XXI, No. 3 (27 May 1938), 7.
22 *CKCSYKHCS*, p. 236; and Hu Shih, *Nan-yu tsa-i* (Shanghai, 1935), p. 65.
23 *China Weekly Review*, 24 March 1934, p. 151; and Huai Hsiang (*pseud.*), *Lun Li Tsung-jen yü Chung-Mei fan-tung p'ai* (Hong Kong, 1948), p. 70.
24 Huai Hsiang, *ibid.*, p. 3; and *Kuang-hsi yin-hsiang chi*, p. 13, p. 20.
25 *BSME*, 149 (May 1934), 314.
26 *Kuang-hsi chih chien-she*, p. 298.
27 Laai Y-faai, ' The Part Played by the Pirates of Kwangtung and Kwangsi Provinces in the Taiping Insurrection ', pp. 92–107, 195.
28 Philip Kuhn, *Rebellion and its Enemies in Late Imperial China* (Cambridge, Mass., 1970), p. 62.
29 *Ibid.*, p. 104.
30 *Kuang-hsi chien-she chi-p'ing*, p. 173. *Kuei hsien chih*, p. 359. Clan rivalry in southeastern Kwangsi led to the creation of clan militia units. See Huang Heng, ' Kuang-hsi chih min-t'uan chi ch'i i-i ', *KWCP*, XI, No. 17. 1–2.
31 For a general discussion of the relationship between the formation of militia units and militarisation, see Kuhn, *Rebellion and its Enemies*, pp. 13–15.
32 Huang Shao-hsiung, *Wu-shih hui-i*, p. 210; and Lai Yen-yü, *Kuang-hsi i-lan*, ' The People's Militia ', p. 3.
33 *Ibid.*, pp. 16–17.
34 *Kuang-hsi chien-she chi-p'ing*, p. 216.
35 The men had time to spare. Kwangsi men were notorious for their idleness; it was usual for women to do the bulk of farm work, and to sell their labour to rich peasants and landlords. Along the West River, large numbers of women worked as coolies. See *Kuang-hsi chien-she chi-p'ing*, p. 242; *Kuang-hsi yin-hsiang chi*, p. 4, p. 10; *TFTC*, XXXII, No. 6 (16 March 1935), 98–9. Ma Chün-wu, then President of Kwangsi University, calculated that many Kwangsi men worked only 40 days a year; he saw militia service as a cure for sloth. Huang Heng, *Kuang-hsi chih min-t'uan chi ch'i i-i*, *KWCP*, XI, No. 7, 2.
36 *Kuang-hsi chih chien-she*, p. 67.
37 *Kuang-hsi yin-hsiang chi*, p. 33; *Kuang-hsi chien-she chi-p'ing*, p. 223.
38 Kuo-min ko-ming-chün ti-ssu chi-t'uan-chün tsung-ssu-ling-pu t'uan-wu ch'u, *Kuang-hsi min-t'uan kai-yao* (n.p., n.d.), no pagination.
39 *Kuang-hsi chih chien-she*, pp. 200–1.
40 Kuang-hsi sheng cheng-fu t'ung-chi ch'u, *Kuang-hsi nien-chien ti-er hui* (Kweilin, 1936), pp. 114–17. Hereafter cited by title.
41 *Liu-chiang hsien chih*, p. 2.
42 *Kuei hsien chih*, p. 162. Throughout the province, the militia performed many police functions. In 1934 the province's regular police force consisted of only 2,842 men. *Kuang-hsi nien-chien*, p. 1,122.
43 Chang Kuo-p'ing, *Pai Ch'ung-hsi chiang-chün chuan*, p. 53.
44 League of Nations, *Report of the Council Committee on Technical Cooperation Between the League of Nations and China* (Geneva, 1935), p. 233. The report gives high praise to the Kwangsi militia and the Kwangsi Reconstruction

Movement, and makes implicit criticism of the areas controlled by the Nanking Government.

[45] *Kuang-hsi chih chien-she*, p. 321.
[46] Yeh Kung-ch'o, *Kuei-yu pan-yüeh chi* (Canton, 1934), p. 27; and Wu Sheng-chi, *Kuang-hsi jen-shih hsing-cheng* (Kweilin, 1940), p. 2.
[47] Details of the training of local officials are found in *Kuang-hsi chien-she chi-p'ing*, pp. 35, 59; and *Kuang-hsi chih chien-she*, pp. 68–9, and 321–8.
[48] *CKCSYKHCS*, p. 242; and *Kuang-hsi chih chien-she*, pp. 328–9.
[49] Kuang-hsi min-cheng t'ing, *Kuang-hsi ko-hsien kai-k'uang* (Nanning, 1934), Appendix 1, no pagination.
[50] *People's Tribune*, I, No. 1 (1 August 1933).
[51] *Kuang-hsi chien-she ch'i-p'ing*, p. 36.
[53] Feng Ho-fa (ed.), *Chung-kuo nung-t'sun ching-chi tzu-liao, hsü-pien*, p. 330.
[54] T'ao Chü-yin, *Chin-tai i-wen*, p. 93.
[55] *BSME*, 149 (May 1934), 313.
[56] *Kuang-hsi chih chien-she*, pp. 96, 139.
[57] Li Tsung-huang, *Chung-kuo Kuo-min-tang tang-shih*, p. 460.
[58] See, for example, *Ho hsien chih* (Ho hsien, 1934; reprinted Taipei, 1967).
[59] *Kuang-hsi ko hsien kai-k'uang*, Appendix 1.
[60] Feng Ho-fa (ed.), *Chung-kuo nung-ts'un ching-chi tzu-liao, hsü-pien*, pp. 503–6.
[61] *Ibid.*, pp. 305–10.
[62] *Ibid.*, p. 326.
[63] Ch'ien Chia-chü *et al.*, *Kuang-hsi sheng ching-chi kai-k'uang*, p. 2.
[64] Fen Ho-fa (ed.), *Chung-kuo nung-ts'un ching-chi tzu-liao, hsü-pien*, p. 988.
[65] Wu Pan-nung, ' Fan t'ang hua ', in Ch'ien Chia-chü (ed.), *Chung-kuo nung-ts'un ching-chi lun-wen chi* (Shanghai, 1936), pp. 639–43.
[66] Feng Ho-fa (ed.), *Chung-kuo nung-ts'un ching-chi tzu-liao, hsü-pien*, pp. 779–80.
[67] *Ibid.*, p. 330.
[68] *Ibid.*, p. 323.
[69] Ch'ien Chia-chü, *et al.*, *Kuang-hsi sheng ching-chi kai-k'uang*, p. 3.
[70] *Kuang-hsi chih chien-she*, p. 90.
[71] *Kuei hsien chih*, pp. 491ff.
[72] *Ibid.*, p. 493.
[73] *Kuang-hsi chih chien-she*, pp. 209, 334.
[74] *CKCSYKHCS*, pp. 244–7.
[75] *Ibid.*, p. 4.
[76] P'ang Tun-chih, *Kuang-hsi she-hui t'e-chih*, p. 13.
[77] T'ien Shu-lan, *Kuang-hsi lü-hsing chi* (Shanghai, 1935), p. 89; and Hu Shih, *Nan-yu tsa-i*, pp. 56–7.
[78] Li Ch'i-pao, ' Kuang-hsi yung-shun ti hsiang-ts'un chien-she yü nung-min ', *TFTC*, XXXII, No. 2 (16 January 1935), 10.
[79] *China Weekly Review*, 9 September 1933, p. 64.
[80] *BSME*, 149 (May 1934), 315.
[81] *Kuang-hsi chih chien-she*, pp. 66ff.
[82] *Ibid.*, p. 50.
[83] *Ibid.*, pp. 264–5.
[84] Cheng Chien-lu, *Kuei yu i-yüeh chi* (Shanghai, 1935), p. 11.
[85] Chiang Heng-yüan, *Hsi-nan lü-hsing tsa-hsieh* (Shanghai, 1937), p. 52.
[86] Quoted in Li Tou-sheng, ' Hsin Kuang-hsi, 3 ', *San-min chu-i yüeh-k'an*, V, No. 2 (15 February 1935), 86ff.
[87] Mary R. Anderson, *Protestant Mission Schools for Girls in South China* (New York), 1943), p. 6.
[88] *BSME*, 154 (October 1934), 682.
[89] Chiang Heng-yüan, *Hsi-nan lü-hsing tsa-hsieh*, pp. 74–6.
[90] Expensive marriages were forbidden; and it was decreed that wedding guests must be offered only tea. *China Weekly Review*, 30 December 1933, p. 214.

[91] *P'ing-lo hsien chih* (P'inglo, 1940; reprinted Taipei, 1967), p. 93.

[92] Lai Yen-yü, ' Society ', p. 15.

[93] *BSME*, 137 (May 1933), 356.

[94] Madame Pai Ch'ung-hsi, as the wife of a Moslem, was seldom seen in public. T'ao Chü-yin, *Chin-tai i-wen*, p. 94.

[95] *Kuang-hsi chih chien-she*, p. 70.

[96] Chang Kuo-p'ing, *Pai Ch'ung-hsi chiang-chün chuan*, pp. 62–4. Agnes Smedley gives a similar account of Kwangsi natives, told to her by a veteran of the Long March: ' As our Army passed through the northern Kwangsi mountains officials beat gongs in the villages and cried that bandits were coming! The peasants fled. We marched through empty villages, but never molested a home. I fell ill with malaria, and along with a great many sick and wounded men fell behind the Army. We sometimes saw officials and policemen, thinking our Army had passed, return to the villages, burn or loot homes, and then, when the peasants returned, tell them that the crimes were the work of the Red Army. The people were turned against us.' *Battle Hymn of China* (London, 1944), p. 91.

[97] Hollington Tong, *Chiang Kai-shek, Soldier and Statesman*, p. 537.

[98] For a discussion of the behaviour of the Kwangsi Clique, see Jerome Ch'en's account of the early stages of the March in his article, ' Resolutions of the Tsunyi Conference ', *China Quarterly*, 40 (October–December 1969), 31–2.

[99] Ch'ien Chia-chü, *et al.*, *Kuang-hsi sheng ching-chi kai-k'uang*, p. 181.

[100] K. P. King, ' The Economic Reconstruction of Kwangsi ', *Chinese Economic Journal*, XV, No. 3 (September 1934), 275.

[101] Ch'ien Chia-chü, *et al.*, *Kuang-hsi sheng ching-chi kai-k'uang*, p. 21.

[102] *Ibid.*, p. 22.

[103] *Ibid.*, p. 20.

[104] Cheng Chien-lu, *Kuei-yu i-yüeh chi*, p. 10.

[105] Ch'ien Chia-chü, *et al.*, *Kuang-hsi sheng ching-chi kai-k'uang*, pp. 21, 178.

[106] F. Tamagana, *Banking and Finance in China* (New York, 1942), p. 153.

[107] Huang Heng, ' Kuang-hsi chih min-t'uan chi ch'i i-i ', *KWCP*, XI, No. 17, 2; and King, ' Economic Reconstruction of Kwangsi ', pp. 298–9.

[108] *Kuei hsien chih*, p. 283; and *Ch'ien-chiang hsien chih* (Ch'ienchiang, 1935; reprinted Taipei, 1967), p. 36.

[109] *Kuang-hsi chih chien-she*, p. 375.

[110] *Ibid.*, p. 60; and Hu Shih, *Nan-yu tsa-i*, p. 55.

[111] *CYB* (1933), p. 139; and *BSME*, 152 (August 1934), 528. After the Mukden Incident (1931), there was an officially-organised invasion scare in Kwangsi. ' At night criers went round the streets shouting " sleepers, awake, China is in danger ".' *BSME*, 120 (December 1931), 907.

[112] King, ' Economic Reconstruction of Kwangsi ', p. 307, describes the extent of smuggling from Kwangtung to Kwangsi.

[113] Ch'ien Chia-chü *et al.*, *Kwang-hsi sheng ching-chi kai-k'uang*, p. 4.

[114] Sun Yü-t'ang (ed.), *Chung-kuo chin-tai kung-yeh shih tzu-liao* (Peking, 1961–), Vol. IV, pp. 540, 596; and P'ang Tun-chih, *Kuang-hsi she-hui i'e-chih*, p. 9.

[115] *Kuang-hsi chih chien-she*, p. 61. The interest rates offered to potential investors in Kwangsi were too low to attract private capital. In 1934, however, Huang Hsü-ch'u was able to negotiate a loan of US $9,000,000 from a group of Shanghai financiers. *China Weekly Review*, 19 May 1934, p. 472.

[116] A. H. George, *Trade and Economic Conditions in China* (London, 1935), p. 94.

[117] Huang Hung-ch'ao, *Kuang-hsi shih-yeh tiao-ch'a chuan-k'an* (Canton, 1933), p. 5.

[118] Ch'ien Chia-chü *et al.*, *Kuang-hsi sheng ching-chi kai-k'uang*, pp. 10–15. By 1937 there had been a considerable increase in mining activity; tin, antimony, manganese and coal were mined in quantity. *Chinese Economic Journal*, XVIII, No. 2 (September 1937), 398–404.

[119] *Kuang-hsi chih chien-she*, p. 398.
[120] *Ibid.*, pp. 343–4, p. 351; and *Kuei hsien chih*, p. 498.
[121] *Kuang-hsi chih chien-she*, pp. 352–4.
[122] Clubb, *Opium Traffic in China*, p. 75.
[123] *Kuang-hsi chien-she chi-p'ing*, p. 61.
[124] Ch'ien Chia-chü *et al.*, *Kuang-hsi sheng ching-chi kai-k'uang*, p. 19.
[125] E. Fischer, *Travels in China* (Tientsin, 1941), pp. 266–7; and *China Weekly Review*, 3 February 1934, p. 382.
[126] Clubb, *Opium Traffic in China*, p. 38.
[127] *BSME*, 159 (March 1935), 197.
[128] D. H. Lew, ' Southwest China: A Survey of a Great Potential ', unpublished Ph.D. dissertation, Harvard University, 1939, p. 51.
[129] Tong, *Chiang Kai-shek*, p. 399; and Lew, *ibid.*, pp. 31, 52.
[130] Lo Yun-yen, *The Opium Problem in the Far East* (Shanghai, 1933), p. 70.
[131] Taylor, *Reconstruction Movement in China*, p. 225.
[132] Ch'ien Chia-chü *et al.*, *Kuang-hsi sheng ching-chi kai-k'uang*, p. 16.
[133] King, ' Economic Reconstruction of Kwangsi ', p. 294.
[134] *Kuang-hsi nien-chien ti-er hui*, pp. 906–7.
[135] Chiang Heng-yüan, *Hsi-nan lü-hsing tsa-hsieh*, p. 83.
[136] *Kuang-hsi chien-she chi-p'ing*, pp. 245–9.
[137] Huang Shao-hsiung, *Wu-shih hui-i*, p. 163.

Chapter 10

[1] *Kuang-hsi chih chien-she*, p. 82.
[2] *Ibid.*, p. 672.
[3] G. E. Taylor, *The Struggle for North China* (New York, 1940), p. 21.
[4] *China Weekly Review*, 9 December 1933, pp. 54–5. Li's arrest in 1929 had broken his links with the Kwangsi Clique, and he played no role in the Kwangsi Reconstruction Movement. Without an independent power-base, he became a bitter, peripatetic opponent of Chiang Kai-shek.
[5] Hallett Abend, *My Years in China* (London, 1944), p. 196.
[6] K. B. Vaidya, *Reflections on the Recent Canton Revolt and After* (Canton, 1936), Vol. II, p. 4, gives the lower estimate; the higher estimate is cited in Abend, *My Years in China*, p. 197.
[7] Wu Hsiang-hsiang, ' Wu Chung-hsin an-ting pien-chiang ', *Chuan-chi wen-hsüeh*, VII, No. 1 (July 1965), 27.
[8] The Kwangsi leaders were accused of being openly anti-Japanese but secretly in league with Japan. In 1934 and 1935, Japanese emissaries were rumoured to have visited the province, to arrange the supply of munitions and arsenal equipment. Reports of these visits are found in sources which are strongly hostile to the Kwangsi Clique. See Chou Ch'üan, *Kuei-hsi chieh-p'ou*, p. 11; and Vaidya, *Reflections on the Recent Canton Revolt*, Vol. II, p. 8.
[9] Chang Kuo-p'ing, *Pai Ch'ung-hsi chiang-chün chuan*, p. 65.
[10] Ts'ai T'ing-k'ai, *Ts'ai T'ing-k'ai tzu-chuan*, p. 545.
[11] Feng Chü-p'ei, *K'ang-chan chung ti ti-wu lu-chün*, p. 11.
[12] Abend, *My Years in China*, pp. 197–8.
[13] *Compte rendu, 1938* (Paris, 1937), p. 107; *Kuang-hsi chih chien-she*, p. 378; and *BSME*, 177 (September 1936), 685.
[14] Chang Kuo-p'ing, *Pai Ch'ung-hsi chiang-chün chuan*, p. 68; Ts'ai T'ing-k'ai, *Ts'ai T'ing-k'ai tzu-chuan* p. 547; Vaidya, *Reflections on the Recent Canton Revolt*, Vol. II, p. 15.
[15] Pai Ch'ung-hsi was apparently concerned about his fate at Nanking; he did not go there until the summer of 1937, when the national crisis had reached its height, in spite of many guarantees for his safety. Chang Kuo-p'ing, *Pai Ch'ung-hsi chiang-chün chuan*, p. 70.

[16] The full conditions of settlement are listed in Vaidya, *Reflections on the Recent Canton Revolt*, Vol. II, p. 27.

[17] *Voice of China*, I, No. 3 (1 July 1936), 3.

[18] Gillin, *Warlord*, p. 128.

[19] *Ibid.*, pp. 130, 166.

[20] *Ibid.*, p. 149.

[21] *Ibid.*, pp. 208–18.

[22] A monument was erected to Shih Ta-k'ai in Kuei hsien city; various sites in Kuei hsien connected with the Taipings were marked with commemorative plaques. Two of the historical studies on the Taipings commissioned by the Kwangsi authorities are Chien Yu-wen's *T'ai-p'ing chün Kuang-hsi shou-i shih* (Shanghai, 1946) and his *Chin-t'ien chih yu* (Kweilin, 1944).

[23] Lai Yen-yü, *Kuang-hsi i-lan*, ' Appendix ', p. 6.

[24] Gillin, *Warlord*, p. 63.

[25] Jerome Ch'en, review of *Warlord* by Donald Gillin, in *Bulletin of the School of Oriental and African Studies*, XXXI, pt 1 (1968), 181.

[26] Huai Hsiang, *Lun Li Tsung-jen yü Chung-Mei fan-tung p'ai*, p. 28.

[27] *Ibid.*, p. 21.

[28] Shu-pao chien-hsün she, *Biographies of Kuomintang Leaders* (Yenan, 1945; translated and privately distributed, Harvard, 1948), pp. 6–8.

[29] Jack Belden, *China Shakes the World* (New York, 1949), p. 443.

[30] Tso Shun-sheng, ' Autobiography ', unpublished manuscript deposited in the Butler Library, Columbia University, p. 259. For a full but partisan description of the election battles, see Yin Shih, *Li-Chiang kuan-hsi yü Chung-kuo*.

[31] It was believed in some quarters that the US government was supporting Li in a last ditch attempt to save the mainland. The US ambassador, J. Leighton Stuart, certainly proposed that the US should abandon Chiang Kai-shek and throw its weight behind Li. But this was in late 1948, when Washington wanted to avoid any further embroilment in the Chinese situation; Stuart was over-ruled. When Li became Acting President, he apparently received little comfort from Washington. See Tsou Tang, *America's Failure in China* (Chicago, 1963), pp. 488, 497–8.

[32] L. Chassin, *The Communist Conquest of China* (London, 1966), p. 215.

[33] J. Leighton Stuart, *Fifty Years in China* (New York, 1954), p. 216.

[34] *New York Times*, 21 July 1965.

[35] *Ta-kung pao*, 21 July 1965.

[36] *Ibid.*, 28 July 1965.

[37] *Wen wüi pao*, 17 May 1966.

[38] *Jen-min jih-pao*, 2 February 1969.

Select bibliography

Periodicals in Chinese

Chin-tai shih tzu-liao 近代史資料 (Materials on Modern History). Peking, 1957– .
Chuan-chi wen-hsüeh 傳記文學 (Biographical Literature). Taipei, 1962– .
Ch'un-ch'iu 春秋 (Spring and Autumn). Hong Kong, 1957– .
Chung-yang chou-pao 中央週報 (Centre Weekly). Nanking, 1928–37.
Hsiang-tao chou-pao 向導週報 (Guide Weekly). Shanghai, 1922–7.
Hsien-tai shih-liao 現代史料 (Materials on Contemporary History). Shanghai, 1934–5.
Hung-ch'i p'iao-p'iao 紅旗飄飄 (The Red Flag Flutters), Peking, 1957– .
Kuang-hsi ko-ming chün pan-yüeh k'an 廣西革命軍半月刊 (Bi-weekly Journal of the Kwangsi Revolutionary Army). Nanning, 1926– .
Kuo-wen chou-pao 國聞週報 (The Weekly Gazette). Tientsin, 1924–37.
Min-tsu t'uan-chieh 民族團結 (Nationalities Unity). Peking, 1959– .
Min-tsu yen-chiu 民族研究 (Nationalities Research). Peking, 1959–8.
San-min chu-i yüeh-k'an 三民主義月刊 (Three People's Principles Monthly). Canton, 1933–7.
Tu-li p'ing-lun 獨立評論 (The Independent Critic). Peking, 1932–7.
Tung-fang tsa-chih 東方雜誌 (Eastern Miscellany). Shanghai, 1904–48.

Books and articles in Chinese

Chang Chi 張繼. *Chang P'u-ch'üan hsien-sheng ch'üan-chi* 張溥泉先生全集 (Complete Works of Mr Chang P'u-ch'uan). Taipei, 1952.
Chang Ch'i-yüan 張其昀. *Tang-shih kai-yao* 黨史概要 (A Résumé of the History of the Party). Taipei, 1951–2.
  Chung-hua min-kuo shih-kang 中華民國史綱 (An Outline History of the Chinese Republic). Taipei, 1954.
Chang Hsien-ch'en 張先辰. *Kuang-hsi ching-chi ti-li* 廣西經濟地理 (Economic Geography of Kwangsi). Kweilin, 1941.
Chang Kuo-p'ing 張國平. *Pai Ch'ung-hsi chiang-chün chuan* 白崇禧將軍傳 (Biography of General Pai Ch'ung-hsi). Hankow, 1938.
Chang Tzu-sheng 張梓生. *Kuo-min ko-ming chün Pei-fa chan-cheng shih* 國民革命軍北伐戰爭史 (The History of the Battles of the National Revolutionary Army on the Northern Expedition). Shanghai, 1933.
Chang Yu-i (ed.) 章有義. *Chung-kuo chin-tai nung-yeh shih tzu-liao* 中國近代農業史資料 (Materials on the History of China's Modern Agriculture). Vols. II and III, Peking, 1957.

Chao-p'ing hsien chih 昭平縣誌 (Chaop'ing Hsien Gazetteer). Chaop'ing, 1934; reprinted Taipei, 1967.

Ch'en Hui 陳暉. *Kuang-hsi chiao-t'ung wen-t'i* 廣西交通問題 (Kwangsi's Communication Question). Ch'angsha, 1938.

Ch'en Kung-po Chou Fo-hai hui-i lu ho-pien 陳公博周佛海回憶錄合編 (Collected Reminiscences of Ch'en Kung-po and Chou Fo-hai). Hong Kong, 1967.

Cheng Chien-lu 鄭健盧. *Kuei-yu i-yüeh chi* 桂游一月記 (Record of a Month's Travelling in Kwangsi). Shanghai, 1935.

Chiang Heng-yüan 江恆源. *Hsi-nan lü-hsing tsa-hsieh* 西南旅行雜寫 (Jottings from Travel in the Southwest). Shanghai, 1937.

Chiang-shang-ch'ing 江上清. *Cheng-hai pi-wen* 政海秘聞 (Secrets from the Sea of Politics). Hong Kong, 1966.

Chiang Tsung-t'ung yen-lun hui-pien pien-chi wei-yüan-hui 蔣總統言論彙編編輯委員會 *Chiang Tsung-t'ung yen-lun hui-pien* 蔣總統言論彙編 (The Collected Speeches of President Chiang). Taipei, 1956.

Chiang Yung-ching 蔣永敬. *Pao-lo-ting yü Wu-han cheng-ch'üan* 鮑羅廷與武漢政權 (Borodin and the Political Authority at Wuhan). Taipei, 1963.

Ch'ien Chia-chü (ed.) 錢家駒. *Chung-kuo nung-ts'un ching-chi lun-wen chi* 中國農材經濟論問集 (Collected Discussions on China's Agricultural Economy). Shanghai, 1936.

Ch'ien Chia-chü 錢家駒, Han Te-chang 韓德章 and Wu Pan-nung 吳半農. *Kuang-hsi sheng ching-chi kai-k'uang* 廣西省經濟概況 (Outline of the Economy of Kwangsi). Shanghai, 1936.

Chien Yu-wen 簡又文. *Chin-t'ien chih yu* 金田之游 (A Trip through Chint'ien). Kweilin, 1944.

T'ai-p'ing chün Kuang-hsi shou-i shih 太平軍廣西首義史 (A History of the Rising of the Taiping Army in Kwangsi). Shanghai, 1946.

Chou Ch'üan 周全. *Kuei-hsi chieh-p'ou* 桂系解剖 (The Banditry of the Kwangsi Clique). Hong Kong, 1949.

Chu Chung-yü (ed.) 朱仲玉. *Wei Pa-ch'ün* 韋拔羣. Peking, 1960.

Chung-kuo jen-min cheng-chih hsieh-shang hui-i ch'üan-kuo wei-yüan-hui, Wen-shih tzu-liao yen-chiu wei yüan-hui (ed.) 中國人民政治協商會議全國委員會文史資料研究委員會編. *Hsin-hai ko-ming hui-i lu* 辛亥革命回憶錄 (Reminiscences of the Hsin-hai Revolution). Peking, 1962.

Chung-kuo Kuo-min-tang chung-yang chih-hsing wei-yüan-hui 中國國民黨中央執行委員會. *Chung-kuo Kuo-min-tang ti-er-t'zu tai-piao ta-hui hsüan-yen chi chüeh-i an* 中國國民黨第二次代表大會宣言及決議案 (Proclamations and Resolutions of the First Congress of the Kuomintang). Canton, 1926.

Chung-shan hsien chih 鍾山縣誌. (Chungshan Hsien Gazetteer). Chungshan, 1933; reprinted Taipei, 1967.

Feng Chü-p'ei 馮菊沛. *K'ang-chan chung ti ti-wu lu-chün* 抗戰中的第五路軍 (The Fifth Route Army During the War of Resistance). Hankow, 1938.

Feng Ho-fa (ed.) 馮合法. *Chung-kuo nung-ts'un ching-chi tzu liao* 中國農村經濟資料 (Materials on the Agricultural Economy of China). Shanghai, 1935.

Feng Yü-hsiang 馮玉祥. *Feng Yü-hsiang hui-i lu* 馮玉祥回憶錄 (Feng Yu-hsiang's Reminiscences). Shanghai, 1949.

Hatano Ken'ichi 波多野乾一. *Gendai Shihna no kiroku* 現代支那之記錄 (Records of Contemporary China). N.p., n.d.

Ho hsien chih 賀縣誌. (Ho Hsien Gazetteer). Ho hsien, 1934; reprinted Taipei, 1967.

Ho P'ing-ti 何炳棣. *Chung-kuo hui-kuan shih-lun* 中國會館史論 (A Discussion of the History of China's *Landsmannschaften*). Taipei, 1966.

Ho Shao-ch'iung, *et al.* (ed.) 何紹夒. *Ch'en Chi-t'ang hsien-sheng chi-nien chi* 陳濟棠先生紀念集 (Collected Memorials to Mr Ch'en Chi-t'ang). Hong Kong, 1957.

Hsieh Hsing-yao 謝興堯. *T'ai-p'ing t'ien-kuo ch'ien-hou Kuang-hsi ti fan-Ch'ing yün-tung* 太年天國前後廣西的反清運動 (The Anti-Ch'ing Movement in Kwangsi Before and After the Taiping Tien-kuo). Peking, 1950.

Hsü Pi-hsü (ed.) 許璧序. *Kuang-hsi chien-she chi-p'ing* 廣西建設集評 (Collected Critiques of Kwangsi's Reconstruction). N.p., 1935.

Hu Hua 胡華. *Chung-kuo hsin min-chu chu-i ko-ming shih* 中國新民主主義革命史 (A History of the New Democratic Revolution in China). Peking, 1950.

Hu Lin 胡霖. *Kuang-hsi yin-hsiang chi* 廣西印象記 (Collected Impressions of Kwangsi). Nanning, 1935.

Hu Shih 胡適. *Nan-yu tsa-i* 南游雜憶 (Assorted Impressions from a Southern Journey). Shanghai, 1935.

Huai Hsiang (*pseud.*) 懷鄉. *Lun Li Tsung-jen yü Chung-Mei fan-tung p'ai* 論李宗仁與中美反動派(A Discussion of Li Tsung-jen and the Sino-American Reactionary Clique). Hong Kong, 1948.

Huang Hsü-ch'u 黃旭初. *Huang Hsü-ch'u hsien-sheng yen-chiang chi* 黃旭初先生言講集 (The Collected Speeches of Mr Huang Hsu-ch'u). Nanning, 1935.

Chung-kuo chien-she yü Kuang-hsi chien-she 中國建設與廣西建設 (China's Reconstruction and Kwangsi's Reconstruction). Kweilin, 1939.

Wo ti mu-ch'in 我的母親 (My Mother). Hong Kong, 1969.

Huang Hung-ch'ao 黃弘超. *Kuang-hsi shih-yeh tiao-ch'a chuan-k'an* 廣西實業調查專刊 (Special Report of an Investigation of Kwangsi's Industry). Canton, 1933.

Huang Shao-hsiung 黃紹雄. *Wu-shih hui-i* 五十回憶 (Reminiscences at Fifty). Shanghai, 1945.

Jen-min ch'u-pan she 人民出版社. *Ti-i-tz'u kuo-nei ko-ming chan-cheng shih-ch'i ti nung-min yün-tung* 第一次國內革命戰爭時期的農民運動 (The Peasant Movement During the First Period of Revolutionary Struggle Within the Country). Peking, 1953.

Kuang-hsi chuang-tsu tzu-chih-ch'ü ch'ou-pei wei-yüan-hui 廣西僮族自治區籌備委員會. *Kuang-hsi chuang-tsu tzu-chih-ch'ü* 廣西僮族自治區 (The Kwangsi-Chuang Autonomous Region). Peking, 1958.

Kuang-hsi chuang-tsu wen-hsüeh shih-pien chi-shih 廣西僮族文學史編輯室. *Kuang-hsi chuang-tsu wen-hsüeh* 廣西僮族文學 (Kwangsi-Chuang Literature). Nanning, 1961.

Kuang-hsi chün-ch'u cheng-chih pu 廣西軍區政治部. *Kuang-hsi ko-ming hui-i lu* 廣西革命回憶錄 (Revolutionary Reminiscences of Kwangsi). Nanning, 1959.

Kuang-hsi min-cheng t'ing 廣西民政庭. *Kuang-hsi ko-hsien kai-k'uang* 廣西各縣概况 (An Outline of Kwangsi's *Hsien*). Nanning, 1934.

Kuang-hsi shao-shu min-tsu she-hui li-shih tiao-ch'a tsu 廣西小數民族組會歷史調查社. *Kuang-hsi Hsin-hai ko-ming tzu-liao* 廣西辛亥革命資料 (Materials on the Hsin-hai Revolution in Kwangsi). Nanning, 1960.

Kuang-hsi sheng cheng-fu t'ung-chi ch'u 廣西省政府統計處. *Ku-chin Kuang-hsi lü-Kuei jen-ming chien* 古今廣西旅桂人名鑑 (Biographical Examination of Kwangsi Men and Visitors to Kwangsi, Ancient and Modern). Kweilin, 1934.

Kuang-hsi t'ung-chi ts'ung-shu 廣西統計叢書 (Collected Statistics of Kwangsi). Nanning, 1934–5.

Kuang-hsi nien-chien, ti-er hui 廣西年鑑第二會 (Second Kwangsi Yearbook). Kweilin, 1936.

Kuang-hsi sheng hsüan-ch'uan pu 廣西省宣傳部. *Ch'ing-tang ts'ung-shu* 清黨叢書 (Collected Documents on the Party Purge). Nanning, 1927.

Kuang-hsi-sheng tang-cheng-chün lien-hsi hui-i 廣西省黨政軍聯系會議. *Kuang-hsi chien-she kang-ling* 廣西建設綱領 (Outline of Kwangsi's Reconstruction). N.p., n.d.

Kuei hsien-chih 貫縣志 (Kuei hsien Gazetteer). Kuei hsien, 1935; reprinted Taipei, 1967.

K'ung Ch'u 龔楚. *Wo yü hung-chün* 我與紅軍 (The Red Army and I). Hong Kong, 1955.

Kuo-min cheng-fu hsing-cheng yüan nung-ts'un fu-hsing wei-yüan-hui 國民政府行政院農村復興委員會. *Kuang-hsi sheng nung-ts'un tiao-ch'a* 廣西省農村調查 (An Investigation of the Agriculture of Kwangsi). Shanghai, 1935.

Kuo-min ko-ming-chün ti-ssu chi-t'uan chün tsung-ssu-ling-pu t'uan-wu ch'u 國民革命軍第四集團軍總司領部團務處. *Kuang-hsi min-t'uan kai-yao* 廣西民團概要 (A Résumé of the Kwangsi Militia). N.p., n.d.

Kuang-hsi min-t'uan t'iao-li chang-ts'e 廣西民團條例章則 (Articles and Rules of the Kwangsi Militia). N.p., 1934.

Kuo Mo-jo 郭沫若. *Pei-fa t'u-t'zu* 北伐途次 (The Path of the Northern Expedition). Shanghai, 1947.

Lai Hsin-hsia 來新夏. 'Shih lun ch'ing Kuang-hsü mo-nien ti Kuang-hsi jen-min ta ch'i-i 試論清光緒末年的廣西人民大起義' (A Preliminary Discussion of Popular Rebellion in Kwangsi at the End of the Kuang-hsu Period). *Li-shih yen-chiu* (Historical Research), 11 (1957), 57–77.

Lai Yen-yü 賴彥于. *Kuang-hsi i-lan* 廣西一覽 (Glimpses of Kwangsi). Nanning, 1935.

Lei Hsiao-ts'en 雷嘯岑. *San-shih-nien tung-luan Chung-kuo* 三十年動亂中國 (Thirty Years of Upheaval in China). Hong Kong, 1955.

Li Ang 李昂, *Hung-se wu-t'ai* 紅色舞台 (The Red Stage). Chungking, 1942.

Li P'ei-sheng 李陪生. *Kuei Hsi chu Yüeh chih you-lai chi ch'i ching-kuo* 桂系據粵之由來及其經過 (The Origin and Process of the Kwangsi Clique's Occupation of Kwangtung). Canton, 1921.

Li Tsung-huang 李宗黃. *Ching-kuo Kuo-min-tang tang-shih* 中國國民黨黨史 (A History of the Kuomintang). Nanking, 1935.

Chung-kuo ti-fang tzu-chih tsung-lun 中國地方自治總論 (A General Account of Local Self-Government in China). Taipei, 1954.

Li Tsung-jen 李宗仁. *Li Tsung-ssu-ling tsui-chin yen-chiang chi* 李總司領最近言講集 (Collection of Commander-in-Chief Li's Recent Speeches). Nanning, 1935.

San-min chu-i tsai Kuang-hsi 三民主義在廣西 (The Three People's Principles in Kwangsi). Nanning, 1938.

Li Te-lin hsien-sheng lun Kuang-hsi chien-she yü fu-hsing Chung-kuo 李德鄰 先生論廣西建設與復興中國 (Mr Li Te-lin Discusses the Reconstruction of Kwangsi and the Restoration of China). Nanning, 1939.

Min-t'uan yü chün-hsün 民團與軍訓 (The Militia and Military Training). Nanning, 1939.

T'ai-er-chuang k'ang-chan hui-i lu 台兒莊抗戰回憶錄 (Memoirs of the War of Resistance at Taierchuang). Hong Kong, 1954.

Li Tsung-jen et al. 李宗仁. *Kuang-hsi chih chien-she* 廣西之建設 (The Reconstruction of Kwangsi). Kweilin, 1939.

'Li Tsung-jen Battle Collection'. Collection of military documents, battle orders, maps, etc., on microfilm in the East Asian Library, Columbia University.

Li Tsung-jen ti sheng-yin 李宗仁的聲音 (The Voice of Li Tsung-jen). Hong Kong, 1965.

Li Tsung-jen yin-hsiang chi 李宗仁印象記 (Impressions of Li Tsung-jen). Hong Kong, 1937.

Li Yün-han 李雲漢. *Ts'ung jung-kung tao ch'ing-tang* 從容共到清黨 (From the Policy of Co-operation with the Communists to their Purge from the Party). Taipei, 1966.

Liang Sheng-chün 梁升俊. *Chiang-Li tou-cheng nei-mu* 蔣李鬥爭內幕 (The Inside Story of the Struggle Between Chiang and Li). Hong Kong, 1954.

Liang Shu-ming 梁漱溟. *Chung-kuo min-tsu tzu-chiu yün-tung tsui-hou chüeh-wu* 中國民族自救運動最後覺悟 (Recent Perceptions on the Chinese People's Movement for Salvation). Shanghai, 1936.

Liu-ch'eng hsien chih 柳城縣誌. (Liuch'eng Hsien Gazetteer). Liuch'eng, 1940; reprinted Taipei, 1967.

Liu-chiang hsien chih 榴江縣誌. (Liuchiang Hsien Gazetteer). Liuchiang, 1937; reprinted Taipei, 1967.

Liu Chieh 劉介. 'Kuang-hsi liang ta hsi-p'ai min-tsu ti you-lai chi ch'i yen-chin'. 廣西兩大系派民族的由來及其演進 (The Origins and Evolution of Kwangsi's Two Great Racial Strains), *Kuang-hsi t'ung-chih-kuan kuan-k'an* 廣西通誌館館刊 (Journal of the Kwangsi Gazetteer Office). Kweilin, 1948.

Lo Chia-lun (ed.) 羅家倫. *Ko-ming wen-hsien* 革命文獻 (Documents of the Revolution). Taipei, 1953– .

Kuo-fu nien-p'u ch'u-kao 國父年譜初稿 (First Draft of a Chronology of Sun Yat-sen). Taipei, 1959.

Lo-jung hsien chih 雒容縣誌 (Lojung Hsien Gazetteer). Lojung, 1934; reprinted Taipei, 1967.

Mao Ssu-ch'eng 毛思城. *Min-kuo shih-wu-nien i-ch'ien chih Chiang Chieh-shih hsien-sheng* 民國十五年以前之蔣介石先生 (Mr Chiang Kai-shek Before 1926). Shanghai, 1936.

Pai Ch'ung-hsi 白崇禧. *Pai Fu tsung-ssu-ling yen-chiang chi* 白副總司領言講集 (The Collected Speeches of Deputy Commander-in-Chief Pai). N.p., 1935.

Min-t'uan cheng-ts'e yü min-tsu ko-ming 民團政策與民族革命 (The Militia Policy and the National Revolution). Nanning, 1938.

P'ang Tun-chih 龐敦志. *Ch'ing-suan Kuei-hsi* 淸算桂系 (Wipe Out the Kwangsi Clique). Canton, 1950.

Kuang-hsi she-hui t'e-chih 廣西社會特質 (Special Characteristics of Kwangsi Society). Hong Kong, 1950.

P'ing-lo hsien chih 平樂縣誌 (P'inglo Hsien Gazetteer). P'inglo, 1940; reprinted Taipei, 1967.

Sun Yü-t'ang (ed.) 孫毓棠. *Chung-kuo chin-tai kung-yeh shih tzu-liao* 中國近代工業史資料 (Materials on the History of China's Modern Industry). Peking, 1961– .

T'ao Chü-yin 陶菊隱. *Chin-tai i-wen* 近代軼聞 (Anecdotes of the Modern Age). Shanghai, 1945.

Pei-yang chün-fa t'ung-chih shih-ch'i shih-hua 北洋軍閥統治時期史話 (A History of the Peiyang Warlords' Period of Control). Peking, 1957.

T'ien Shu-lan 田曙嵐. *Kuang-hsi lü-hsing chi* 廣西旅行記 (Record of Travel in Kwangsi). Shanghai, 1935.

Ts'ai T'ing-k'ai 蔡廷鍇. *Ts'ai T'ing-k'ai tzu-chuan* 蔡廷鍇自傳 (Autobiography of Ts'ai T'ing-k'ai). Hong Kong, 1946.

Ts'ao Chü-jen 曹聚仁. *Chiang Pai-li p'ing-chuan* 蔣百理評傳 (A Critical Biography of Chiang Pai-li). Hong Kong, 1963.

Ts'en Ch'un-hsüan 岑春煊. *Lo-chai man-pi* 樂齋漫筆 (Jottings from the Studio of Happiness). Peking, 1933; reprinted Taipei, 1962.

Tsou Lu 鄒魯. *Chung-kuo Kuo-min-tang shih-kao* 中國國民黨史稿 (A Draft History of the Kuomintang). Canton, 1938; reprinted Taipei, 1965.

Hui-ku lu 回顧錄 (Reminiscences). Chungking, 1943.

Wang Tsao-shih 王造時. *Chung-kuo wen-t'i ti fen-hsi* 中國問題的分析 (An Analysis of China's Problems). Shanghai, 1935.

Wen Kung-chih 文公直. *Tsui-chin san-shih-nien Chung-kuo chün-shih shih* 最近三十年中國軍事史 (A History of Chinese Military Affairs of the Last Thirty Years). Shanghai, 1930; reprinted Taipei, 1962.

Wu Hsiang-hsiang 吳相湘. *Ho Chien ti i-sheng* 何鍵的一生 (A Life of Ho Chien). Taipei, 1964.

Wu Sheng-chi 吳胜己. *Kuang-hsi jen-shih hsing-cheng* 廣西人事行政 (The Personnel Administration of Kwangsi). Kweilin, 1940.

Yang Chia-ming 楊家銘. *Min-kuo shih-wu-nien hsüeh-sheng yün-tung* 民國十五年學生運動 (The 1926 Student Movement). Shanghai, 1927.

Yang Yi-t'ang 楊逸棠. *Teng Yen-ta hsien-sheng i-chu* 鄧遠達先生遺著 (Obituary of Mr Teng Yen-ta). Hong Kong, 1949.

Yeh Kung-ch'o 葉恭綽. *Kuei-yu pan-yüeh chi* 桂遊平月記 (Record of Two Weeks in Kwangsi). Canton, 1934.

Yin Shih (*pseud.*) 隱士. *Li-chiang kuan-hsi yü Chung-kuo* 李蔣關系與中國 (The Li-Chiang Relationship and China). Hong Kong, 1954.

Periodicals in Western languages

Asia. New York, 1917–44.

Bulletin de l'Association amicale Franco-Chinoise. Paris, 1909.

Bulletin de la Société des Missions-Etrangères de Paris. Paris, 1922– .

China Weekly Review (Millard's Review). Shanghai, 1918–49.

China Year Book. Tientsin and Shanghai, 1912–39.

Chinese Economic Journal. Shanghai, 1926–37.

Compte rendu des travaux de la Société des Missions-Etrangères de Paris. Paris, 1918– .

North China Herald. Shanghai, 1910–41.

Oriental Affairs. Shanghai, 1933–7.

People's Tribune (new series). Shanghai, 1933–7.

Voice of China. Shanghai, 1936–7.

Books and articles in Western languages

Abend, Hallett. *My Years in China.* London, 1944.

Amann, Gustav. *Chiang Kai-shek und die Regierung der Kuomintang in China.* Berlin, 1936.

Anderson, Mary R. *Protestant Mission Schools for Girls in South China.* New York, 1943.

Baudrit, André. *Bétail humain : rapt, vente et infanticide dans l'Indochine et dans la Chine du sud.* Saigon, 1942.

Belden, Jack. *China Shakes the World.* New York, 1949.

Brandt, Conrad. *Stalin's Failure in China.* Cambridge, Mass., 1958.

Buck, J. L. *Land Utilisation in China.* Shanghai, 1937.

Burton, Wilbur. *The French Stranglehold on Yunnan.* Shanghai, 1933.

Carlson, Evans. *The Chinese Army.* New York, 1940.

Chang, C. C. *China Tung Oil and Its Future.* Hong Kong, 1940.

Chapman, H. O. *The Chinese Revolution, 1926/7.* London, 1928.

Chassin, L. *The Communist Conquest of China.* London, 1966.

Ch'en, Jerome. *Yuan Shih-k'ai.* London, 1961.
   Mao and the Chinese Revolution. London, 1965.

Chesneaux, Jean. *Le mouvement ouvrier en Chine.* Paris, 1962.
   Les syndicats chinois. Paris, 1965.
   The Chinese Labor Movement. Stanford, 1968.
   ' The Federalist Movement in China, 1930–1933 ', in Jack Gray (ed.), *Modern China's Search for a Political Form.* London, 1969.

Chesneaux, Jean, and Feiling Davis and Nguyen Nguyet Ho (eds.). *Mouvements populaires et sociétés secrètes en Chine au XIX et XX siècles.* Paris, 1970.

Chi Ch'ao-ting. *Key Economic Areas in Chinese History.* London, 1936.

Chien Tuan-sheng. ' The Role of the Military in Chinese Government '. *Pacific Affairs*, XXI, No. 3 (September 1948), 239–51.

Clubb, O. E. *The Opium Traffic in China.* Hankow, 1934. Report of the US Consul at Hankow.

Cohen, Maurice, and Charles Drage. *Two Gun Cohen.* London, 1954.

Cordier, Andrew (ed.). *Columbia Essays in International Affairs*, Vol. III. New York, 1967.

Cuenot, Joseph. *Au pays des pavillons noirs.* Hong Kong, 1925.

Feuerwerker, Albert, Rhoads Murphey and Mary Wright (eds.). *Approaches to Modern Chinese History.* Berkeley, 1967.

Fincher, John. 'Political Provincialism and the National Revolution', in Mary Wright (ed.), *China in Revolution : The First Phase*. New Haven, 1968.

Fischer, E. *Travels in China*. Tientsin, 1941.

Fischer, Louis. *The Soviets in World Affairs*. London, 1930.

Furth, Charlotte. *Ting Wen-chiang : Science and China's New Culture*. Cambridge, Mass., 1970.

George, A. H. *Trade and Economic Conditions in China*. London, 1935.

Gillin, Donald. *Warlord : Yen Hsi-shan in Shansi Province, 1911–1949*. Princeton, 1967.

Gray, Jack (ed.). *Modern China's Search for a Political Form*. London, 1969.

Ho, Franklin. *Rural Economic Reconstruction in China*. Honolulu, 1936.

Ho P'ing-ti. *Studies on the Population of China*. Cambridge, Mass., 1959.

Ho P'ing-ti and Tang Tsou (eds.). *China in Crisis*. Chicago, 1968.

Hobart, Alice T. *Within the Walls of Nanking*. London, 1928.

Hsieh Pao-chao. *The Government of China, 1644–1911*. Baltimore, 1925.

Hsieh, Winston. 'The Ideas and Ideals of a Warlord: Ch'en Chiung-ming (1878–1933)', in *Harvard Papers on China*, XVI (1962), 198–244.

Ilionchetchkine, Vassili. 'Les sociétés secrètes et les sectes herétiques en Chine au milieu de XIXe siècle ', in Jean Chesneaux, Feiling Davis and Nguyen Nguyet (eds.), *Mouvements populaires et sociétés secrètes en Chine au XIX et XX siècles*. Paris, 1970.

Iriye Ikeda. *After Imperialism*. Cambridge, Mass., 1965.

Isaacs, Harold. *The Tragedy of the Chinese Revolution*. Second revised edition, New York, 1966.

Jensen, Merrill (ed.). *Regionalism in America*. Madison, 1951.

Johnson, Chalmers. *Peasant Nationalism and the Rise of Communist Power*. Stanford, 1963.

Kotenev, Anatole. *New Lamps for Old*. Shanghai, 1931.

Laai Yi-faai. 'The River Strategy of the Taipings'. *Oriens*, V, No. 2 (1952).

'The Use of Maps in Social Research'. *Geographical Review*, LII (1962).

'The Part Played by the Pirates of Kwangtung and Kwangsi Provinces in the Taiping Insurrection'. Unpublished Ph.D. dissertation, University of California, 1950.

Laffay, Ella. 'La formation d'un rebelle : Liu Yong-fu et la création de l'armée des pavillons noirs ', in Jean Chesneaux.

League of Nations. *Report of the Council Committee on Technical Cooperation Between the League of Nations and China*. Geneva, 1935.

Levenson, Joseph. 'The Province, the Nation and the World: The Problem of Chinese Identity ', in Albert Feuerwerker, Rhoads Murphey and Mary Wright (eds.), *Approaches to Modern Chinese History*. Berkeley, 1967.

Lew, D. H. 'Southwest China: A Survey of a Great Potential '. Unpublished Ph.D. dissertation, Harvard, 1939.

Li Chien-nung. *The Political History of China, 1840–1928*. New York, 1956.

'Li Tsung-jen Autobiography'. Unpublished manuscript deposited in the Butler Library, Columbia University.

Linebarger, Paul. *The China of Chiang Kai-shek*. Boston, 1941.

Liu, F. F. *A Military History of Modern China*. Princeton, 1956.

Lo Yun-yen. *The Opium Problem in the Far East*. Shanghai, 1933.

McAleavy, Henry. *The Black Flags in Vietnam*. London, 1968.

Michael, Franz. *The Taiping Rebellion*. Seattle, 1966.

'Regionalism in Nineteenth-Century China', introduction to Stanley Spector, *Li Hung-chang and the Huai Army*. Princeton, 1964.

Nathan, Andrew. 'Factionalism in Chinese Politics: The Case of the Cultural Revolution'. Paper presented to the 1971 Annual Meeting of the American Political Science Association.

Needham, Joseph. *Science and Civilisation in China*. Cambridge, 1956– .

North, Robert. *Kuomintang and Chinese Communist Elites*. Stanford, 1952.

Paauw, Douglas. 'The Kuomintang and Economic Stagnation'. *JAS*, XVI, No. 2 (1957).

Powell, R. L. *The Rise of Chinese Military Power*. Princeton, 1955.

Ransome, Arthur. *The Chinese Puzzle*. London, 1927.

Ray, Rex. *Cowboy Missionary in Kwangsi*. Nashville, Tennessee, 1964.

Roy, M. N. *Revolution and Counter-revolution in China*. Calcutta, 1946.

Schiffrin, H. *Sun Yat-sen and the Origins of the Chinese Revolution*. Berkeley, 1968.

Schulze, Dieter. *Das politisch-geographisches Kräfterverhältnis zwischen den drei chinesischen sudwest Provinzen*. Heidelberg, 1940.

Sheridan, James. *Chinese Warlord : The Career of Feng Yü-hsiang*. Stanford, 1966.

Shu-pao chien-hsün she. *Biographies of Kuomintang Leaders*. Yenan, 1945; translated and privately distributed, Harvard, 1948.

Sih, Paul K. T. (ed.). *The Strenuous Decade : China's Nation-Building Efforts, 1927–1937*. New York, 1970.

Smedley, Agnes. *Battle Hymn of China*. London, 1944.

The Great Road : The Life and Times of Chu Te. London, 1958.

Snow, Edgar. *Far Eastern Front*. New York, 1934.

Sokolsky, George. *China*, Shanghai, 1920.

The Tinder Box of Asia. New York, 1932.

Spector, Stanley. *Li Hung-chang and the Huai Army*. Princeton, 1964.

Spencer, J. E. 'On Regionalism in China'. *Journal of Geography*, XLVI, I, No. 4 (1947).

Stuart, J. Leighton. *Fifty Years in China*. New York, 1954.

Tamagana, F. *Banking and Finance in China*. New York, 1942.

Tang Leang-li. *The Inner History of the Chinese Revolution*. London, 1930.

Taylor, George E. *The Reconstruction Movement in China*. London, 1936.

The Struggle for North China. New York, 1940.

Teng Ssu-yu. *New Light on the History of the Taiping Rebellion*. Cambridge, Mass., 1950.

Tong, Hollington. *Chiang Kai-shek, Soldier and Statesman*. Shanghai, 1937. Authorised biography.

Trois mois au Kouangsi : souvenirs d'un officier en mission. Paris, 1906.

'Tso Shun-sheng Autobiography'. Unpublished manuscript deposited in the Butler Library, Columbia University.

Tsou Tang. *America's Failure in China*. Chicago, 1963.

Vaidya, K. B. *Reflections on the Recent Canton Revolt and After*. Canton, 1936.

Van Slyke, Lyman P. 'Liang Sou-ming and the Rural Reconstruction Movement'. *JAS*, XVIII, No. 4 (1959).

Vance, Rupert. 'The Regional Concept as a Tool for Social Research', in Merrill Jensen (ed.), *Regionalism in America*. Madison, 1951.

Vishryakova-Akimova, Vera Vladimirovna. *Two Years in Revolutionary China, 1925–1927*, translated by Stephen Levine. Cambridge, Mass., 1971.

Whiting, Allen S. *Sinkiang : Pawn or Pivot?* Ann Arbor, 1958.

Wiens, Herold J. *Han Chinese Expansion in South China*. Hampden, Conn., 1967.

Wilbur, C. M. 'Military Separatism and the Process of Reunification under the Nationalist regime, 1922–1937', in Ho P'ing-ti and T'ang Tsou (eds.), *China in Crisis*. Chicago, 1968.

Wilson, Dick. *The Long March*. London, 1971.

Wright, Mary (ed.). *China in Revolution : The First Phase*. New Haven, 1968.

Wou, Odoric Y. K. 'A Chinese "Warlord" Faction: the Chihli Clique, 1918–1924', in Andrew Cordier (ed.), *Columbia Essays in International Affairs*, Vol. III. New York, 1967.

Wu T'ien-wei. 'Chiang Kai-shek's March Twentieth Coup d'Etat of 1926'. *JAS*, XXVII (1968).

Glossary

With a few exceptions, place-names are given only for Kwangsi.

Chang Chi 張繼
Chang Chih-pen 張知本
Chang Ching-chiang 張靜江
Chang Fa-k'uei 張發奎
Chang Hsüeh-liang 張學良
Chang Jen-min 張任民
Chang Kan 張淦
Chang Tsung-ch'ang 張宗昌
Chang Yi-ch'i 張一氣
Chang Yün-i 張雲逸
Chaoch'ing, Kwangtung 肇慶
Chao Heng-t'i 趙恒惕
Chaop'ing, Kwangsi 昭平
Chennankuan 鎮南關
Chenp'ing, Honan 鎮平
Ch'en Ch'eng 陳誠
Ch'en Chi-t'ang 陳濟棠
Ch'en Chiung-ming 陳烱明
Ch'en Hsiung 陳雄
Ch'en Mien-shu 陳勉恕
Ch'en Ming-shu 陳銘樞
Ch'en Ping-k'un 陳丙焜
Ch'en T'iao-yüan 陳調元
Ch'en T'ien-t'ai 陳天太
Ch'en Yi 陳儀
Cheng-li shui-wu wei-yüan-hui 整理稅務委員會: Tax Regulation Committee.
Ch'eng Ch'ien 程潛
Ch'eng Ssu-yüan 程思遠
chi-kuan kuan-nien 籍貫觀念: localism.
Ch'i-min 旗民: Manchus; lit. banner people.
chia 甲: unit of collective security system.
Chiang Hua 江華
Chiang Kai-shek (Chiang Chieh-shih) 蔣介石
Chiang Kuang-nai 蔣光鼐

Chien-kuo ta-kang 建國大綱: *Fundamentals of National Reconstruction.*

chien-she 建設: reconstruction.

Ch'ien Ta-chün 錢大鈞

Ch'ien-ti ts'ung-chih-hui 前敵總指揮: field commander.

ching ping fei 警兵費: police subsidies.

Ch'ing-nien t'uan 青年團: (Communist) Youth League.

Ch'ing-tang 清黨: Party purge.

Chint'ien, Kwangsi 金田

Chiu Ch'ang-wei 邱昌渭

ch'iung tso-fa 窮作法: shoe-string approach.

Chou En-lai 周恩來

Chou Feng-ch'i 周鳳岐

Chou Fo-hai 周佛海

Chou Tsu-huang 周祖晃

Chu Chao-sen 朱朝森

Chu P'ei-te 朱陪德

Chuang 僮

Chung-kuo Hui-chiao hui 中國回教會: China Moslim Society.

Chung Tsu-p'ei 鍾祖培

Chung-yang chih-hsing wei-yüan-hui hsi-nan chih-hsing pu 中央執行委員會西南執行部: Southwest Executive Branch of the Central Executive Committee.

chü-jen 舉人: recommended man; graduate of the second level of examinations in the traditional examination system.

chün 軍: army.

chün-tui hua 軍隊化: militarisation.

Fan Chung-hsiu 樊鍾秀

Fan Shih-sheng 範石生

Fang Pen-jen 方木仁

fen-chih ho-tso 分治合作: co-operation between separate governments.

Fengshan, Kwangsi 鳳山

Feng Yü-hsiang 馮玉祥

fu-chia shui 附價稅: tax supplements.

Fu-hsing P'ai 復興派: Revivalist Faction.

Fu Tso-yi 傅作義

hao t'ieh pu tang ting, hao jen pu tang ping 好鐵不當釘, 好人不當兵: good iron is not used for nails, good men are not used as soldiers.

hao-wan ti tung-hsi 好玩的東西: game, plaything.

Ho Chien 何鍵

Ho Chung-ch'üan 何中權

Ho Lung 賀龍

Ho Yao-tsu 賀耀祖

Ho Ying-ch'in 何應欽

hou pei tui 後備隊: militia reserve unit.

Hsia Ch'ao 夏超

Hsia Wei 夏威

hsiang 鄉: district.

hsiao Chu-ko Liang 小諸葛亮

hsiao-ch'ün kuan-nien 小群觀念: particularism.

hsien 縣: county.

hsien-chang 縣長: *hsien* head.

hsiu-ts'ai 秀才: nature talent; graduate of first level of examinations in the traditional examination system.

Hsiung K'o-wu 熊克武

Hsiung Shih-hui 熊式輝

Hsü Chi-ming 徐啓明

Hsü Ching-t'ang 徐景唐

Hsü Ch'ung-chih 許崇智

Hsüeh-chung 血鐘: *Bell of Blood* (journal).

hu 戶: household.

Hu Han-min 胡漢民

Hu Fa yün-tung 護法運動: Movement to Protect the Constitution.

Hu Kuo yün-tung 護國運動: Movement to Protect the Nation.

Hu-Tang Chiu-Kuo Chün 護黨救國軍: Protect the Party, Save the Country Army.

Hu Tsung-to 胡宗鐸

huan t'ang pu huan yao 換湯不換藥: superficial change; literally, to change the medicine without changing the drug.

Huang Chen-kuo 黃鎮國

Huang Chi 黃薊

Huang Chih-hsi 黃植溪

Huang Chung-chin 黃中匾

Huang Chung-yüeh 黃鍾岳

Huang Hsü-ch'u 黃旭初

Huang Jih-k'uei 黃日葵

Huang P'u-hsin 黃樸心

Huang Shao-hsiung 黃紹雄

hui-kuan 會館: *Landsmannschaft.*

Jen Ying-chih 仁應岐

Jung hsien, Kwangsi 容縣

jung-kung 容共: policy of co-operation with the Communists.

Kai-liang feng-su kuei-lü 改良風俗規條: *Regulations for the Improvement of Social Customs.*

Kai-tsu P'ai 改組派: Reorganisation Faction.

Kan Nai-kuang 甘乃光

Kan-pu P'ai 幹部派: Cadre Faction.

kao-teng yu-min 高等游民: high-level vagabonds.

Ko-ming chih hua 革命之花: *Flowers of Revolution* (Journal).

k'o-chün 客軍: guest army.

Kuang-hsi chien-she kang-ling 廣西建設綱領: *Kwangsi Reconstruction Programme.*

Kuang-hsi lu-chün hsiao-hsüeh 廣西陸軍小學: Kwangsi Military Elementary School.

Kuang-hsi lu-chün su-ch'eng hsiao-hsüeh 廣西陸軍速成小學: Kwangsi Short Course Military Elementary School.

Kuang-hsi mo-fan ying 廣西模範營: Kwangsi Model Battalion.

Kuang-hsi sheng cheng-fu ho-shu 廣西省政府合署: Kwangsi Combined Government Office.

Kuang-hsi sheng-li hsüan-ch'uan-yüan yang-ch'eng suo 廣西省立宣傳院養成所: Kwangsi Provincial Propaganda Training School.

Kuei hsien, Kwangsi 貴縣

Kueip'ing, Kwangsi 桂平

kung-tse 工賊: scab.

kuo-huo 國貨: Chinese products.

Kuo-min cheng-fu hsi-nan cheng-wu wei-yüan-hui 國民政府西南政務委員會: Southwest Political Council of the National Government.

Kuo-min cheng-fu hsi-nan chün-shih fen-hui 國民政府西南軍事分會: Southwest Military Branch Council of the National Government.

Kuo-min jih-pao 國民日報: *National Daily.*

Kuomintang 國民黨: Nationalist Party.

K'uo-ta hui-i 擴大會議: Enlarged Congress (of the Kuomintang).

Kweilin (Kueilin), Kwangsi 桂林

Lai Hsin-hui 賴心輝

Lei Ching-t'ien 雷嗣天

Lei Pei-hung 雷沛鴻

Lei Pei-t'ao 雷沛濤

Lei Yin 雷殷

Li Ch'ao-fang 李朝芳

Li Chi-shen 李濟琛

Li Fu-lin 李福林

Li Hung-chang 李鴻章

Li Jen-jen 李任仁

Li Li-san 李立三

Li Lieh-chün 李烈鈞

Li Ming-jui 李明瑞

Li Pai-yün 李白雲

Li P'in-hsien 李品仙

Li Shih-tseng 李石曾

Li Tsung-jen 李宗仁

Liang Ch'i-ch'ao 梁啓超

Liang Han-sung 梁瀚嵩

Liang-Hu 兩湖: Hunan and Hupei provinces.

Liang Hua-t'ang 梁華堂

Liang Kuang 兩廣: Kwangtung and Kwangsi provinces.

Liang Liu-tu 梁六度

Liang Shu-ming 梁漱溟

Liao Lei 廖磊

Lin Chün-t'ing 林俊廷

Lin Mo 林茂

Lin Sen 林森

Linkuei, Kwangsi 臨桂

Liu Chen-huan 劉震寰
Liu Ch'eng-chih 劉成助
Liu Chih 劉峙
Liuchow (Liuchow), Kwangsi 柳州
Liu Ch'üan-chung 劉權中
Liu Hsiang 劉湘
Liu Hsing 劉興
Liu Jih-fu 劉日福
Liu Tso-lung 劉佐龍
Liu Wen-hui 劉文輝
Liu Wen-tao 劉文島
Liu Yung-fu 劉永福
Lü Ching-ts'un 呂競存
Lu Fu-hsiang 陸福祥
Lu Han 盧漢
Lü Huan-yen 呂煥炎
Lu Jung-t'ing 陸榮廷
Lu Ti-p'ing 魯滌平
Lu Yün-kao 陸雲高
Lung Chi-kuang 龍濟光
Lungchow (Lungchou), Kwangsi 龍州
Ma Chün-wu 馬君武
Ma Hsiao-chün 馬曉軍
Mai Huan-chang 麥煥章
Mao Ping-wen 毛秉文
Meng Chih 蒙志
Meng Jen-chien 蒙仁潛
Miao 苗
Miao Pei-nan 繆培南
Min-cheng hui-i 民政會議: Civil Government conference.
Min-cheng kung-shu 民政公署: Office of Civil Government.
Min-ch'üan chu-i 民權主義: Democracy.
Min-sheng chu-i 民生主義: People's Livelihood.
Min-tsu chu-i 民族主義: Nationalism.
Min-t'uan 民團: militia.
mou 畝: Chinese acre.
Nanlu (Kwangtung) 南路
Nanning, Kwangsi 南寧
Pai Ch'ung-hsi 白崇禧
Pai Pao-shan 白寶山
P'an Chu-chi 盤珠祁
P'an Yi-chih 潘宜之
pao-chia 保甲: collective security system.
pao-ching an-min 保境安民: protect the frontiers and pacify the people.
pen-ti 本地: local, native.
P'eng Han-chang 彭漢章

P'eng Yü-t'ing 彭禹廷

Pi Yün Ssu 碧雲寺: Temple of the Azure Clouds.

Pose, Kwangsi 百色

P'u Yi 溥儀

San-Chiang 三江: Kiangsu, Anhwei, Kiangsi, and Chekiang provinces.

San-tzu cheng-ts'e 三自政策: Policy of Three-fold Self-reliance.

San-wei i-t'i 三位一體: Three in One.

San-yü cheng-ts'e 三寓政策: policy of three ' incorporations '.

Shanhaikuan 山海關

Shan-hou hui-i 善後會議: Rehabilitation Conference.

Shan-hou tu-pan, hui-pan 善後督辦，會辦: Rehabilitation Commissioner and Deputy Commissioner.

Shan-hsi sheng cheng-fu shih-nien chien-she chi-hua 山西省政府十年建設計畫: Ten Year Plan for the Reconstruction of Shansi.

Shao Li-tzu 邵力子

Shen Hung-ying 沈鴻英

shih 師: army division.

ssu-mien Ch'u-ke 四面楚歌: *in extremis.*

Sun Ch'uan-fang 孫傳芳

Sun Fo (Sun K'e) 孫科

Sun Yat-sen (Sun Chung-shan) 孫中山

Ta Kuang-hsi chu-i 大廣西主義: Greater Kwangsi-ism.

ta-tui 大隊: large militia unit.

T'an Hao-ch'ing 譚浩清

T'an Hao-ming 譚浩明

T'an Lien-fang 覃連芳

T'an Yen-k'ai 譚延闓

T'ang Chi-yao 唐繼堯

T'ang Shao-i 唐紹儀

T'ang Sheng-chih 唐生智

T'ao Chün 陶鈞

T'ao-fa Kuei-hsi hsüan-ch'uan ta-kang 討伐桂系宣傳大綱: Denunciation of the Kwangsi Clique.

T'ao-tse chün 討賊軍: Anti-bandit Army.

Teng Hsi-hou 鄧錫侯

t'e huo 特貨: 'special goods ' – opium.

Teng Hsiao-p'ing 鄧小平

ti-fang chu-i 地方主義: regionalism.

ti-fang kuan-nien 地方觀念: regionalism.

ti-yü kuan-nien 地域觀念: regionalism.

T'ien Sung-yao 田頌堯

T'ien Ti Hui 天地會: Heaven and Earth Society.

Ting-Kuei Chün 定桂軍: Army to Settle Kwangsi.

Ting Wen-chiang 丁文江

to-ch'iang chieh-chi 多槍階級: class with guns.

Ts'ai T'ing-k'ai 蔡廷鍇

Ts'ai Yuan-p'ei 蔡元培

Ts'ao Wan-shun 曹萬順

Ts'en Ch'un-hsüan 岑春煊

Ts'en Yü-ying 岑毓英

Tsou Lu 鄒魯

Tsoup'ing, Shantung 鄒平

ts'un kung suo 村公所: village community centre.

tu-chün 督軍: military governor of a province.

tu-tu 都督: provincial governor.

t'u-ssu chih-tu 土司制度: local governor system.

Tuan Chi-jui 段祺瑞

t'uan-lien 團連: local protection units.

t'uan-wu 團務: militia affairs.

Tunglan, Kwangsi 東蘭

t'ung, t'ung-yu 桐, 桐油: tung tree, tung oil.

t'ung chih kuo 桐之國: the Land of Tung.

t'ung-hsiang 同鄉: fellow-native.

t'ung-hsiang hui 同鄉會: Landsmannschaft.

t'ung-hsiang kuan-nien 同鄉觀念: local particularism.

T'ung Meng Hui 同盟會: Alliance Society.

Tzu-chih Chün 自治軍: Autonomous Army.

tzu li wei wang 自立爲王: to set oneself up as king.

Tzu-wei, Tzu-chih, Tzu-fu 自衛自治富: Self-defence, Self-government and Self-enrichment.

Wang Ching-wei 汪精衛

Wang Kung-tu 王公度

Wang T'ien-p'ei 王天培

Wei Keng-t'ang 韋賡唐

Wei Pa-ch'ün 韋拔羣

Wei Yün-sung 韋雲淞

Wei Yung-ch'eng 韋永成

wu-ch'iang chieh-chi 無槍階級: gunless classes.

Wu Chih-hui 吳稚輝

Wuchow (Wuchou), Kwangsi 梧州

Wu P'ei-fu 吳佩孚

Wu-sheng lien-fang hui-i 五省聯防會議: Five province meeting for common defence.

Wu T'ing-yang 伍廷颺

yamen 衙門: government office.

Yang Hsi-min 楊希閔

yang nu 洋奴: foreign slave.

Yang Sen 楊森

Yang Teng-hui 楊騰輝

Yao 徭

Yeh Ch'i 葉琪

Yeh T'ing 葉挺

Yen Hsi-shan 閻西山
yu-min 游民: vagrants.
yü chiang yü hsüeh 寓將於學: military training of students, to produce officers.
Yü Chih-fang 余志芳
yü mu yü cheng 寓募於徵: troop-raising through conscription.
yü ping yü t'uan 寓兵於團: militia training of able-bodied men to produce soldiers.
Yü Shao-chieh 余少傑
Yü Tso-po 俞作柏
Yü Tso-yü 俞作預
yüan 元: Chinese dollar.
Yuan Loa P'ai 元老派: Party Elders Faction.
Yüan Shih-k'ai 袁世凱
Yülin, Kwangsi 鬱林

Index